NAKED MASKS

Naked Masks

FIVE PLAYS

By
LUIGI PIRANDELLO

Edited by Eric Bentley

A Dutton dep *Paperback*

NEW YORK
E. P. DUTTON

Published in the United States by E. P. Dutton,
a division of New American Library,
2 Park Avenue, New York, N.Y. 10016.

ISBN: 0-525-48319-5

40 39 38 37 36 35 34 33 32

CONTENTS

LUIGI PIRANDELLO (1867-1936) was born in Girgenti, Sicily. He attended the University of Rome and took a doctorate in philology at Bonn University in 1891. Pirandello began his literary career as a poet, but he soon turned to fiction and in 1904 published his first widely recognized novel, *The Late Mattia Pascal*. With the appearance of *It Is So!* in 1917 Pirandello proved himself to be one of the most original and powerful dramatists of the 20th century, a claim well substantiated by his two greatest plays, *Six Characters in Search of an Author* (1921) and *Henry IV* (1922). Pirandello opened his own Art Theatre in Rome in 1925, and was awarded the Nobel Prize in 1934.

NAKED MASKS was first published in 1952.

INTRODUCTION

I

A GENERATION AGO there was, notoriously, a literature
of ideas. Most of it, like most literature of all movements,
was bad; and fashion, which elevates the bad to the level
of the good, subsequently turns its back on bad and good
alike. Only if there is a body of readers interested in
merit as such can anything like justice be done.

Such readers will rescue the better literature of ideas
from beneath the fashionable ideas about it. Even authors like Ibsen and Shaw, who are by no means unread,
need rescuing from ideas about their ideas. How much
the more so Pirandello, who is suffering fashionable
rejection without ever having had—outside Italy—wide-
spread fashionable acceptance. I have met persons who
rejected him because of his "tiresome ideas" without being able to give me even their own version of what these
ideas are. Pirandello needs rescuing from the very *lack*
of ideas about his ideas.

It is true that all too much of Pirandello, and Pirandello criticism, remains untranslated. The untranslated
essay *L'Umorismo* ("Humor") contains all his principal
ideas (especially its Second Part). The untranslated later
plays are especially full of theory. The untranslated essays
of Adriano Tilgher (especially "Il Teatro di Luigi Pirandello" in *Studi sul Teatro Contemporaneo*) are the standard exposition from the point of view of the famous ideas.
However, I submit that the ideas offer no real difficulty.

They are old ideas—good old ideas—some of which would take us back to Pirandello's fellow-countrymen Empedocles and Gorgias. It was Pascal, not Pirandello, who first said: "there is no man who differs more from another than he does from himself at another time." Illusion and reality—the "mix-up" of illusion and reality —is so far from being a peculiarly Pirandellian theme as to be perhaps the main theme of literature in general.

"No," says the more knowledgeable reader, "it is not that we can't understand the ideas. It's that we can't see why they troubled and obsessed Pirandello to such an extent. Always the *same* ideas! *"Oh, Dio mio, ma questo girar sempre sullo stesso pernio!"*—as he himself has his critics say. "This always harping on the same string!" More important: we can't see why these ideas should trouble and obsess *us*."

Obviously this reader can't mean that Pirandello—in his essay on humor, say—doesn't make a strong enough case for his ideas, in the sense that a lawyer or a logician makes a case. An artist, and no one was more aware of it than Pirandello, makes his ideas matter by rendering them artistically active, that is, by giving them the life of his chosen form in his chosen medium. The question for us here then is whether Pirandello's ideas become active in the dramatic form.

In reconsidering Pirandello today, fifteen years after his death, the first play to read is *Liolà*. It loses more than other plays in translation, but enough of the original comes through (I hope) to remove the anti-Pirandello prejudice. It is a play that lives by an evident loveliness. Sicily is a land of golden light, scarcely of this world, and Agrigento, with its Greek temples, its proud position above Porto Empedocle and the Mediterranean, and its isolation both from the merchants of Palermo and the tourists of Taormina, is perhaps the most charming spot on the island. Without any scene painting whatsoever,

and without (even in the Sicilian text) any attempt to
create "poetic" peasant dialogue, Pirandello has con-
trived to let in the light and distill the essence of the
charm.

If it especially commends itself to those who love Sicily
the play has a quality all can appreciate, the more so for
its rarity both in life and art, and that is joy. High-spirits
and hilarity we can on occasion manage; in the theatre
they are *de rigueur,* in real life they have their allotted
place; but joy—as an actor would say—"there is nothing
harder to do." Not even ecstasy. For ecstasy is extreme
and preternatural, and that is in our line. Joy is hard
for being pure and delicate, but no less hard for having
its feet on the ground. It is bliss without otherworldliness.
It lies tantalizingly in between the extremes of beatitude
and bestiality which are increasingly the postulates of our
world. *Liolà* is a play for the nineteen-fifties. Amid the
spurious apocalyptics of the few and the genuine hysteria
of the many—so far the only spiritual manifestations of
the atomic age—anything that recalls us to sanity is welcome. Pirandello's tidings of great joy are the best "message" any theatrical manager of today could find.

Liolà to be sure is Pirandello on holiday: he made one
of his short trips back home to the island and dashed off
the play in about a week. It is a dream, if you wish, but
in no Celtic twilight or Maeterlinckian mist; it is all
actual, it is all concrete. Sicily is like that: the African
sun shines, the hard rock takes on the soft color of honey,
the trees are laden with almonds and oranges, and vaga-
bonds sing. Granted, Pirandello picked, from this reality,
just those particulars that suited his mood and intention.
The village could be the same village as in *Cavalleria
Rusticana*—it was Verga's mood and intention that were
different. This is not to disregard the reality of the village
itself: if Pirandello has dreamed himself away from the
problems of Agrigento in 1916 it is back into the Agri-

gento of another day. The breath of a happy paganism
is felt in his play, which is the last Sicilian pastoral.

The greatest single creation of the piece is Liolà himself, from whom joy flows as from a fountain:

> *Io, questa notte, ho dormito al sereno,*
> *solo le stelle m'han fatto riparo:*
> *il mio lettuccio, un palmo di terreno,*
> *il mio guanciale, un cardoncello amaro.*
> *Angustie, fame, sete, crepacuore?*
> *non m'importa di nulla: so cantare!*
> *canto e di gioia mi s'allarga il cuore,*
> *è mia tutta la terra e tutto il mare.*
> *Voglio per tutti il sole e la salute,*
> *voglio per me le ragazze leggiadre,*
> *teste di bimbi bionde e ricciolute*
> *e una vecchietta qua come mia madre.*[1]

And Liolà is a holiday creation, a truancy on Pirandello's
part, an exception to the rules of the Maestro's art. He
is one of the few gay characters in Pirandello, and he is
perhaps the only positive one. By positive I mean morally
positive—being an agent, not merely a victim; hammer,
not merely anvil. There is positive will in Henry IV and
in Baldovino (of *The Pleasure of Honesty*) but Life
sweeps in like a flood and decides the issue. Neither of
these protagonists is, like Liolà, master of his fate.

He is master of his fate without being a hero, and

[1]Last night I slept the sleep I love,
My cabin roof the stars above,
A bit of earth, it was my bed,
And there were thistles 'neath my head.
Hunger and thirst and sorrow's sting,
They touch me not: for I can sing!
My heart, it jumps for joy: I sing!
Of all the earth and sea I'm king.
I wish to all men health and sun,
To me may lovely lasses run!
May curly children round me gather
With an old lady like my mother!

that by steadfastly refusing to do what other Pirandello characters do: let himself be exploited. This fact is firmly fixed in Pirandello's plot.

The story is essentially that of Tuzza's attempted revenge on Mita who has both the rich husband (Simone) and the gallant lover (Liolà) that Tuzza would like to have. Tuzza gets herself pregnant by Liolà and then arranges for Simone to pretend that the child is his. This he is eager to do since he has never been able to beget an heir. Mita will therefore fall from grace, and Tuzza become the mistress of Simone's household.

The snag is that Liolà will not stand for it. He warns Tuzza and her aunt: *"badi che, infamità, come non voglio farne io a nessuno così non voglio che ne facciamo gli altri, servendosi di me."* [2] When the plotters ignore the warning, he decides to make Mita pregnant too, so that she can reassume her wifely dignity. (For Simone will now disown Tuzza's child and claim Mita's.) The turning point of the action is therefore Liolà's seduction of Mita. Urging her to cuckold Simone, he uses the same language he had used before: *"No, no, non deve passare quest' infamia, Mita! . . . Non deve approffitarsi di me, quell'infame, per rovinarti!"* [3] He will not be made use of.

Were the opposite the case, as it is with all Pirandello's other characters, the story would not have a happy ending; it would be a normal, unhappy Pirandello play. And indeed, having granted that the character of Liolà, as it works out both in the action and in the tone of the dialogue, turns everything around, one must insist a little on the converse of the proposition: save for a single, central reversal of values, *Liolà* is characteristically Piran-

[2] "Look, I wouldn't like to commit an outrage. But I also wouldn't like others to commit an outrage and make use of me."
[3] "No, no, this outrage must not stand, Mita! . . . The wretch mustn't make use of me to bring about your ruin!"

dellian. It would be hasty for example to congratulate the author on having forgotten for once the famous ideas. On the contrary: we can learn from this play what his ideas are.

The play is about appearance and reality and shows, in what readers have always regarded as Pirandello's characteristically tricky fashion, that reality is not more real than appearance. Further, there are real appearances and—merely apparent appearances. And just as appearance may be more real than reality, so merely apparent appearance may be more real than real appearance.

Now the point is that though this sounds like an undergraduate discussion of Berkeley, in Pirandello's context it is concrete and clear. For Uncle Simone, to appear to be a father is enough: appearance will establish his paternity more surely than actually having done the deed. However, strictly speaking, he does *not* appear to be a father; for the whole town knows the truth. He only appears to appear to be the father. That he appears to be the father is a kind of social pact or legal fiction.

And here a distinction is made. Tuzza excludes Uncle Simone from the pact by actually telling him what has happened and thus preventing him from pretending to himself that the child is his. Mita doesn't make this mistake. It matters nothing that others shout the news in his face. That is unofficial gossip. The understanding—the apparent appearance—is that he is the father of Mita's child. And it is this appearance of an appearance, this shadow of a shadow, that brings back into Mita's grasp the solid realities of Simone's wealth and power.

Tuzza: *Hai saputo farla meglio di me! Tu i fatti, e io le parole!*

Mita: *Parole? Non pare!*

Zia Croce: *Parole, parole, si! Perche qua non c'è l'inganno che pare! L'inganno è in te che non pare! . . . Per te c'è*

> *tuo marito, ora, che ti ripara, ingannato! Mentre mia figlia,*
> *no, suo zio non lo volle ingannare: gli si buttò ai piedi:*
> *piangendo, come Maria Maddalena!*
>
> Zio Simone: *Quest'è vero! quest'è vero!*
>
> Zia Croce: *Ecco, vedi? te lo dice lui stesso! lui ch'è la causa*
> *di tutto il male, per potersi vantare davanti a te, davanti*
> *a tutto il paese—*
>
> Mita: *E voi lo permetteste, zia Croce? Oh guarda! A costo*
> *dell'onore di vostra figlia? Ma l'inganno, sì, è proprio dove*
> *non pare: nelle ricchezze di mio marito, di cui a costo della*
> *vostra stessa vergogna volevate appropriarvi!* [4]

Considering how the theme of reality and illusion is
embedded in the action, particularly in such a passage as
the one just quoted, we see that it is not important for
itself only but as referring to the concrete and indeed
humble circumstances of human society. Brought up in
the liberal tradition we expect an author who, like Pirandello, "exposes illusions" to "champion reality," whereas
he is content to leave the deceit "in Mita," to accept the
veil of illusion. In *Humor,* published eight years before
Liolà was conceived, he had written:

[4] *Tuzza:* You managed it better than I did. You have facts on your
side. I have—words.

Mita: Only words? I don't see it.

Aunt Croce: Words, *words,* WORDS! The deceit people see in
us is no deceit at all. The real deceit is in *you*—but no one sees
it . . . You have your husband again. You deceived him, but
he gives you shelter. Whereas my daughter wouldn't deceive
her uncle, oh no: she threw herself at his feet and wept like
Mary Magdalene!

Uncle Simone: That's true, that's true!

Aunt Croce: You see! He says so himself. He who was the cause
of all the trouble—just so he could boast before the whole
village. . . .

Mita: And you let him do that, Aunt Croce? Come now, at the
cost of your daughter's honor? But I agree with you: the deceit
is where no one sees it—in my husband's riches—which you
wished to take over at the cost of your own shame!

The harder the struggle for life and the more one's weakness is felt, the greater becomes the need for mutual deception. [The word is *inganno*, as in *Liolà*.] The simulation of force, honesty, sympathy, prudence, in short, of every virtue, and of that greatest virtue veracity, is a form of adjustment, an effective instrument of struggle. The "humorist" at once picks out such various simulations; amuses himself by unmasking them; is not indignant about them—he simply is that way!

And while the sociologist describes social life as it presents itself to external observation, the humorist, being a man of exceptional intuition, shows—nay, reveals—that appearances are one thing and the consciousness of the people concerned, in its inner essence, another. And yet people "lie psychologically" even as they "lie socially." And this lying to ourselves—living, as we do, on the surface and not in the depths of our being—is a result of the social lying. The mind that gives back its own reflection is a solitary mind, but our internal solitude is never so great that suggestions from the communal life do not break in upon it with all the fictions and transferences which characterize them.[5]

Mita is not mocked. She needs her "simulations" in her "struggle for life," in her struggle against society, and Pirandello is "not indignant about them." If he is conservative and "Latin" in defending established conventions against the sceptic, he is liberal and "Protestant" in his feeling that society is an enemy against which the individual, in his "inner essence," needs protection. As much as in any of the libertarian literature of the nineteenth century, public opinion in Pirandello is uniformly the opinion of a stupid, heartless, inquisitive outer world. One need not refer back to Stendhal or to the English legend of Mrs. Grundy. Pirandello had met Mrs. Grundy at home and in real life long before he could have met her abroad or in literature.

Pirandello's "liberalism" is protected by his "conservatism": his individuals are protected in their struggle

[5] *Saggi.* Di Luigi Pirandello (Mondadori, Milano, 1939), p. 163.

against society by illusion, convention, mendacity, pretence. Liolà knows this, even if the proverbial, gnomic language he finds to express it shows that such wisdom is for him intuitive and traditional, not arrived at by study, discussion or even observation. He knows it without perhaps fully knowing he knows it, for he is civilized without being educated—a thing which people who are educated without being civilized find hard to grasp. He has the smiling wisdom of an old culture. With his bones if not with his head he knows that life is ironical. The whole play is in one of his first and most casual remarks: *"Fingere è virtu, e chi non sa fingere non sa regnare."* [6] I have spoken already of his seduction of Mita as the turning point of the plot. His chief argument is the very fulcrum of the theme. It is that to bring everything out in the open is foolishness. *"Strilli, bastonate, avvocato, delegato, separazione? . . . Cose da bambino! . . . Chi ci crede? Si, magari, ci crederanno tutti. Ma lui no, lui non ci credera mai, per la ragione appunto che non ci vuol credere!"* [7] If we need a dignified antecedent for this it will not be *An Enemy of the People* but *The Wild Duck.*

II

I have asserted that Liolà himself is the exceptional feature of the play that bears his name and that otherwise it is characteristically Pirandellian. Pirandello, indeed, makes of him an exception not only in the canon of his own work but also in life: Liolà does not belong to modern society, to the bourgeois world. Interesting as his antagonism to private property may be he stands outside the class system, and breathes the spirit of an earlier day.

---

[6] "Pretending is virtue. If you can't pretend, you can't be king."
[7] "Beatings and screechings, the lawyer, the Deputy, a separation? . . . What childishness! . . . Who will believe it? Well: possibly they all will. Except him. He'll never believe it—for the good reason that he doesn't wish to."

He can be independent only at the cost of being a vaga-
bond and having few demands to make on life. Otherwise what would his wisdom avail him?

Even before he left Sicily Pirandello must have known
there was no such future in an ideal, and when he got to
Rome he must have found there was not even a present.
The great bulk of Pirandello's work bears witness to the
sadness of a spirit that reaches back to pagan joy and
Garibaldian heroism but is confronted with the unheroic
joylessness of the urban middle class. It is easy to understand why there is only one Liolà; still easier to overlook
the typicality of his play—and the correlative fact that
the other plays draw their energy from the same sources
and not from books of philosophy and psychology.

This is especially true of the play which is the most
famous statement of Pirandello's "relativism"—*It Is So!*
(*If You Think So*). In this play, pre-eminently, we see the
struggle for life in its inner essence, life in the private
depths. The struggle is caused, or exacerbated, by the
desire of other people to know the truth about a certain
family. Pirandello maintains, we are told, that truth is
relative and subjective, the joke being that people know
the truth already since whatever seems to each of them so
is so. One would think the play philosophical, and the
philosophy cynical, but what is this love of truth that
Pirandello condemns? It is no Socratic dedication, it is
Mrs. Grundy's nosiness, it is the idle curiosity of Ciuzza,
Luzza, and Nela which has gained in malignancy as it has
risen in social station. This love of truth is the pseudo-
religion of the bureaucratic fact, on the altars of which
men are sacrificed to paper and typewriters: the recourse
to documents in acts two and three parallels Aunt Gesa's
rushing to the lawyer in *Liolà*.

In *Liolà,* to stick to the terms of the play itself, deception (*inganno*) leads to outrage (*infamia*), whereupon

a remedy (*rimedio*) is found, not by exposure of the deception but by another and larger deception. The human content of the larger deception is not however deception itself—or evil—but the wisdom of Liolà. This *gaia scienza*, I have said, would have no place in the bourgeois plays, of which *It Is So!* is one of the first. Here there is no active mastery of the situation. There is passive suffering—and an effort to compose matters through affection. When all else has been blasted away, kindness, like joy, is a pearl of great price. For Liolà's serene mastery it is at any rate a handy substitute. Mother-in-law, son-in-law, and wife know it is their most precious possession, their one sure, real possession.

The old lady warns the truth-lovers early in the play. *"E perche si deve allora tormentarlo con questa indagine della sua vita familiare . . . ?"* [8] Ponza explains to the well-wishers how much ill they do: *"Chiedo scusa a lor signori di questo triste spettacolo che ho dovuto dar loro per rimediare al male che, senza volerlo, senza saperlo, con la loro pietà, fanno a questa infelice."* [9] He cries out to them in pain: *". . . non posso tolerare questa inquisizione accanita, feroce sulla mia vita privata, che finirà di compromettere, guasterà irreparabilmente un opera di carità che mi costa tanta pena e tanti sacrifizii!"* [10] The old lady cries out too: *"Loro credono di farmi bene e mi fanno tanto male!"* [11] The veiled wife is even more ex-

---

[8] "And why is it necessary then to torment him with this investigation of his family life?"

[9] "I beg pardon for this sad spectacle which I've had to present before all you ladies and gentlemen to remedy the evil which, without wanting, without knowing, you are doing to this unhappy woman with your compassion."

[10] ". . . I cannot tolerate this fierce, relentless inquisition on my private life. In the end it will compromise—irreparably destroy—a labor of love which is costing me much pain, much sacrifice."

[11] "You think to help me and do me so much harm!"

plicit: *"Qui c'è una sventura, come vedono, che deve restar nascosta, perche solo cosi può valere il rimedio che la pietà le ha prestato."* [12]

The *rimedio* comes to us, as in *Liolà,* as the largest deception of all—*we* feel as much deceived as the people on stage. Yet again the content is human wisdom—this time in the shape of *carità, pietà.* While, certainly, the entrance of the veiled wife carries this "parable" outside the bounds of realism, we are under no obligation to believe, as many have, that she is Truth itself! If she must have a capital letter, she is Love. Just how her birth certificate reads doesn't matter; she has lost her separate interests, her separate existence, in devotion to the others; she exists only in the mother and the husband. This alone, this her love and theirs, is true; the rest?—you can have it your own way.

Henry IV and the "trilogy of the theatre in the theatre" (*Six Characters, Each In His Own Way,* and *Tonight We Improvise*) represent a development of this "system" rather than a break with it. In *Henry IV,* the Pirandellian version of illusion and reality has crystallized in his celebrated confrontation of form and life. The kinetic pattern is still deception, outrage, and remedy by larger deceit. The spatial pattern is still a center of suffering and a periphery of busybodies—the pattern of the Sicilian village.

To Pirandello, form increasingly meant artistic form, and artistic form increasingly meant dramatic form. Theatre and life is the theme. The spatial pattern of the Sicilian village, the drama of suffering before a crowd of onlookers is his standard version of it—Tuzza and all Agrigento looking on; the Ponza-Frola trio and the whole provincial capital looking on; Henry IV— a spectacle for

[12] "There is a misfortune here, as you see, which must remain hidden because only in this way can the remedy which compassion has found avail."

his friends and his servants; the six characters—a drama to amaze actors and stage manager; Delia Morello—with her double out front and actors on stage discussing the author; Mommina—dying in a play within a play while singing in a play within a play within a play.

The heterodox form of *Six Characters* is thus no freak and has nothing to do with the Bohemian experimentalism of the twenties, with which people still associate it. It closely corresponds to Pirandello's sense of life and is but an extension of a pattern he had, as we have seen, used before. In *Liolà* and *It Is So!* he juggles with reality and appearance, interchanging them, subdividing them, mixing them, always urgently aware of different degrees or levels of illusion. Having established a level midway between the audience and the essential drama—namely, that of the spectator-characters—he could go a step further and frankly use the device of the play within a play —which is all that we mean when we talk of the play's formal heterodoxy.

Some think that Pirandello's turning from *Liolà* (and the short story) to more ambitious forms of drama was all to the bad: the more he attempted the less he achieved, the more he tried to be a thinker the less he succeeded in being an artist. When one finds a Liolà giving place to a Laudisi one certainly fears the worst. To give one's wisdom to a spectator-character, a raisonneur, might well mean the weakening of plot and the dilution of dialogue.

Yet *It Is So!* has a strong plot and (in the original) a concise dialogue. Laudisi does not stand at the center of the action because Pirandello has reserved that place for his three sufferers. Laudisi's talk is legitimately and of its nature a commentary; its force is not direct—cannot therefore be judged in quotation—but derives from ironic interaction with the main business. Of course he is a spectator-character. Pirandello is painting the portrait of a spectator at the drama of life.

It is not simply that Pirandello grew garrulous with age. He believed that the essentially human thing was not merely to live, as the beasts do, but also to see yourself living, to think. Thinking is a function of human life. Whereas in his short stories, as in *Liolà,* he is often content to tell the story from outside, reducing it as much as possible to action, and giving full play to the setting, he obviously regarded the dramatic form as a challenge to show more of the inner life of man, to show man seeing himself, to let characters become roles and speak for themselves. Thus, his people "think" a lot, but their thinking is a part of *their* living, not of Pirandello's speculating or preaching. In such a character as the Father in *Six Characters,* the thought is always subordinated to the feeling which produces it. Thought is something he tortures himself with, it is a part of his emotional life.

Of course, there is no denying that Pirandello sometimes failed to bring it off. His emotions sometimes dried up, and we are left with brittle ratiocination that remains external to the drama. His standard situations and patterns remained safer ground for him than the territory his ambition reached after. The "Preface" to *Six Characters* tells us what Pirandello thinks the play is. Despite his assertion that he is describing what he finds there and not merely his intentions, we do not find fully realized in the work all that is in the description. The very idea that is announced in the play's title has less reality, perhaps, in the work itself than the image of Father and Daughter suffering before the uncomprehending eyes of the actors. The other two plays of the trilogy would peter out in talk if, from time to time and especially just before the end, Pirandello did not remember his customary scheme and summon his primitive emotional strength.

In so far as there is a moral conception in the trilogy, it is as much more modest than *It Is So!* as that play,

morally speaking, is more modest than *Liolà*. We find
neither a smiling mastery of the situation, nor even a sad
tenacious affection, but only *a striving towards the genuine,*
starting from the mournful yet horribly justified
realization that we live in an age when it is an achievement
to have a single genuine feeling. We may have little
patience with Delia Morello, the frenetic actress of *Each
In His Own Way* but at least she knows the score and
hasn't given up the game for lost: *"fra tutto questo finto,
fra tutto questo falso, che diventa sempre più finto e più
falso—e non si può sgombrare; perchè, ormai, a rifarla in
noi, attorno a noi, la semplicità, appare falsa—appare?
è, è—falsa, finta anch'essa . . . Non è più vero niente!
E io voglio vedere, voglio sentire, sentire, almeno una
cosa, almeno una cosa sola che sia vera, vera, in me!"* [13]

Delia Morello is only a character but she voices here
what seems to me not only Pirandello's noblest impulse
but also the one he was best able to keep within the
bounds of art (because it was imposed by experience and
not by ambition). *"Non è più vero niente!" Here* is the
sense in which nothing is true! What a pity that critics
have noticed Pirandello's nihilistic flouting of truth in
the philosophic sense and have not noticed that all his
work is an effort of heart and mind to find the true in the
moral sense, to find at least *"una cosa, almeno una cosa
che sia vera, vera in me."*

III

As with Ibsen, as with Shaw, it is not the many more or
less ostentatious ideas that matter but one or two more

---

[13] "in all that is fake, in all that is false, as it gets ever more fake,
more false—and you can't get out from under—because by now simplicity itself, as we remake it within us, around us, simplicity seems
false—seems? no: is—*is* false, *is* fake . . . Nothing is true any more,
nothing! And I want to see, I want to hear just one thing, just one
thing that is true—TRUE—in me!"

persistent ideas that lie concealed behind them. This is the place to remember to how large an extent form is meaning. The degree to which an idea gets expressed in an art—and not merely mentioned—depends on the artistic skill of the writer, his ability to create forms. For many years even Italian criticism of Pirandello was preoccupied with ideas as mentioned rather than as expressed. It is surprising how little has been said as yet of Pirandello's art.

Even against it. For there are surprising lacunae in his equipment as a playwright, lacunae and deficiencies. A first reading of his forty-four plays leaves us with an impression of monotony. A second reading calls our attention to grave faults in dramatic structure and grave limitations in character portrayal. One of the plays most frequently performed in Italy (*Tutto Per Bene—All For The Best*) has a central scene of the rankest ham melodrama. Two that are translated into English, and have been highly praised (*Henry IV* and *The Pleasure of Honesty*) have an expository first act of such cumbersome explanatoriness one would think the author a plodding mediocrity or a careless hack. Over-all structure? Pirandello forces all his full length plays into the three-act mould whether they really fit it or not. Sometimes he has obvious difficulty (e.g. in *L'uomo, la bestia, e la virtù —Man, Beast and Virtue*) in making the material spin out. More often, one simply remains uncertain about the relation of act to act. How many *real* acts are there in *Six Characters* and *Each In His Own Way*? It is hard to resist Tilgher's conclusion that both plays *piétinent sur place* a good deal. Characters? How many of the personages in Pirandello's plays have an effective existence of any sort? Take two or three away during the intermission and no one would miss them afterwards. Many of them are uninteresting in themselves and remarkably like many of the others.

Despite its reputation for experimentalism, the dramaturgy of Pirandello stays all too close to the French drawing-room play—we could more flatteringly say to Ibsen were it not precisely the "French" externals of Ibsenism that we find. Within the French frame, Ibsen unfolded a classic drama: doom flowers in due season, crisis is brought to birth by Time. The Ibsenite exposition is admirable not because the characters give us information without seeming to but because the exposition is itself drama, furthering, even constituting, the action. Now, as Giacomo Debenedetti has pointed out, Pirandello destroys Time. His events do not grow in Time's womb. They erupt on the instant, arbitrarily; just as his characters do not approach, enter, present themselves, let alone have motivated entrances; they are suddenly there, dropped from the sky. In Paris, the six characters were literally lowered on stage in an elevator; it is the quintessence of Pirandellism. In this sort of drama, the Ibsenite exposition is dead wood and breaks in the playwright's hands. For this sort of drama is the aftermath of Ibsenism, drama to end drama.

Not with a whimper, though; with a bang. It is a decadent drama but it rises at times to greatness and is in its full extent (Pirandello's plays being, as Bontempelli says, a single drama in a hundred acts) one of the very few profound versions of modern life in histrionic terms. How could an artist so faulty, limited, and, to boot, so ambitious—so unaware, that is, of his faults and limitations—be profound and great?

His strongest weapon is his prose. Its torrential eloquence and pungent force are unique in the whole range of modern drama, and recall the Elizabethans (in contrast with our verse playwrights who imitate the Elizabethans and don't in the least "recall" them). He gets effects which one would not have thought possible to colloquial prose, thus compelling us to reopen the dis-

cussion of poetry and drama, in which it has always been
assumed that prose was a limitation.

Though it is not clear that the same feats could be
performed in any language but Italian, Pirandello exploited the special resources of that marvellous tongue;
the credit cannot be given to the Italian tradition alone.
Italian critics have themselves borne witness to the origi-
nality of Pirandello's style:

> . . . always extremely simple (the most naked and eco-
> nomic, the furthest removed from literary "equilibrium," the
> most truly "spoken" ever heard on our stage) the language of
> these plays is agile, astute, mobile, full of sap, bursting with
> inner vitality; the dialogue, restrained, exact, with no orna-
> mental appendages, the images immediate and germane,
> bends itself wonderfully to follow the sinuosities of psycho-
> logical processes.[14]

Thus Tilgher. Debenedetti speaks of the obsessive Pirandellian rhythm as "recitative":

> . . . unremitting, throwing itself ever forward towards the
> same cadence, always the same movement, having only its
> own anxiety to keep it from monotony. Broken, and angry
> at its own "openness," it swells outwards, it rushes in pur-
> suit, it turns on itself as if to correct itself, as if, with the
> next touch, to recover its balance, contrite because it has
> never quite succeeded in explaining itself. And it pounces
> on the word and devours it almost as if the word were the
> momentary definition of what should be said but above all
> because it is the quickest and directest track forward.[15]

And, consciously or not, Pirandello describes his own
achievement in setting forth this notion of dramatic
writing:

> . . . so that the characters may leap from the written pages
> alive and self-propelled the playwright needs to find the word

[14] *Studi sul teatro contemporaneo,* p. 244.
[15] *Saggi Critici,* p. 277.

which will be the action itself spoken, the living word that
moves, the immediate expression, having the same nature as
the act itself, the unique expression that cannot but be this,
i.e., appropriate to this given character in this given situation; words, expressions, which are not invented but are
born, when the author has identified himself with his creature to the point of feeling it as it feels itself, wishing it as
it wishes itself.[16]

It is clear that Pirandello, theorizing, did not view his
prose in isolation from his characters and their activities
(the plot). *Liolà, It Is So!*, and his other more successful
plays show us that his practice could conform to his
theory. Even the more discursive plays are discursive in
order that the prose may fully express the nature of men
—who, among other things, have brains and think. In
Pirandello's dialogue, passion does not commit incest
with passion as in D'Annunzio's. It meshes with the rest
of life, and especially with thought; and benefits thereby,
even as passion.

I once had the strange good fortune to see Emma
Gramatica in *La Città Morta* (*The Dead City*) of
D'Annunzio and *La Vita Che Ti Diedi* (*The Life I Gave
Thee*) of Pirandello on successive evenings. I was surprised to find that Italy does not demand two different
styles of acting for the two playwrights. Out of Pirandello has come no "Stanislavsky school" of naturalism
and understatement. Though in Italy he was often called
"anti-rhetorical," in the theatre of any other country he
would be considered rhetorical to a degree. In Pirandello
La Gramatica uses a distinctly elevated style, weaving
all the time a sinuous pattern with voice and arms, weaving a web in which the spectator is caught.

In performance Pirandello differs from D'Annunzio
not in being less stormy but in being more effectively so.
His anti-rhetoric is a counter-rhetoric, to which the per-

[16] *Saggi*, p. 235.

former can bring the traditional technique of the passionate Latin theatre with the happiest results.

Sometimes everything about a Pirandello play is weak except the central role. The cause of this is doubtless to be found in the star-system of Italian theatre, the lack of good ensembles. The quality of the defect is that, when you have a star before you, the whole play takes on life, and you see that after all it is not a mere essay or speech but poetry, theatre, and even a drama *sui generis*. Thus it is with La Gramatica's *The Life I Gave Thee* and Ruggero Ruggeri's *All For The Best*. You may say that even the protagonist in such a play is hardly a character in the traditional sense. He (or she) is more of an impulse than a person. There is nothing in world drama resembling such characters. They fall from the sky, they are whirled hither and yon, they cry out in anguish, they sink into the ground. But is not this, in its way, highly dramatic?

At any rate it is poignant theatre, and it conveys a vision of life that cuts below the celebrated ideas. Conversely: the ideas are a superstructure of the vision and of the pain of the vision. And what are they after all, the ideas that Pirandello calls the pangs of his spirit?

> . . . the deceit of mutual understanding irremediably founded on the empty abstraction of words, the multiple personality of everyone (corresponding to the possibilities of being to be found in each of us), and finally the inherent tragic conflict between life (which is always moving and changing) and form (which fixes it, immutable).

The common denominator of these intellectual propositions is loneliness, isolation, alienation. As we break the bonds between man and man one after another, and find no other bonds to replace them with—or none that are compatible with our humanity—the sense of separateness in the individual grows from mild melancholy to frantic hysteria. As the invisible walls of our culture crumble, and the visible walls collapse in ever increasing quantity, a disintegration sets in within the individual personality and lags, not far perhaps, behind the general disintegration. Pirandello cannot claim the dubious privilege of being the only writer to dramatize this situation; all our profounder spirits have been busy doing so. But he has dramatized it with his own accent and that of his people. His Sicilian intensity and equally Sicilian speculativeness drive him into a sort of metaphysical agony, an arraignment of human life itself. For, if the great human gift is that of words, by what diabolic plan does it happen that words multiply misunderstanding? The very humanity of man increases his isolation. Such is the idea "behind" one of Pirandello's most famous ideas. "Multiple personality" is a similar instance: Pirandellian man is isolated not only from his fellows but also from himself at other times. Further than this, isolation cannot go. This is a "nihilistic vision" with a vengeance.

Perhaps it would nowadays be called an existentialist vision: life is absurd, it fills one with nausea and dread and anguish, it gives us the metaphysical shudder, yet, without knowing why, perhaps just because one is *there,* in life, one faces it, one fights back, one cries out in pain, in rage, in defiance (if one is a Sicilian existentialist), and since all living, all life, is improvisation, one improvises some values. Their Form will last until Living destroys them and we have to improvise some more.

Pirandello's plays grew from his own torment (I overlook for the moment the few precious pages that grew from his joy) but through his genius they came to speak for all the tormented and, potentially, *to* all the tormented, that is, to all men. And they will speak with particular immediacy until the present crisis of mankind —a crisis which trembles, feverishly or ever so gently, through all his plays—is past.

—ERIC BENTLEY

LIOLÀ

(*Liolà*)

A COUNTRY COMEDY

English version by

ERIC BENTLEY and GERARDO GUERRIERI

Translators' Note. The present version is with very minor exceptions based on the text in Pirandello's collected plays (*Maschere Nude,* Mondadori, Milano, 1948-9). There are two earlier versions published together as *Liolà: Commedia Campestre in Tre Atti* (Formiggini, Roma, 1917): the first of these is the original Sicilian text, the second (facing it) an Italian translation.

Producers should regard our text as eminently alterable. In many parts of the English-speaking world it should be given a touch of the local dialect. In all parts of the British Empire its Americanisms could without difficulty be replaced by Anglicisms. We are aware, in short, that our rather American, rather middle-class speech is no equivalent of Pirandello's peasant dialogue; but neither is there a strong case for translating this for all readers into the dialect of one region of one English-speaking country.

E.B.
G.G.

1

CHARACTERS

NICO SCHILLACI, *called Liolà*
    (accent on last syllable)
AUNT NINFA, *Liolà's mother*
UNCLE SIMONE PALUMBO
MITA, *his young wife*
AUNT CROCE AZZARA, *his cousin*
TUZZA, *her daughter*
NEIGHBOR GESA, *Mita's aunt*

CARMINA, *called La Moscardina*
CIUZZA ⎫
LUZZA ⎬ *Peasant girls*
NELA ⎭
TININO ⎫ *Liolà's three little*
CALICCHIO ⎬ *boys*
PALLINO ⎭
OTHER PEASANTS

THE TIME: *The Present (i.e. 1916)*
THE PLACE: *The Sicilian countryside, near Agrigento.*

ACT ONE

Between the little farmhouse and the shop, the stable and the winepress of AUNT CROCE AZZARA, *there is a "tettoia"—a straw roof or awning supported by the house-wall on one side and by wooden posts on the other. In the background, countryside with clumps of prickly pear trees, almond trees, and "Saracen" olive trees. On the audience's right, under the tettoia, the house door, a rough stone seat and a monumental stove. On the left, the shop-door, the winepress window, and another window with bars across it. Rings in the wall to tie the animals to.*

It is September and the almonds are being shelled. On the two benches in the corner are sitting TUZZA, MITA, MOTHER GESA, CARMINA LA MOSCARDINA, LUZZA, CIUZZA *and* NELA. *They shell the almonds by hammering them with a stone against another stone which is placed on their knees.* UNCLE SIMONE *is looking on, seated on an inverted chest.* AUNT CROCE *comes and goes. On the ground, sacks, baskets, chests, and nutshells.*

At the rising of the curtain, the WOMEN *are shelling nuts and singing the Passion.*

Chorus. And when they scourged the Lord
        Mary was at the gate
      "O do not hit so hard,
      His flesh is delicate!"

Aunt Croce [*coming from the shopdoor with a basket of almonds*]. Go to it girls, we're nearly through. With God's help, that'll be all the shelling for this year.

Ciuzza. Give me some almonds, Aunt Croce!

Luzza. Me!

Nela. Me!

Aunt Croce. If you hurry you'll be in time for the last Mass.

Ciuzza. Oh dear, it's too late now!

Nela. We can't get to the village . . .

Luzza. We haven't time to dress . . .

Gesa. Oh well, do you have to get dolled up to hear the Holy Mass?

Nela. What do you want us to do? A church isn't a kitchen.

Ciuzza. I'll dash to church as I am, if I can manage it.

Aunt Croce. And meanwhile lose more time chattering!

Luzza. Let's sing, let's sing! [*And* THEY *go on hammering and singing.*]

Chorus. "Now take me to him, John!"
      "Mary, thou canst not walk!"

Uncle Simone [*interrupting the chorus*]. Get this Passion over once and for all! You've been deafening me all morning with it. Can't you hammer without singing?

Luzza. Don't you know it's the custom to sing while you're shelling?

Nela. Old grumbler!

Gesa. On your conscience be the sin we're committing for you—working on the Holy Sabbath!

Uncle Simone. For me? For Aunt Croce, you mean!

Aunt Croce. Oh yes? What impudence! For three days he's not given me a minute's peace with these almonds he wants to sell! Who knows what might have happened to him if I hadn't shelled them and delivered them right away!

Uncle Simone [*grumbling, with irony*]. I'll get rich from them all right.

La Moscardina. Oh, Uncle Simone, remember you promised to give us something to drink when we've finished.

Aunt Croce. Promised? It's an agreement. Rest easy.

Uncle Simone. Not at all. What agreement's this, cousin? And for a handful of shells? You can't be serious.

Aunt Croce. Aha, you're going back on it? After mak ing me bring in the women to work on Sunday? No cousin, no, you can't do this to me! [*Turning to* MITA. Now, Mita, run and get me a good pitcher of wine They'll drink to your husband's health and prosperity

[*The* WOMEN *approve and clap, crying "Yes, yes Hooray!"*]

Uncle Simone. Thank you, cousin. You've a good heart and no doubt about it!

Aunt Croce [*to* MITA]. Why aren't you off?

Mita. Well, if *he* doesn't order me . . .

Aunt Croce. Do you need him to order you? Aren't you the boss too?

Mita. No, Aunt Croce, *he's* the boss.

Uncle Simone. I'll tell you one thing. You see these eyes? If I'm tempted to buy off the tree again next year, I'll pluck them out with my own hands!

Ciuzza. Time enough to think of that when next year comes!

Luzza. As if we didn't all know almond trees and their ways.

Nela. One year heavy with fruit, another—nearly barren.

Uncle Simone. The almonds! If it was only the almonds! The vines are stricken with blight as well! Just take a look out there: the olive trees are eaten away at the tips and a pitiful sight to see.

La Moscardina. Merciful heavens, watch the man weep, rich as he is! You looked the crop over, made an estimate, and it was wrong. Well, think of it this way: your loss was your cousin's gain—your widow cousin and her orphan niece. Let the dead bury their dead.

Ciuzza. It's money that stays in the family . . .

Luzza. . . . or do you want to take it with you underground?

La Moscardina. If you had a son . . . ooh, it slipped out!

[She *claps her hand on her mouth. The other* Women *are petrified.* Uncle Simone *looks daggers at them; then, seeing his wife, unburdens his wrath on* her.]

Uncle Simone [*to* Mita]. Go away, go away, good-for-nothing, go away!

[As Mita *is abashed and stays put,* He *goes over to her, makes her get up, rudely takes hold of her, and shakes her.*]

Now you see what you're good for, don't you? To set them all a-pecking at me like mosquitoes! Go away! Go home this minute! Or by Christ I don't know what foul misdeed I'll be doing this fair morning!

[*At the back,* Mita *leaves, mortified, weeping.* Uncle Simone *kicks the chest he had been sitting on and goes into the shop.*]

Aunt Croce [*to* La Moscardina]. Bless you, woman, you can't control your tongue.

La Moscardina. He forces the words out of a person's mouth!

Ciuzza [*with an air of naiveté*]. Maybe it's a disgrace for a man—not having any children?

Aunt Croce. You be quiet! Young girls can't meddle in matters of this sort.

Luzza. What's wrong about it?

Nela. It means God didn't want to give him any.

Luzza. Then why does he blame it all on his wife?

Aunt Croce. For heaven's sake, will you hush? And get on with your shelling?

Ciuzza. We've finished, Aunt Croce.

Aunt Croce. Then go and attend to your own affairs.

[*At the back of the stage, the three* Girls *go and surround* Tuzza *who hasn't opened her mouth but has been sulking all this time.* They *try to start a conversation with her. But* Tuzza *pushes them off with her shoulders. Then, gradually and one after another, they go over to hear what* Aunt Croce, Mother Gesa, *and* Mother Carmina *are saying to one another: each girl reporting it to the other two, and warning them not to laugh or they'll be overheard.*]

Oh my dears, my head's blown up like a balloon, the way he talks and talks! There he is, the whole blessed time, and every day from morning to night, harping on the same string . . .

La Moscardina. . . . about the child that's not been born? And how *should* he be born?

Gesa. If weeping would do the trick, who knows?

Aunt Croce. Weeping? Now let's be fair: he's weeping for the property—all those wonderful things that'll go out of the family when he dies. He can't get over it.

La Moscardina. Let him weep, Aunt Croce. So long as *he's* weeping, *you* have every reason to laugh, it seems to me.

Aunt Croce. You mean the inheritance? I don't give it a moment's thought, my dear. He has more relatives than I have hairs on my head.

La Moscardina. All the same—much or little accord-

ing to your place in the family—some part will come to
you, won't it?—I'm sorry for your niece, Aunt Gesa, but
the law's the law: when there are no children, the husband's property . . .

Gesa. . . . may the devil run off with it all, the property and its owner too! It'll be the death of my niece—is
that what you want? Poor Christian soul, unhappy from
her birth! Abandoned by her mother before she was out
of her baby clothes! Left without a father at the age of
three! I've raised her myself, the good Lord knows how!
If she had but a brother the old man wouldn't treat her
that way, I can assure you! He does everything but tread
her under foot: you saw for yourselves! [She *starts crying.*]

La Moscardina. It's true, poor Mita! Who would have
said it four years ago? When she married Uncle Simone
Palumbo everyone thought she was very lucky! Well,
[*Singing*]
            "The plum and the cherry are lovely . . ."
but if there's no bread . . .

Aunt Croce. Oh, come on now: do you mean to say
it wasn't a great piece of luck for Mita in the end? A fine
girl, Mita, I don't deny it, but, look, even in her fondest
dreams she couldn't have expected to become my cousin's
wife!

Gesa. All the same, my dear Aunt Croce, I'd like to
know who asked your cousin to take my niece for his
wife. I certainly didn't, let alone Mita herself.

Aunt Croce. You know as well as I do that Uncle
Simone's first wife was a real lady . . .

La Moscardina. . . . and he wept for her, I must say
that, he wept his heart out for her, when she passed away!

Gesa. Ay, for all the sons *she* could give him!

Aunt Croce. What sons would you've had her give
him, the poor thing? She was no fatter than this. [*Showing her little finger.*] She held her soul in with her teeth!
And once he was a widower there could hardly be a

shortage of candidates for his hand, could there? To start with me: if he'd asked for my daughter, I'd have given her to him. But he didn't want anyone from our family—or our neighborhood—in the dead woman's place. Your niece was just someone to have a son by.

Gesa. May I ask what you mean by that? That it's my niece who's been found wanting?

[*At this point* LUZZA *comes over to listen, and in turning to make signs to her companions, bumps against* AUNT CROCE. *The latter wheels round, and in a rage pushes her against the others;* THEY *shout and laugh.*]

Aunt Croce. Jumping Juniper, what a pest of a girl! I told you to keep away. You're gossips!

La Moscardina [*picking up the conversation*]. A fine figure of a woman, Mita. A rose, that's what she is, a picture of health.

Aunt Croce. That may not mean anything. Very often . . .

Gesa. Oh, you can't be serious, Aunt Croce? Just put those two together, gracious God! and I defy anyone to say which has been found wanting!

Aunt Croce. Pardon me, if he does so much shouting about having a child, that means he could have one, it seems to me; otherwise he'd keep quiet.

Gesa. He should thank God my niece is a good girl—so there's no putting her to the test! But take it from me, Aunt Croce, a saint from heaven wouldn't put up with the old rascal's ill-treatment and the scoldings he gives her in front of everybody. The Virgin Mary herself wouldn't stand for it. "So you want me to have a baby, do you?" she'd shout back at him. "Just wait here, I'll have a baby all right!"

La Moscardina. Oh, the Lord forbid!

Gesa [*suddenly correcting herself*]. You don't think I mean my niece would . . . !

La Moscardina. It would be a mortal sin!

Gesa. My niece? She'd rather be hanged than do a thing like that!

La Moscardina. A golden girl if ever there was one, and wise from the time she was small! [*Wondering if she's overdone it.*] No offense, I hope?

Aunt Croce. Why no, who denies it?

Ciuzza [*from the back, seeing* AUNT NINFA *pass in front of the tettoia with* TININO, CALICCHIO, *and* PALLINO]. Oh, here's Aunt Ninfa with Liolà's three canaries!

Luzza and *Nela* [*clapping their hands*]. Aunt Ninfa! Aunt Ninfa!

Ciuzza [*calling*]. Tinino!

[TININO *runs up and jumps into her arms.*]

Luzza [*calling*]. Calicchio!

[CALICCHIO *runs up and jumps into her arms.*]

Nela [*calling*]. Pallino!

[PALLINO *runs up and jumps into her arms.*]

Aunt Ninfa. For heaven's sake, girls, let them be! They've been making my head turn like a spinning-wheel. And you see how late it's getting for me to go to Mass.

Ciuzza [*to* TININO]. Who's your sweetheart?

Tinino. You! [*And kisses her.*]

Luzza [*to* CALICCHIO]. What about you, Calicchio?

Calicchio. You! [*And kisses her.*]

Nela [*to* PALLINO]. Pallino, what about you?

Pallino. You! [*And kisses her.*]

La Moscardina. "A wolf's offspring are born with their teeth!"

Gesa. Poor Aunt Ninfa, she's like an old hen with her chicks!

Aunt Ninfa. Three poor little innocents without a mother . . .

La Moscardina. He should thank God they're but three! Since he makes a rule of *keeping* all the children the women pour in his lap—three? Why, there could be thirty.

Aunt Croce [*indicating the girls with a look*]. Quiet, Mother Carmina, sh!

La Moscardina. I'm not saying anything bad. We can all see he has a good heart.

Aunt Ninfa. He wants a whole brood of chicks, he says. He'll teach them all singing, carry them off to town in a cage, and sell them.

Ciuzza. Will you live in a cage, Tinino, like a canary? Can you sing?

La Moscardina [*stroking* PALLINO'S *fine hair*]. Is he Rose of Favara's son?

Aunt Ninfa. Who? Pallino? What if I told you I don't know myself any more? No, Tinino is Rosa's son, it seems to me.

Ciuzza. No, no, not Tinino. He's *my* son, Tinino!

Gesa. Ay, and woe betide you if it were so!

Aunt Ninfa [*resentfully*]. And why?

La Moscardina. Wife of Liolà?!

Aunt Ninfa. You shouldn't talk that way, Mother Carmina. If ever there was a loving and dutiful lad it's my son Liolà.

La Moscardina. Loving? And how! He sees a hundred and wants a hundred.

Aunt Ninfa. That means he hasn't yet found *one*— [SHE *looks intently at* TUZZA.]—the right one . . . Well, well, let me be on my way, girls. [SHE *goes over to* TUZZA.] What's the matter, Tuzza, aren't you feeling all right?

La Moscardina. She's had the sulks ever since morning, Tuzza has.

Tuzza [*rudely*]. There's nothing wrong with me!

Aunt Croce. Let her alone, Aunt Ninfa: she was feverish last night.

Gesa. I'll come with you, Aunt Ninfa, if there's nothing else to do here.

La Moscardina. You'll only be in time for the ladies' Mass.[1]

Aunt Ninfa. For heaven's sake, don't talk to me of the ladies' Mass! I was there last Sunday and didn't see the service. The devil tempted me. My eyes fell on the ladies' fans, and I took to staring at them till I couldn't see the Mass!

Ciuzza. Why? What did you see in the fans?

Luzza. Tell us, tell us.

Aunt Ninfa. The devil, my daughters. It was as if he was sitting nearby to show me how the ladies made a breeze. I'll show you. [SHE *sits down and they all make a circle around her.*] The unmarried girls, like this—[SHE *mimics the rapid shaking of a fan while at the same time sticking out her chest and saying very fast.*] "I shall have him! I shall have him! I shall have him! I shall have him! I shall have him!" The married ladies like this—[*Moving her hand with calm and serious satisfaction.*] "I have him! I have him! I have him!" And the poor widows— [SHE *moves her hand with mournful abandon from her bosom down to her lap.*] "I had him but have him no more! I had him but have him no more! I had him but have him no more!" [THEY *all laugh.*] I kept crossing myself, but it was no use: I couldn't get rid of the temptation.

Ciuzza, Nuzza and *Nela* [*in chorus, using their hands as little fans*]. Oh, what fun! I shall have him! I shall have him! I shall have him! I shall have him! I shall have him!

La Moscardina. How crazy they are, just look!

[*At this point, the voice of* LIOLÀ *is heard from a distance.* HE *is coming home from the village in his cart, singing.*]

[1] The fashionable, late Mass.

Liolà's voice.

Two and twenty days I have not seen thee
I'm straining at the leash, I'm barking madly . . .

Gesa. Oh, here's Liolà coming home with his cart.

Ciuzza, Nuzza and *Nela* [*running in front of the tettoia with the children in their arms.*] Liolà! Liolà! Liolà! [THEY *shout gaily and signal to him to come near.*]

Aunt Ninfa. Down, girls, put the children down, or he won't let me get to Mass, the madcap!

[LIOLÀ *comes in wearing his Sunday clothes: a green velvet coat, a close-fitting jacket, and bell-bottomed trousers. On his head, a boat-shaped beret, "English" style, with two ribbons hanging down behind.*]

Liolà. Aha! So they've gone and found their mothers, these boys! Their three mothers—it's plenty! [*Putting the children down: first,* TININO, *then,* CALICCHIO, *and last* PALLINO.] And this one is LI, this one is O, and LÀ! The three together make up LIOLÀ! [*While the girls laugh and clap their hands,* HE *goes up to his mother.*] How's this, it's you? Still here?

Aunt Ninfa. No, look, I'm going, I'm going . . .

Liolà. Where to? Into the village? At this hour? Come on with you! Never mind about Mass for today—Aunt Croce, God be with you!

Aunt Croce. Amen, and you stay over there, my lad!

Liolà. Over here? What if I wanted to come over *there?*

Aunt Croce. I'd take the rolling-pin and . . .

Ciuzza [*approvingly*]. . . . let out some of your crazy blood!

Liolà. You'd like that, would you? You'd like to let some of the crazy blood out of me? [HE *makes a game of taking hold of her.*]

Luzza and *Nela* [*taking hold of him to defend their comrade*]. Hands off her! Hands off her!

La Moscardina. What a madcap! Let him alone, girls! Don't you see how he's dolled up?

Ciuzza. Oh yes, in his Sunday best! Why?

Luzza. What elegance!

Nela. Whence comes this—Englishman?

Liolà [*strutting*]. Am I handsome or am I not? I'm going to be married.

Ciuzza. To what she-devil straight from hell?

Liolà. Yourself, my beauty. Don't you want me?

Ciuzza. My God, I'd prefer fire and brimstone!

Liolà. Then you, Luzza! Come, if I really wanted you . . .

Luzza [*very saucily*]. I wouldn't want *you!*

Liolà. No?

Luzza [*stamping her foot*]. No.

Liolà. You act proud because you know I don't want you, any of you. Otherwise, I'd only need to breathe— [He *breathes*] and you'd come flying to me! Well, what do you expect me to do with three butterflies like you? A little pinch, a little squeeze—they'd be wasted—you are not for me.

>She that will reign, a tyrant, over me
>Beauty's queen and Virtue's must she be.

Ciuzza, Luzza and *Nela* [*clapping their hands*]. Hooray for Liolà, hooray! Let's have another verse! Another, Liolà!

Gesa. He unwinds them like a rosary!

La Moscardina. Another one, come on! Don't wait to be persuaded!

The Girls. Yes, yes, another, another!

Liolà. Here I am! I never needed persuading! [*To his three "canaries," placing them around him.*] Pay attention, all of you. [He *sings:*]

>My brain it is a windmill:
>When the wind blows, it's never still.

With me the world
(Sea, sky, and ground)
Also is twirled
Is twirled and seems a merry-go-round.

[HE *strikes up a dance melody, beating out a rhythm with feet and hands, the three children bounding about him. Then* HE *stops and starts singing again.*]

Today my heart
With love doth smart
I languish
In anguish
Sweet girl, for thee!
But tomorrow thou must not wait for me:
My brain is like the fruit on the tree,
My brain it is a windmill:
The wind blows and it's never still.

[*Dance melody and children's dance as above. The* GIRLS *laugh and clap. But* AUNT CROCE *shows annoyance.*]

La Moscardina. Well done! [*Mockingly.*] Is this how you want to find your queen?

Liolà. Who says I haven't found her already and she simply doesn't know why I laugh and sing this way? Pretending is a virtue. "If you can't pretend, you can't be king."

Aunt Croce. That's enough, boys! Let's stop now: I have a lot of things to straighten out.

La Moscardina. What about the agreement with Uncle Simone? He's supposed to give us something to drink!

Aunt Croce. Something to drink? Forget it—after what you just blurted out!

La Moscardina. That's good, that is! Liolà, do you know why he doesn't want to give us anything to drink— Uncle Simone? Because I told him he hadn't any sons to leave his inheritance to!

Ciuzza. As if that was a reason!

Liolà. Let me handle it. [*Goes to the shop door and calls out.*] Uncle Simone, Uncle Simone, come here, I have a piece of good news for you.

Uncle Simone [*coming out of the shop*]. What do you want, you scheming rogue?

Liolà. They've made a new law, especially for us— I mean, to relieve the condition of our people. Listen. If a man has a sow and it brings him twenty little pigs, he's rich, isn't he? He sells them, and the more little pigs she brings him, the richer he is. The same with a cow —the more calves she brings. Now these women of ours, God save the mark, you merely touch them and they've a pain in the belly: what can a poor fellow do? He's ruined, isn't he? Very well: the government has thought of this. They've passed a law that from now on little boys can be sold. Bought and sold, Uncle Simone. As for me, look. [He *shows him the three children.*] I can open a shop. Would you like a little boy? I'll sell you one. Here, this one. Look what a fat piece of meat he is! Firm as can be! Weighs fifty pounds! Nothing but juice! Take him and weigh him! I'll let you have him for a mere nothing—one barrel of your cherry wine.

[*The* Women *laugh, while the* Old Man, *antagonized, fights back.*]

Uncle Simone. Go away! And stop it! I don't like to joke about such things.

Liolà. You think I'm joking? What I say is serious. If you don't have any, you buy yourself one. Now don't stand there like a sick old capon with ruffled feathers!

Uncle Simone [*between bursts of laughter from the* Women; *in a rage*]. Let me go, let me go, I tell you, or, by God, I won't answer for what I'll do!

Liolà [*detaining him*]. No, sir! Stay there and don't take offence! We're neighbors here, we have country blood in our veins, and one good turn deserves another. I am fertile, you are not . . .

Uncle Simone. I'm not, aren't I? You know, do you? Wouldn't I just like to show you!

Liolà [*pretending to be terrified*]. Show me? No! God forbid! You're going to show me a miracle? [*Pushing towards him one of the three girls after another.*] Try yourself out with this one—or this one—or this!

Aunt Croce. Now, now, now, children, what are we coming to? I don't like this joke, let's be done with it.

Liolà. No harm meant, Aunt Croce. We're in the country—where some take the high road and some take the low road. Uncle Simone takes the low road: he's flabby and feeble and getting on in years. Prod him with your finger, and it leaves a mark.

Uncle Simone [*with raised hands, hurling himself forward*]. You filthy rascal, just wait till I leave a mark on you!

[Liolà *defends himself by jumping quickly to one side.*
    Uncle Simone *is about to fall.*]

Liolà [*holding him up*]. Tch, tch, Uncle Simone, you should drink ironized wine!

Ciuzza, Luzza and *Nela.* What's that? What *is* ironized wine?

Liolà. What is it? You take a piece of iron, fire it till it's red hot, stick it in a glass of wine, and knock it down! It works wonders. Thanks be to God they haven't dispossessed you yet, Uncle Simone!

Uncle Simone. Would you have them dispossess me as well?

Liolà. Why, sure. That's another law they could make any time. Listen. Here is a piece of earth. If you stand staring at it and doing nothing, what does the earth yield? Nothing. Just like a woman. She doesn't give you children . . . Good. Then *I* come along, on this piece of earth. I hoe it, I manure it, I dig a hole in it, I throw seed in the hole. A tree starts sprouting. Who has the earth given this tree to?—Why, me!—You come along and say: No, it's yours . . . Why yours? Because the earth is yours?—But the earth, Uncle Simone, does it know who it belongs to? It gives its fruit to anybody who works it. You can grab it because your foot is planted on it and the law supports you. But tomorrow the law may change, and you'll be thrown aside with a push of the hand. The earth remains, and I toss seed into it, and look: the tree is in leaf!

Uncle Simone. Ah, you're clever, I can see that.

Liolà. Me? No. Don't be afraid of *me,* Uncle Simone. I don't want anything. I leave it to you to worry about your money and stand guard over them with your snakes' eyes darting hither and yon.

> Last night I slept the sleep I love,
> My cabin roof the stars above,
> A bit of earth, it was my bed,
> And there were thistles 'neath my head.
> Hunger and thirst and sorrow's sting,
> They touch me not: for I can sing!
> My heart, it jumps for joy: I sing!
> Of all the earth and sea I'm king.
> I wish to all men health and sun,
> To me may lovely lasses run!
> May curly children round me gather
> With an old lady like my mother!

[HE *embraces and kisses his mother while the* GIRLS, *much moved, clap their hands. Then, turning to* AUNT CROCE.] Come on, then, what's left to do, Aunt Croce? The shelled almonds have to be carried into Uncle Simone's shop?—Forward march! Hurry, girls, and Uncle Simone will give us something to drink! [HE *enters the shop and, from the door, starts loading the full sacks of almonds on the women's shoulders.*] Now, who's first?— This one's for you, Nela. Okay!—This one for you,

Ciuzza. Okay!—This one for you, Moscardina, keep your chin up!—This little one for you, Aunt Gesa.—And here's the biggest of the lot for me to carry.—Come on, let's get going, girls! Let's get going, Uncle Simone!

Uncle Simone [to Aunt Croce]. I'll come back later and bring you the money, cousin.

Aunt Croce. Don't put yourself out, cousin. Give it me at your convenience.

Liolà [to Aunt Ninfa]. You come behind me with the children. We'll sell him one of them, that's certain. [He is leaving with the Women and Uncle Simone. But when they have all gone off, He turns back.] Wait for a minute, Aunt Croce. I'll be back—to tell you something.

Aunt Croce. Tell me?

[Tuzza jumps angrily to her feet.]

Liolà [turning to look at her]. What's the matter with you?

Aunt Croce [also turning to look at her daughter]. Ah! What does this mean?

Liolà. Nothing, Aunt Croce. She's probably been taken with a cramp. Don't take any notice. I'll be back in a minute. [He goes off at the rear with the sack on his shoulders.]

Tuzza [at once, angrily]. Now look: I don't want him, I don't want him, I don't want him!

Aunt Croce [suddenly still]. You don't want him? What are you saying?

Tuzza. He'll come and ask for my hand, as you'll see. I don't want him!

Aunt Croce. Are you mad? Who wants to give him to you?—Tell me something: how could the fellow have the cheek to come and ask me for your hand?

Tuzza. I don't want him, I tell you! I don't want him!

Aunt Croce. Answer me, you bad girl: have you—been with him?—Ah! So it's true!—Where? When?

Tuzza. Don't shout like that. In front of everybody!

Aunt Croce. You wretch, you wretch! So you're lost? [*Seizing her by the arms and looking her in the eyes.*] Tell me, tell me!—Come inside, come inside!

[SHE *drags her into the house and shuts the door. From the interior crying and shouts are heard. Meanwhile songs and the sound of tambourines are heard from* UNCLE SIMONE'S *farmhouse in the distance.* AUNT CROCE *emerges a little later in a state of confusion and tearing her hair. Like a madwoman, not knowing what she is doing,* SHE *distractedly starts putting things in order under the tettoia.*]

Aunt Croce. Dear God, on the holy sabbath, on the holy sabbath! And what's to be done now? I'll kill her, I'll kill her! Hold Thou my hand, O Lord, or I shall kill her! She has the gall to tell me *I'm* to blame, the shameless hussy. Me! Because marrying her to Uncle Simone was my idea! But for me, she says, she'd never have dreamt of it! [*Going back to the door.*] Even if this was so, would it be any reason why you should give yourself to a crook?

Tuzza [*looking out of the door, all bruised and dishevelled, but saucy and stubborn*]. Yes, yes, yes!

Aunt Croce. Stay indoors, you jailbird! Don't you show yourself to me now or as sure as God's in heaven . . .

Tuzza. Will you let me speak or won't you?

Aunt Croce. Listen to her impudence! She dares to speak, she dares to speak!

Tuzza. Just now, it was all "Speak, girl, speak!" I didn't speak and you tried to force me with slapping and hitting. Now that I *want* to speak . . .

Aunt Croce. What more could you want to tell me? Isn't it enough, what you've already let me know?

Tuzza. I want to tell you *why* I've—been with Liolà.

Aunt Croce. Why? Because you're a shameless hussy, that's why!

Tuzza. No. Because when Uncle Simone took this little saint of a Mita instead of me, I knew the little saint was Liolà's sweetheart.

Aunt Croce. What of that? How did Liolà come into it once Mita was married to Uncle Simone?

Tuzza. He came into it because after four years of marriage he was still around her like a butterfly around a flame. I wanted to take him from her!

Aunt Croce. Ah! So that's it?

Tuzza. Yes, that's it! Must the little guttersnipe have all those things? Wasn't a rich husband enough? Without a gallant lover?

Aunt Croce. Stupid girl! Don't you see that the only person you've hurt is yourself? Now there's nothing left but for you to marry . . .

Tuzza [*interrupting*]. . . . what? *I,* marry *him? I* take a husband I'd have to share with all the other girls? I'd be crazy. I'm happy as a lost woman, do you know why? Because I can hand my hurt right back to the person who brought it me. If I'm ruined, so will she be. That's what I wanted to say.

Aunt Croce. How will you do it? Oh Lord, I think she's gone crazy, that's what I think.

Tuzza. No. I'm not crazy. Listen. Yesterday wasn't the first time Uncle Simone . . .

Aunt Croce. Uncle Simone . . . ?

Tuzza. . . . told me he was sorry it wasn't me he married, instead of Mita. [*As* SHE *speaks,* SHE *starts smoothing out her hair and combing it. Her eyes light up with malicious fire.*]

Aunt Croce. I know. He's told me, too. [*Shocked of a sudden.*] Is it possible you . . .

Tuzza [*pretending to be horrified*]. What? Me? With my uncle? Pah!

Aunt Croce. What then? What do you wish to do? I don't understand.

Tuzza. How many relatives has Uncle Simone? More than we have hairs on our heads, isn't that so? [*And* SHE *shows the hair* SHE *is busy plaiting.*] And children? Not a one. Good. Before, it couldn't be; but now it can.

Aunt Croce [*stunned*]. You're trying to have him understand that the baby . . .

Tuzza. Not to "have him understand." There'll be no need. I'll throw myself at his feet. I'll confess all.

Aunt Croce. And then?

Tuzza. And then he'll have the others understand— and his wife above all—that the child is his. This will give him so much satisfaction, he won't ask questions.

Aunt Croce. You're a devil, you're a devil! Do you want to make everyone believe . . .

Tuzza. Lost is lost. Now that I've done the evil deed with that . . .

Aunt Croce [*interrupting*]. Be off with you indoors, indoors! Here he comes with Liolà! [TUZZA *disappears indoors.*] Mother of God, how'll I be able to bear it? How? [SHE *takes the broom and starts sweeping up all the almond shells that are still on the ground, pretending to be enormously happy.*]

Liolà [*entering with* UNCLE SIMONE]. Very well, give your cousin the money, Uncle Simone, and be gone. I must talk with Aunt Croce at once.

Aunt Croce. You? And who are you to tell my cousin to be gone? My cousin—for your information—is thoroughly at home here. Come in, come in, Cousin, Tuzza is over there.

Uncle Simon. I can give the money to you?

Aunt Croce. If you want. If you don't want, that's all right too. You are the master here and can do what you please. Come in and let me hear what this madcap wants to tell me.

Uncle Simone. Don't pay any attention, Cousin. He'll make your head spin round, as he has mine. He *is* crazy, it's a fact! [HE *enters the farmhouse, and* AUNT CROCE *shuts the door.*]

Liolà [*almost to himself*].　Ah well, I realize now . . .

Aunt Croce.　What do you say?

Liolà.　Nothing. I was going to say something, but why? It seems . . . it seems there's no longer any need. You say I'm crazy. And I realize now you're right, both of you! Imagine: I was wanting to sell him a son. *Sell* a son, to Uncle Simone! He wants one for nothing! And I'll be blessed if he hasn't seen his way to *getting* one for nothing!

Aunt Croce.　What do you say? This is wild talk!

Liolà.　I saw your daughter Tuzza jump a foot in the air when I said I'd come back and talk to you . . .

Aunt Croce.　I noticed it too. And so . . . ?

Liolà.　In addition you receive Uncle Simone into your house with all your best flattery and gush, and there he is from morning to night . . .

Aunt Croce.　Do you have any orders to give in my house? If Uncle Simone may come in or go out?

Liolà.　No orders, Aunt Croce. I have only come to do my duty. I don't want anyone to say I was found wanting.

Aunt Croce.　What might this duty of yours be? Let's hear.

Liolà.　This: I'll tell you at once. But you already know. I can't live caged up, Aunt Croce, *I'm* a bird that must fly—here today, there tomorrow, in the sun, the water, the wind. I sing and am drunk—on song and sun— I hardly know which affects me more. For all that, here I am: I'm clipping my wings and have come to shut myself in a cage of my own making. I am asking for your daughter Tuzza's hand.

Aunt Croce.　You? Ha! You must have gone off your head in good earnest. My daughter? See here: I'd hand her over to the hangman rather than give her to you. You understand? The hangman . . . Aren't you satisfied to have ruined *three* poor girls? Tell me.

Liolà. Oh, come on, drop it, Aunt Croce, *I* haven't ruined anyone—ever!

Aunt Croce. Three sons—did you give birth to them by yourself? You're like those snakes that bewitch our cows!

Liolà. Be quiet. You know very well how my children were born and who bore them. Everybody knows . . . Wenches off the streets.—"It is bad to force a well-guarded gate," but he who travels an open and beaten track . . . Well, no one on these beaten tracks, I can tell you, would scruple to kick aside any obstacle that crosses his path: *I* didn't do it. Three poor little innocents . . . They live with my mother and wouldn't dream of giving trouble, Aunt Croce. They're boys, and when they grow up . . . Well, as you know, in the country the more arms and legs we have, the richer we are. And I'm a breadwinner: stableman, day-laborer, I reap, I clip hedges, I cut hay, I do a bit of everything, I'm never at a loss. I'm like an oven at Easter, Aunt Croce, I could feed a whole village.

Aunt Croce. Very good, my lad. Now see if you can find someone to take this fine speech to. It leaves me cold.

Liolà. Aunt Croce, don't talk like that. Look: I wouldn't like to commit an outrage. But I also wouldn't like others to commit an outrage and make use of me . . . I desire your daughter to tell me in the presence of Uncle Simone that she doesn't want me.

Aunt Croce. She doesn't want you, she doesn't want you! She told me so herself just a short time ago. And she repeated it. She doesn't want you!

Liolà [*to himself, holding a lip between two fingers*]. Ah! so it's true? [HE *is going to make a dash for the door.*

But AUNT CROCE *forestalls him and places herself in the way.* THEY *stand looking into each other's eyes for a moment.*] Aunt Croce!

Aunt Croce. Liolà!

Liolà. I want Tuzza to tell me, you understand? Tuzza, with her own lips, and in front of Uncle Simone!

Aunt Croce. Yet again: Tuzza has nothing further to say to you. I'm telling you myself. Let that suffice! Go away! It'll be better for you!

Liolà. Better for me, certainly; but not for a certain other person, you understand? Look: you won't succeed, Aunt Croce! [HE *puts his arm under her nose.*] Smell!

Aunt Croce. Go away! What do you want me to smell?

Liolà. Don't you smell anything?

Aunt Croce. Yes, I smell you: you're a bad egg!

Liolà. No, just a spoilsport! The cards are badly shuffled, but I shan't lose the game because of *that,* you watch!—For the moment let's say I've lost one trick and part friends.

Aunt Croce. Yes, yes, good, now go away. Go away and stay away. Stay away!

Liolà [*ruminating, laughing to himself, and taking a wide sweep in order to pass before* TUZZA's *door.* HE *sings. After every line, a derisive burst of laughter*].

Today no one gives it a thought (ha! ha! ha!)
If you jump you may be caught (ha! ha! ha!)
And you'll be left with a handful of naught . . .

[*Exit at the back.* AUNT CROCE *stays, lost in thought. A little later the farmhouse door is opened and out of it come* UNCLE SIMONE *and* TUZZA. *The latter is quite overcome with weeping—spurious or genuine. The former is troubled and flustered.* THEY *don't speak for a time because* AUNT CROCE *has immediately signalled to them to keep quiet.*]

Uncle Simone [*softly interrogatory*].   What did he say?
What did he want?

The Voice of Liolà [*in the distance*].
And you'll be left with a handful of naught . . .

Uncle Simone [*to* TUZZA]. Ah! With him? [TUZZA
hides her face in her hands.] But . . . but tell me: does
he know?

Tuzza [*immediately*]. No, no, he doesn't know a
thing! Nobody knows!

Uncle Simone.   Very good. [*To* AUNT CROCE.] Only on
this condition, cousin: that nobody knows! As for the
boy—he's mine!

The Voice of Liolà [*from further off still*].
And you'll be left with a handful of naught . . .

ACT TWO

*Part of the farmstead. At the audience's left, almost in
the middle of the stage,* GESA's *little house. We see the
front of it and, receding from us, the side (which is
shorter). In front there is a little door facing the orchard.
The orchard is shut in at the side (i.e. from the corner of
the house down to the proscenium) by a bramble hedge
with a little gate across the passage-way in the middle. In
the side of the house a larger door is seen—the "street"
door.*

To the audience's right is LIOLÀ's *house (his mother
NINFA and the three children also live there) with a
door and two windows. Between the orchard hedge and
LIOLÀ's house is the "street" (an unpaved pathway).*

As the CURTAIN RISES, GESA *is sitting in the orchard,
busy peeling potatoes, with a great lead colander between
her knees.* LIOLÀ's *three little boys are with her.*

Gesa.   Are you really a clever boy, Pallino?

Pallino. Yes, I am.

Calicchio. Me too!

Gesa. You too?

Tinino. And me too! Me too!

Gesa. But who's the cleverest of the three?

Pallino. Me, me!

Calicchio. No, me, me!

Tinino. No, no! Me, me, me!

Gesa. All three then! You're all equally clever. Pallino's the big boy, of course, you can't deny that! So tell me something, Pallino, will you? Could you run over there—you see where I mean—[She *points to a certain spot in the orchard, off stage at right.*]—and pick me three onions?

Pallino. Oh, yes. [He *starts to run.*]

Gesa. Wait!

Calicchio. Me too! Me too!

Tinino. Me too!

Gesa. Careful, boys: one onion each, one each! Pallino will take you there.

All Three [*running to the point she indicates*]. Oh, yes, yes!

Gesa. Steady! Only three! Three! Well done, that'll be enough! [*The* THREE BOYS *come back, each with an onion in his hand.*] Well, so it's true: you're all equally clever!

[*At this point the* VOICE *of* AUNT NINFA *is heard from* LIOLÀ'S *house calling out a refrain which must be habitual to her.*]

Voice of Aunt Ninfa. Pallino, Calicchio, Tinino!

Gesa. They're here with me, Aunt Ninfa, don't worry.

Aunt Ninfa [*showing herself at the door*]. They stick to you like flies. Come inside! Inside this minute! [*Goes back in the house.*]

Gesa. Let them stay, Aunt Ninfa: they don't bother me—why, they help me!

Aunt Ninfa. If they bother you, just pack them off!

Gesa. Don't worry. With me they'll be as quiet as three tortoises.

Aunt Ninfa. That's all right then. [*Goes back in the house.*]

Gesa. Otherwise, as soon as Daddy comes home . . . tell me something what does Daddy do? What does he do?

Pallino [*with complete gravity*]. He teaches us singing.

Gesa. And doesn't he play a tune on your backsides too if you're the despair of your granny and won't be good?

[CIUZZA *is seen coming down the "street."* SHE *stops at the hedge and looks over.*]

Ciuzza. Please, Aunt Gesa, do you have a little sprig of garlic to lend my mother?

Gesa. Oh, yes, come in, Ciuzza. [SHE *indicates the house door behind her.*] Just go and take it for yourself.

Ciuzza [*pushing the lattice and coming through*]. Thanks, Aunt Gesa. Do you always have these boys with you? They're sweet! Who wouldn't enjoy being a mother to them?

Gesa. Mm! *You* would, I imagine, with all your heart!

Ciuzza. As an act of charity, I mean! Don't misunderstand me, Aunt Gesa!

Gesa. Oh, certainly: as an act of charity! Who'd doubt it?

Ciuzza. Anyway, tell me one thing: Liolà . . .

[LUZZA *and* NELA *also come down the "street."* THEY *also stop at the hedge and look over.*]

Luzza. Do you want us, Aunt Gesa? Ooh, look: Ciuzza's there!

Gesa [*aside*]. Here come the other two!

Nela. We've come to help you, Aunt Gesa. Are you peeling the potatoes?

Gesa. You want to help me? God bless you; so you're housewives now! [*Aside.*] There must be birdlime in this orchard, and it sticks. Come in, come in. He hasn't come back yet though. [*A malicious allusion to* LIOLÀ.]

Nela [*pretending not to understand*]. Who, Aunt Gesa?

Gesa. Who? Don't play the simpleton!

Luzza [*sitting on her heels in front of* GESA]. Give me some. I have the knife. I'll help you with your peeling.

Gesa. But not that way! Pallino, run and bring a chair!

Nela. No, *I'll* go, Aunt Gesa! [*Goes and comes back with three chairs.*]

Gesa. Three lovely girls sitting here just to be of use to me? Meanwhile I wouldn't like your mother to be kept waiting for that sprig of garlic!

Ciuzza. Oh, it's for this evening.

Gesa. Ah! It's evening already, it seems to me! . . . He's practically here now! [*Another allusion to* LIOLÀ.]

Ciuzza [*also pretending not to understand*]. Who, Aunt Gesa?

Gesa. The cat! . . . Don't *you* play the simpleton either!

Luzza. Do you mean Liolà.

Gesa. I'm malicious, didn't you know?

Ciuzza. I wanted to ask you, Aunt Gesa, if it's true Tuzza has refused him?

Gesa [*now* SHE *pretends not to understand*]. Refused? Who?

Luzza [*as the others laugh*]. Don't *you* play the simpleton, Aunt Gesa!

Nela. I've heard it was her mother—Aunt Croce.

Luzza. You don't know a thing about it?

Ciuzza. Oh no, they say it was really her—Tuzza.

Nela. Tuzza . . . but if . . . [*shutting her mouth*] —stop, don't make me speak!

Luzza. What about him—Liolà? What does *he* say? We'd like to know!

Gesa. You want *me* to tell you! Go and ask *him*!

Ciuzza. Serve him right if it were true!

Nela. Serve him right!

Ciuzza. He thought he'd only to do this—[*making a small gesture*]—with his hand and all the women'd throw themselves out of the window for him!

Gesa. Not any of *you* three!

Luzza. Who ever gave him a thought!

Ciuzza. Who's after him?

Nela. Who wants him?

Gesa. Hm! Anyone can see it!

Luzza. Why are we here now to ask you . . . ?

Nela. We've come because we'd like to hear how he sings when he sings for spite!

Ciuzza. He must be *boiling* with rage, I should think.

Luzza. What is he doing? Is he singing?

Nela. Do tell us, Aunt Gesa. Is he singing?

Gesa [*stopping up her ears*]. Oho, what do you want from me, girls? Look, over there's Aunt Ninfra. Ask *her* if he's singing or not!

[AUNT NINFA *shows herself in the doorway as if on call.*]

Aunt Ninfa. What is it? Do you have grasshoppers in your garden, Neighbor Gesa?

Luzza, Ciuzza and *Nela* [*suddenly confused, all together*]. Not at all, Aunt Ninfa. . . . Good afternoon, Aunt Ninfa. . . . [*Aside.*] Oooh, look, *she* was there!

Gesa. It's not grasshoppers, it's three wasps, I think, that have fastened themselves onto me, Aunt Ninfa. They want to know . . .

Luzza, Ciuzza and *Nela.* No, not at all!—It's not true —It's not true.

Gesa. But it is! They want to know if Liolà is singing for very spite—because Tuzza didn't want him for a husband?

Aunt Ninfa. My son? Who said that?

Luzza, Ciuzza and *Nela.* They all say it! . . . Is it true?! It's God's truth! Don't deny it, Aunt Ninfa!

Aunt Ninfa. I know nothing about it. If it's true, Tuzza has done well and Aunt Croce, her mother, has done better, refusing to give her. If I had daughters, I wouldn't give one to a man like Liolà, I wouldn't give him a bitch from my kennels! Tch, tch, tch! Keep an eye on yourselves, girls! He has all the blackest sins to his account. Beware of him as of the devil! Then again, with the three little ones here . . . Be off, kiddies, into the house with you!

[*At this point the cries of* LA MOSCARDINA *are heard from up the "street."* SHE *enters, thoroughly agitated, her hands in the air.*]

La Moscardina. Holy Jesus, what goings-on! It's not to be believed! This is the end!

Ciuzza. Ah! La Moscardina! You hear how she shouts?

Luzza. What's the matter with you?

Nela. What are you shouting about?

Là Moscardina [*entering the orchard*]. Ruin, Neighbor Gesa, ruin has come to your niece's house!

Gesa [*leaping to her feet*]. My niece? What's happened to her? Speak!

La Moscardina. She's like a Mourning Mary, with her hands in her hair!

Gesa. But *why?* Mother of God! Let me go! Let me go! [SHE *runs up the "street," turning and disappearing at the left.*]

The Others [*in one voice*]. What's happened to Mita? Speak! What was it?

La Moscardina. Uncle Simone, her husband . . . [SHE *looks at them and says nothing more.*]

The Others [*at once, urging her on*]. . . . Well?—Say it!—What has he done?

La Moscardina. He's—taken up with his niece!

Luzza, Ciuzza, Nela and *Aunt Ninfa* [*all together*]. —With Tuzza?—Is it possible?—Just think! Lord, what are you saying?

La Moscardina. That's how it is. And it seems that Tuzza is already . . . [*Surreptitiously she makes a sign to* AUNT NINFA *giving her to understand* TUZZA *is pregnant.*]

Aunt Ninfa [*with horror*]. Madonna save us!

Luzza, Ciuzza and *Nela.* What's this, what's this?— Tuzza? It seems what? *What* has she done?

La Moscardina. Be off with you, girls, these matters are none of your business, run along!

Aunt Ninfa. But it's certain? Certain?

La Moscardina. He's gone to his wife and boasted of it!

Aunt Ninfa. He had the impertinence!

La Moscardina. Yes. He boasted that it wasn't him who'd been found wanting—if he'd married his niece, says he, by this time he could have had *three* children!

Ciuzza [*to* AUNT NINFA]. Pardon me, wasn't Tuzza running around with your son Liolà up to yesterday?

Aunt Ninfa. I told you I know nothing about it!

La Moscardina. Now, Aunt Ninfa, no fairy tales! Would you deny it? Or can you really swallow the idea of Uncle Simone . . . by himself . . . ? Mother and daughter have got together and pushed the old man's head in a sack!

Aunt Ninfa. Tch, tch, tch, tch!

La Moscardina. Is it slander?

Aunt Ninfa. To bring my son into it *is,* yes!

La Moscardina. Aunt Ninfa: if so, I'll cut my hands open, first one, then the other!

Ciuzza. Me too!

Luzza. Me too!

Nela. Everybody knows it!

Aunt Ninfa. Everybody but me!

La Moscardina. Because you don't wish to know. Let's drop it!

Luzza. Oh, here *is* Mita! Here's Mita with her aunt!

[MITA *comes down the "street" with* AUNT GESA, *all dishevelled and sobbing. Hands on hips, running from the top of the "street" to the hedge and from the hedge to the top of the "street,"* AUNT GESA *shouts the following, while in the orchard the* WOMEN *comfort* MITA.]

Gesa. My daughter, my daughter! May God's thunder strike him! That he dared lay hands on her, the hoary old murderer, the hoary old scoundrel! Lay hands on her, on top of everything else! He grabbed her by the hair and dragged her through the house, the jailbird! All right: just let me go to the village! I place her in your hands, good neighbors! I'll have recourse to justice! Into jail with him!

La Moscardina. You're doing the right thing. Yes: go to the Deputy, do that!

Aunt Ninfa. No, not the Deputy. It's a lawyer you should go to: listen to me.

Gesa. I'll go to both! Into jail with the hoary old ruffian! He has the nerve to say the child is his as sure as the blood of Jesus is in the cup at Holy Mass!

Aunt Ninfa [*stopping up her ears*]. Heavens, what's going on!

Gesa. Into jail with the other two wretches as well, mother and daughter! Harlots!—Just let me go. It'll be night when I get to the village. No matter. I'll go sleep at my sister's place. You are at home here, Mita, among these good neighbors. Lock the doors carefully, front and side. I'm going. Into jail with them, into jail! . . . Scoundrel . . . Harlots . . . [*Still shouting,* SHE *disappears at the top of the "street."*]

La Moscardina. When you're separated, you have the right to a maintenance, don't you worry!

Aunt Ninfa. Separated! What are you saying! You intend to let him win? You're his wife, you must stay his wife!

Mita. No! I've had enough! I'll never go back to him, you can be certain of that! Not if they were to kill me!

Aunt Ninfa. Don't you see that's just what they want?

La Moscardina. Surely! Mother and daughter are planning to lord it in the old man's house and give all the other relatives garlic to eat!

Mita. You wish me to let myself be trodden under foot? I won't! I have nothing in common with him now, Aunt Ninfa. He's got what he desired from another and now they'd like me dead, all three of them!

La Moscardina. Dead? A mere word! There's the law, my dear. Your aunt has run to the village.

Mita. The law! Ha! It's four years I've been suffering. And you know what he came and shouted in my face? That I mustn't *dare* speak ill of his niece! Just that. Because his niece—says he—is a *good* girl!

Aunt Ninfa. Good? He said that?

La Moscardina. Unbelievable, unbelievable!

Ciuzza [*to* LUZZA *and* NELA]. Good! Well, I say!

Mita. That's what he said! Because she's taken up with him. And he'll leave her everything, says he. Because she's proved, says he, that it wasn't him that was found wanting, but me. And the law, says he, should provide a remedy for a poor fellow that has the misfortune to meet with a woman like me! Oh, Aunt Ninfa, my heart always told me not to take him. And I wouldn't have taken him if I hadn't been . . .

La Moscardina. . . . a poor helpless orphan, how true! . . .

. *Mita.* ... dependent on my aunt so I couldn't say no to her.—I was so peaceful and happy right here—in this little house, in this little orchard. You can bear me out, Aunt Ninfa, you saw it all. But God will find a way to punish the man who betrayed me!

La Moscardina [*with determination*]. Liolà will have to speak, Aunt Ninfa!

Aunt Ninfa. Liolà again! Will you ever stop naming my son?

La Moscardina. Now girls, *you* say if it isn't true!

Ciuzza, Luzza and *Nela.* Of course it's true! It was him, it was him!

Mita. I knew Liolà was fond of me when I lived here, Aunt Ninfa. But what fault of mine was it if I had to marry another?

Aunt Ninfa. Can you seriously think Liolà did this to spite you? After four years?

La Moscardina. No, no, I don't believe it myself. But if he's a gentleman, Liolà must go now and shout in the hoary old ruffian's face, telling him of the deceit practised by two foul females for the ruination of a fellow creature! That's what he must do if he has any conscience at all, this son of yours, Aunt Ninfa! Put to shame those two infamous wretches and thwart a conspiracy against a poor innocent girl!

[*Evening has arrived.* LIOLÀ *is heard singing as he returns home.*]

The Voice of Liolà.

What all my friends agree on is no riddle:
A man who takes a wife plays second fiddle . . .

La Moscardina. Here he comes, singing his way home! Now I'll talk to him, I'll tell him!

Ciuzza, Luzza and *Nela* [*leaning over the hedge and calling*]. Liolà, Liolà, Liolà!

Aunt Ninfa. Come along, my son!

La Moscardina. Here, Liolà!

Liolà [*to* LA MOSCARDINA]. At your service! [*Then,*
to the GIRLS.] Ah! The turtle doves!

La Moscardina. Let the turtle doves alone! Come
here. Look who's with us: Mita!

Liolà. Well, it's Mita . . . what's the matter?

La Moscardina. Have a conscience, Liolà. It's your
fault that Mita is crying.

Liolà. My fault?

La Moscardina. Yes. It's what you did with Tuzza,
Aunt Croce's daughter.

Liolà. Me? What *did* I do?

La Moscardina. Mother and daughter mean to have
Uncle Simone understand that the child . . .

Liolà. . . . the child? what child? . . .

La Moscardina. . . . ah! You ask? Why, Tuzza's
child . . .

Liolà. . . . Tuzza's? What do you say? So Tuzza
is . . . [*Makes a sign for "pregnant."*]

Aunt Ninfa. Off with you, girls, run along! As a favor
to me!

Luzza. Heavens above, always that "run along, run
along" . . .

Ciuzza. And the conversation that's "none of our
business"!

Liolà. Actually I don't understand this conversation
myself.

La Moscardina. Very well, go on playing simple
Simon!—Hey, are you going, girls? I can't talk with you
here!

Ciuzza. All right, we're going. Good evening, Aunt
Ninfa.

Luzza. Good evening, Mita.

Nela. Good evening, Neighbor Carmina.

Liolà. Not a word for me? Not even a greeting?

Ciuzza. Be off with you, impostor!

Luzza. Bad egg!

Nela.   Brazen fellow!

[ALL THREE *leave by the "street."*]

La Moscardina [*immediately starting in afresh, with determination*].   Tuzza's son is yours, Liolà!

Liolà.   Come now: enough! It's become a vicious habit with you people—all over our part of the country. A girl has more saliva in her mouth than usual—who did it?— Liolà!

La Moscardina.   Oh! You deny it?

Liolà.   Enough, I tell you! I don't know a thing about it.

La Moscardina.   Then why did you ask Aunt Croce for Tuzza's hand?

Liolà.   Ah! So that's it! I was wondering how I came into all this.

La Moscardina.   You're not denying it, are you?

Liolà.   I asked her . . . for fun . . . I was passing by . . .

La Moscardina [*to* AUNT NINFA].   You hear him, Aunt Ninfa? Now it's your turn: give him a motherly talking to. With me he laughs it off and plays the man about town. We have a weeping woman with us! [*Shouting.*] Have a little conscience! Look at her!

Liolà.   Surely, I see she's crying. But what for?

La Moscardina.   What for, you say? [*Turning on* AUNT NINFA *and stamping her foot.*] *You* talk!

Aunt Ninfa.   Because Uncle Simone . . . or so it seems . . .

La Moscardina [*aside*].   At last she's got around to it! —So it seems?—why, he even laid hands on her . . . !

Aunt Ninfa.   Yes, because he says he doesn't know what to do with her any more—now, says he, that he's going to have a child by his niece . . .

Liolà.   Ah! So it was him? Uncle Simone? Oh dear, oh dear: he's taken up with his niece?

Aunt Ninfa [to LA MOSCARDINA, *pointing at* LIOLÀ]. You see? My son is sincere. If it were as you say . . .

La Moscardina [taking no notice, turning to LIOLÀ]. You'd like me to swallow this? You who never wanted to have anything to do with marriage . . . ?

Liolà. . . . Me? Who told you that? Nothing to do with marriage? You're wrong: every five minutes . . .

La Moscardina. Pah! As a joke!

Liolà. No! With all my heart! I beg your pardon: it isn't my fault if no woman wants me. They all want me— all—and none! For five minutes, yes, when I first take the plunge . . . the priest should come running up at once with the holy water—but he doesn't and the marriage is off. . . . Let's think now, Tuzza . . . Hm, there's no denying that Aunt Croce chose her son-in-law well!—Hooray for Uncle Simone, he managed it at last! —He's a very cock . . . Old but of the best quality, that's clear . . . Well, I bet Tuzza . . . With the fine reception he prepared for Mita. . . . Don't take it hard, Mita, what can you do, you poor girl?

La Moscardina [blazing]. Is that all you have to say? All? Be off with you then! I'm boiling with bile! Just let me go. To have to fight with people who trample conscience under foot! [*And* SHE *goes off in a temper, her hands in the air.*]

Aunt Ninfa. She's completely crazy! Conscience, says she! She's pig-headed, good people, she can't believe it's not just as she suspects!

Liolà. Don't worry your head about it. Go—go and put the three little ones to bed. Look there: Tinino has gone to sleep.

[*Indeed the* CHILD *has gone to sleep, lying prone on the ground. The* TWO OTHERS *are dozing where they sit.*]

Aunt Ninfa. So he has, poor little chap . . . just look at him! [SHE *runs up; bends over him, and calls:*]

Tinino . . . Tinino . . . [*To* LIOLÀ.] Go on, take him, pick him up, give him to me. [SHE *holds out her arms to receive him.*]

[LIOLÀ *stoops, first making the sign of the cross over the sleeping child, then whistling to wake him up. But seeing that the child does not wake,* HE *quietly goes into the usual dance tune, clapping his hands as he does so.* TININO *then gets up. So do his* TWO BROTHERS. *And rubbing their eyes with their little hands—fists closed—*THEY *start bounding about. Still bounding along,* ALL THREE *enter the house, accompanied by their father who goes on singing and clapping.*]

Mita [*getting up*]. I'm going into the house. Good night, Aunt Ninfa.

Aunt Ninfa. If you need me, daughter, as soon as I've put these kiddies to bed, I'll come back.

Mita. No thank you. I'm shutting myself up for the night. Good night to you, too, Liolà.

[AUNT NINFA *goes into the house.*]

Liolà. You'll stay and sleep here tonight?

Mita. My aunt is up in the village.

Liolà. She's run to the Authorities?

Mita. She said she was going to a lawyer.

Liolà. Then you really don't wish to go back to your husband?

Mita. I've nothing in common with my husband now. Good night.

Liolà. Oh, how silly you are, Mita!

Mita. What do you expect? We can't all be bright like you, Liolà. You mean that *God* will look after it for me.

Liolà. God? Oh, sure. . . . He's *supposed* to look after it. He *did* look after it one time.—But however good you may be, my pious friend, you can hardly compare yourself with the Virgin Mary!

Mita. I? You blaspheme!

Liolà. Pardon me, but you said God must look after it. How? Through the medium of His Holy Spirit?

Mita. Stop, stop! It would be better for me to leave. I can't stand here listening to such heresies!

Liolà. Heresies . . . You are saying, rather, that God cannot help you in *that* way . . .

Mita. But I didn't mean "that way" at all, I didn't!

Liolà. Then how? By the scenes that La Moscardina has just been making here? Or your aunt's useless errands in the village? Beatings and screechings, the lawyer, the Deputy, a separation . . . ? Or else, dragging me into it, sending me to shout in Uncle Simone's face that Tuzza's child is mine?—These are things children would think of, things that could have come into your head and mine in the days when we played husbands and wives in this very orchard—and every now and then got in each other's hair—and ran off to put our case before your aunt or my mother, do you remember?

Mita. Yes, I remember. But, Liolà, it wasn't my fault —I said so just now to your mother—*God* knew where my heart was when I married . . .

Liolà. I know where it was too, Mita. . . . But that doesn't apply any longer. You are married. Let's say no more about it.

Mita. *You* introduced the subject: you asked if I remembered . . .

Liolà. But now we're talking of something else. . . . You are wrong and your husband is right.

Mita. I'm wrong?

Liolà. Pardon me, haven't you lost . . . how many years? Four? Five?—That's where you're wrong!—Your husband is worn out. You knew all along he made you his wife in order to have a son. Have you given him that son? No. He waited and waited, day in, day out. He tried everything, and came to the end of his tether. So finally, he's found another—to give him what you didn't give.

Mita. But . . . this favor . . . suppose God in His goodness didn't wish to show it to me?

Liolà. So you expect it to rain figs? You seriously want *God* to do it for you? Then you say *I* blaspheme! Ask Tuzza: go and ask who gave her this child.

Mita. The devil gave it her!

Liolà. No: Uncle Simone!

Mita. The devil, the devil!

Liolà. Uncle Simone!

Mita. Do you have the gall to say so to *me*? It's an outrage, Liolà, an outrage!

Liolà. That's why I say you're silly! [*Picking up the thread.*] Look! Suppose we do what La Moscardina says. I go to Uncle Simone. I even tie a cowbell round my neck and start shouting all over the countryside and in all the streets of the village: "Ding, dong, ding, dong! Uncle Simone's child is mine! Ding, dong, ding, dong! Uncle Simone's child is mine!" Who will believe it? Well, possibly they all will. Except him. He'll never believe it—for the good reason that he doesn't wish to. Make him believe it if you can!—And anyway, let's be fair—do you think Tuzza's child will be born tomorrow with a board on his forehead reading: LIOLÀ?—These things are not always clear even to the mother. . . . You can kill him and he'll *still* believe the child is his. Nor is there any way I can prove to him it's mine. But *you,* if you're not really silly, *you* above all should tell him it's true.

Mita. True—that the child is his?

Liolà. Yes, that it's his, and that it wasn't him that was found wanting, but you! Don't you see he's going to have a child by Tuzza and that—if he has a child now by Tuzza—he can have one tomorrow by you!

Mita. How?

Liolà. How? You ask you? *How* he's going to have a child by Tuzza?

Mita. Oh! [*Suddenly realizing.*] No! Not that! Never that!

Liolà. Good night then! Keep calm and don't cry any more. Who will you turn to? Why are you running away? Who are you complaining about? The others advise you what to do and you don't take their advice. It's you who let Tuzza commit this outrage, not me. That's why I denied it, that's why I deny it now. I deny it for you. For you and for your good—and because there's no other way out of this deceit, this outrage. Oh, you think you make trouble for yourself alone? God only knows what *I've* had to swallow! When I went there, to do my duty as a gentleman, and before my very eyes that wretch of a mother brought your husband in where Tuzza was—ha! —I saw the whole betrayal as in a picture. I saw you, Mita, and I saw what would become of you, and I swore to myself: they shall not have the best of it! I sealed my lips. I waited for this moment. No: this outrage must not stand, Mita. *You* shall punish them. God himself bids you do so. The wretch mustn't make use of me to bring about your ruin! [*On these last words,* HE *puts his arm round her waist.*]

Mita [*tearing herself free*]. No, no . . . let me alone . . . I'll never do it . . . no, I don't want to, I don't want . . . [*All of a sudden she stops, terrified, and listens:*] Ah! Sh! Wait! I hear someone coming . . . who's there?

Liolà [*drawing her toward the door of* AUNT GESA'S *house*]. Let's go in—at once!

Mita. No, it's him . . . it's him . . . it's my husband's step . . . Get away from here for heaven's sake!

[LIOLÀ *is at his own door with a bound. Bent double,* MITA *runs softly and hides in her aunt's house, closing the smaller door very quietly.*

Uncle Simone *is seen coming down the "street" with a lantern on a chain in his hand. He approaches the larger door of the house—the "street" door—and knocks several times.*]

Uncle Simone. Aunt Gesa! Aunt Gesa! Open, it's me —[*Hearing* Mita's *voice from inside.*] Ah! You? Open . . . I say, open!—Open, or I'll knock the door down!— No, I want to tell you something.—Yes, yes, I'll go away, but first, open!

[*The door opens and* Uncle Simone *enters. From the door of his own house,* Liolà's *head emerges. He peers out into the darkness of the night, into the silence. He withdraws his head as he hears the smaller door of* Aunt Gesa's *house opening.*]

Mita [*going out through this door into the orchard and calling*]. Aunt Ninfa! Aunt Ninfa! [*Then turing to her husband who emerges from the interior of the house, lantern in hand.*] No! I told you NO! I'm not coming! I don't want to be with you any more!—Aunt Ninfa, Aunt Ninfa!

Uncle Simone. You're calling for help?

Aunt Ninfa [*running from* Liolà's *house and entering the orchard*]. Mita, Mita! What is it?—Ah! It's you, Uncle Simone?

Mita [*taking refuge behind* Aunt Ninfa]. For heaven's sake, *you* tell him to let me alone, Aunt Ninfa, *you* tell him!

Uncle Simone. You are my wife, you must come with me!

Mita. No, no! I'm not your wife any longer! You can go and seek out your wife where she is—in the house of that filthy cousin of yours!

Uncle Simone. You be quiet, or by God I'll let you feel the weight of my hands again!

Aunt Ninfa [*stepping between them*]. Hey, enough of

this, Uncle Simone. Let her at least blow off steam, in God's name!

Uncle Simone. No, she should be quiet. If she couldn't be a mother, she can at least be a wife—and not soil her lips with talk against my family.

Aunt Ninfa. But let's be fair, Uncle Simone, what claims are you making? It eats away at the poor girl, what you've been doing to her!

Uncle Simone. I've done nothing to her! Don't forget: I was doing her a kindness when I took her off the street and put her in a position she didn't deserve.

Aunt Ninfa. Bless the man! And you think that's the way to persuade her to go home with you?

Uncle Simone. Oh, Aunt Ninfa, believe me, I'd never have shown this disrespect to my first wife, God rest her soul. Only I didn't know who to leave the property to! All the things I sweated blood for in sun and rain!

Aunt Ninfa. Well and good. But how is this poor girl to blame, in the name of God?

Uncle Simone. She may not be to blame—but she can't push it off on someone who's doing what she failed to do!

Mita [*to* AUNT NINFA]. You hear? [*To* UNCLE SIMONE.] Then what do you want of *me?* Go to her who can do your business for you and leave me in peace. As for your name and your riches, I don't know what to do with them anyway.

Uncle Simone. You're my wife, I said, and she's my niece. What has been has been, and there's an end. I need a woman to help me in the house, Aunt Ninfa.

Mita. And as for me, I can tell you, I'd rather go out when night falls and roam the countryside!

Aunt Ninfa. Come, let her calm down a bit, Uncle Simone. You struck her too hard a blow. Now be patient. Mita will calm down and come back home, you'll see!

Mita. He can just wait. I'm not coming.

Aunt Ninfa. He's come here, hasn't he? To take you back. And he's told you that it's all over now and he won't go to Aunt Croce's any more, isn't that so?

Uncle Simone. Not any more. But when the child is born—I'll take him with me.

Mita. There, did you hear? So the mother will come and tread on me in my own house?

Aunt Ninfa. Why, no! Why should she?

Mita. When she has the excuse that she's the mother, can I shut the door in her face? Do you want to put up with such an injury? Oh, Aunt Ninfa, must I make them a bed, in my own house, with my own hands? After all this, do you have the heart to send me back to him?

Aunt Ninfa. I, daughter? What have I to do with it? I mustn't keep you with me. I'm speaking for your own good.

Uncle Simone. Come on, let's be going, it's night.

Mita. No, no! If you don't go away I'll run and throw myself off the bridge!

Aunt Ninfa. Pay attention to me, Uncle Simone, leave her here at least for tonight. Bit by bit, if you're nice with her, she'll be persuaded and tomorrow you'll see . . . tomorrow she'll come back home, you can be sure.

Uncle Simone. But why does she want to stay here tonight?

Aunt Ninfa. Because . . . well, for one thing . . . she must look after the house for her aunt who's gone up to the village . . .

Uncle Simone. . . . to bring an action against me?

Aunt Ninfa. Oh come, don't take any notice of the first fit of anger. Just go and sleep, it's late. Mita will shut herself in the house now. [*To* Mita.] Go and see your husband off. You close this door first. Then that one. Good night! Good night to you, Uncle Simone!

[UNCLE SIMONE *enters the house first, forgetting he has left his lantern alight in the orchard. Following him in,* MITA *closes the door.*]

Aunt Ninfa [*crossing the orchard and the "street"*]. It seems to me Aunt Gesa has made the wolf a present of the lamb! [SHE *stops before the door of her house, sees* LIOLÀ *in ambush, and speaks to him softly.*] Go indoors, my son, go indoors and no foolishness . . .

Liolà. Sh! Wait . . . I want to see how this will finish . . . Go away, go away and sleep . . .

Aunt Ninfa. Be reasonable, son, be reasonable! [SHE *goes into the house.*]

[LIOLÀ *draws the door to and at once hides in the orchard crouching against the hedge. Silent and bowed,* HE *goes up to the corner of* AUNT GESA'S *house and stands pressed against the wall. All of a sudden the smaller door opens and* MITA, *seeing* LIOLÀ, *lets out a cry, but at once represses it and turns to her husband, blocking his path.*]

Mita. I told you! Go away! Or I'll call Aunt Ninfa again! Go away!

Uncle Simone [*from the interior of the house*]. I'm going, I'm going, rest easy! [MITA *re-enters, leaving the smaller door half-open. Then as* UNCLE SIMONE *goes out through the "street" door,* LIOLÀ, *crawling along the wall, goes in through the smaller door and immediately closes it. The departure of* UNCLE SIMONE *at one door and the entry of* LIOLÀ *at the other door should happen simultaneously. But* UNCLE SIMONE, *as soon as the "street" door is shut, turns and says.*] Oh, the lantern . . . I've left the lantern behind . . . What do you say? Ah, in the orchard?—Very good . . . I'll go round that way . . . . [*Gropingly* HE *goes down the "street," enters the orchard by the gate in the hedge, takes up the lantern from the ground, raises it to see if it's well lit, and by its light peers into the darkness.*] Phew! [HE *sighs with re-*

lief.] I was seeing things! [HE *shakes his head.*] In the country, when it's dark, a man is easily deceived! [HE *goes slowly back up the "street."*]

ACT THREE

The scene is the same as Act One. It is the time of the grape harvest. By the shop door, hampers and baskets are seen.

TUZZA *is sitting on the rustic stone seat sewing clothes for the expected baby.* AUNT CROCE, *her "mantle" on her shoulders and a kerchief on her head, comes from the back.*

Aunt Croce.   They've all got rich. Nobody wants to come.

Tuzza.   You should have expected this.

Aunt Croce.   I certainly didn't go and invite them to sit at table with me! With all the dirt on them, filthier than the stone on the corner;[2] they haven't even straw to sleep on, and look! I call on them to earn a piece of bread: and one has a sore arm, another a sore leg . . .

Tuzza.   I told you not to go and plead with them.

Aunt Croce.   It's envy that's eating at them, and they pretend to be angry! There's nothing for it: I must go up to the village and find workers for this handful of grapes if I don't want the wasps to eat them. . . . Is the winepress in order now?

Tuzza.   Yes, it's in order.

Aunt Croce.   The baskets are here and ready, everything's ready, it's labor I'm short of. *He's* the only one who's promised to come—Liolà.

Tuzza.   Ah! Did you have to go out of your way to call *him!*

---

[2] Where the whole village leaves its droppings.

Aunt Croce. I did it on purpose, silly girl! So they'll all see there's nothing to it.

Tuzza. But by now the very stones know, don't they?

Aunt Croce. Not from him, anyway; he's always denied it, so I'm told, and I'm grateful for that. I'd never have believed it. And when *he* denies it the others can talk like grasshoppers—till they burst!

Tuzza. All right. But I'm telling you, *I* shall shut myself in the house and you won't see the tip of my nose! I can't endure the sight of him any more!

Aunt Croce. Now, huh? *Now* you can't bear the sight of him?—Monster that he is!—Meanwhile it's several days since your uncle showed himself.

Tuzza. He sent to say he doesn't feel well.

Aunt Croce. If *he'd* been around, anyway, he'd have relieved me of the burden of this grape harvest. But this child *will* be born! I long for the time. When his child is here, now that he's given it recognition in front of everybody, his wife can go and sing for him! His home will be here. "The home is where the children are."

[*At this point* LA MOSCARDINA *appears before the tettoia, lively and excited.*]

La Moscardina. May I, Aunt Croce?

Aunt Croce. Oh, it's you, Moscardina?

La Moscardina. At your service. I'm announcing their coming, see? All of them!

Aunt Croce. Ha! So what's happened? You look so happy!

La Moscardina. Yes, I'm happy, I really am, Aunt Croce!

Aunt Croce. Eh! And red as peppers! Did you *run* here?

La Moscardina. I always run, Aunt Croce. You know what they say?

> The hen that runs about
> Comes home good and stout!

And it's harvest time. They're gay too, the girls, as you'll see!

Aunt Croce. How can that be? I saw them a short while ago all moping their heads off. None of them wanted to come. And now they're all ready and gay?

Tuzza. If I were you, I'd have no use for their services now. I'd go up to the village to find my crew.

Aunt Croce. No. I'd rather see all resentment among neighbors removed. And I'd like to know the reason for these high spirits . . .

La Moscardina. Maybe it's because they knew Liolà will come. This Liolà, Aunt Croce, believe me, he's awful . . . awful . . . it seems he's made a pact with the devil!

Aunt Croce. What has he been cooking up now?

La Moscardina. I don't know. But the fact is he sows good humor in all hearts. "He does one thing and thinks a hundred," as they say. And wherever he is the girls are willing!—He sings, ah! you hear him? Here he comes with the girls and the three kiddies bounding round about him. Look, look!

[*And indeed* LIOLÀ *is heard striking up a pastoral chorus. Then* HE *comes under the tettoia with* CIUZZA, LUZZA, NELA *and other* PEASANTS, *both men and women, and his three "canaries."* HE *starts improvising, beating his feet to the rhythm.*]

Liolà.   Ullarallà! Ullarallà!
          Press the grape! Make haste!
          The harder you press in the vat
          The stronger the wine will taste
          Stronger than that
          Of yesteryear, Liolà!

Chorus. Ullarallà! Ullarallà!

Liolà.   Each cluster
          You muster
          Press it well, friend:

'Twill fill a barrel in the end.
'Twill be a drink
To make my head go round
And fell me to the ground:
I'm seasick, I sink!

Chorus. Ullarallà! Ullarallà!

Liolà [*adding a rhyme*]. Dear Aunt Croce, here is Liolà!

[*The crew laughs, bounds about, and claps.*]

Aunt Croce. Oh, what high spirits! You certainly are gay! What miracle is this?

Liolà. No miracle, Aunt Croce. "He who seeks shall find and he who perseveres shall win!"

[*The* GIRLS *laugh.*]

Aunt Croce. What do you mean?

Liolà. Nothing. It's a proverb.

Aunt Croce. It is? Then hear this one: "Songs and sounds are things of wind."

Liolà [*promptly*]. "And the tavernkeeper wants to be paid."

Aunt Croce. Correct! Agreements in black and white! Shall we make it like last year, eh?

Liolà. Yes, but don't give it a thought: I said it to let you see I knew the proverb—and its sequel.

Aunt Croce. Let's hurry then, girls! Take the baskets and be careful—but you need no advice from me.

Liolà. I've brought the children to pick up any grapes left lying around.

Aunt Croce. As long as they don't swing on the supports when they can't reach the fruit.

Liolà. Oh, there's no danger. They've been reared in their daddy's school. When a grape's so high you can't reach it, you leave it there—and don't say it's sour! [*Another burst of laughter from the* GIRLS.] What's there to laugh at in that? Don't you know the fable of the fox? —Okay. Is everything ready here in the winepress?

Aunt Croce. Oh yes, everything's ready.

Liolà [*taking the baskets and hampers and distributing them to the boys and girls*]. Very well then, let's start, take a basket . . . here you are! take one . . . And let's sing! "Ullarallà! Ullarallà! . . ." [HE *goes off at the back with the crew, singing.*]

Aunt Croce [*shouting after them*]. Begin at the bottom, girls, row by row, and work your way up! Keep an eye on the kiddies, too! [*Then, to* TUZZA.] You go down with them, bestir yourself! Must I look after our interests all alone?

Tuzza. No, no! I told you I'm not going.

Aunt Croce. Who knows what sort of a pigsty they'll be making, they're like hungry beasts!—And, by the way, did you see their eyes? All aslant and asparkle?

Tuzza. I saw them, I saw them.

Aunt Croce. For that crazy man! [*Looking up at this moment,* SHE *sees* UNCLE SIMONE.] Oh, here's your uncle . . . But look, he's pushing his legs along as if they didn't belong to him . . . He really *must* be ill!

[UNCLE SIMONE *comes under the tettoia in a bad humor.*]

Uncle Simone. Good morning, dear cousin. Good morning, Tuzza.

Tuzza. Good morning.

Aunt Croce. Aren't you well, cousin? What's wrong with you?

Uncle Simone [*scratching his head under his Paduan beret*]. Troubles, cousin, troubles.

Aunt Croce. Troubles? What troubles can *you* have?

Uncle Simone. Not me . . . I mean . . . on the contrary, I . . .

Aunt Croce. Is your wife not in good health, maybe?

Uncle Simone. Hm . . . she says . . . she says that . . . well . . .

Aunt Croce. "Well" what? Speak: the workers are
out there and I must go and look after them.

Uncle Simone. Have you started harvesting?

Aunt Croce. Yes, we've just started.

Uncle Simone. Without a word to me?

Aunt Croce. You haven't showed up for two days!
And I've been boiling with bile! These—vipers! They
didn't mean to come. Then, all of a sudden, who knows
why? here they all are, and at this moment they're down
with the baskets.

Uncle Simone. Always in a hurry, cousin, aren't you?

Aunt Croce. Me? In a hurry? In a hurry? The wasps
were busy eating everything . . .

Uncle Simone. I don't mean just in the harvesting
. . . I mean in other things . . . with me for instance
. . . I don't see what pleasure there is in breaking your
neck and not letting time take its course!

Aunt Croce. May a person know what you have up
your sleeve? Out with it! I see you want to blame something on me . . .

Uncle Simone. Oh no, cousin, I'm blaming nothing
on you, I blame it all on myself. On myself!

Aunt Croce. Being in a hurry?

Uncle Simone. Surely. Being in a hurry.

Aunt Croce. In what connection?

Uncle Simone. What connection! You think the burden I carry is an easy one? Yesterday, Neighbor Randisi
came to see me . . .

Aunt Croce. . . . Oh yes, I saw him pass by here . . .

Uncle Simone. . . . Did he stop and talk with you?

Aunt Croce. No, he walked right on . . .

Tuzza. . . . Everybody walks right on, nowadays,
when they pass by here!

Uncle Simone. They walk right on, my daughter,
because people, seeing me here imagine . . . imagine

what, by the grace of God, is not so and never was so! Our conscience is clean. But appearances, unfortunately. . . .

Aunt Croce. All right, all right . . . We knew all those who envied us would behave like this, Uncle Simone. We had to expect it from the start. To talk of it now . . . [*To* Tuzza.] You too, silly!

Uncle Simone. Oh, but all these people who walk right on when passing by here come and peck *me* in the face!

Aunt Croce. Well, well, tell me what the devil this Neighbor Randisi came to you to say.

Uncle Simone. He came to say just this, if you want to know: "Thou shalt not be in a hurry!" He maintained to my wife's face that there've been cases of children not after four but after fifteen years of marriage.

Aunt Croce. I was wondering what he could have said to make you so thoughtful!—Tell me something: what did *you* say?—Fifteen years?—Sixty plus fifteen, how many's that? Seventy-five, I believe.—When the answer's NO at sixty, cousin, will it be YES at seventy-five?

Uncle Simone. Who said the answer is No at sixty?

Aunt Croce. The fact of the matter, cousin.

Uncle Simone. No, cousin. The fact of the matter is . . . [He *hesitates.*]

Aunt Croce. . . . that the answer is . . .

Uncle Simone. . . . Yes at sixty!

Aunt Croce. What?

Uncle Simone. Yes. Just that.

Aunt Croce. Your wife?

Uncle Simone. She gave me the news this morning.

Tuzza [*biting her hands*]. Ha! Liolà!

Aunt Croce [*to* Uncle Simone]. He's done you!

Tuzza. So that's why they were all so gay, the vipers!

"He who seeks shall find and he who perseveres shall win!"

Uncle Simone. Tch, tch! Let's not carry on this way!

Aunt Croce. Do you have the gall to believe the child is yours?

Tuzza. Liolà! Liolà! He's done you! He's done you and he's done me, the murderer!

Uncle Simone. Let's not carry on . . . let's not carry on . . .

Aunt Croce. Is that how you keep a watch on your wife, you old idiot?

Tuzza. And I told you! I told you a hundred times: keep a watch on Liolà!

Uncle Simone. Oho! be careful! Don't have *his* name on your lips! I made my wife shut up when that accusation was made about *you* and flung in my face to boot—though it was true!

Aunt Croce. And now it *isn't* true? In your wife's case, it *isn't* true, you old cuckold?

Uncle Simone. By Christ, cousin, do you want me to do some foul misdeed?

Aunt Croce. Oh, stop it. As if we didn't know . . .

Uncle Simone. What?

Aunt Croce. . . . what *you* know better than anyone else!

Uncle Simone. I know I've never had a thing in common with your daughter here. What I did was charity, that's all. But with my wife, I was in on it, I was in on it!

Aunt Croce. And for four years you didn't get anywhere! Just you go and ask who has been with your wife!

Tuzza. Charity he has the gall to call it!

Aunt Croce. Yes! After boasting in front of everybody, boasting in front of his own wife, that the child was his—just for the satisfaction it gave him to do so, knowing that it was this way or none!

Tuzza [*with a sudden change of tone*]. Stop, stop! From now on no more shouting! Stop!

Aunt Croce. Oh no, my dear girl! Do you want me to give up like that?

Tuzza. What else can you do? If he took mine, knowing who the father was, do you imagine he won't give recognition to the child his wife is going to give him . . .

Uncle Simone. . . . and which is mine, mine, mine! Woe to him who has a word to say against my wife . . .

[*At this point* MITA, *very tranquil, appears at the back.*]

Mita. What's all the disturbance?

Tuzza. Go away, Mita, go away: don't provoke me!

Mita. Provoke you, Tuzza, I? May that never be!

Tuzza [*rushing forward to take hold of her*]. Take her out of my sight! Out of my sight!

Uncle Simone [*intercepting her*]. Oho! I'm here!

Aunt Croce. You have the nerve to turn up here? Get out! Get out!

Mita [*pointing her out to her husband*]. Just look who's talking of nerve!

Uncle Simone. No, no! *You* mustn't meddle here, wife. Go back home! And leave me to defend you!

Mita. Wait a moment. I want to remind Tuzza of an ancient motto of ours: "Who tarries but is not found wanting shall not be said to want." I tarried, it is true; but I was not found wanting. You went ahead; I followed after.

Tuzza. You certainly followed after—on the road I'm travelling!

Mita. No, my dear. My road is straight and right, yours winding and wrong.

Uncle Simone. Don't excite yourself, dear wife, don't

excite yourself like this! They're doing it on purpose, don't you see? Just to make you angry? Come along, pay attention to me! Back home, back home!

Aunt Croce. Just look at him! Just listen to him! "Dear wife!"

Tuzza [*to* MITA]. You're right! You managed it better than I did. You have facts on your side. I have—words.

Mita. Only words? I don't see it.

Aunt Croce. Words, *words,* WORDS! The deceit people see in us is no deceit at all. The real deceit is in you—but nobody sees it!

Uncle Simone. For heaven's sake, shall we be done with this or not?

Aunt Croce. You understand? You have your husband again. You deceived him, but he gives you shelter. Whereas my daughter wouldn't deceive her uncle, oh no: she threw herself at his feet and wept like Mary Magdalene!

Uncle Simone. That's true, that's true!

Aunt Croce. You see? He says so himself. He who was the cause of all the trouble—just so he could boast before you, before the whole village . . .

Mita. And you let him do that, Aunt Croce? Come now: at the cost of your daughter's honor? But I agree with you: the deceit is where one sees it—in my husband's riches—which you wished to take over at the cost of your own shame!

Uncle Simone. Stop, stop, stop! Instead of chattering to no avail and quarrelling without settling a thing let's try now to arrive at the remedy and be agreed. We're in the family here!

Aunt Croce. Remedy? What remedy could you want to find now, you old fool? We're in the family, you say. *You* must find the remedy for all the harm you've done my daughter—for what you hoped to get out of it.

Uncle Simone. Me? I have my child to think of. Yours is for its father to think of. . . . Liolà can't deny to my face that the child is his.

Tuzza. Which child?

Uncle Simone [*stunned by the question as by a treacherous blow*]. What do you mean: which child?

Mita [*promptly*]. Why, yours, my dear! Which do you think? I have my husband who cannot doubt me.

Uncle Simone. Well? Have you finished, you two, mother and daughter? Now that my wife has brought me this solace you'll not trouble with your words! Let *me* speak to Liolà.

[*A chorus of* HARVESTERS *is heard gradually approaching from the distance.*]

Tuzza. No, stop! Don't you dare speak for me! Woe to you if you do!

Uncle Simone. You will take him because it's right you should. He alone can give you your rightful place and ensure that his child is born legitimate. For the rest, *I* will think how best to persuade him, according to the dictates of my heart. Here he comes. Let me do the talking!

[LIOLÀ *returns with the crew.* THEY *are singing a harvest song in chorus. Once under the tettoia, carrying in triumph the full baskets of grapes, the crew see* MITA *and* UNCLE SIMONE *and the flabbergasted faces of* AUNT CROCE *and* TUZZA *and stop in their tracks. The song is interrupted. Only* LIOLÀ, *as if he hadn't wished to notice anything, continues singing and walking.* HE *is going over to empty his basket through the winepress window.*]

Aunt Croce [*going towards them*]. Stop! Empty the baskets, girls, and then throw them over here. At the moment, I don't have the peace of mind to look after you.

Liolà. And why not? What has happened?

Aunt Croce [*to the women*]. Go, I tell you, go! Then, if necessary, I'll call you!

Uncle Simone. You come here, Liolà!

[*At the back of the tettoia* LA MOSCARDINA, CIUZZA, LUZZA, NELA, *and the other women surround* MITA *and shower greetings and embraces on her for the consolation she has brought to all.* TUZZA *stares at her and is consumed with anger.* SHE *slowly withdraws to the house door and finally goes in with a quick, angry movement.*]

Liolà. Do you want me? Here I am.

Uncle Simone. Cousin, you come here too.

Liolà [*with an air of command*]. Come on, Aunt Croce!

Uncle Simone. Today is a red-letter day. We must all celebrate.

Liolà. Wonderful! We'll sing. Not that songs and sounds are things of wind, as Aunt Croce said. Anyway, things of wind are after my own heart; the wind and I are brothers, Uncle Simone.

Uncle Simone. We all know how windy and giddy you are, we all know. But now is the time to be still and reasonable!

Liolà. Reasonable? I die!

Uncle Simone. Just listen to me, Liolà. [*Pompously.*] First of all, I must make you party to the fact that God in His goodness has at last seen fit to do me the favor . . .

Aunt Croce. . . . Listen, Liolà, listen, you who never knew a thing about it!

Uncle Simone. . . . Look, I told you to leave the talking to me . . .

Liolà. Let him talk.

Aunt Croce. Very well, talk, talk! You're sure it was

God in His goodness who saw fit to do you the favor?

Uncle Simone. Yes, yes! After four years my wife has finally . . .

Liolà. She has? Really? Your wife? I'll drum her out a poem this minute!

Uncle Simone. Wait, wait, why a poem?

Liolà. Allow me to go and drink her health at least!

Uncle Simone. Wait, I say, for the love of . . .

Liolà. Oh, don't get angry. You must be in the seventh heaven of joy—and you get angry?—Look, I have it on the tip of my tongue.

Uncle Simone. Let the poem be, I said. You have something else to do right now.

Liolà. I have? But I don't know *how* to do anything else, Uncle Simone!

Aunt Croce. Ha! . . . surely . . . he doesn't know anything else, poor thing . . . [SHE *comes up to him, takes hold of him by the arm, and says through her teeth in a low voice.*] It's two times you've ruined my daughter, murderer!

Liolà. I? Your daughter? You dare to say that to me in front of Uncle Simone? *He* has ruined your daughter two times, not I!

Aunt Croce. He hasn't! It was you!

Liolà. It was Uncle Simone! Don't let's change the cards in our hands, Aunt Croce! I came here honestly to ask your daughter's hand. I couldn't suppose . . .

Aunt Croce. No? Not after what you did with her?

Liolà. I? You mean Uncle Simone!

Aunt Croce. Uncle Simone, ha! Uncle Simone indeed!

Liolà. You talk to her, Uncle Simone! You'd like to deny it now and throw the child on *my* back?—Let's not play around!—I've been thanking God for keeping me out of the trap which—all unaware—I'd nearly got caught in. I'll keep my distance from you, Uncle Simone!

What strange species of old men do you belong to, may one know? A child by your niece wasn't enough? You wanted another by your wife? What do you have in your body? The flames of hell or the fire divine? The devil? Mount Etna? God save and protect every mother's lass in these parts!

Aunt Croce. Ha! It's Uncle Simone the mothers' lasses should beware of, it's Uncle Simone!

Uncle Simone. Liolà, don't make me speak. Don't make me do what I needn't do and don't wish to do. You can see that between me and my niece there was not and could not be such a sin. It was just that she threw herself at my feet repenting for what she'd done with you and confessing to me the state she found herself in. My wife knows all now. And I am ready to swear by our Blessed Lord Jesus and in front of everybody that I boasted wrongly about the child—which is, in all conscience, yours!

Liolà. And by this you mean I should now take Tuzza?

Uncle Simone. You can and must take her, Liolà, because, as sure as God and the Holiest Madonna are above, she's been yours only!

Liolà. Tch, tch, tch. How you do run on, my dear Uncle Simone.—I did want her once, it's true. It was my conscience, nothing else. I knew that, marrying her, all the songs would die in my heart.—Then Tuzza didn't want me.—"The barrel full and your wife drunk?"—You'd like to have both at the same time?— Now you've lost the game?—No thank you, Uncle Simone. No thank you, Aunt Croce. [HE *takes two of the boys by the hand.*] Let us go, let us go away, boys! [HE *is going, then* HE *turns back.*] Oh, there's something I can do with a good conscience. After all these ups and downs the net result is another child. Good, it presents me with no problem. My mother will have more work to do. Tell Tuzza, Aunt Croce, if she wants to give me the child, I'll take him!

Tuzza [*who has been crouching in a corner with fire darting from her eyes rushes at* LIOLÀ *as he speaks these last words, a knife in her hand*]. You'll take the child? Take this instead!

[ALL *shout, raise their arms, and run to hold her.* MITA *faints, is at once supported and comforted by* UNCLE SIMONE.]

Liolà [*was ready and has gripped Tuzza's arm. With his other hand* HE *smacks her fingers till she lets the knife fall to the ground.* HE *laughs and assures everyone that it was nothing*]. Nothing at all . . . it was nothing . . . [*As soon as* TUZZA *lets the knife fall,* HE *puts his foot on it and again says with a great burst of laughter.*] Nothing! [HE *bends down to kiss the head of one of the three children. Then, seeing a trickle of blood on his chest.*] A scratch, it grazed the skin . . . [HE *passes his finger along it and then puts the finger on* TUZZA'S *lips.*] Here you are, taste!—Sweet, isn't it?— [*To the women holding her.*] Let her go! [HE *looks at her, then at the three children.* HE *places his hands on their little heads and says, turning to* TUZZA.]

No weeping now! And no complaining!
When he is born, give him to me!
Three, and a fourth: I'll teach him singing!

IT *IS* SO! (IF YOU THINK SO)

(*Così è, se vi pare!*)

A PARABLE IN THREE ACTS

English version by

ARTHUR LIVINGSTON

CHARACTERS

LAMBERTO LAUDISI
SIGNORA FROLA
PONZA, *Son-in-law of Signora Frola*
SIGNORA PONZA, *Ponza's wife*
COMMENDATORE AGAZZI, *a provincial councillor*
AMALIA, *his wife*
DINA, *their daughter*

SIRELLI
SIGNORA SIRELLI, *his wife*
THE PREFECT
CENTURI, *a police commissioner*
SIGNORA CINI
SIGNORA NENNI
A BUTLER
A NUMBER OF LADIES AND GENTLEMEN

Our Own Times, in a Small Italian Town, the Capital of a Province

ACT I

The parlor in the house of COMMENDATORE AGAZZI.

A door, the general entrance, at the back; doors leading to the wings, left and right.

LAUDISI *is a man nearing the forties, quick and energetic in his movements. He is smartly dressed, in good taste. At this moment he is wearing a semi-formal street suit: a sack coat, of a violet cast, with black lapels, and with black braid around the edges; trousers of a light but different color.*

AMALIA, AGAZZI'S *wife, is* LAUDISI'S *sister. She is a*

*woman of forty-five more or less. Her hair is already quite
grey.* Signora Agazzi *is always showing a certain sense of
her own importance from the position occupied by her
husband in the community; but she gives you to understand that if she had a free rein she would be quite
capable of playing her own part in the world and, perhaps, do it somewhat better than* Commendatore Agazzi.

Dina *is the daughter of* Amalia *and* Agazzi. *She is
nineteen. Her general manner is that of a young person
conscious of understanding everything better than papa
and mamma; but this defect must not be exaggerated to
the extent of concealing her attractiveness and charm as
a good-looking winsome girl.*

As the curtain rises Laudisi *is walking briskly up and
down the parlor to give vent to his irritation.*

Laudisi. I see, I see! So he did take the matter up
with the prefect!

Amalia. But Lamberto *dear,* please remember that
the man is a subordinate of his.

Laudisi. A subordinate of his . . . very well! But a
subordinate in the office, not at home nor in society!

Dina. And he hired an apartment for that woman, his
mother-in-law, right here in this very building, and on
our floor.

Laudisi. And why not, pray? He was looking for an
apartment; the apartment was for rent, so he leased it—
for his mother-in-law. You mean to say that a mother-in-
law is in duty bound to make advances to the wife and
daughter of the man who happens to be her son-in-law's
superior on his job?

Amalia. That is not the way it is, Lamberto. We
didn't ask her to call on us. Dina and I took the first step
by calling on her and—she *refused* to *receive* us!

Laudisi. Well, is that any reason why your husband
should go and lodge a complaint with the man's boss? Do

you expect the government to order him to invite you to tea?

Amalia. I think he deserves all he gets! That is not the way to treat two ladies. I hope he gets fired! The idea!

Laudisi. Oh, you women! I say, making that complaint is a dirty trick. By Jove! If people see fit to keep to themselves in their own houses, haven't they a right to?

Amalia. Yes, but you don't understand! We were trying to do her a favor. She is new in the town. We wanted to make her feel at home.

Dina. Now, now, uncle dear, don't be so cross! Perhaps we did go there out of curiosity more than anything else; but it's all so funny, isn't it! Don't you think it was natural to feel just a little bit curious?

Laudisi. Natural be damned! It was none of your business!

Dina. Now, see here, uncle, let's suppose—here you are right here minding your own business and quite indifferent to what other people are doing all around you. Very well! I come into the room and right here on this table, under your very nose, and with a long face like an undertaker's, or, rather, with the long face of that jail-bird you are defending, I set down—well, what?—anything—a pair of dirty old shoes!

Laudisi. I don't see the connection.

Dina. Wait, don't interrupt me! I said a pair of old shoes. Well, no, not a pair of old shoes—a flat iron, a rolling pin, or your shaving brush for instance—and I walk out again without saying à word to anybody! Now I leave it to you, wouldn't you feel justified in wondering just a little, little, bit as to what in the world I meant by it?

Laudisi. Oh, you're irresistible, Dina! And you're clever, aren't you? But you're talking with old uncle, remember! You see, you have been putting all sorts of crazy things on the table here; and you did it with the idea of making me ask what it's all about; and, of course, since you were doing all that on purpose, you can't blame me if I do ask, why those old shoes just there, on that table, dearie? But what's all that got to do with it? You'll have to show me now that this Mr. Ponza of ours, that jailbird as you say, or that rascal, that boor, as your father calls him, brought his mother-in-law to the apartment next to ours with the idea of stringing us all! You've got to show me that he did it on purpose!

Dina. I don't say that he did it on purpose—not at all! But you can't deny that this famous Mr. Ponza has come to this town and done a number of things which are unusual, to say the least; and which he must have known were likely to arouse a very natural curiosity in everybody. Look uncle, here is a man: he comes to town to fill an important public position, and—what does he do? Where does he go to live? He hires an apartment on the *top* floor, if your please, of that dirty old tenement out there on the very outskirts of the town. Now, I ask you —did you ever see the place? Inside?

Laudisi. I suppose you went and had a look at it?

Dina. Yes, uncle dear, I went—with mamma! And we weren't the only ones, you know. The whole town has been to have a look at it. It's a five story tenement with an interior court so dark at noontime you can hardly see your hand before your face. Well, there is an iron balcony built out from the fifth story around the courtyard. A basket is hanging from the railing . . . They let it up and down—on a rope! [1]

Laudisi. Well, what of it?

Dina [*looking at him with astonished indignation*]. What of it? Well, there, if you please, is where he keeps his wife!

Amalia. While her mother lives here next door to us!

Laudisi. A fashionable apartment, for his mother-in-law, in the residential district!

[1] Quite customary in Italy.

Amalia. Generous to the old lady, eh? But he does that to keep her from seeing her daughter!

Laudisi. How do you know that? How do you know that the old lady, rather, does not prefer this arrangement, just to have more elbow room for herself?

Dina. No, no, uncle, you're wrong. Everybody knows that it is he who is doing it.

Amalia. See here, Lamberto, everybody understands, if a girl, when she marries, goes away from her mother to live with her husband in some other town. But supposing this poor mother can't stand being separated from her daughter and follows her to the place, where she herself is also a complete stranger. And supposing now she not only does not live with her daughter, but is not even allowed to see her? I leave it to you . . . is that so easy to understand?

Laudisi. Oh say, you have about as much imagination as so many mud turtles. A mother-in-law and a son-in-law! Is it so hard to suppose that either through her fault or his fault or nobody's fault, they should find it hard to get along together and should therefore consider it wiser to live apart?

Dina [*with another look of pitying astonishment at her uncle*]. How stupid of you, uncle! The trouble is not between the mother-in-law and the son-in-law, but between the mother and the daughter.

Laudisi. How do you know that?

Dina. Because he is as thick as pudding with the old lady; because they are always together, arm in arm, and as loving as can be. Mother-in-law and son-in-law, if you please! Whoever heard the like of that?

Amalia. And he comes here every evening to see how the old lady is getting on!

Dina. And that is not the worst of it! Sometimes he comes during the daytime, once or twice!

Laudisi.   How scandalous! Do you think he is making love to the old woman?

Dina.   Now don't be improper, uncle. No, we will acquit him of that. She is a poor old lady, quite on her last legs.

Amalia.   But he never, never, never brings his wife! A daughter kept from seeing her mother! The idea!

Laudisi.   Perhaps the young lady is not well; perhaps she isn't able to go out.

Dina.   Nonsense! The old lady goes to see *her!*

Amalia.   Exactly! And she never gets in! She can see her only from a distance. Now will you explain to me why, in the name of common sense, that poor mother should be forbidden ever to enter her daughter's house?

Dina.   And if she wants to talk to her she has to shout up from the courtyard!

Amalia.   Five stories, if you please! . . . And her daughter comes out and looks down from the balcony up there. The poor old woman goes into the courtyard and pulls a string that leads up to the balcony; a bell rings; the girl comes out and her mother talks up at her, her head thrown back, just as though she were shouting from out of a well. . . .

[*There is a knock at the door and the* BUTLER *enters.*]

Butler.   Callers, madam!

Amalia.   Who is it, please?

Butler.   Signor Sirelli, and the Signora with another lady, madam.

Amalia.   Very well, show them in.

[*The* BUTLER *bows and withdraws.*]

SIRELLI, SIGNORA SIRELLI, SIGNORA CINI *appear in the doorway, rear.*

SIRELLI, *also a man of about forty, is a bald, fat gentle-man with some pretensions to stylish appearance that do not quite succeed: the overdressed provincial.*

Signora Sirelli, *his wife, plump, petite, a faded blonde, still young and girlishly pleasing. She, too, is somewhat overdressed with the provincial's fondness for display. She has the aggressive curiosity of the small-town gossip. She is chiefly occupied in keeping her husband in his place.*

Signora Cini *is the old provincial lady of affected manners, who takes malicious delight in the failings of others, all the while affecting innocence and inexperience regarding the waywardness of mankind.*

Amalia [*as the visitors enter, and taking* Signora Sirelli's *hands effusively*].   Dearest! Dearest!

Signora Sirelli.   I took the liberty of bringing my good friend, Signora Cini, along. She was so anxious to know you!

Amalia.   So good of you to come, Signora! Please make yourself at home! My daughter Dina, Signora Cini, and this is my brother, Lamberto Laudisi.

Sirelli [*bowing to the ladies*].   Signora, Signorina. [He *goes over and shakes hands with* Laudisi.]

Signora Sirelli.   Amalia dearest, we have come here as to the fountain of knowledge. We are two pilgrims athirst for the truth!

Amalia.   The truth? Truth about what?

Signora Sirelli.   Why . . . about this blessed Mr. Ponza of ours, the new secretary at the prefecture. He is the talk of the town, take my word for it, Amalia.

Signora Cini.   And we are all just dying to find out!

Amalia.   But we are as much in the dark as the rest of you, I assure you, madam.

Sirelli [*to his wife*].   What did I tell you? They know no more about it than I do. In fact, I think they know less about it than I do. Why is it this poor woman is not allowed to see her daughter? Do you know the reason, you people, the real reason?

Amalia. Why, I was just discussing the matter with my brother.

Laudisi. And my view of it is that you're all a pack of gossips!

Dina. The reason is, they say, that Ponza will not allow her to.

Signora Cini. Not a sufficient reason, if I may say so, Signorina.

Signora Sirelli. Quite insufficient! There's more to it than that!

Sirelli. I have a new item for you, fresh, right off the ice: he keeps her locked up at home!

Amalia. His mother-in-law?

Sirelli. No, no, his wife!

Signora Cini. Under lock and key!

Dina. There, uncle, what have you to say to that? And you've been trying to defend him all along!

Sirelli [*staring in astonishment at* LAUDISI]. Trying to defend that man? Really . . .

Laudisi. Defending him? No! I am not defending anybody. All I'm saying, if you ladies will excuse me, is that your curiosity is unbearable if only because it's quite useless.

Sirelli. Useless? Useless?

Laudisi. Useless!

Signora Cini. But we're trying to get somewhere—we are trying to find out!

Laudisi. Excuse me, what can you find out? What can we really know about other people—who they are—what they are—what they are doing, and why they are doing it?

Signora Sirelli. How can we know? Why not? By asking, of course! You tell me what you know, and I tell you what I know.

Laudisi. In that case, madam, you ought to be the best informed person in the world. Why, your husband knows more about what others are doing than any other man—or woman, for that matter—in this neighborhood.

Sirelli [*deprecating but pleased*]. Oh I say, I say . . .

Signora Sirelli [*to her husband*]. No dear, he's right, he's right. [*Then turning to* AMALIA.] The real truth, Amalia, is this: for all my husband says he knows, I never manage to keep posted on anything!

Sirelli. And no wonder! The trouble is—that woman never trusts me! The moment I tell her something she is convinced it is not *quite* as I say. Then, sooner or later, she claims that it *can't* be as I say. And at last she is certain it is the exact opposite of what I say!

Signora Sirelli. Well, you ought to hear all he tells me!

Laudisi [*laughing aloud*]. May I speak, madam? Let me answer your husband. My dear Sirelli, how do you expect your wife to be satisfied with things as you explain them to her, if you, as is natural, represent them as they seem to you?

Signora Sirelli. And that means—as they cannot possibly be!

Laudisi. Why no, Signora, now you are wrong. From your husband's point of view things are, I assure you, exactly as he represents them.

Sirelli. As they are in reality!

Signora Sirelli. Not at all! You are always wrong.

Sirelli. No, not a bit of it! It is you who are always wrong. I am always right.

Laudisi. The fact is that neither of you is wrong. May I explain? I will prove it to you. Now here you are, you, Sirelli, and Signora Sirelli, your wife, there; and here I am. You see me, don't you?

Sirelli. Well . . . er . . . yes.

Laudisi. Do you see me, or do you not?

Sirelli.   Oh, I'll bite! Of course I see you.

Laudisi.   So you see me! But that's not enough. Come here!

Sirelli [*smiling, he obeys, but with a puzzled expression on his face as though he fails to understand what* LAUDISI *is driving at*].   Well, here I am!

Laudisi.   Yes! Now take a better look at me . . . Touch me! That's it—that's it! Now you are touching me, are you not? And you see me! You're sure you see me?

Sirelli.   Why, I should say . . .

Laudisi.   Yes, but the point is, you're sure! Of course you're sure! Now if you please, Signora Sirelli, you come here—or rather . . . no . . . [*Gallantly.*] it is my place to come to you! [*He goes over to* SIGNORA SIRELLI *and kneels chivalrously on one knee.*] You see me, do you not, madam? Now that hand of yours . . . touch me! A pretty hand, on my word! [*He pats her hand.*]

Sirelli.   Easy! Easy!

Laudisi.   Never mind your husband, madam! Now, you have touched me, have you not? And you see me? And you are absolutely sure about me, are you not? Well now, madam, I beg of you; do not tell your husband, nor my sister, nor my niece, nor Signora Cini here, what you think of me; because, if you were to do that, they would all tell you that you are completely wrong. But, you see, you are really right; because I am really what you take me to be; though, my dear madam, that does not prevent me from also being really what your husband, my sister, my niece, and Signora Cini take me to be—because they also are absolutely right!

Signora Sirelli.   In other words you are a different person for each of us.

Laudisi.   Of course I'm a different person! And you, madam, pretty as you are, aren't you a different person, too?

Signora Sirelli [*hastily*].   No siree! I assure you, as far as I'm concerned, I'm always the same always, yesterday, today, and forever!

Laudisi.   Ah, but so am I, from my point of view, believe me! And, I would say that you are all mistaken unless you see me as I see myself; but that would be an inexcusable presumption on my part—as it would be on yours, my dear madam!

Sirelli.   And what has all this rigmarole got to do with it, may I ask?

Laudisi.   What has it got to do with it? Why . . . I find all you people here at your wits' ends trying to find out who and what other people are; just as though other people had to be this, or that, and nothing else.

Signora Sirelli.   All you are saying is that we can never find out the truth! A dreadful idea!

Signora Cini.   I give up! I give up! If we can't believe even what we see with our eyes and feel with our fingers . . .

Laudisi.   But you must understand, madam! All I'm saying is that you should show some respect for what other people see and feel, even though it be the exact opposite of what you see and feel.

Signora Sirelli.   The way to answer you is to refuse to talk with you. See, I turn my back on you! You're driving me mad!

Laudisi.   Oh, I beg your pardon. Don't let me interfere with your party. Please go on! Pray continue your argument about Signora Frola and Signor Ponza—I promise not to interrupt again!

Amalia.   You're right for once, Lamberto; and I think it would be even better if you should go into the other room.

Dina.   Serves you right, uncle! Into the other room with you, into the other room!

Laudisi. No, I refuse to budge! Fact is, I enjoy hearing you gossip; but I promise not to say anything more, don't fear! At the very most, with your permission, I shall indulge in a laugh or two.

Signora Sirelli. How funny . . . and our idea in coming here was to find out . . . But really, Amalia, I thought this Ponza man was your husband's secretary at the Provincial building.

Amalia. He is his secretary—in the office. But here at home what authority has Agazzi over the fellow?

Signora Sirelli. Of course! I understand! But may I ask . . . haven't you even tried to see Signora Frola, next door?

Dina. Tried? I should say we had! Twice, Signora!

Signora Cini. Well . . . so then . . . you have probably talked to her . . .

Dina. We were not *received,* if you please!

Signora Sirelli, Sirelli, Signora Cini [*in chorus*]. Not received? Why! Why! Why!

Dina. This very forenoon!

Amalia. The first time we waited fully fifteen minutes at the door. We rang and rang and rang, and no one came. Why, we weren't even able to leave our cards! So we went back today . . .

Dina [*throwing up her hands in an expression of horror*]. And *he* came to the door.

Signora Sirelli. Why yes, with that face of his . . . you can tell by just looking at the man . . . Such a face! Such a face! You can't blame people for talking! And then, with that black suit of his . . . Why, they all dress in black. Did you ever notice? Even the old lady! And the man's eyes, too! . . .

Sirelli [*with a glance of pitying disgust at his wife*]. What do you know about his eyes? You never saw his eyes! And you never saw the woman. How do you know she

dresses in black? *Probably* she dresses in black . . . By
the way, they come from a village in the next county.
Had you heard that? A village in Marsica! [2]

Amalia. Yes, the village that was destroyed a short
time ago.

Sirelli. Exactly! By an earthquake! Not a house left
standing in the place.

. *Dina.* And all their relatives were lost, I have heard.
Not one of them left in the world!

Signora Cini [*impatient to get on with the story*]. Very
well, very well, so then . . . he came to the door . . .

Amalia. Yes . . . And the moment I saw him in front
of me with that weird face of his I had hardly enough
gumption left to tell him that we had just come to call
on his mother-in-law, and he . . . well . . . not a word,
not a word . . . not even a "thank you," if you please!

Dina. That is not quite fair, mama: . . . he did bow!

Amalia. Well, yes, a bow . . . if you want to call it
that. Something like this! . . .

Dina. And his eyes! You ought to see his eyes—the
eyes of a devil, and then some! You never saw a man with
eyes like that!

Signora Cini. Very well, what did he say, finally?

Dina. He seemed quite taken aback.

Amalia. He was all confused like; he hitched about
for a time; and at last he said that Signora Frola was
not feeling well, but that she would appreciate our kindness in having come; and then he just stood there, and
stood there, apparently waiting for us to go away.

Dina. I never was more mortified in my life!

Sirelli. A boor, a plain boor, I say! Oh, it's his fault,
I am telling you. And . . . who knows? Perhaps he has
got the old lady also under lock and key.

[2] A region in Abruzzi. In 1915 there was a great earthquake there;
the town of Avezzano, e.g. was destroyed.

Signora Sirelli. Well, I think something should be done about it! . . . After all, you are the wife of a superior of his. You can *refuse* to be treated like that.

Amalia. As far as that goes, my husband did take it rather badly—as a lack of courtesy on the man's part; and he went straight to the prefect with the matter, insisting on an apology.

[SIGNOR AGAZZI, *commendatore and provincial councillor, appears in the doorway rear.*]

Dina. Oh goody, here's papa now!

[AGAZZI *is well on toward fifty. He has the harsh, authoritarian manner of the provincial of importance. Red hair and beard, rather unkempt; gold-rimmed eyeglasses.*]

Agazzi. Oh Sirelli, glad to see you! [*He steps forward and bows to the company.*]

Agazzi. Signora! . . . [*He shakes hands with* SIGNORA SIRELLI.]

Amalia [*introducing* SIGNORA CINI]. My husband, Signora Cini!

Agazzi [*with a bow and taking her hand*]. A great pleasure, madam! [*Then turning to his wife and daughter in a mysterious voice.*] I have come back from the office to give you some real news! Signora Frola will be here shortly.

Signora Sirelli [*clapping her hands delightedly*]. Oh, the mother-in-law! She is coming? Really? Coming here?

Sirelli [*going over to* AGAZZI *and pressing his hand warmly as an expression of admiration*]. That's the talk, old man, that's the talk. What's needed here is some show of authority.

Agazzi. Why I had to, you see, I had to! . . . I can't let a man treat my wife and daughter that way! . . .

Sirelli. I should say not! I was just expressing myself to that effect right here.

Signora Sirelli. And it would have been entirely proper to inform the prefect also . . .

Agazzi [*anticipating*]. . . . of all the talk that is going around on this fine gentleman's account? Oh, leave that to me! I didn't miss the opportunity.

Sirelli. Fine! Fine!

Signora Cini. And such talk!

Amalia. For my part, I never heard of such a thing. Why, do you know, he has them both under lock and key!

Dina. No, mamma, we are not *quite* sure of that. We are not *quite* sure about the old lady, yet.

Amalia. Well, we know it about his wife, anyway.

Sirelli. And what did the prefect have to say?

Agazzi. Oh the prefect . . . well, the prefect . . . he was very much impressed, *very* much impressed, with what I had to say.

Sirelli. I should hope so!

Agazzi. You see, some of the talk had reached his ears already. And he agrees that it is better, as a matter of his own official prestige, for all this mystery in connection with one of his assistants to be cleared up, so that once and for all we shall know the truth.

Laudisi [*bursts out laughing*].

Amalia. That is Lamberto's usual contribution. He laughs!

Agazzi. And what is there to laugh about?

Signora Sirelli. Why he says that no one can ever know the truth.

[*The* BUTLER *appears at the door in back set.*]

The Butler. Excuse me, Signora Frola!

Sirelli. Ah, here she is now!

Agazzi. Now we'll see if we can settle it!

Signora Sirelli. Splendid! Oh, I am so glad I came.

Amalia [*rising*]. Shall we have her come in?

Agazzi. Wait, you keep your seat, Amalia! Let's have

her come right in here. [*Turning to the butler.*] Show
her in!

[*Exit* BUTLER.]

[*A moment later all rise as* SIGNORA FROLA *enters, and*
AMALIA *steps forward, holding out her hand in greeting.* SIGNORA FROLA *is a slight, modestly but neatly
dressed old lady, very eager to talk and apparently
fond of people. There is a world of sadness in her
eyes, tempered however, by a gentle smile that is
constantly playing about her lips.*]

Amalia. Come right in, Signora Frola! [*She takes the
old lady's hand and begins the introduction.*] Mrs. Sirelli,
a good friend of mine; Signora Cini; my husband; Mr.
Sirelli; and this is my daughter, Dina; my brother Lamberto Laudisi. Please take a chair, Signora!

Signora Frola. Oh, I am so very, very sorry! I have
come to excuse myself for having been so negligent of my
social duties. You, Signora Agazzi, were so kind, so very
kind, to have honored me with a first call—when really
it was my place to leave my card with you!

Amalia. Oh, we are just neighbors, Signora Frola!
Why stand on ceremony? I just thought that you, being
new in town and all alone by yourself, would perhaps like
to have a little company.

Signora Frola. Oh, how very kind of you it was!

Signora Sirelli. And you are quite alone, aren't you?

Signora Frola. Oh no! No! I have a daughter, married, though she hasn't been here very long, either.

Sirelli. And your daughter's husband is the new secretary at the prefecture, Signor Ponza, I believe?

Signora Frola. Yes, yes, exactly! And I hope that
Signor Agazzi, as his superior, will be good enough to excuse me—and him, too!

Agazzi. I will be quite frank with you, madam! I
was a bit put out.

Signora Frola [*interrupting*]. And you were quite

right! But I do hope you will forgive him. You see, we
are still—what shall I say—still so upset by the terrible
things that have happened to us . . .

Amalia. You went through the earthquake, didn't
you?

Signora Sirelli. And you lost all your relatives?

Signora Frola. Every one of them! All our family—
yes, madam. And our village was left just a miserable
ruin, a pile of bricks and stones and mortar.

Sirelli. Yes, we heard about it.

Signora Frola. It wasn't so bad for me, I suppose. I
had only one sister and her daughter, and my niece had
no family. But my poor son-in-law had a much harder
time of it. He lost his mother, two brothers, and their
wives, a sister and her husband, and there were two little
ones, his nephews.

Sirelli. A massacre!

Signora Frola. Oh, one doesn't forget such things!
You see, it sort of leaves you with your feet off the ground.

Amalia. I can imagine.

Signora Sirelli. And all over-night with no warning at
all! It's a wonder you didn't go mad.

Signora Frola. Well, you see, we haven't quite gotten
our bearings yet; and we do things that may seem impolite, without in the least intending to. I hope you
understand!

Agazzi. Oh please, Signora Frola, of course!˙

Amalia. In fact it was partly on account of your
trouble that my daughter and I thought we ought to go
to see you first.

Signora Sirelli [*literally writhing with curiosity*]. Yes,
of course, since they saw you all alone by yourself, and
yet . . . excuse me, Signora Frola . . . if the question
doesn't seem impertinent . . . how is it that when you
have a daughter here in town and after a disaster like
the one you have been through . . . I should think you

people would all stand together, that you would need one another.

Signora Frola. Whereas I am left here all by myself?

Sirelli. Yes, exactly. It does seem strange, to tell the honest truth.

Signora Frola. Oh, I understand—of course! But you know, I have a feeling that a young man and a young woman who have married should be left a good deal to themselves.

Laudisi. Quite so, quite so! They should be left to themselves. They are beginning a life of their own, a life different from anything they have led before. One should not interfere in these relations between a husband and a wife!

Signora Sirelli. But there are limits to everything, Laudisi, if you will excuse me! And when it comes to shutting one's own mother out of one's life . . .

Laudisi. Who is shutting her out of the girl's life? Here, if I have understood the lady, we see a mother who understands that her daughter cannot and must not remain so closely associated with her as she was before, for now the young woman must begin a new life on her own account.

Signora Frola [*with evidence of keen gratitude and relief*]. You have hit the point exactly, sir. You have said what I would like to have said. You are exactly right! Thank you!

Signora Cini. But your daughter, I imagine, often comes to see you . . .

Signora Frola [*hesitating, and manifestly ill at ease*]. Why yes . . . I . . . I . . . we do see each other, of course!

Sirelli [*quickly pressing the advantage*]. But your daughter never goes out of her house! At least no one in town has ever seen her.

Signora Cini. Oh, she probably has her little ones to take care of.

Signora Frola [*speaking up quickly*]. No, there are no children yet, and perhaps there won't be any, now. You see, she has been married seven years. Oh, of course, she has a lot to do about the house; but that is not the reason, really. You know, we women who come from the little towns in the country—we are used to staying indoors much of the time.

Agazzi. Even when your mothers are living in the same town, but not in your house? You prefer staying indoors to going and visiting your mothers?

Amalia. But it's Signora Frola probably who visits her daughter.

Signora Frola [*quickly*]. Of course, of course, why not! I go there once or twice a day.

Sirelli. And once or twice a day you climb all those stairs up to the fifth story of that tenement, eh?

Signora Frola [*growing pale and trying to conceal under a laugh the torture of that cross-examination*]. Why . . . er . . . to tell the truth, I don't go up. You're right, five flights would be quite too much for me. No, I don't go up. My daughter comes out on the balcony in the courtyard and . . . well . . . we see each other . . . and we talk!

Signora Sirelli. And that's all, eh? How terrible! You never see each other more intimately than that?

Dina. I have a mamma and certainly I wouldn't expect her to go up five flights of stairs to see me, either; but at the same time I could never stand talking to her that way, shouting at the top of my lungs from a balcony on the fifth story. I am sure I should want a kiss from her occasionally, and feel her near me, at least.

Signora Frola [*with evident signs of embarrassment and confusion*]. And you're right! Yes, exactly . . .

quite right! I must explain. Yes . . . I hope you people
are not going to think that my daughter is something she
really is not. You must not suspect her of having so little
regard for me and for my years, and you mustn't believe
that I, her mother, am . . . well . . . five, six, even more
stories to climb would never prevent a real mother, even
if she were as old and infirm as I am, from going to her
daughter's side and pressing her to her heart with a real
mother's love . . . oh no!

Signora Sirelli [*triumphantly*]. There you have it,
there you have it, just as we were saying!

Signora Cini. But there must be a reason, there must
be a reason!

Amalia [*pointedly to her brother*]. Aha, Lamberto,
now you see, there *is* a reason, after all!

Sirelli [*insisting*]. Your son-in-law, I suppose?

Signora Frola. Oh please, please, please, don't think
badly of *him*. He is such a very good boy. Good is no
name for it, my dear sir. You can't imagine all he does for
me! Kind, attentive, solicitous for my comfort, everything! And as for my daughter—I doubt if any girl ever
had a more affectionate and well-intentioned husband.
No, on that point I am proud of myself! I could not
have found a better man for her.

Signor Sirelli. Well then . . . What? What? *What?*

Signora Cini. So your son-in-law is not the reason?

Agazzi. I never thought it was his fault. Can you
imagine a man forbidding his wife to call on her mother,
or preventing the mother from paying an occasional visit
to her daughter?

Signora Frola. Oh, it's not a case of forbidding! Who
ever dreamed of such a thing! No, it's we, Commendatore,
I and my daughter, that is. Oh, please, believe me! We
refrain from visiting each other of our own accord, out of
consideration for him, you understand.

Agazzi. But excuse me . . . how in the world could he be offended by such a thing? I *don't* understand.

Signora Frola. Oh, please don't be angry, Signor Agazzi. You see it's a . . . what shall I say . . . a feeling . . . that's it, a feeling, which it would perhaps be very hard for anyone else to understand; and yet, when you do understand it, it's all so simple, I am sure . . . so simple . . . and believe me, my dear friends, it is no slight sacrifice that I am making, and that my daughter is making, too.

Agazzi. Well, one thing you will admit, madam. This is a very, very unusual situation.

Sirelli. Unusual, indeed! And such as to justify a curiosity even more persistent than ours.

Agazzi. It is not only unusual, madam. I might even say it is suspicious.

Signora Frola. Suspicious? You mean you suspect Signor Ponza? Oh please, Commendatore, don't say that. What fault can you possibly find with him, Signor Agazzi?

Agazzi. I didn't say just that . . . Please don't misunderstand! I said simply that the situation is so very strange that people might legitimately suspect . . .

Signora Frola. Oh, no, no, no! What could they suspect. We are in perfect agreement, all of us; and we are really quite happy, very happy, I might even say . . . both I and my daughter.

Signora Sirelli. Perhaps it's a case of jealousy?

Signora Frola. Jealousy of me? It would be hardly fair to say that, although . . . really . . . oh, it is so hard to explain! . . . You see, he is in love with my daughter . . . so much so that he wants her whole heart, her every thought, as it were, for himself; so much so that he insists that the affections which my daughter must have for me, her mother—he finds that love quite natural of course, why not? Of course he does!—should reach me

through him—that's it, through him—don't you understand?

Agazzi. Oh, that is going pretty strong! No, I don't
understand. In fact it seems to me a case of downright
cruelty!

Signora Frola. Cruelty? No, no, please don't call it
cruelty, Commendatore. It is something else, believe me!
You see it's so hard for me to explain the matter. Nature,
perhaps . . . but no, that's hardly the word. What shall
I call it? Perhaps a sort of disease. It's a fullness of love,
of a love shut off from the world. There, I guess that's
it . . . a fullness . . . a completeness of devotion in
which his wife must live without ever departing from it,
and into which no other person must ever be allowed to
enter.

Dina. Not even her mother, I suppose?

Sirelli. It is the worst case of selfishness I ever heard
of, if you want my opinion!

Signora Frola. Selfishness? Perhaps! But a selfishness,
after all, which offers itself wholly in sacrifice. A case
where the selfish person gives all he has in the world to
the one he loves. Perhaps it would be fairer to call me
selfish; for selfish it surely is for me to be always trying
to break into this closed world of theirs, break in by
force if necessary; when I know that my daughter is
really so happy, so passionately adored—you ladies understand, don't you? A true mother should be satisfied when
she knows her daughter is happy, oughtn't she? Besides
I'm not completely separated from my daughter, am I? I
see her and I speak to her [*She assumes a more confidential tone.*] You see, when she lets down the basket
there in the courtyard I always find a letter in it—a short
note, which keeps me posted on the news of the day; and
I put in a little letter that I have written. That is some
consolation, a great consolation indeed, and now, in
course of time, I've grown used to it. I am resigned, there!

Resignation, that's it! And I've ceased really to suffer from it at all.

Amalia. Oh well then, after all, if you people are satisfied, why should . . .

Signora Frola [*rising*]. Oh yes, yes! But, remember, I told you he is such a good man! Believe me, he couldn't be better, really! We all have our weaknesses in this world, haven't we! And we get along best by having a little indulgence, for one another. [*She holds out her hand to* AMALIA.] Thank you for calling, madam. [*She bows to* SIGNORA SIRELLI, SIGNORA CINI, *and* DINA; *then turning to* AGAZZI, *she continues*.] And I do hope you have forgiven me!

Agazzi. Oh, my dear madam, please, please! And we are extremely grateful for your having come to call on us.

Signora Frola [*offering her hand to* SIRELLI *and* LAUDISI *and again turning to* AMALIA *who has risen to show her out*]. Oh no, please, Signora Agazzi, please stay here with your friends! Don't put yourself to any trouble!

Amalia. No, no, I will go with you; and believe me, we were very, very glad to see you!

[*Exit* SIGNORA FROLA *with* AMALIA *showing her the way.* AMALIA *returns immediately.*]

Sirelli. Well, there you have the story, ladies and gentlemen! Are you satisfied with the explanation?

Agazzi. An explanation, you call it? So far as I can see she has explained nothing. I tell you there is some big mystery in all this business.

Signor Sirelli. That poor woman! Who knows what torment she must be suffering?

Dina. And to think of that poor girl!

Signor Cini. She could hardly keep in her tears as she talked.

Amalia. Yes, and did you notice when I mentioned all those stairs she would have to climb before really being able to see her daughter?

Laudisi. What impressed me was her concern, which amounted to a steadfast determination, to protect her son-in-law from the slightest suspicion.

Signor Sirelli. Not at all, not at all! What could she say for him? She couldn't really find a single word to say for him.

Sirelli. And I would like to know how anyone could condone such violence, such downright cruelty!

The Butler [*appearing again in the doorway.*] Beg pardon, sir! Signor Ponza calling.

Signora Sirelli. The man himself, upon my word!

[*An animated ripple of surprise and curiosity, not to say of guilty self-consciousness, sweeps over the company.*]

Agazzi. Did he ask to see me?

Butler. He asked simply if he might be received. That was all he said.

Signora Sirelli. Oh please, Signor Agazzi, please let him come in! I am really afraid of the man; but I confess the greatest curiosity to have a close look at the monster.

Amalia. But what in the world can he be wanting?

Agazzi. The way to find that out is to have him come in. [*To the* BUTLER.] Show him in, please.

[*The* BUTLER *bows and goes out. A second later* PONZA *appears, aggressively, in the doorway.*]

[PONZA *is a short, thick set, dark complexioned man of a distinctly unprepossessing appearance; black hair, very thick and coming down low over his forehead; a black mustache upcurling at the ends, giving his face a certain ferocity of expression. He is dressed entirely in black. From time to time he draws a black-bordered handkerchief and wipes the perspiration from his brow. When he speaks his eyes are invariably hard, fixed, sinister.*]

Agazzi. This way please, Ponza, come right in! [*Introducing him.*] Signor Ponza, our new provincial secretary;

my wife; Signora Sirelli; Signora Cini; my daughter Dina.
This is Signor Sirelli; and here is Laudisi, my brother-in-
law. Please join our party, won't you, Ponza?

Ponza. So kind of you! You will pardon the intru-
sion. I shall disturb you only a moment, I hope.

Agazzi. You had some private business to discuss with
me?

Ponza. Why yes, but I could discuss it right here. In
fact, perhaps as many people as possible should hear what
I have to say. You see it is a declaration that I owe, in a
certain sense, to the general public.

Agazzi. Oh my dear Ponza, if it is that little matter
of your mother-in-law's not calling on us, it is quite all
right; because you see . . .

Ponza. No, that was not what I came for, Commendatore. It was not to apologize for her. Indeed I may say that
Signora Frola, my wife's mother, would certainly have
left her cards with Signora Agazzi, your wife, and Signorina Agazzi, your daughter, long before they were so
kind as to honor her with their call, had I not exerted
myself to the utmost to prevent her coming, since I am
absolutely unable to consent to her paying or receiving
visits!

Agazzi [*drawing up into an authoritative attitude and
speaking with some severity*]. Why? if you will be so
kind as to explain, Ponza?

Ponza [*with evidences of increasing excitement in spite
of his efforts to preserve his self-control*]. I suppose my
mother-in-law has been talking to you people about her
daughter, my wife. Am I mistaken? And I imagine she
told you further that I have forbidden her entering my
house and seeing her daughter intimately.

Amalia. Oh not at all, not at all, Signor Ponza! Signora Frola had only the nicest things to say about you.
She could not have spoken of you with greater respect
and kindness.

Dina. She seems to be very fond of you indeed.

Agazzi. She says that she refrains from visiting your house of her own accord, out of regard for feelings of yours which we frankly confess we are unable to understand.

Signora Sirelli. Indeed, if we were to express our honest opinion . . .

Agazzi. Well, yes, why not be honest? We think you are extremely harsh with the woman, extremely harsh, perhaps cruel would be an exacter word.

Ponza. Yes, that is what I thought; and I came here for the express purpose of clearing the matter up. The condition this poor woman is in is a pitiable one indeed —not less pitiable than my own perhaps; because, as you see, I am compelled to come here and make apologies— a public declaration—which only such violence as has just been used upon me could ever bring me to make in the world . . . [*He stops and looks about the room. Then he says slowly with emphatic emphasis on the important syllables.*] Signora Frola is mad.

All [*with a start*]. Mad?

Ponza. She's been mad for four years.

Signora Sirelli [*with a cry*]. Dear me, she doesn't seem mad in the least!

Agazzi [*amazed*]. What? Mad?

Ponza. She doesn't seem mad: she *is* mad. And her madness consists precisely in believing that I don't want to let her see her daughter. [*His face takes on an expression of cruel suffering mingled with a sort of ferocious excitement*]. What daughter, for God's sake? Why her daughter died four years ago! [*A general sensation*].

Everyone at once. Died? She is dead? What do you mean? Oh, really? Four years ago? Why! Why!

Ponza. Four years ago! In fact it was the death of the poor girl that drove her mad.

Sirelli.   Are we to understand that the wife with whom you are now living . . .

Ponza.   Exactly! She is my second wife. I married her two years ago.

Amalia.   And Signora Frola believes that her daughter is still living, that she is your wife still?

Ponza.   Perhaps it was best for her that way. She was in charge of a nurse in her own room, you see. Well, when she chanced to see me passing by inadvertence on her street one day, with this woman, my second wife, she suddenly began to laugh and cry and tremble all over in an extreme of happiness. She was sure her daughter, whom she had believed dead, was alive and well; and from a condition of desperate despondency which was the first form of her mental disturbance, she entered on a second obsession, believing steadily that her daughter was not dead at all; but that I, the poor girl's husband, am so completely in love with her that I want her wholly for myself and will not allow anyone to approach her. She became otherwise quite well, you might say. Her nervousness disappeared. Her physical condition improved, and her powers of reasoning returned quite clear. Judge for yourself, ladies and gentlemen! You have seen her and talked with her. You would never suspect in the world that she is mad.

Amalia.   Never in the world! Never!

Signora Sirelli.   And the poor woman says she is so happy, so happy!

Ponza.   That is what she says to everybody; and for that matter she really has a wealth of affection and gratitude for me; because, as you may well suppose, I do my very best, in spite of the sacrifices entailed, to keep up this beneficial illusion in her. The sacrifices you can readily understand. In the first place I have to maintain two homes on my small salary. Then it is very hard on my wife, isn't it? But she, poor thing, does the very best she can to help me out! She comes to the window when the old lady appears. She talks to her from the balcony. She writes letters to her. But you people will understand that there are limits to what I can ask of my poor wife. Signora Frola, meanwhile, lives practically in confinement. We have to keep a pretty close watch on her. We have to lock her up, virtually. Otherwise, some fine day she would be walking right into my house. She is of a gentle, placid disposition fortunately; but you understand that my wife, good as she is, could never bring herself to accepting caresses intended for another woman, a dead woman! That would be a torment beyond conception.

Amalia. Oh, of course! Poor woman! Just imagine!

Signora Sirelli. And the old lady herself consents to being locked up all the time?

Ponza. You, Commendatore, will understand that I couldn't permit her calling here except under absolute constraint.

Agazzi. I understand perfectly, my dear Ponza, and you have my deepest sympathy.

Ponza. When a man has a misfortune like this fall upon him he must not go about in society; but of course when, by complaining to the prefect, you practically compelled me to have Signora Frola call, it was my duty to volunteer this further information; because, as a public official, and with due regard for the post of responsibility I occupy, I could not allow any discredible suspicions to remain attached to my reputation. I could not have you good people suppose for a moment that, out of jealousy or for any other reason, I could ever prevent a poor suffering mother from seeing her own daughter. [*He rises.*] Again my apologies for having intruded my personal troubles upon your party. [*He bows.*] My compliments, Commendatore. Good afternoon, good afternoon! Thank

you! [*Bowing to* LAUDISI, SIRELLI, *and the others in turn,
he goes out through the door, rear.*]

Amalia [*with a sigh of sympathy and astonishment*].
Uhh! Mad! What do you think of that?

Signora Sirelli. The poor old thing! But you wouldn't
have believed it, would you?

Dina. I always knew there was something under it all.

Signora Cini. But who could ever have guessed . . .

Agazzi. Oh, I don't know, I don't know! You could
tell from the way she talked . . .

Laudisi. You mean to say that you thought . . . ?

Agazzi. No, I can't say that. But at the same time, if
you remember, she could never quite find her words.

Signora Sirelli. How could she, poor thing, out of her
head like that?

Sirelli. And yet, if I may raise the question, it seems
strange to me that an insane person . . . oh, I admit
that she couldn't really talk rationally . . . but what
surprises me is her trying to find a reason to explain why
her son-in-law should be keeping her away from her
daughter. This effort of hers to justify it and then to
adapt herself to excuses of her own invention . . .

Agazzi. Yes, but that is only another proof that she's
mad. You see, she kept offering excuses for Ponza that
really were not excuses at all.

Amalia. Why, yes! She'd say a thing and then take it
right back again.

Agazzi. If she weren't downright mad, how could she
or any other woman ever accept such a situation from a
man? How could she ever consent to talk with her own
daughter only by shouting up from the bottom of a well
five stories deep?

Sirelli. But if I remember rightly she has you there!
Notice, she doesn't accept the situation. She says she is
resigned to it. That's different! No, I tell you, there is

still something funny about this business. What do you say, Laudisi?

Laudisi. Why, I say nothing, nothing at all!

The Butler [*appearing at the door and visibly excited*]. Beg pardon, Signora Frola is here again!

Amalia [*with a start*]. Oh dear me, again? Do you suppose she'll be pestering us all the time now?

Signora Sirelli. I understand how you feel now that you know she's mad.

Signora Cini. My, my, what do you suppose she is going to say now?

Sirelli. For my part I'd really like to hear what she's got to say.

Dina. Oh yes, mamma, don't be afraid! Ponza said she was quite harmless. Let's have her come in.

Agazzi. Of course, we can't send her away. Let's have her come in; and, if she makes any trouble, why . . . [*Turning to the* BUTLER.] Show her in. [*The* BUTLER *bows and withdraws.*]

Amalia. You people stand by me, please! Why, I don't know what I am ever going to say to her now!

[SIGNORA FROLA *appears at the door.* AMALIA *rises and steps forward to welcome her. The others look on in astonished silence.*]

Signora Frola. May I please . . . ?

Amalia. Do come in, Signora Frola, do come in! You know all these ladies. They were here when you came before.

Signora Frola [*with an expression of sadness on her features, but still smiling gently*]. How you all look at me—and even you, Signora Agazzi! I am sure you think I am mad, don't you!

Amalia. My dear Signora Frola, what in the world are you talking about?

Signora Frola. But I am sure you will forgive me if I disturb you for a moment. [*Bitterly.*] Oh, my dear

Signora Agazzi, I wish I had left things as they were. It was hard to feel that I had been impolite to you by not answering the bell when you called that first time; but I could never have supposed that you would come back and force me to call upon you. I could foresee the consequences of such a visit from the very first.

Amalia. Why, not at all, not at all! I don't understand. Why?

Dina. What consequences could you foresee, madam?

Signora Frola. Why, my son-in-law, Signor Ponza, has just been here, hasn't he?

Agazzi. Why, yes, he was here! He came to discuss certain office matters with me . . . just ordinary business, you understand!

Signora Frola [*visibly hurt and quite dismayed*]. Oh, I know you are saying that just to spare me, just in order not to hurt my feelings.

Agazzi. Not at all, not at all! That was really why he came.

Signora Frola [*with some alarm*]. But he was quite calm, I hope, quite calm?

Agazzi. Calm? As calm as could be! Why not? Of course!

[*The members of the company all nod in confirmation.*]

Signora Frola. Oh, my dear friends, I am sure you are trying to reassure me; but as a matter of fact I came to set you right about my son-in-law.

Signora Sirelli. Why no, Signora, what's the trouble?

Agazzi. Really, it was just a matter of politics we talked about . . .

Signora Frola. But I can tell from the way you all look at me . . . Please excuse me, but it is not a question of me at all. From the way you all look at me I can tell that he came here to prove something that I would never have confessed for all the money in the world. You will

all bear me out, won't you? When I came here a few
moments ago you all asked me questions that were very
cruel questions to me, as I hope you will understand.
And they were questions that I couldn't answer very well;
but anyhow I gave an explanation of our manner of living which can be satisfactory to nobody, I am well aware.
But how could I give you the real reason? How could I
tell you people, as he's doing, that my daughter has been
dead for four years and that I'm a poor mad mother who
believes that her daughter is still living and that her
husband will not allow me to see her?

Agazzi [*quite upset by the ring of deep sincerity he finds
in* SIGNORA FROLA's *manner of speaking*]. What do you
mean, your daughter?

Signora Frola [*hastily and with anguished dismay
written on her features*]. You know that's so. Why do
you try to deny it? He did say that to you, didn't he?

Sirelli [*with some hesitation and studying her features
warily*]. Yes . . . in fact . . . he did say that.

Signora Frola. I know he did; and I also know how
it pained him to be obliged to say such a thing of me. It is
a great pity, Commendatore! We have made continual
sacrifices, involving unheard of suffering, I assure you;
and we could endure them only by living as we are living now. Unfortunately, as I well understand, it must
look very strange to people, seem even scandalous, arouse
no end of gossip! But after all, if he is an excellent secretary, scrupulously honest, attentive to his work, why
should people complain? You have seen him in the office,
haven't you? He is a good worker, isn't he?

Agazzi. To tell the truth, I have not watched him
particularly, as yet.

Signora Frola. Oh he really is, he really is! All the
men he ever worked for say he's most reliable; and I beg
of you, please don't let this other matter interfere. And
why then should people go tormenting him with all this

prying into his private life, laying bare once more a misfortune which he has succeeded in mastering and which, if it were widely talked about, might upset him again personally, and even hurt him in his career?

Agazzi.   Oh no, no, Signora, no one is trying to hurt him. Nor would we hurt you either.

Signora Frola.   But my dear sir, how can you help hurting me when you force him to give almost publicly an explanation which is quite absurd—ridiculous I might even say! Surely people like you can't seriously believe what he says? You can't possibly be taking me for mad. You don't really think that this woman is his second wife? And yet it is all so necessary! He needs to have it that way. It is the only way he can pull himself together; get down to his work again . . . the only way . . . the only way! Why he gets all wrought up, all excited, when he is forced to talk of this other matter; because he knows himself how hard it is for him to say certain things. You may have noticed it . . .

Agazzi.   Yes, that is quite true. He did seem very much excited.

Signora Sirelli.   Well, well, well, so then it's he!

Sirelli [*triumphantly*].   I always said it was he.

Agazzi.   Oh, I say! Is that really possible? [*He motions to the company to be quiet.*]

Signora Frola [*joining her hands beseechingly*].   My dear friends, what are you really thinking? It is only on this subject that he is a little queer. The point is, you must simply not mention this particular matter to him. Why, really now, you could never suppose that I would leave my daughter shut up with him all alone like that? And yet just watch him at his work and in the office. He does everything he is expected to do and no one in the world could do it better.

Agazzi.   But this is not enough, madam, as you will understand. Do you mean to say that Signor Ponza, your son-in-law, came here and made up a story out of whole cloth?

Signora Frola. Yes, sir, yes sir, exactly . . . only I will explain. You must understand—you must look at things from his point of view.

Agazzi. What do you mean? Do you mean that your daughter is not dead?

Signora Frola. God forbid! Of course she is not dead!

Agazzi. Well, then, he is mad!

Signora Frola. No, no, look, look! . . .

Sirelli. I always said it was he! . . .

Signora Frola. No, look, look, not that, not that! Let me explain . . . You have noticed him, haven't you? Fine, strong looking man . . . violent . . . when he married my daughter he was seized with a veritable frenzy of love . . . he risked my little daughter's life almost, she was frail . . . On the advice of doctors and relatives, even *his* relatives—dead now, poor things—they had to take his wife off in secret and shut her up in a sanatorium. And he came to think she was dead.

Just imagine when we brought my daughter back to him—and a pretty thing she was to look at, too—he began to scream and say, no, no, no, she wasn't his wife, his wife was dead! He looked at her: No, no, no, not at all! She wasn't the woman! Imagine my dear friends, how terrible it all was. Finally he came up close to her and for a moment it seemed that he was going to recognize her again; but once more it was "No, no, no, she is not my wife!" And do you know, to get him to accept my daughter at all again, we were obliged to pretend having a second wedding, with the collusion of his doctors and his friends, you understand!

Signora Sirelli. Ah, so that is why he says that . . .

Signora Frola. Yes, but he doesn't really believe it, you know; and he hasn't for a long time, I am sure. But he seems to feel a need for maintaining the pretense. He can't do without it. He feels surer of himself that way. He is seized with a terrible fear, from time to time, that this little wife he loves may be taken from him again. [*Smiling and in a low, confidential tone.*] So he keeps her locked up at home where he can have her all for himself. But he worships her—he worships her; and I am really quite convinced that my daughter is happy. [*She gets up.*] And now I must be going. You see, my son-in-law is in a terrible state of mind at present. I wouldn't like to have him call, and find me not at home. [*With a sigh, and gesturing with her joined hands.*] Well, I suppose we must get along as best we can; but it is hard on my poor girl. She has to pretend all along that she is not herself, but another, his second wife; and I . . . oh, as for me, I have to pretend that I am mad when he's around, my dear friends; but I'm glad to, I'm glad to, really, so long as it does him some good. [*The* LADIES *rise as* SHE *steps nearer to the door.*] No, no, don't let me interrupt your party. I know the way out! Good afternoon! Good afternoon! [*Bowing and smiling, she hurries out through the rear door.* THEY *all remain standing, astonished, stunned, looking into each other's eyes. Silence.*]

Laudisi [*coming forward among them*]. So you're having a look at each other? Well! And the truth? [*He bursts out laughing.*]

ACT II

COUNCILLOR AGAZZI's *study in the same house. Antique furnishings with old paintings on the walls. A portière over the rear entrance and over the door to the left which opens into the drawing room shown in the first act. To the right a substantial fireplace with a big mirror above the mantel. A flat top desk with a telephone. A sofa, armchairs, straight back chairs, etc.*

As the curtain rises AGAZZI *is shown standing beside*

his desk with the telephone receiver pressed to his ear.
LAUDISI *and* SIRELLI *sit looking at him expectantly.*

Agazzi. Yes, I want Centuri. Hello . . . hello . . .
Centuri? Yes, Agazzi speaking. That you, Centuri? It's
me, Agazzi. Well? [*He listens for some time.*] What's that?
Really? [*Again he listens at length.*] I understand, but
you might go at the matter with a little more speed . . .
[*Another long pause.*] Well, I give up! How can that pos-
sibly be? [*A pause.*] Oh, I see, I see . . . [*Another pause.*]
Well, never mind, I'll look into it myself. Goodbye,
Centuri, goodbye! [*He lays down the receiver and steps
forward on the stage.*]

Sirelli [*eagerly*]. Well?

Agazzi. Nothing! Absolutely nothing!

Sirelli. Nothing at all?

Agazzi. You see the whole blamed village was wiped
out. Not a house left standing! In the collapse of the
town hall, followed by a fire, all the records of the place
seem to have been lost—births, deaths, marriages, everything.

Sirelli. But not everybody was killed. They ought to
be able to find somebody who knows them.

Agazzi. Yes, but you see they didn't rebuild the place.
Everybody moved away, and no record was ever kept of
the people, of course. So far they have found nobody who
knows the Ponzas. To be sure, if the police really went
at it, they might find somebody; but it would be a
tough job.

Sirelli. So we can't get anywhere along that line! We
have got to take what they say and let it go at that.

Agazzi. That, unfortunately, is the situation.

Laudisi [*rising*]. Well, you fellows take a piece of
advice from me: believe them both!

Agazzi. What do you mean—"believe them
both"? . . .

Sirelli. But if she says one thing, and he says another . . .

Laudisi. Well, in that case, you needn't believe either of them!

Sirelli. Oh, you're just joking. We may not be able to verify the stories; but that doesn't prove that either one or the other may not be telling the truth. Some document or other . . .

Laudisi. Oh, documents! Documents! Suppose you had them? What good would they do you?

Agazzi. Oh, I say! Perhaps we can't get them now, but there were such documents once. If the old lady is mad, there was, as there still may be somewhere, the death certificate of the daughter. Or look at it from the other angle: if we found all the records, and the death certificate were not there for the simple reason that it never existed, why then, it's Ponza, the son-in-law. He would be mad.

Sirelli. You mean to say you wouldn't give in if we stuck that certificate under your nose tomorrow or the next day? Would you still deny . . .

Laudisi. Deny? Why . . . why . . . I'm not denying anything! In fact, I'm very careful not to be denying anything. You're the people who are looking up the records to be able to affirm or deny something. Personally, I don't give a rap for the documents; for the truth in my eyes is not in them but in the mind. And into their minds I can penetrate only through what they say to me of themselves.

Sirelli. Very well— She says he's mad and he says she's mad. Now one of them must be mad. You can't get away from that. Well which is it, she or he?

Agazzi. There, that's the way to put it!

Laudisi. But just observe; in the first place, it isn't true that they are accusing each other of madness. Ponza, to be sure, says his mother-in-law is mad. She denies this, not only of herself, but also of him. At the most, she says that he was a little off once, when they took her daughter from him; but that now he is quite all right.

Sirelli. I see! So you're rather inclined, as I am, to trust what the old lady says.

Agazzi. The fact is, indeed, that if you accept his story, all the facts in the case are explained.

Laudisi. But all the facts in the case are explained if you take her story, aren't they?

Sirelli. Oh, nonsense! In that case neither of them would be mad! Why, one of them must be, damn it all!

Laudisi. Well, which one? You can't tell, can you? Neither can anybody else! And it is not because those documents you are looking for have been destroyed in an accident—a fire, an earthquake—what you will; but because those people have concealed those documents in themselves, in their own souls. Can't you understand that? She has created for him, or he for her, a world of fancy which has all the carmarks of reality itself. And in this fictitious reality they get along perfectly well, and in full accord with each other; and this world of fancy, this reality of theirs, no document can possibly destroy because the air they breathe is of that world. For them it is something they can see with their eyes, hear with their ears, and touch with their fingers. Oh, I grant you—if you could get a death certificate or a marriage certificate or something of the kind, you might be able to satisfy that stupid curiosity of yours. Unfortunately, you can't get it. And the result is that you are in the extraordinary fix of having before you, on the one hand, a world of fancy, and on the other, a world of reality, and you, for the life of you, are not able to distinguish one from the other.

Agazzi. Philosophy, my dear boy, philosophy! And I have no use for philosophy. Give me facts, if you please! Facts! So, I say, keep at it; and I'll bet you we get to the bottom of it sooner or later.

Sirelli. First we got her story and then we got his; and

then we got a new one from her. Let's bring the two of them together—and you think that then we won't be able to tell the false from the true?

Laudisi. Well, bring them together if you want to! All I ask is permission to laugh when you're through.

Agazzi. Well, we'll let you laugh all you want. In the meantime let's see . . . [*He steps to the door at the left and calls.*] Amalia, Signora Sirelli, won't you come in here a moment?

[*The* LADIES *enter with* DINA.]

Signora Sirelli [*catching sight of* LAUDISI *and shaking a finger at him*]. But how is it a man like you, in the presence of such an extraordinary situation, can escape the curiosity we all feel to get at the bottom of this mystery? Why, I lie awake nights thinking of it!

Agazzi. As your husband says, that man's impossible! Don't bother about him, Signora Sirelli.

Laudisi. No, don't bother with me; you just listen to Agazzi! He'll keep you from lying awake tonight.

Agazzi. Look here, ladies. This is what I want—I have an idea: won't you just step across the hall to Signora Frola's?

Amalia. But will she come to the door?

Agazzi. Oh, I imagine she will!

Dina. We're just returning the call, you see . . .

Amalia. But didn't he ask us not to call on his mother-in-law? Hasn't he forbidden her to receive visits?

Sirelli. No, not exactly! That's how he explained what had happened; but at that time nothing was known. Now that the old lady, through force of circumstance, has spoken, giving her version at least of her strange conduct, I should think that . . .

Signora Sirelli. I have a feeling that she'll be awfully glad to see us, if for nothing else, for the chance of talking about her daughter.

Dina. And she really is a jolly old lady. There is no doubt in my mind, not the slightest: Ponza is mad!

Agazzi. Now, let's not go too fast. You just listen to me [*He looks at his wife.*]—don't stay too long—five or ten minutes at the outside!

Sirelli [*to his wife*]. And for heaven's sake, keep your mouth shut!

Signora Sirelli. And why such considerate advice to me?

Sirelli. Once *you* get going . . .

Dina [*with the idea of preventing a scene*]. Oh, we are not going to stay very long, ten minutes—fifteen, at the outside. I'll see that no breaks are made.

Agazzi. And I'll just drop around to the office, and be back at eleven o'clock—ten or twenty minutes at the most.

Sirelli. And what can I do?

Agazzi. Wait! [*Turning to the* LADIES.] Now, here's the plan! You people invent some excuse or other so as to get Signora Frola in here.

Amalia. What? How can we possibly do that?

Agazzi. Oh, find some excuse! You'll think of something in the course of your talk; and if you don't, there's Dina and Signora Sirelli. But when you come back, you understand, go into the drawing room. [*He steps to the door on the left, makes sure that it is wide open, and draws aside the portière.*] This door must stay open, wide open, so that we can hear you talking from in here. Now, here are some papers that I ought to take with me to the office. However, I forget them here. It is a brief that requires Ponza's immediate personal attention. So then, I forget it. And when I get to the office I have to bring him back here to find them— See?

Sirelli. But just a moment. Where do I come in? When am I expected to appear?

Agazzi. Oh, yes! . . . A moment or two after eleven,

when the ladies are again in the drawing room, and I am back here, you just drop in—to take your wife home, see? You ring the bell and ask for me, and I'll have you brought in here. Then I'll invite the whole crowd in! That's natural enough, isn't it?—into my office? . . .

Laudisi [*interrupting*].   And we'll have the Truth, the whole Truth with a capital T!

Dina.   But look, uncle, of course we'll have the truth —once we get them together face to face—capital T and all!

Agazzi.   Don't get into an argument with that man. Besides, it's time you ladies were going. None of us has any too much leeway.

Signora Sirelli.   Come, Amalia, come Dina! And as for you, sir [*Turning to* LAUDISI.], I won't even shake hands with you.

Laudisi.   Permit me to do it for you, madam. [*He shakes one hand with the other.*] Good luck to you, my dear ladies.

[*Exit* DINA, AMALIA, SIGNORA SIRELLI.]

Agazzi [*to Sirelli*].   And now we'd better go, too. Suppose we hurry!

Sirelli.   Yes, right away. Goodbye, Lamberto!

Laudisi.   Goodbye, good luck, good luck! [AGAZZI *and* SIRELLI *leave.* LAUDISI, *left alone, walks up and down the study a number of times, nodding his head and occasionally smiling. Finally he draws up in front of the big mirror that is hanging over the mantelpiece. He sees himself in the glass, stops, and addresses his image.*]

Laudisi.   So there you are! [*He bows to himself and salutes, touching his forehead with his fingers.*] I say, old man, who is mad, you or I? [*He levels a finger menacingly at his image in the glass; and, of course, the image in turn levels a finger at him. As he smiles, his image smiles.*] Of course, I understand! I say it's you, and you say it's me. You—you are mad! No? It's me? Very well!

It's me! Have it *your* way. Between you and me, we get along very well, don't we! But the trouble is, others don't think of you just as I do; and that being the case, old man, what a fix you're in! As for me, I say that here, right in front of you, I can see myself with my eyes and touch myself with my fingers. But what are you for other people? What are you in their eyes? An image, my dear sir, just an image in the glass! They're all carrying just such a phantom around inside themselves, and here they are racking their brains about the phantoms in other people; and they think all that is quite another thing!

[*The* Butler *has entered the room in time to catch* Laudisi *gesticulating at himself in the glass. He wonders if the man is crazy. Finally he speaks up.*]

Butler. Ahem! . . . Signor Laudisi, if you please . . .

Laudisi [*coming to himself*]. Uff!

Butler. Two ladies calling, sir! Signora Cini and another lady!

Laudisi. Calling to see me?

Butler. Really, they asked for the signora; but I said that she was out—on a call next door; and then . . .

Laudisi. Well, what then?

Butler. They looked at each other and said, "Really! Really!" and finally they asked me if anybody else was at home.

Laudisi. And of course you said that everyone was out!

Butler. I said that you were in!

Laudisi. Why, not at all! I'm miles and miles away! Perhaps that fellow they call Laudisi is here!

Butler. I don't understand, sir.

Laudisi. Why? You think the Laudisi they know is the Laudisi I am?

Butler. I don't understand, sir.

Laudisi. Who are you talking to?

Butler.   Who am I talking to? I thought I was talking to you.

Laudisi.   Are you really sure the Laudisi you are talking to is the Laudisi the ladies want to see?

Butler.   Why, I think so, sir. They said they were looking for the brother of Signora Agazzi.

Laudisi.   Ah, in that case you are right! [*Turning to the image in the glass.*] You are not the brother of Signora Agazzi? No, it's me! [*To the* BUTLER.] Right you are! Tell them I am in. And show them in here, won't you? [*The* BUTLER *retires.*]

Signora Cini.   May I come in?

Laudisi.   Please, please, this way, madam!

Signora Cini.   I was told Signora Agazzi was not at home, and I brought Signora Nenni along. Signora Nenni is a friend of mine, and she was most anxious to make the acquaintance of . . .

Laudisi.   . . . of Signora Frola?

Signora Cini.   Of Signora Agazzi, your sister!

Laudisi.   Oh, she will be back very soon, and Signora Frola will be here, too.

Signora Cini.   Yes, we thought as much.

[SIGNORA NENNI *is an oldish woman of the type of* SIGNORA CINI, *but with the mannerisms of the latter somewhat more pronounced. She, too, is a bundle of concentrated curiosity, but of the sly, cautious type, ready to find something frightful under everything.*]

Laudisi.   Well, it's all planned in advance! It will be a most interesting scene! The curtain rises at eleven, precisely!

Signora Cini.   Planned in advance? What is planned in advance?

Laudisi [*mysteriously, first with a gesture of his finger and then aloud*].   Why, bringing the two of them together! [*A gesture of admiration.*] Great idea, I tell you!

Signora Cini. The two of them—together—who?

Laudisi. Why, the two of them. He—in here! [*Pointing to the room about him.*]

Signora Cini. Ponza, you mean?

Laudisi. And she—in there! [*He points toward the drawing room.*]

Signora Cini. Signora Frola?

Laudisi. Exactly! [*With an expressive gesture of his hands and even more mysteriously.*] But afterwards, all of them—in here! Oh, a great idea, a great idea!

Signora Cini. In order to get . . .

Laudisi. The truth! But it's already known: all that remains is the unmasking.

Signora Cini [*with the greatest surprise*]. Oh, really? So they know the truth! And which is it— He or she?

Laudisi. Well, I'll tell you . . . you just guess! Who do you think it is?

Signora Cini [*ahemming*]. Well . . . I say . . . really . . . you see . . .

Laudisi. Is it she or is it he? You don't mean to say you don't know! Come now, give a guess!

Signora Cini. Why, for my part I should say . . . well, I'd say . . . it's *he.*

Laudisi [*looks at her admiringly*]. Right you are! It *is* he!

Signora Cini. Really? I always thought so! Of course, it was perfectly plain all along. It had to be he!

Signora Nenni. All of us women in town said it was he. We always said so!

Signora Cini. But how did you get at it? I suppose Signor Agazzi ran down the documents, didn't he—the birth certificate, or something?

Signora Nenni. Through the prefect, of course! There was no getting away from those people. Once the police start investigating . . . !

Laudisi [*motions to them to come closer to him; then in*

a low voice and in the same mysterious manner, and stressing each syllable]. The certificate!—Of the second marriage!

Signora Cini [*starting back with astonishment*]. What?

Signora Nenni [*likewise taken aback*]. What did you say? The second marriage?

Signora Cini. Well, in that case he was *right*.

Laudisi. Oh, documents, ladies, documents! This certificate of the second marriage, so it seems, talks as plain as day.

Signora Nenni. Well, then, *she* is mad.

Laudisi. Right! She must be, mustn't she?

Signora Cini. But I thought you said . . .

Laudisi. Yes, I did say . . . but this certificate of the second marriage may very well be, as Signora Frola said, a fictitious document, gotten up through the influence of Ponza's doctors and friends to pamper him in the notion that his wife was not his first wife, but another woman.

Signora Cini. But it's a public document. You mean to say a public document can be a fraud?

Laudisi. I mean to say—well, it has just the value that each of you chooses to give it. For instance, one could find somewhere, possibly, those letters that Signora Frola said she gets from her daughter, who lets them down in the basket in the courtyard. There are such letters, aren't there?

Signora Cini. Yes, of course!

Laudisi. They are documents, aren't they? Aren't letters documents? But it all depends on how you read them. Here comes Ponza, and he says they are just made up to pamper his mother-in-law in her obsession . . .

Signora Cini. Oh, dear, dear, so then we're never sure about anything?

Laudisi. Never sure about anything? Why not at all,

not at all! Let's be exact. We are sure of many things, aren't we? How many days are there in the week? Seven —Sunday, Monday, Tuesday, Wednesday . . . How many months in the year are there? Twelve: January, February, March . . .

Signora Cini. Oh, I see, you're just joking! You're just joking! [DINA *appears, breathless, in the doorway, at the rear.*]

Dina. Oh, uncle, won't you please . . . [*She stops at the sight of* SIGNORA CINI.] Oh, Signora Cini, you here?

Signora Cini. Why, I just came to make a call! . . .

Laudisi. . . . with Signora Cenni.

Signora Nenni. No, my name is Nenni.

Laudisi. Oh yes, pardon me! She was anxious to make Signora Frola's acquaintance . . .

Signora Nenni. Why, not at all!

Signora Cini. He has just been making fun of us! You ought to see what fools he made of us!

Dina. Oh, he's perfectly insufferable, even with mamma and me. Will you excuse me for just a moment? No, everything is all right. I'll just run back and tell mamma that you people are here and I think that will be enough. Oh, uncle, if you had only heard her talk! Why, she is a perfect *dear,* and what a good, kind soul! . . . She showed us all those letters her daughter wrote . . .

Signora Cini. Yes, but as Signora Laudisi was just saying . . .

Dina. He hasn't even seen them!

Signora Nenni. You mean they are not really fictitous?

Dina. Fictitious nothing! They talk as plain as day. And such things! You can't fool a mother when her own daughter talks to her. And you know—the letter she got yesterday! . . . [*She stops at the sound of voices coming into the study from the drawing room.*] Oh, here they are, here they are, already! [*She goes to the door and peeps into the room.*]

Signora Cini [*following her to the door*]. Is *she* there, too?

Dina. Yes, but you had better come into the other room. All of us women must be in the drawing room. And it is just eleven o'clock, uncle!

Amalia [*entering with decision from the door on the left*]. I think this whole business is quite unnecessary! We have absolutely no further need of proofs . . .

Dina. Quite so! I thought of that myself. Why bring Ponza here?

Amalia [*taken somewhat aback by* SIGNORA CINI's *presence*]. Oh, my dear Signora Cini! . . .

Signora Cini [*introducing* SIGNORA NENNI]. A friend of mine, Signora Nenni! I ventured to bring her with me . . .

Amalia [*bowing, but somewhat coolly, to the visitor*]. A great pleasure, Signora! [*After a pause.*] There is not the slightest doubt in the world: . . . it's he!

Signora Cini. It's he? Are you sure it's he?

Dina. And such a trick on the poor old lady!

Amalia. Trick is not the name for it! It's downright dishonest!

Laudisi. Oh, I agree with you: it's outrageous! Quite! So much so, I'm quite convinced it must be *she!*

Amalia. She? What do you mean? How can you say that?

Laudisi. I say, it is *she*, it is *she*, it's *she!*

Amalia. Oh, I say! If you had heard her talk . . . !

Dina. It is absolutely clear to us now.

Signora Cini and *Signora Nennin* [*swallowing*]. Really? You are sure?

Laudisi. Exactly! Now that you are sure it's he, why, obviously—it must be she.

Dina. Oh dear me, why talk to that man? He is just impossible!

Amalia. Well, we must go into the other room . . . This way, if you please!

[SIGNORA CINI, SIGNORA NENNI *and* AMALIA *withdraw through the door on the left.* DINA *starts to follow, when* LAUDISI *calls her back.*]

Laudisi. Dina!

Dina. I refuse to listen to you! I refuse!

Laudisi. I was going to suggest that, since the whole matter is closed, you might close the door also.

Dina. But papa . . . he told us to leave it open. Ponza will be here soon; and if papa finds it closed—well, you know how papa is!

Laudisi. But you can convince him! . . . You especially. You can show him that there really was no need of going any further. You are convinced yourself, aren't you?

Dina. I am as sure of it, as I am that I'm alive!

Laudisi [*putting her to the test with a smile*]. Well, close the door then!

Dina. I see, you're trying to make me say that I'm not really sure. Well, I won't close the door, but it's just on account of papa.

Laudisi. Shall I close it for you?

Dina. If you take the responsibility yourself! . . .

Laudisi. But you see, *I* am sure! I *know* that Ponza is mad!

Dina. The thing for you to do is to come into the other room and just hear her talk a while. Then you'll be sure, absolutely sure. Coming?

Laudisi. Yes, I'm coming, and I'll close the door behind me—on my own responsibility, of course.

Dina. Ah, I see. So you're convinced even before you hear her talk.

Laudisi. No, dear, it's because I'm sure that your papa, who has been with Ponza, is just as certain as you are that any further investigation is unnecessary.

Dina. How can you say that?

Laudisi. Why, of course, if you talk with Ponza, you're sure the old lady is mad. [*He walks resolutely to the door.*] I am going to shut this door.

Dina [*restraining him nervously, then hesitating a moment*]. Well, why not . . . if you're really sure? What do you say—let's leave it open!

Laudisi [*bursts out laughing*].

Dina. But just because papa told us to!

Laudisi. And papa will tell you something else by and by. Say . . . let's leave it open!

[*A piano starts playing in the adjoining room—an ancient tune, sweet, graceful, full of pain, from "Nina Dead of Love" by Paisiello.*]

Dina. Oh, there she is. She's playing! Do you hear? Actually playing the piano!

Laudisi. The old lady?

Dina. Yes! And you know? She told us that her daughter used to play this tune, always the same tune. How well she plays! Come! Come!

[THEY *hurry through the door.*]

The stage, after the exit of LAUDISI *and* DINA, *remains empty for a space of time while the music continues from the other room.* PONZA, *appearing at the door with* AGAZZI, *catches the concluding notes and his face changes to an expression of deep emotion—an emotion that will develop into a virtual frenzy as the scene proceeds.*

Agazzi [*in the doorway*]. After you, after you, please! [*He takes* PONZA's *elbow and motions him into the room. He goes over to his desk, looks about for the papers which he pretends he had forgotten, finds them eventually and says.*] Why, here they are! I was sure I had left them here. Won't you take a chair, Ponza? [PONZA *seems not to hear. He stands looking excitedly at the door into the drawing room, through which the sound of the piano is still coming.*]

Agazzi. Yes, they are the ones! [HE *takes the papers and steps to* PONZA'S *side, opening the folder.*] It is an old case, you see. Been running now for years and years! To tell you the truth I haven't made head or tail of the stuff myself. I imagine you'll find it one big mess. [*He, too, becomes aware of the music and seems somewhat irritated by it. His eyes also rest on the door to the drawing room.*] That noise, just at this moment! [*He walks with a show of anger to the door.*] Who is that at the piano anyway? [*In the doorway he stops and looks, and an expression of astonishment comes into his face.*] Ah!

Ponza [*going to the door also. On looking into the next room he can hardly restrain his emotion*]. In the name of God, is *she* playing?

Agazzi. Yes—Signora Frola! And how well she does play!

Ponza. How is this? You people have brought her in here, again! And you're letting her play!

Agazzi. Why not? What's the harm?

Ponza. Oh, please, please, no, not that song! It is the one her daughter used to play.

Agazzi. Ah, I see! And it hurts you?

Ponza. Oh, no, not me—but her—it hurts her—and you don't know how much! I thought I had made you and those women understand just how that poor old lady was!

Agazzi. Yes, you did . . . quite true! But you see . . . but see here, Ponza! [*Trying to pacify the man's growing emotion.*]

Ponza [*continuing*]. But you *must* leave her alone! You *must* not go to her house! She *must* not come in here! I am the only person who can deal with her. You are killing her . . . killing her!

Agazzi.   No, I don't think so. It is not so bad as that.
My wife and daughter are surely tactful enough . . .
[*Suddenly the music ceases. There is a burst of applause.*]

Agazzi.   There, you see. Listen! Listen!

[*From the next room the following conversation is distinctly heard.*]

Dina.   Why, Signora Frola, you are perfectly *marvellous* at the piano!

Signora Frola.   But you should hear how my Lena
plays!

[PONZA *digs his nails into his hands.*]

Agazzi.   Her daughter, of course!

Ponza.   Didn't you hear? "How my Lena plays! How
my Lena *plays!*"

[*Again from inside.*]

Signora Frola.   Oh, no, not now! . . . She hasn't
played for a long time—since that happened. And you
know, it is what she takes hardest, poor girl!

Agazzi.   Why, that seems quite natural to me! Of
course, she thinks the girl is still alive!

Ponza.   But she shouldn't be allowed to say such
things. She *must* not—she *must* not say such things!
Didn't you hear? "She hasn't played since that happened"! She said "she *hasn't* played since that happened"!
Talking of the piano, you understand! Oh, you don't
understand, no, of course! My first wife had a piano and
played that tune. Oh, oh, oh! You people are determined
to ruin me!

[SIRELLI *appears at the back door at this moment, and
hearing the concluding words of* PONZA *and noticing
his extreme exasperation, stops short, uncertain as
to what to do.* AGAZZI *is himself very much affected
and motions to* SIRELLI *to come in.*]

Agazzi.   Why, no, my dear fellow, I don't see any
reason . . . [*To* SIRELLI.] Won't you just tell the ladies
to come in here?

[SIRELLI, *keeping at a safe distance from* PONZA, *goes to the door at the left and calls.*]

Ponza. The ladies in here? In here with me? Oh, no, no, please, rather . . .

[*At a signal from* SIRELLI, *who stands in the doorway to the left, his face taut with intense emotion, the* LADIES *enter. They all show various kinds and degrees of excitement and emotion.* SIGNORA FROLA *appears, and catching sight of* PONZA *trembling from head to foot, worked up into a state of positively animal passion, stops, quite overwhelmed. As* HE *assails her during the lines that follow,* SHE *exchanges glances of understanding from time to time with the* LADIES *about her. The action here is rapid, nervous, tense with excitement, and extremely violent.*]

Ponza. You? Here? How is this? You! Here! Again! What are you doing here?

Signora Frola. Why, I just came . . . don't be cross!

Ponza. You come here to tell these ladies . . . What did you tell these ladies?

Signora Frola. Nothing! I swear to God, nothing!

Ponza. Nothing? What do you mean, nothing? I heard you with my own ears, and this gentleman here heard you also. You said "she plays." Who plays? Lena plays! And you know very well that Lena has been dead for four years. Dead, do you hear! Your daughter has been dead—for four years!

Signora Frola. Yes, yes, I know . . . Don't get excited, my dear . . . Oh, yes, oh yes. I know . . .

Ponza. And you said "she hasn't been able to play since that happened." Of course she hasn't been able to play since that happened. How could she, if she's dead?

Signora Frola. Why, of course, certainly. Isn't that what I said? Ask these ladies. I said that she hasn't been able to play since that happened. Of course. How could she, if she's dead?

Ponza.   And why were you worrying about that piano, then?

Signora Frola.   No, no! I'm not worrying about any piano . . .

Ponza.   I broke that piano up and destroyed it. You know that, the moment your daughter died, so that my second wife couldn't touch it. She can't play in any case. You know she doesn't play.

Signora Frola.   Why, of course, dear! Of course! She doesn't know how to play!

Ponza.   And one thing more: Your daughter was Lena, wasn't she? Her name was Lena. Now, see here! You just tell these people what my second wife's name is. Speak up! You know very well what her name is! What is it? What is it?

Signora Frola.   Her name is Julia! Yes, yes, of course, my dear friends, her name is Julia! [*Winks at someone in the company.*]

Ponza.   Exactly! Her name is Julia, and not Lena! Who are you winking at? Don't you go trying to suggest by those winks of yours that she's not Julia!

Signora Frola.   Why, what do you mean? I wasn't winking! Of course I wasn't!

Ponza.   I saw you! I saw you very distinctly! You are trying to ruin me! You are trying to make these people think that I am keeping your daughter all to myself, just as though she were not dead. [*He breaks into convulsive sobbing.*] . . . just as though she were not dead!

Signora Frola [*hurrying forward and speaking with infinite kindness and sympathy*].   Oh no! Come, come, my poor boy. Come! Don't take it so hard. I never said any such thing, did I, madam!

Amalia, Signora Sirelli, Dina.   Of course she never said such a thing! She always said the girl was dead! Yes! Of course! No!

Signora Frola.   I did, didn't I? I said she's dead,

didn't I? And that you are so very good to me. Didn't I, didn't I? I, trying to ruin you? I, trying to get you into trouble?

Ponza. And you, going into other people's houses where there are pianos, playing your daughter's tunes on them! Saying that Lena plays them that way, or even better!

Signora Frola. No, it was . . . why . . . you see . . . it was . . . well . . . just to see whether . . .

Ponza. But you *can't* . . . you *mustn't!* How could you ever dream of trying to play a tune that your dead daughter played!

Signora Frola. You are quite right! . . . Oh, yes! Poor boy! Poor boy! [*She also begins to weep.*] I'll never do it again: Never, never, never again!

Ponza [*advancing upon her threateningly*]. What are you doing here? Get out of here! Go home at once! Home! Home! Go home!

Signora Frola. Yes, yes! Home! I am going home! Oh dear, oh dear!

[*She backs out the rear door, looking beseechingly at the company, as though urging everyone to have pity on her son-in-law. She retires, sobbing. The others stand there looking at* PONZA *with pity and terror; but the moment* SIGNORA FROLA *has left the room, he regains his normal composure.*]

Ponza. I beg pardon for the sad spectacle I've had to present before all you ladies and gentlemen to remedy the evil which, without wanting, without knowing, you are doing to this unhappy woman—with your compassion.

Agazzi [*astonished like all the others*]. What? You were only pretending?

Ponza. I had to, my good people! It's the only way to keep up the illusion for her, don't you see? I have to roar out the truth that way—as if it were madness, *my* madness! Forgive me, I must be going, I must go to her. [*He hurries out through the rear door. Once more* THEY *stand astonished and silent looking at each other.*]

Laudisi [*coming forward*]. And so, ladies and gentlemen, we learn the truth! [*He bursts out laughing*].

ACT III

The same scene. As the curtain rises, LAUDISI *is sprawling in an easy chair, reading a book. Through the door that leads into the parlor on the left comes the confused murmur of many voices.*

The BUTLER *appears in the rear door, introducing the police commissioner,* CENTURI. CENTURI *is a tall, stiff, scowling official, with a decidedly professional air. He is in the neighborhood of forty.*

The Butler. This way, sir. I will call Signor Agazzi at once.

Laudisi [*drawing himself up in his chair and looking around*]. Oh, it's you, Commissioner! [*He rises hastily and recalls the butler, who has stepped out through the door.*] One moment, please! Wait! [*To* CENTURI.] Anything new, Commissioner?

Commissioner [*stiffly*]. Yes, something new!

Laudisi. Ah! Very well. [*To the* BUTLER.] Never mind. I'll call him myself. [*He motions with his hand toward the door on the left. The* BUTLER *bows and withdraws.*] You have worked miracles, Commissioner! You're the savior of this town. Listen! Do you hear them! You are the lion of the place! How does it feel to be the father of your country? But say, what you've discovered is all solid fact?

Commissioner. We've managed to unearth a few people.

Laudisi. From Ponza's town? People who know all about him?

Commissioner. Yes! And we have gathered from them a few facts,—not many, perhaps, but well authenticated.

Laudisi. Ah, that's nice. Congratulations! For example . . .

Commissioner. For example? Why, for instance, here . . . well, here are all the communications I have received. Read 'em yourself! [*From an inner pocket he draws a yellow envelope, opened at one end, from which he takes a document and hands it to* LAUDISI.]

Laudisi. Interesting, I am sure. Very interesting! . . . [*He stands, reading the document carefully, commenting from time to time with exclamations in different tones. First an "ah" of satisfaction, then another "ah" which attenuates this enthusiasm very much. Finally an "eh" of disappointment, which leads to another "eh" of complete disgust.*] Why, no, what's all this amount to, Commissioner?

Commissioner. Well, it's what we were able to find out.

Laudisi. But this doesn't prove anything, you understand! It leaves everything just where it was. There's nothing of any significance whatever here. [*He looks at the* COMMISSIONER *for a moment and then, as though suddenly making up his mind, he says:*] I wonder, Commissioner, would you like to do something really great—render a really distinguished service to this town; and meanwhile lay up a treasure in heaven?

Commissioner [*looking at him in perplexity*]. What are you thinking of, sir?

Laudisi. I'll explain. Here, please, take this chair! [*He sets the chair in front of* AGAZZI's *desk.*] I advise you, Mr. Commissioner, to tear up this sheet of paper that you've brought and which has absolutely no significance at all. But here on this other piece of paper, why don't you write down something that will be precise and clear?

Commissioner. Why . . . why . . . myself? What do you mean? What should I write?

Laudisi [*insisting*]. Just say something—anything— that these two old acquaintances of Ponza's whom you managed to get hold of might have said. Come, Commissioner, rise to the occasion! Do something for the commonwealth! Bring this town back to normal again! Don't you see what they are after? They all want the truth—*a* truth that is: Something specific; something concrete! They don't care what it is. All they want is something categorical, something that speaks plainly! Then they'll quiet down.

Commissioner. *The* truth—*a* truth? Excuse me, have I understood you clearly? You were suggesting that I commit a forgery? I am astonished that you dare propose such a thing, and when I say I am astonished, I'm not saying half what I actually feel. Be so good as to tell the Commendatore that I am here!

Laudisi [*dropping his arms dejectedly*]. As you will, Commissioner!

[*He steps over to the door on the left. As he draws the portières and swings the door more widely open, the voices become louder and more confused. As he steps through, there is a sudden silence. The* POLICE COMMISSIONER *stands waiting with a satisfied air, twirling one of the points of his mustache. All of a sudden, there is commotion and cheering in the next room. Cries of delight and applause, mixed with handclapping. The* POLICE COMMISSIONER *comes out of his reverie and looks up with an expression of surprise on his features, as though not understanding what it's all about. Through the door to the left come* AGAZZI, SIRELLI, LAUDISI, AMALIA, DINA, SIGNORA SIRELLI, SIGNORA CINI, SIGNORA NENNI, *and many other ladies and gentlemen.* AGAZZI *leads the proces-*

*sion. They are all still talking and laughing ex-
citedly, clapping their hands, and crying "I told you
so! Fine! Fine! Good! How wonderful! Now we'll
know!" etc.]*

Agazzi [stepping forward cordially]. Ah, my dear
Centuri, I was sure you could! Nothing ever gets by *our*
chief!

Company. Fine! Good! What did you find out! Have
you brought something? Is it she? Is it he? Tell us?

*Commissioner [who doesn't yet understand what all the
excitement is about. For him it has been a mere matter
of routine].* Why, no . . . why, Commendatore, simply . . . you understand . . .

Agazzi. Hush! Give him a chance! . . .

Commissioner. I have done my best. I . . . but what
did Signor Laudisi tell you?

Agazzi. He told us that you have brought news, real
news!

Sirelli. Specific data, clear, precise! . . .

Laudisi [amplifying]. . . . not many, perhaps, but
well authenticated! The best they've managed to trace!
Old neighbors of Ponza, you see; people well acquainted
with him . . .

Everybody. Ah! At last! At last! Now we'll know! At
last!

[The Commissioner *hands the document to* Agazzi.]

Commissioner. There you have it, Commendatore!

Agazzi [opening the sheet, as all crowd around him].
Let's have a look at it!

Commissioner. But you, Signor Laudisi . . .

Laudisi. Don't interrupt, please, the document speaks
for itself! Agazzi, you read it.

Agazzi [to Laudisi]. But give me a chance, won't you?
Please! Please! Now! There you are!

Laudisi. Oh, I don't care. I've read the thing already.

Everybody [*crowding around him*].   You've read it already? What did it say? Is it he? Is it she?

Laudisi [*speaking very formally*].   There is no doubt whatever, as a former neighbor of Ponza's testifies, that the woman Frola was once in a sanatorium!

The Group [*cries of disappointment*].   Oh really! Too bad! Too bad!

Signora Sirelli.   Signora Frola, did you say?

Dina.   Are you sure it was she?

Agazzi.   Why, no! Why, no, it doesn't say anything of the kind! [*Coming forward and waving the document triumphantly.*] It doesn't say anything of the kind! [*General excitement.*]

Everybody.   Well, what does it say? What does it say?

Laudisi [*insisting*].   It does too! It says "the Frola woman"—the Frola woman, categorically.

Agazzi.   Nothing of the kind! The witness says that he *thinks* she was in a sanatorium. He does not assert that she was. Besides, there is another point. He doesn't know whether this Frola woman who was in a sanatorium was the mother or the daughter, the first wife, that is!

Everybody [*with relief*].   Ah!

Laudisi [*insistingly*].   But I say he does. It must be the mother! Who else could it be?

Sirelli.   No, of course, it's the daughter! It's the daughter!

Signora Sirelli.   Just as the old lady said herself!

Amalia.   Exactly! That time when they took her away by force from her husband! . . .

Dina.   Yes, she says that her daughter was taken to a home.

Agazzi.   Furthermore, observe another thing. The witness does not really belong to their town. He says that he used to go there frequently, but that he does not remember particularly. He remembers that he heard something or other! . . .

Sirelli. Ah! How can you depend on such a man's testimony? Nothing but hearsay!

Laudisi. But, excuse me! If all you people are so sure that Signora Frola is right, what more do you want? Why do you go looking for documents? This is all nonsense!

Sirelli. If it weren't for the fact that the prefect has accepted Ponza's side of the story, I'll tell you . . .

Commissioner. Yes, that's true. The prefect said as much to me . . .

Agazzi. Yes, but that's because the prefect has never talked with the old lady who lives next door.

Signora Sirelli. You bet he hasn't. He talked only with Ponza.

Sirelli. But, for that matter, there are other people of the same mind as the prefect.

A Gentleman. That is my situation, my situation exactly. Yes sir! Because I know of just such a case where a mother went insane over the death of her daughter and insists that the daughter's husband will not allow her to see the girl. The same case to a *T*.

A Second Gentleman. Not exactly to a *T*! Not exactly to a *T*! In the case you mention the man didn't marry again. Here, this man Ponza is living with another woman . . .

Laudisi [*his face brightening with a new idea that has suddenly come to him*]. I have it, ladies and gentlemen! Did you hear that? It's perfectly simple. Dear me, as simple as Columbus's egg!

Everybody. What? What? What? What?

The Second Gentleman. What did I say? I didn't realize it was important.

Laudisi. Just a moment, ladies and gentlemen! [*Turning to* AGAZZI.] Is the prefect coming here, by chance?

Agazzi. Yes, we were expecting him. But what's the new idea?

Laudisi. Why, you were bringing him here to talk

with Signora Frola. So far, he is standing by Ponza. When he has talked with the old lady, he'll know whether to believe Ponza or her. That's *your* idea! Well, I've thought of something better that the prefect can do. Something that only he can do.

Everybody. What is it? What is it? What is it?

Laudisi [*triumphantly*]. Why, this wife of Ponza's, of course . . . at least, the woman he is living with! What this gentleman said suggested the idea to me.

Sirelli. Get the second woman to talk? Of course! Of course!

Dina. But how can we, when she is kept under lock and key?

Sirelli. Why, the prefect can use his authority—order her to speak!

Amalia. Certainly, she is the one who can clear up the whole mystery.

Signora Sirelli. I don't believe it. She'll say just what her husband tells her to say.

Laudisi. She must speak before the prefect. Of course!

Sirelli. She must speak with the prefect privately, all by himself.

Agazzi. And the prefect, as the final authority over the man, will insist that the wife make a formal explicit statement before him. Of course, of course! What do you say, Commissioner?

Commissioner. Why certainly, there's no doubt that if the prefect were so inclined . . .

Agazzi. It is the only way out of it, after all. We ought to phone him and explain that he needn't go to the trouble of coming here. You attend to that, will you, Commissioner?

Commissioner. Very glad to! My compliments, ladies! Good afternoon, gentlemen!

Signora Sirelli. A good idea for once, Laudisi.

Dina. Oh, uncle, how clever of you! Wise old uncle!

The Company. The only way out of it! Yes! Yes! Fine! At last!

Agazzi. Curious none of us thought of that before!

Sirelli. Not so curious! None of us ever set eyes on the woman. She might as well be in another world, poor girl.

Laudisi [*as though suddenly impressed by this latter reflection*]. In another world? Why yes,—are you really sure there is such a woman?

Amalia. Oh I say! Please, please, Lamberto!

Sirelli [*with a laugh*]. You mean to say you think there is no such woman?

Laudisi. How can you be sure there is? You can't guarantee it!

Dina. But the old lady sees her and talks with her every day.

Signora Sirelli. And Ponza says that, too. They both agree on that point!

Laudisi. Yes, yes, I don't deny that. But just a moment! To be strictly logical: there must be a phantom in that house.

All. A phantom?

Agazzi. Oh, go on with you!

Laudisi. Let me finish.—It's the phantom of the second wife, if Signora Frola is right. It's the phantom of the daughter, if Signor Ponza is right. It remains to be seen if what is a phantom for him and her is actually a person for herself. At this point it seems to me there's some reason to doubt it.

Amalia. Oh, come on! You'd like us all to be as mad as you are!

Signora Nenni. Heavens: how he makes my flesh creep!

Signora Cini. I can't think why you enjoy frightening us like this!

All. Nonsense! It's a joke, a joke!

Sirelli. She's a woman of flesh and bones, rest assured. And we'll have her talk, we'll have her talk!

Agazzi. You suggested it yourself, didn't you?—having her talk with the prefect?

Laudisi. Certainly the woman from that house should talk with the prefect—if there is such a woman—and if she *is* a woman!

Signora Sirelli. Dear me, dear me! That man simply drives me mad.

Laudisi. Well, supposing we wait and see!

Everybody. Well, who is she then? But people have seen her! His wife! On the balcony! She writes letters!

Police Commissioner [*in the heat of the confusion comes into the room, excitedly announcing*]. The prefect is coming! The prefect!

Agazzi. What do you mean? Coming here? But you went to . . .

Commissioner. Why yes, but I met him hardly a block away. He was coming here; and Ponza is with him.

Sirelli. Ah, Ponza!

Agazzi. Oh, if Ponza is with him, I doubt whether he is coming here. They are probably on their way to the old lady's. Please, Centuri, you just wait on the landing there and ask him if he won't step in here as he promised?

Commissioner. Very well! I'll do so! [*He withdraws hurriedly through the door in the rear.*]

Agazzi. Won't you people just step into the other room?

Signora Sirelli. But remember now, be sure to make him see the point! It's the only way out, the only way.

Amalia [*at the door to the left*]. This way, ladies, if you please!

Agazzi. Won't you just stay here, Sirelli; and you, too, Lamberto?

[*All the others go out through the door to the left.*]

Agazzi [*to* LAUDISI]. But let me do the talking, won't you!

Laudisi. Oh, as for that, don't worry. In fact, if you prefer, I'll go into the other room . . .

Agazzi. No, no, it's better for you to be here. Ah, here he is now!

[THE PREFECT *is a man of about sixty, tall, thick set, good natured, affable.*]

Prefect. Ah, Agazzi, glad to see you. How goes it, Sirelli? Good to see you again, Laudisi. [*He shakes hands all around.*]

Agazzi [*motioning toward a chair*]. I hope you won't mind my having asked you to come here.

Prefect. No, I was coming, just as I promised you!

Agazzi [*noticing the* POLICE COMMISSIONER *at the door*]. Oh, I'm sorry, Commissioner! Please come in! Here, have a chair!

Prefect [*good-naturedly to* SIRELLI]. By the way, Sirelli, they tell me that you've gone half nutty over this blessed affair of our new secretary.

Sirelli. Oh, no, governor, believe me. I'm not the only one! The whole village is worked up.

Agazzi. And that's putting it very mildly.

Prefect. What's it all about? What's it all about? Good heavens!

Agazzi. Of course, governor, you're probably not posted on the whole business. The old lady lives here next door. . . .

Prefect. Yes, I understand so.

Sirelli. No, one moment, please, governor. You haven't talked with the poor old lady yet.

Prefect. I was on my way to see her. [*Turning to* AGAZZI.] I had promised you to see her here, but Ponza came and begged me, almost on his knees, to see her in her own house. His idea was to put an end to all this talk that's going around. Do you think he would have done such a thing if he weren't absolutely sure?

Agazzi. Of course, he's sure! Because when she's talking in front of him, the poor woman . . .

Sirelli [*suddenly getting in his oar*]. She says just what he wants her to say, governor; which proves that she is far from being as mad as he claims.

Agazzi. We had a sample of that, here, yesterday, all of us.

Prefect. Why, I understand so. You see he's trying all the time to make her believe he's mad. He warned me of that. And how else could he keep the poor woman in her illusion? Do you see any way? All this talk of yours is simply torture to the poor fellow! Believe me, pure torture!

Sirelli. Very well, governor! But supposing *she* is the one who is trying to keep *him* in the idea that her daughter is dead; so as to reassure him that his wife will not be taken from him again. In that case, you see, governor, it's the old lady who is being tortured, and not Ponza!

Agazzi. The moment you see the possibility of that, governor . . . Well, you ought to hear her talk; but all by herself, when he's not around. Then you'd see the possibility all right . . .

Sirelli. Just as we all see it!

Prefect. Oh, I wonder! You don't seem to me so awfully sure; and for my part, I'm quite willing to confess that I'm not so sure myself. How about you, Laudisi?

Laudisi. Sorry, governor, I promised Agazzi here to keep my mouth shut.

Agazzi [*protesting angrily*]. Nothing of the kind! How dare you say that? When the governor asks you a plain question . . . It's true I told him not to talk, but do you know why? He's been doing his best for the past two days to keep us all rattled so that we can't find out anything.

Laudisi. Don't you believe him, governor. On the contrary. I've been doing my best to bring these people to common sense.

Sirelli. Common sense! And do you know what he calls common sense? According to him it is not possible to discover the truth; and now he's been suggesting that Ponza is living not with a woman, but with a ghost!

Prefect [*enjoying the situation*]. That's a new one! Quite an idea! How do you make that out, Laudisi?

Agazzi. Oh, I say! . . . You know how he is. There's no getting anywhere with him!

Laudisi. I leave it to you, governor. I was the one who first suggested bringing you here.

Prefect. And do you think, Laudisi, I ought to see the old lady next door?

Laudisi. No, I advise no such thing, governor. In my judgment you are doing very well in depending on what Ponza tells you.

Prefect. Ah, I see! Because you, too, think that Ponza . . .

Laudisi. No, not at all . . . because I'm also satisfied to have all these people stand on what Signora Frola says, if that does them any good.

Agazzi. So you see, eh, governor? That's what you call arguing, eh?

Prefect. Just a moment! Let me understand! [*Turning to* LAUDISI.] So you say we can also trust what the old lady says?

Laudisi. Of course you can! Implicitly! And so you can depend upon what Ponza says. Implicitly!

Prefect. Excuse me, I don't follow you!

Sirelli. But man alive, if they both say the exact opposite of each other! . . .

Agazzi [*angrily and with heat*]. Listen to me, governor, please. I am prejudiced neither in favor of the old lady nor in favor of Ponza. I recognize that he may be

right and that she may be right. But we ought to settle
the matter, and there is only one way to do it.

Sirelli. The way that Laudisi here suggested.

Prefect. He suggested it? That's interesting? What
is it?

Agazzi. Since we haven't been able to get any positive
proof, there is only one thing left. You, as Ponza's final
superior, as the man who can fire him if need be, can obtain a statement from his wife.

Prefect. Make his wife talk, you mean?

Sirelli. But not in the presence of her husband, you
understand.

Agazzi. Yes, making sure she tells the truth!

Sirelli. . . . tell whether she's the daughter of Signora Frola, that is, as we think she must be . . .

Agazzi. . . . or a second wife who is consenting to
impersonate the daughter of Signora Frola, as Ponza
claims.

Prefect. . . . and as I believe myself, without a
shadow of doubt! [*Thinking a moment.*] Why, I don't
see any objection to having her talk. Who could object?
Ponza? But Ponza, as I know very well, is more eager than
anybody else to have this talk quieted down. He's all upset over this whole business, and said he was willing to do
anything I proposed. I'm sure he will raise no objection.
So if it will ease the minds of you people here . . . Say,
Centuri [*The* POLICE COMMISSIONER *rises.*], won't you just
ask Ponza to step in here a moment? He's next door with
his mother-in-law.

Commissioner. At once, Your Excellency! [*He bows
and withdraws through the door at the rear.*]

Agazzi. Oh well, if he consents . . .

Prefect. He'll consent, all right. And we'll be through
with it in a jiffy. We'll bring her right in here so that you
people . . .

Agazzi. Here, in my house?

Sirelli. You think he'll let his wife come in here?

Prefect. Just leave it to me, just leave it to me! I prefer to have her right here because, otherwise you see, you people would always suppose that I and Ponza had . . .

Agazzi. Oh, please, governor, no! That's not fair!

Sirelli. Oh, no, governor, we trust you implicitly!

Prefect. Oh, I'm not offended, not at all! But you know very well that I'm on his side in this matter; and you'd always be thinking that to hush up any possible scandal in connection with a man in my office . . . No, you see. I must insist on having the interview here . . . Where's your wife, Agazzi?

Agazzi. In the other room, governor, with some other ladies.

Prefect. Other ladies? Aha, I see! [*Laughing.*] You have a regular detective bureau here, eh? [*The* POLICE COMMISSIONER *enters with* PONZA.]

Commissioner. May I come in? Signor Ponza is here.

Prefect. Thanks, Centuri. This way, Ponza, come right in! [PONZA *bows.*]

Agazzi. Have a chair, Ponza. [PONZA *bows and sits down.*]

Prefect. I believe you know these gentlemen? [PONZA *rises and bows.*]

Agazzi. Yes, I introduced them yesterday. And this is Laudisi, my wife's brother. [PONZA *bows.*]

Prefect. I venture to disturb you, my dear Ponza, just to tell you that here with these friends of mine . . . [*At the first words of the prefect,* PONZA *evinces the greatest nervousness and agitation.*]

Prefect. Was there something you wanted to say, Ponza?

Ponza. Yes, there is something I want to say, governor. I want to present my resignation here and now.

Prefect. Oh, my dear fellow, I'm so sorry! But just a few moments ago down at the office you were talking . . .

Ponza. Oh, really, this is an outrage, governor! This is just plain persecution, plain persecution!

Prefect. Oh, now, don't take it that way, old man. See here. These good people . . .

Agazzi. Persecution, did you say? On my part? . . .

Ponza. On the part of all of you! And I am sick and tired of it! I am going to resign, governor. I refuse to submit to this ferocious prying into my private affairs which will end by undoing a work of love that has cost me untold sacrifice these past two years. You don't know, governor! Why, I've treated that dear old lady in there just as tenderly as though she were my own mother. And yesterday I had to shout at her in the most cruel and terrible way! Why, I found her just now so worked up and excited that . . .

Agazzi. That's queer! While she was in here Signora Frola was quite mistress of herself. If anybody was worked up, Ponza, it was you. And even now, if I might say . . .

Ponza. But you people don't know what you're making me go through!

Prefect. Oh, come, come, my dear fellow, don't take it so hard. After all, I'm here, am I not? And you know I've always stood by you! And I always will!

Ponza. Yes, governor, and I appreciate your kindness, really!

Prefect. And then you say that you're as fond of this poor old lady as you would be if she were your own mother. Well, now, just remember that these good people here seem to be prying into your affairs because they, too, are fond of her! . . .

Ponza. But they're killing her, I tell you, governor! They're killing her, and I warned them in advance.

Prefect. Very well, Ponza, very well! Now we'll get through with this matter in no time. See here, it is all very simple. There is one way that you can convince these people without the least doubt in the world. Oh, not me—I don't need convincing. I believe *you*.

Ponza. But *they* won't believe me, no matter what I say.

Agazzi. That's not so! When you came here after your mother-in-law's first visit and told us that she was mad, all of us . . . well, we were surprised, but we believed you. [*Turning to the* PREFECT.] But after he left, you understand, the old lady came back . . .

Prefect. Yes, yes, I know. He told me. [*Turning to* PONZA *again.*] She came back here and said that she was trying to do with you exactly what you say you were trying to do with her. It's natural, isn't it, that people hearing both stories, should be somewhat confused. Now you see that these good people, in view of what your mother-in-law says, can't possibly be sure of what you say. So there you are. Now, such being the case, you and your mother-in-law—why, it's perfectly simple—you two just step aside. Now you know you're telling the truth, don't you? So do I! So you can't possibly object to their hearing the testimony of the only person who does know, aside from you two.

Ponza. And who may that be, pray?

Prefect. Why, your wife!

Ponza. My wife! [*Decisively and angrily.*] Ah, no! I refuse! Never in the world! Never!

Prefect. And why not, old man?

Ponza. Bring my wife here to satisfy the curiosity of these strangers?

Prefect [*sharply*]. And my curiosity, too, if you don't mind! What objection can you have?

Ponza. Oh, but governor, no! My wife! Here? No! Why drag my wife in? These people ought to believe me!

Prefect. But don't you see, my dear fellow, that the

course you're taking now is just calculated to discredit what you say?

Agazzi.   His mistake in the first place, governor, was trying to prevent his mother-in-law from coming here and calling—a double discourtesy, mark you, to my wife and to my daughter!

Ponza.   But what in the name of God do you people want of me? You've been nagging and nagging at that poor old woman next door; and now you want to get your clutches on my wife! No, governor! I refuse to submit to such an indignity! She owes nothing to anybody. My wife is not making visits in this town. You say you believe me, governor? That's enough for me! Here's my resignation! I'll go out and look for another job!

Prefect.   No, no, Ponza, I must speak plainly. In the first place I have always treated you on the square; and you have no right to speak in that tone of voice to me. In the second place you are beginning to make me doubt your word by refusing to furnish me—not other people —but me, the evidence that I have asked for in your interest, evidence, moreover, that so far as I can see, cannot possibly do you any harm. It seems to me that my colleague here, Signor Agazzi, can ask a lady to come to his house! But no, if you prefer, we'll go and see her.

Ponza.   So you really insist, governor?

Prefect.   I insist, but as I told you, in your own interest. You realize, besides, that I might have the legal right to question her . . .

Ponza.   I see, I see! So that's it! An official investigation! Well, why not, after all? I will bring my wife here, just to end the whole matter. But how can you guarantee me that this poor old lady next door will not catch sight of her?

Prefect.   Why, I hadn't thought of that! She does live right next door.

Agazzi [*speaking up*].   We are perfectly willing to go to Signor Ponza's house.

Ponza.   No, no, I was just thinking of you people. I don't want you to play any more tricks on me. Any mistakes might have the most frightful consequences, set her going again! ·

Agazzi.   You're not very fair to us, Ponza, it seems to me.

Prefect.   Or you might bring your wife to my office, rather . . .

Ponza.   No, no! Since you're going to question her anyway, we might as well get through with it. We'll bring her here, right here. I'll keep an eye on my mother-in-law myself. We'll have her here right away, governor, and get an end of this nonsense once and for all, once and for all! [*He hurries away through the rear exit.*]

Prefect.   I confess I was not expecting so much opposition on his part.

Agazzi.   Ah, you'll see. He'll go and cook up with his wife just what she's to say!

Prefect.   Oh, don't worry as to that! I'll question the woman myself.

Sirelli.   But he's more excited than he's ever been before.

Prefect.   Well, I confess I never saw him just in this state of mind. Perhaps it is the sense of outrage he feels in having to bring his wife . . .

Sirelli.   In having to let her loose for once, you ought to say!

Prefect.   A man isn't necessarily mad because he wants to keep an eye on his wife.

Agazzi.   Of course he says it's to protect her from the mother-in-law.

Prefect.   I wasn't thinking of just that—he may be jealous of the woman!

Sirelli.   Jealous to the extent of refusing her a servant?

For you know, don't you, he makes his wife do all the housework?

Agazzi. And he does all the marketing himself every morning.

Commissioner. That's right, governor! I've had him shadowed. An errand boy from the market carries the stuff as far as the door.

Sirelli. But he never lets the boy inside.

Prefect. Dear me, dear me! He excused himself for that servant business when I took the matter up with him.

Laudisi. And that's information right from the source!

Prefect. He says he does it to save money.

Laudisi. He has to keep two establishments on one salary.

Sirelli. Oh, we weren't criticizing how he runs his house; but I ask you as a matter of common sense: he is a man of some position, and do you think that this second wife of his, as he calls her, who ought to be a lady, would consent to do all the work about the house? . . .

Agazzi. The hardest and most disagreeable work, you understand . . .

Sirelli. . . . just out of consideration for the mother of her husband's first wife?

Agazzi. Oh, I say, governor, be honest now! That doesn't seem probable, does it?

Prefect. I confess it does seem queer . . .

Laudisi. . . . in case this second woman is an ordinary woman!

Prefect. Yes, but let's be frank. It doesn't seem reasonable. But yet, one might say—well, you could explain it as generosity on her part, and even better, as jealousy on his part. Mad or not mad, there is no denying that he's jealous!

[*A confused clamor of voices is heard from the next door.*]

Agazzi. My, I wonder what's going on in there!

[AMALIA *enters from the door on the left in a state of great excitement.*]

Amalia. Signora Frola is here!

Agazzi. Impossible! How in the world did she get in? Who sent for her?

Amalia. Nobody! She came of her own accord!

Prefect. Oh, no, please—just a moment! No! Send her away, madam, please!

Agazzi. We've got to get rid of her. Don't let her in here! We must absolutely keep her out!

[SIGNORA FROLA *appears at the door on the left, trembling, beseeching, weeping, a handkerchief in her hand. The people in the next room are crowding around behind her.*]

Signora Frola. Oh, please, please! You tell them, Signor Agazzi! Don't let them send me away!

Agazzi. But you must go away, madam! We simply can't allow you to be here now!

Signora Frola [*desperately*]. Why? Why? [*Turning to* AMALIA.] I appeal to you, Signora Agazzi.

Amalia. But don't you see? The prefect is there! They're having an important meeting.

Signora Frola. Oh, the prefect! Please, governor, please! I was intending to go and see you.

Prefect. No, I am so sorry, madam. I can't see you just now! You must go away!

Signora Frola. Yes, I am going away. I am going to leave town this very day! I am going to leave town and never come back again!

Agazzi. Oh, we didn't mean that, my dear Signora Frola. We meant that we couldn't see you here, just now, in this room. Do me a favor, please! You can see the governor by and by.

Signora Frola. But why? I don't understand! What's happened!

Agazzi. Why, your son-in-law will soon be here! There, now do you see?

Signora Frola. Oh, he's coming here? Oh, yes, in that case . . . Yes, yes, . . . I'll go! But there was something I wanted to say to you people. You must stop all this. You must let us alone. You think you are helping me. You are trying to do me a favor; but really, what you're doing is working me a great wrong. I've got to leave town this very day because he must not be aroused. What do you want of him anyway? What are you trying to do to him? Why are you having him come here? Oh, Mr. Governor . . .

Prefect. Come, Signora Frola, don't worry, don't worry. I'll see you by and by and explain everything. You just step out now, won't you?

Amalia. Please, Signora Frola . . . yes, that's right! Come with me!

Signora Frola. Oh, my dear Signora Agazzi, you are trying to rob me of the one comfort I had in life, the chance of seeing my daughter once in a while, at least from a distance! [*She begins to weep.*]

Prefect. What in the world are you thinking of? We are not asking you to leave town. We just want you to leave this room, for the time being. There, now do you understand?

Signora Frola. But it's on his account, governor . . . it's on his account I was coming to ask you to help him! It was on his account, not on mine!

Prefect. There, there, everything will be all right. We'll take care of him. And we'll have this whole business settled in a jiffy.

Signora Frola. But how . . . how can I be sure? I can see that everybody here hates him. They are trying to do something to him.

Prefect. No, no, not at all! And even if they were,

I would look after him. There, there, don't worry, don't worry!

Signora Frola. Oh, so you believe him? Oh, thank you; thank you, sir! That means that at least *you* understand!

Prefect. Yes, yes, madam, I understand, I understand! And I cautioned all these people here. It's a misfortune that came to him long, long ago. He's all right now! He's all right now!

Signora Frola. . . . Only he must not go back to all those things.

Prefect. You're right, you're quite right, Signora Frola, but as I told you, I understand!

Signora Frola. Yes, governor, that's it! If he compels us to live this way—well, what does it matter. That doesn't do anybody any harm so long as we're satisfied, and my daughter is happy this way. That's enough for me, and for her! But you'll look after us, governor. They mustn't spoil anything. Otherwise there's nothing left for me except to leave town and never see her again—never, not even from a distance. You must not irritate him. You must leave him alone. Oh, please!

[*At this moment a wave of surprise, anxiety, dismay, sweeps over the company. Everybody falls silent and turns to the door. Suppressed exclamations are audible.*]

Voices. Oh! Oh! Look! There she is! Oh! Oh!

Signora Frola [*noticing the change in people, and groaning, all of a tremble*]. What's the matter? What's the matter?

[*The* COMPANY *divides to either hand. A* LADY *has appeared at the door in back. She is dressed in deep mourning and her face is concealed with a thick, black, impenetrable veil.*]

Signora Frola [*uttering a piercing shriek of joy*]. Oh, Lena! Lena! Lena! Lena!

[*She dashes forward and throws her arms about the veiled woman with the passionate hysteria of a mother who has not embraced her daughter for years and years. But at the same time from beyond the door in the rear another piercing cry comes.* PONZA *dashes into the room.*]

Ponza. No! Julia! Julia! Julia!

[*At his voice* SIGNORA PONZA *draws up stiffly in the arms of* SIGNORA FROLA *who is clasping her tightly.* PONZA *notices that his mother-in-law is thus desperately entwined about his wife and he shrieks desperately.*]

Ponza. Cowards! Liars! I knew you would! I knew you would! It is just like the lot of you!

Signora Ponza [*turning her veiled head with a certain austere solemnity toward her husband*]. Don't be afraid! Just take her away! Go!

[SIGNORA FROLA, *at these words, turns to her son-in-law and humbly, tremblingly, goes over and embraces him.*]

Signora Frola. Yes, yes, you poor boy, come with me, come with me!

[*Their arms about each other's waists, and holding each other up affectionately,* PONZA *and his mother-in-law withdraw through the rear door. They are both weeping. Profound silence in the company.* ALL *those present stand there with their eyes fixed upon the departing couple. As* SIGNORA FROLA *and* PONZA *are lost from view, all eyes turn expectantly upon the veiled lady. Some of the women are weeping.*]

Signora Ponza [*having looked at them through her veil, speaking with dark solemnity*]. What else do you want of me, after this, ladies and gentlemen? There is a misfortune here, as you see, which must stay hidden: otherwise the remedy which our compassion has found cannot avail.

The Prefect [*moved*]. We want to respect your compassion, madam. It's only that we'd like you to tell us . . .

Signora Ponza [*slowly, and with clear articulation*]. Tell you what? The truth? Simply this: I am the daughter of Signora Frola . . .

All [*with a happy intake of breath*]. Ah!

Signora Ponza. . . . and the second wife of Signor Ponza . . .

All [*amazed and disenchanted, quietly*]. . . . What?

Signora Ponza [*continuing*]. . . . and, for myself, I am nobody!

The Prefect. No, no, madam, for yourself you must be either one or the other!

Signora Ponza. No! I am she whom you believe me to be. [*She looks at them all through her veil for a moment, then leaves. Silence.*]

Laudisi. And there, my friends, you have the truth! [*With a look of derisive defiance at them all.*] Are you satisfied? [*He bursts out laughing.*]

HENRY IV

(*Enrico IV*)

A TRAGEDY IN THREE ACTS

English version by
EDWARD STORER

CHARACTERS

HENRY IV		
THE MARCHIONESS MATILDA SPINA	HAROLD (FRANK)	*The four pri-*
FRIDA, *her daughter*	LANDOLPH (LOLO)	*vate counsel-*
CHARLES DI NOLLI, *the young*	ORDULPH (MOMO)	*lors (The*
Marquis	BERTHOLD (FINO)	*names in*
BARON TITO BELCREDI		*brackets are*
DOCTOR DIONYSIUS GENONI		*nicknames)*
	JOHN, *the old waiter*	
	THE TWO VALETS IN COSTUME	

A Solitary Villa in Italy in Our Own Time

ACT I

Salon in the villa, furnished and decorated so as to look exactly like the throne room of Henry IV in the royal residence at Goslar. Among the antique decorations there are two modern life-size portraits in oil painting. They are placed against the back wall, and mounted in a wooden stand that runs the whole length of the wall. (It is wide and protrudes, so that it is like a large bench.) One of the paintings is on the right; the other on the left of the throne, which is in the middle of the wall and divides the stand.

The Imperial chair and Baldachin.

The two portraits represent a lady and a gentleman, both young, dressed up in carnival costumes: one as "Henry IV," the other as the "Marchioness Matilda of Tuscany." Exits to right and left.

When the curtain goes up, the two valets jump down, as if surprised, from the stand on which they have been lying, and go and take their positions, as rigid as statues, on either side below the throne with their halberds in their hands. Soon after, from the second exit, right, enter HAROLD, LANDOLPH, ORDULPH *and* BERTHOLD, *young men employed by the* MARQUIS CHARLES DI NOLLI *to play the part of "Secret Counsellors" at the court of "Henry IV." They are, therefore, dressed like German knights of the XIth century.* BERTHOLD, *nicknamed Fino, is just entering on his duties for the first time. His companions are telling him what he has to do and amusing themselves at his expense. The scene is to be played rapidly and vivaciously.*

Landolph [*to* BERTHOLD *as if explaining*]. And this is the throne room.

Harold. At Goslar.

Ordulph. Or at the castle in the Hartz, if you prefer.

Harold. Or at Wurms.

Landolph. According as to what's doing, it jumps about with us, now here, now there.

Ordulph. In Saxony.

Harold. In Lombardy.

Landolph. On the Rhine.

One of the Valets [*without moving, just opening his lips*]. I say . . .

Harold [*turning round*]. What is it?

First Valet [*like a statue*]. Is he coming in or not? [*He alludes to* HENRY IV.]

Ordulph. No, no, he's asleep. You needn't worry.

Second Valet [*releasing his pose, taking a long breath*

and going to lie down again on the stand]. You might have told us at once.

First Valet [*going over to* HAROLD]. Have you got a match, please?

Landolph. What? You can't smoke a pipe here, you know.

First Valet [*while* HAROLD *offers him a light*]. No; a cigarette. [*Lights his cigarette and lies down again on the stand.*]

Berthold [*who has been looking on in amazement, walking round the room, regarding the costumes of the others*]. I say . . . this room . . . these costumes . . . Which Henry IV is it? I don't quite get it. Is he Henry IV of France or not? [*At this* LANDOLPH, HAROLD, *and* ORDULPH, *burst out laughing.*]

Landolph [*still laughing; and pointing to* BERTHOLD *as if inviting the others to make fun of him*]. Henry of France he says: ha! ha!

Ordulph. He thought it was the king of France!

Harold. Henry IV of Germany, my boy: the Salian dynasty!

Ordulph. The great and tragic Emperor!

Landolph. He of Canossa. Every day we carry on here the terrible war between Church and State, by Jove.

Ordulph. The Empire against the Papacy!

Harold. Antipopes against the Pope!

Landolph. Kings against anti-kings!

Ordulph. War on the Saxons!

Harold. And all the rebels Princes!

Landolph. Against the Emporer's own sons!

Berthold [*covering his head with his hands to protect himself against this avalanche of information*]. I understand! I understand! Naturally, I didn't get the idea at first. I'm right then: these aren't costumes of the XVIth century?

Harold. XVIth century be hanged!

Ordulph. We're somewhere between a thousand and eleven hundred.

Landolph. Work it out for yourself: if we are before Canossa on the 25th of January, 1071 . . .

Berthold [*more confused than ever*]. Oh my God! What a mess I've made of it!

Ordulph. Well, just slightly, if you supposed you were at the French court.

Berthold. All that historical stuff I've swatted up!

Landolph. My dear boy, it's four hundred years earlier.

Berthold [*getting angry*]. Good Heavens! You ought to have told me it was Germany and not France. I can't tell you how many books I've read in the last fifteen days.

Harold. But I say, surely you knew that poor Tito was Adalbert of Bremen, here?

Berthold. Not a damned bit!

Landolph. Well, don't you see how it is? When Tito died, the Marquis Di Nolli . . .

Berthold. Oh, it was he, was it? He might have told me.

Harold. Perhaps he thought you knew.

Landolph. He didn't want to engage anyone else in substitution. He thought the remaining three of us would do. But *he* began to cry out: "With Adalbert driven away . . .": because, you see, he didn't imagine poor Tito was dead; but that, as Bishop Adalbert, the rival bishops of Cologne and Mayence had driven him off . . .

Berthold [*taking his head in his hand*]. But I don't know a word of what you're talking about.

Ordulph. So much the worse for you, my boy!

Harold. But the trouble is that not even we know who you are.

Berthold. What? Not even you? You don't know who I'm supposed to be?

Ordulph. Hum! "Berthold."

Berthold. But which Berthold? And why Berthold?

Landolph [*solemnly imitating* HENRY IV]. "They've driven Adalbert away from me. Well then, I want Berthold! I want Berthold!" That's what he said.

Harold. We three looked one another in the eyes: who's got to be Berthold?

Ordulph. And so here you are, "Berthold," my dear fellow!

Landolph. I'm afraid you will make a bit of a mess of it.

Berthold [*indignant, getting ready to go*]. Ah, no! Thanks very much, but I'm off! I'm out of this!

Harold [*restraining him with the other two, amid laughter*]. Steady now! Don't get excited!

Landolph. Cheer up, my dear fellow! We don't any of us know who we are really. He's Harold; he's Ordulph; I'm Landolph! That's the way he calls us. We've got used to it. But who are we? Names of the period! Yours, too, is a name of the period: Berthold! Only one of us, poor Tito, had got a really decent part, as you can read in history: that of the Bishop of Bremen. He was just like a real bishop. Tito did it awfully well, poor chap!

Harold. Look at the study he put into it!

Landolph. Why, he even ordered his Majesty about, opposed his views, guided and counselled him. We're "secret counsellors"—in a manner of speaking only; because it is written in history that Henry IV was hated by the upper aristocracy for surrounding himself at court with young men of the bourgeoise.

Ordulph. Us, that is.

Landolph. Yes, small devoted vassals, a bit dissolute and very gay . . .

Berthold.   So I've got to be gay as well?

Harold.   I should say so! Same as we are!

Ordulph.   And it isn't too easy, you know.

Landolph.   It's a pity; because the way we're got up, we could do a fine historical reconstruction. There's any amount of material in the story of Henry IV. But, as a matter of fact, we do nothing. We have the form without the content. We're worse than the real secret counsellors of Henry IV; because certainly no one had given them a part to play—at any rate, they didn't feel they had a part to play. It was their life. They looked after their own interests at the expense of others, sold investitures and—what not! We stop here in this magnificent court—for what?—Just doing nothing. We're like so many puppets hung on the wall, waiting for some one to come and move us or make us talk.

Harold.   Ah, no, old sport, not quite that! We've got to give the proper answer, you know. There's trouble if he asks you something and you don't chip in with the cue.

Landolph.   Yes, that's true.

Berthold.   Don't rub it in too hard! How the devil am I to give him the proper answer, if I've swatted up Henry IV of France, and now he turns out to be Henry IV of Germany? [*The other three laugh.*]

Harold.   You'd better start and prepare yourself at once.

Ordulph.   We'll help you out.

Harold.   We've got any amount of books on the subject. A brief run through the main points will do to begin with.

Ordulph.   At any rate, you must have got some sort of general idea.

Harold.   Look here! [*Turns him around and shows him the portrait of the Marchioness Matilda on the wall.*] Who's that?

Berthold [*looking at it*]. That? Well, the thing seems to me somewhat out of place, anyway: two modern paintings in the midst of all this respectable antiquity!

Harold. You're right! They weren't there in the beginning. There are two niches there behind the pictures. They were going to put up two statues in the style of the period. Then the places were covered with those canvases there.

Landolph [*interrupting and continuing*]. They would certainly be out of place if they really were paintings!

Berthold. What are they, if they aren't paintings?

Landolph. Go and touch them! Pictures all right . . . but for him! [*Makes a mysterious gesture to the right, alluding to* HENRY IV.] . . . who never touches them! . . .

Berthold. No? What are they for him?

Landolph. Well, I'm only supposing, you know; but I imagine I'm about right. They're images such as . . . well—such as a mirror might throw back. Do you understand? That one there represents himself, as he is in this throne room, which is all in the style of the period. What's there to marvel at? If we put you before a mirror, won't you see yourself, alive, but dressed up in ancient costume? Well, it's as if there were two mirrors there, which cast back living images in the midst of a world which, as you well see, when you have lived with us, comes to life too.

Berthold. I say, look here . . . I've no particular desire to go mad here.

Harold. Go mad, be hanged! You'll have a fine time!

Berthold. Tell me this: how have you all managed to become so learned?

Landolph. My dear fellow, you can't go back over 800 years of history without picking up a bit of experience.

Harold. Come on! Come on! You'll see how quickly you get into it!

Ordulph. You'll learn wisdom, too, at this school.

Berthold. Well, for Heaven's sake, help me a bit! Give me the main lines, anyway.

Harold. Leave it to us. We'll do it all between us.

Landolph. We'll put your wires on you and fix you up like a first-class marionette. Come along! [THEY *take him by the arm to lead him away.*]

Berthold [*stopping and looking at the portrait on the wall*]. Wait a minute! You haven't told me who that is. The Emperor's wife?

Harold. No! The Emperor's wife is Bertha of Susa, the sister of Amadeus II of Savoy.

Ordulph. And the Emperor, who wants to be young with us, can't stand her, and wants to put her away.

Landolph. That is his most ferocious enemy: Matilda, Marchioness of Tuscany.

Berthold. Ah, I've got it: the one who gave hospitality to the Pope!

Landolph. Exactly: at Canossa!

Ordulph. Pope Gregory VII!

Harold. Our *bête noir*! Come on! come on! [*All four move toward the right to go out, when, from the left, the old servant* JOHN *enters in evening dress.*]

John [*quickly, anxiously*]. Hss! Hss! Frank! Lolo!

Harold [*turning round*]. What is it?

Berthold [*marvelling at seeing a man in modern clothes enter the throne room*]. Oh! I say, this is a bit too much, this chap here!

Landolph. A man of the XXth century, here! Oh, go away! [THEY *run over to him, pretending to menace him and throw him out.*]

Ordulph [*heroically*]. Messenger of Gregory VII, away!

Harold. Away! Away!

John [*annoyed, defending himself*].   Oh, stop it! Stop it, I tell you!

Ordulph.   No, you can't set foot here!

Harold.   Out with him!

Landolph [*to* BERTHOLD].   Magic, you know! He's a demon conjured up by the Wizard of Rome! Out with your swords! [*Makes as if to draw a sword.*]

John [*shouting*].   Stop it, will you? Don't play the fool with me! The Marquis has arrived with some friends . . .

Landolph.   Good! Good! Are there ladies too?

Ordulph.   Old or young?

John.   There are two gentlemen.

Harold.   But the ladies, the ladies, who are they?

John.   The Marchioness and her daughter.

Landolph [*surprised*].   What do you say?

Ordulph.   The Marchioness?

John.   The Marchioness! The Marchioness!

Harold.   Who are the gentlemen?

John.   I don't know.

Harold [*to* BERTHOLD].   They're coming to bring us a message from the Pope, do you see?

Ordulph.   All messengers of Gregory VII! What fun!

John.   Will you let me speak, or not?

Harold.   Go on, then!

John.   One of the two gentlemen is a doctor, I fancy.

Landolph.   Oh, I see, one of the usual doctors.

Harold.   Bravo Berthold, you'll bring us luck!

Landolph.   You wait and see how we'll manage this doctor!

Berthold.   It looks as if I were going to get into a nice mess right away.

John.   If the gentlemen would allow me to speak . . . they want to come here into the throne room.

Landolph [*surprised*].   What? She? The Marchioness here?

Harold. Then this is something quite different! No play-acting this time!

Landolph. We'll have a real tragedy: that's what!

Berthold [*curious*]. Why? Why?

Ordulph [*pointing to the portrait*]. She is that person there, don't you understand?

Landolph. The daughter is the fiancée of the Marquis. But what have they come for, I should like to know?

Ordulph. If he sees her, there'll be trouble.

Landolph. Perhaps he won't recognize her any more.

John. You must keep him there, if he should wake up . . .

Ordulph. Easier said than done, by Jove!

Harold. You know what he's like!

John. —even by force, if necessary! Those are my orders. Go on! Go on!

Harold. Yes, because who knows if he hasn't already wakened up?

Ordulph. Come on then!

Landolph [*going towards* JOHN *with the others*]. You'll tell us later what it all means.

John [*shouting after them*]. Close the door there, and hide the key! That other door too. [*Pointing to the other door on right.*]

John [*to the* TWO VALETS]. Be off, you two! There! [*Pointing to exit right.*] Close the door after you, and hide the key!

[*The* TWO VALETS *go out by the first door on right.* JOHN *moves over to the left to show in:* DONNA MATILDA SPINA, *the young* MARCHIONESS FRIDA, DR. DIONYSIUS GENONI, *the* BARON TITO BELCREDI *and the young* MARQUIS CHARLES DI NOLLI, *who, as master of the house, enters last.*

DONNA MATILDA SPINA *is about 45, still handsome, although there are too patent signs of her attempts to remedy the ravages of time with make-up. Her head is thus rather like a Walkyrie. This facial make-up contrasts with her beautiful sad mouth. A widow for many years, she now has as her friend the* BARON TITO BELCREDI, *whom neither she nor anyone else takes seriously—at least so it would appear.*

What TITO BELCREDI *really is for her at bottom, he alone knows; and he is, therefore, entitled to laugh, if his friend feels the need of pretending not to know. He can always laugh at the jests which the beautiful Marchioness makes with the others at his expense. He is slim, prematurely gray, and younger than she is. His head is bird-like in shape. He would be a very vivacious person, if his ductile agility (which among other things makes him a redoubtable swordsman) were not enclosed in a sheath of Arab-like laziness, which is revealed in his strange, nasal drawn-out voice.*

FRIDA, *the daughter of the Marchioness is 19. She is sad; because her imperious and too beautiful mother puts her in the shade, and provokes facile gossip against her daughter as well as against herself. Fortunately for her, she is engaged to the* MARQUIS CHARLES DI NOLLI.

CHARLES DI NOLLI *is a stiff young man, very indulgent towards others, but sure of himself for what he amounts to in the world. He is worried about all the responsibilities which he believes weigh on him. He is dressed in deep mourning for the recent death of his mother.*

DR. DIONYSIUS GENONI *has a bold rubicund Satyr-like face, prominent eyes, a pointed beard (which is silvery and shiny) and elegant manners. He is nearly bald. All enter in a state of perturbation, almost as if afraid, and all (except* DI NOLLI) *looking curiously about the room. At first, they speak sotto voce.*

Di Nolli [*to* JOHN]. Have you given the orders properly?

John. Yes, my Lord; don't be anxious about that.

Belcredi. Ah, magnificent! magnificent!

Doctor. How extremely interesting! Even in the surroundings his raving madness—is perfectly taken into account!

Donna Matilda [*glancing round for her portrait, discovers it, and goes up close to it*]. Ah! Here it is! [*Going back to admire it, while mixed emotions stir within her.*] Yes . . . yes . . . [*Calls her daughter* FRIDA.]

Frida. Ah, your portrait!

Donna Matilda. No, no . . . look again; it's you, not I, there!

Di Nolli. Yes, it's quite true. I told you so, I . . .

Donna Matilda. But I would never have believed it! [*Shaking as if with a chill.*] What a strange feeling it gives one! [*Then looking at her daughter.*] Frida, what's the matter? [*She pulls her to her side, and slips an arm round her waist.*] Come: don't you see yourself in me there?

Frida. Well, I really . . .

Donna Matilda. Don't you think so? Don't you, really? [*Turning to* BELCREDI.] Look at it, Tito! Speak up, man!

Belcredi [*without looking*]. Ah, no! I shan't look at it. For me, *a priori*, certainly not!

Donna Matilda. Stupid! You think you are paying me a compliment! [*Turning to* DOCTOR GENONI.] What do you say, Doctor? Do say something, please!

Doctor [*makes a movement to go near to the picture*].

Belcredi [*with his back turned, pretending to attract his attention secretly*]. —Hss! No, Doctor! For the love of Heaven, have nothing to do with it!

Doctor [*getting bewildered and smiling*]. And why shouldn't I?

Donna Matilda. Don't listen to him! Come here! He's insufferable!

Frida. He acts the fool by profession, didn't you know that?

Belcredi [*to the* DOCTOR, *seeing him go over*]. Look at your feet, Doctor! Mind where you're going!

Doctor. Why?

Belcredi. Be careful you don't put your foot in it!

Doctor [*laughing feebly*]. No, no. After all, it seems to me there's no reason to be astonished at the fact that a daughter should resemble her mother!

Belcredi. Hullo! Hullo! He's done it now; he's said it.

Donna Matilda [*with exaggerated anger, advancing towards* BELCREDI]. What's the matter? What has he said? What has he done?

Doctor [*candidly*]. Well, isn't it so?

Belcredi [*answering the* MARCHIONESS]. I said there was nothing to be astounded at—and you are astounded! And why so, then, if the thing is so simple and natural for you now?

Donna Matilda [*still more angry*]. Fool! fool! It's just because it is so natural! Just because it isn't my daughter who is there. [*Pointing to the canvas.*] That is my portrait; and to find my daughter there instead of me fills me with astonishment, an astonishment which, I beg you to believe, is sincere. I forbid you to cast doubts on it.

Frida [*slowly and wearily*]. My God! It's always like this . . . rows over nothing . . .

Belcredi [*also slowly, looking dejected, in accents of apology*]. I cast no doubt on anything! I noticed from the beginning that you haven't shared your mother's astonishment; or, if something did astonish you, it was because the likeness between you and the portrait seemed so strong.

Donna Matilda. Naturally! She cannot recognize herself in me as I was at her age; while I, there, can very well recognize myself in her as she is now!

Doctor. Quite right! Because a portrait is always there fixed in the twinkling of an eye: for the young lady something far away and without memories, while, for the Marchioness, it can bring back everything: movements, gestures, looks, smiles, a whole heap of things . . .

Donna Matilda. Exactly!

Doctor [*continuing, turning towards her*]. Naturally enough, you can live all these old sensations again in your daughter.

Donna Matilda. He always spoils every innocent pleasure for me, every touch I have of spontaneous sentiment! He does it merely to annoy me.

Doctor [*frightened at the disturbance he has caused, adopts a professorial tone*]. Likeness, dear Baron, is often the result of imponderable things. So one explains that . . .

Belcredi [*interrupting the discourse*]. Somebody will soon be finding a likeness between you and me, my dear Professor!

Di Nolli. Oh! let's finish with this, please! [*Points to the two doors on the right, as a warning that there is someone there who may be listening.*] We've wasted too much time as it is!

Frida. As one might expect when *he's* present. [*Alludes to* BELCREDI.]

Di Nolli. Enough! The Doctor is here; and we have come for a very serious purpose which you all know is important for me.

Doctor. Yes, that is so! But now, first of all, let's try to get some points down exactly. Excuse me, Marchioness, will you tell me why your portrait is here? Did you present it to him then?

Donna Matilda. No, not at all. How could I have given it to him? I was just like Frida then—and not

even engaged. I gave it to him three or four years after
the accident. I gave it to him because his mother wished
it so much . . . [*Points to* DI NOLLI.]

Doctor. She was his sister? [*Alludes to* HENRY IV.]

Di Nolli. Yes, Doctor; and our coming here is a debt
we pay to my mother who has been dead for more than a
month. Instead of being here, she and I [*Indicating*
FRIDA.] ought to be traveling together . . .

Doctor. . . . taking a cure of quite a different kind!

Di Nolli. —Hum! Mother died in the firm conviction
that her adored brother was just about to be cured.

Doctor. And can't you tell me, if you please, how she
inferred this?

Di Nolli. The conviction would appear to have derived from certain strange remarks which he made, a little
before mother died.

Doctor. Oh, remarks! . . . Ah! . . . It would be extremely useful for me to have those remarks, word for
word, if possible.

Di Nolli. I can't remember them. I know that mother
returned awfully upset from her last visit with him. On
her death-bed, she made me promise that I would never
neglect him, that I would have doctors see him, and examine him.

Doctor. Um! Um! Let me see! let me see! Sometimes very small reasons determine . . . and this portrait
here then? . . .

Donna Matilda. For Heaven's sake, Doctor, don't attach excessive importance to this. It made an impression
on me because I had not seen it for so many years!

Doctor. If you please, quietly, quietly . . .

Di Nolli. —Well, yes, it must be about fifteen years
ago.

Donna Matilda. More, more: eighteen!

Doctor. Forgive me, but you don't quite know what
I'm trying to get at. I attach a very great importance to

these two portraits . . . They were painted, naturally, prior to the famous—and most regrettable pageant, weren't they?

Donna Matilda. Of course!

Doctor. That is . . . when he was quite in his right mind—that's what I've been trying to say. Was it his suggestion that they should be painted?

Donna Matilda. Lots of the people who took part in the pageant had theirs done as a souvenir . . .

Belcredi. I had mine done—as "Charles of Anjou!"

Donna Matilda. . . . as soon as the costumes were ready.

Belcredi. As a matter of fact, it was proposed that the whole lot of us should be hung together in a gallery of the villa where the pageant took place. But in the end, everybody wanted to keep his own portrait.

Donna Matilda. And I gave him this portrait of me without very much regret . . . since his mother . . . [*Indicates* DI NOLLI.]

Doctor. You don't remember if it was he who asked for it?

Donna Matilda. Ah, that I don't remember . . . Maybe it was his sister, wanting to help out . . .

Doctor. One other thing: was it his idea, this pageant?

Belcredi [*at once*]. No, no, it was mine!

Doctor. If you please . . .

Donna Matilda. Don't listen to him! It was poor Belassi's idea.

Belcredi. Belassi! What had he got to do with it?

Donna Matilda. Count Belassi, who died, poor fellow, two or three months after . . .

Belcredi. But if Belassi wasn't there when . . .

Di Nolli. Excuse me, Doctor; but is it really necessary to establish whose the original idea was?

Doctor. It would help me, certainly!

Belcredi. I tell you the idea was mine! There's nothing to be proud of in it, seeing what the result's been. Look here, Doctor, it was like this. One evening, in the first days of November, I was looking at an illustrated German review in the club. I was merely glancing at the pictures, because I can't read German. There was a picture of the Kaiser, at some University town where he had been a student . . . I don't remember which.

Doctor. Bonn, Bonn!

Belcredi. —You are right: Bonn! He was on horseback, dressed up in one of those ancient German student guild-costumes, followed by a procession of noble students, also in costume. The picture gave me the idea. Already someone at the club had spoken of a pageant for the forthcoming carnival. So I had the notion that each of us should choose for this Tower of Babel pageant to represent some character: a king, an emperor, a prince, with his queen, empress, or lady, alongside of him—and all on horseback. The suggestion was at once accepted.

Donna Matilda. I had my invitation from Belassi.

Belcredi. Well, he wasn't speaking the truth! That's all I can say, if he told you the idea was his. He wasn't even at the club the evening I made the suggestion, just as he [*Meaning* HENRY IV.] wasn't there either.

Doctor. So he chose the character of Henry IV?

Donna Matilda. Because I . . . thinking of my name, and not giving the choice any importance, said I would be the Marchioness Matilda of Tuscany.

Doctor. I . . . don't understand the relation between the two.

Donna Matilda. —Neither did I, to begin with, when he said that in that case he would be at my feet like Henry IV at Canossa. I had heard of Canossa of course; but to tell the truth, I'd forgotten most of the story; and I remember I received a curious impression when I had to get up my part, and found that I was the faithful and zealous friend of Pope Gregory VII in deadly enmity with the Emperor of Germany. Then I understood why, since I had chosen to represent his implacable enemy, he wanted to be near me in the pageant as Henry IV.

Doctor. Ah, perhaps because . . .

Belcredi. —Good Heavens, Doctor, because he was then paying furious court to her! [*Indicates the* MARCHIONESS.] And she, naturally . . .

Donna Matilda. Naturally? Not naturally at all . . .

Belcredi [*pointing to her*]. She shouldn't stand him . . .

Donna Matilda. —No, that isn't true! I didn't dislike him. Not at all! But for me, when a man begins to want to be taken seriously, well . . .

Belcredia [*continuing for her*]. He gives you the clearest proof of his stupidity.

Donna Matilda. No, dear; not in this case; because he was never a fool like you.

Belcredi. Anyway, I've never asked you to take me seriously.

Donna Matilda. Yes, I know. But with him one couldn't joke. [*Changing her tone and speaking to the* DOCTOR.] One of the many misfortunes which happen to us women, Doctor, is to see before us every now and again a pair of eyes glaring at us with a contained intense promise of eternal devotion. [*Bursts out laughing.*] There is nothing quite so funny. If men could only see themselves with that eternal look of fidelity in their faces! I've always thought it comic; then more even than now. But I want to make a confession—I can do so after twenty years or more. When I laughed at him then, it was partly out of fear. One might have almost believed a promise from those eyes of his. But it would have been very dangerous.

Doctor [*with lively interest*]. Ah! ah! This is most interesting! Very dangerous, you say?

Donna Matilda. Yes, because he was very different

from the others. And then, I am . . . well . . . what
shall I say? . . . a little impatient of all that is pondered,
or tedious. But I was too young then, and a woman. I had
the bit between my teeth. It would have required more
courage than I felt I possessed. So I laughed at him too—
with remorse, to spite myself, indeed; since I saw that my
own laugh mingled with those of all the others—the
other fools—who made fun of him.

Belcredi. My own case, more or less!

Donna Matilda. You make people laugh at you, my
dear, with your trick of always humiliating yourself. It
was quite a different affair with him. There's a vast difference. And you—you know—people laugh in your face!

Belcredi. Well, that's better than behind one's back!

Doctor. Let's get to the facts. He was then already
somewhat exalted, if I understand rightly.

Belcredi. Yes, but in a curious fashion, Doctor.

Doctor. How?

Belcredi. Well, cold-bloodedly so to speak.

Donna Matilda. Not at all! It was like this, Doctor!
He was a bit strange, certainly; but only because he was
fond of life: eccentric, there!

Belcredi. I don't say he simulated exaltation. On the
contrary, he was often genuinely exalted. But I could
swear, Doctor, that he saw himself at once in his own
exaltation. Moreover, I'm certain it made him suffer.
Sometimes he had the most comical fits of rage against
himself.

Doctor. Yes?

Donna Matilda. That is true.

Belcredi [*to* DONNA MATILDA]. And why? [*To the*
DOCTOR.] Evidently, because that immediate lucidity that
comes from acting, assuming a part, at once put him out
of key with his own feelings, which seemed to him not
exactly false, but like something he was obliged to give
the value there and then of—what shall I say—of an act

of intelligence, to make up for that sincere cordial warmth he felt lacking. So he improvised, exaggerated, let himself go, so as to distract and forget himself. He appeared inconstant, fatuous, and—yes—even ridiculous, sometimes.

Doctor. And may we say unsociable?

Belcredi. No, not at all. He was famous for getting up things: *tableaux vivants,* dances, theatrical performances for charity: all for the fun of the thing, of course. He was a jolly good actor, you know!

Di Nolli. Madness has made a superb actor of him.

Belcredi. —Why, so he was even in the old days. When the accident happened, after the horse fell . . .

Doctor. Hit the back of his head, didn't he?

Donna Matilda. Oh, it was horrible! He was beside me! I saw him between the horse's hoofs! It was rearing!

Belcredi. None of us thought it was anything serious at first. There was a stop in the pageant, a bit of disorder. People wanted to know what had happened. But they'd already taken him off to the villa.

Donna Matilda. There wasn't the least sign of a wound, not a drop of blood.

Belcredi. We thought he had merely fainted.

Donna Matilda. But two hours afterwards . . .

Belcredi. He reappeared in the drawing-room of the villa . . . that is what I wanted to say . . .

Donna Matilda. My God! What a face he had. I saw the whole thing at once!

Belcredi. No, no! that isn't true. Nobody saw it, Doctor, believe me!

Donna Matilda. Doubtless, because you were all like mad folk.

Belcredi. Everybody was pretending to act his part for a joke. It was a regular Babel.

Donna Matilda. And you can imagine, Doctor, what

terror struck into us when we understood that he, on the contrary, was playing his part in deadly earnest . . .

Doctor. Oh, he was there too, was he?

Belcredi. Of course! He came straight into the midst of us. We thought he'd quite recovered, and was pretending, fooling, like all the rest of us . . . only doing it rather better; because, as I say, he knew how to act.

Donna Matilda. Some of them began to hit him with their whips and fans and sticks.

Belcredi. And then—as a king, he was armed, of course—he drew out his sword and menaced two or three of us . . . It was a terrible moment, I can assure you!

Donna Matilda. I shall never forget that scene—all our masked faces hideous and terrified gazing at him, at that terrible mask of his face, which was no longer a mask, but madness, madness personified.

Belcredi. He was Henry IV, Henry IV in person, in a moment of fury.

Donna Matilda. He'd got into it all the detail and minute preparation of a month's careful study. And it all burned and blazed there in the terrible obsession which lit his face.

Doctor. Yes, that is quite natural, of course. The momentary obsession of a dilettante became fixed, owing to the fall and the damage to the brain.

Belcredi [*to* FRIDA *and* DI NOLLI]. You see the kind of jokes life can play on us. [*To* DI NOLLI.] You were four or five years old. [*To* FRIDA.] Your mother imagines you've taken her place there in that portrait; when, at the time, she had not the remotest idea that she would bring you into the world. My hair is already grey; and he—look at him—[*Points to portrait*]—ha! A smack on the head, and he never moves again: Henry IV for ever!

Doctor [*seeking to draw the attention of the others, looking learned and imposing*]. —Well, well, then it comes, we may say, to this . . .

[*Suddenly the first exit to right, the one nearest foot-lights, opens, and* BERTHOLD *enters all excited.*]

Berthold [*rushing in*]. I say! I say! [*Stops for a moment, arrested by the astonishment which his appearance has caused in the others.*]

Frida [*running away terrified*]. Oh dear! oh dear! it's he, it's . . .

Donna Matilda [*covering her face with her hands so as not to see*]. Is it, is it he?

Di Nolli. No, no, what are you talking about? Be calm!

Doctor. Who is it then?

Belcredi. One of our masqueraders.

Di Nolli. He is one of the four youths we keep here to help him out in his madness . . .

Berthold. I beg your pardon, Marquis . . .

Di Nolli. Pardon be damned! I gave orders that the doors were to be closed, and that nobody should be allowed to enter.

Berthold. Yes, sir, but I can't stand it any longer, and I ask you to let me go away this very minute.

Di Nolli. Oh, you're the new valet, are you? You were supposed to begin this morning, weren't you?

Berthold. Yes, sir, and I can't stand it, I can't bear it.

Donna Matilda [*to* DI NOLLI *excitedly*]. What? Then he's not so calm as you said?

Berthold [*quickly*]. —No, no, my lady, it isn't he; it's my companions. You say "help him out with his madness," Marquis; but they don't do anything of the kind. They're the real madmen. I come here for the first time, and instead of helping me . . .

[LANDOLPH *and* HAROLD *come in from the same door, but hesitate on the threshold.*]

Landolph. Excuse me?

Harold. May I come in, my Lord?

Di Nolli. Come in! What's the matter? What are you all doing?

Frida. Oh God! I'm frightened! I'm going to run away. [*Makes towards exit at left.*]

Di Nolli [*restraining her at once*]. No, no, Frida!

Landolph. My Lord, this fool here . . . [*Indicates* BERTHOLD.]

Berthold [*protesting*]. Ah, no thanks, my friends, no thanks! I'm not stopping here! I'm off!

Landolph. What do you mean—you're not stopping here?

Harold. He's ruined everything, my Lord, running away in here!

Landolph. He's made him quite mad. We can't keep him in there any longer. He's given orders that he's to be arrested; and he wants to "judge" him at once from the throne: What is to be done?

Di Nolli. Shut the door, man! Shut the door! Go and close that door! [LANDOLPH *goes over to close it.*]

Harold. Ordulph, alone, won't be able to keep him there.

Landolph. —My Lord, perhaps if we could announce the visitors at once, it would turn his thoughts. Have the gentlemen thought under what pretext they will present themselves to him?

Di Nolli. —It's all been arranged! [*To the* DOCTOR.] If you, Doctor, think it well to see him at once. . . .

Frida. I'm not coming! I'm not coming! I'll keep out of this. You too, mother, for Heaven's sake, come away with me!

Doctor. —I say . . . I suppose he's not armed, is he?

Di Nolli. —Nonsense! Of course not. [*To* FRIDA.] Frida, you know this is childish of you. You wanted to come!

Frida. I didn't at all. It was mother's idea.

Donna Matilda. And I'm quite ready to see him. What are we going to do?

Belcredi. Must we absolutely dress up in some fashion or other?

Landolph. —Absolutely essential, indispensable, sir. Alas! as you see . . . [*Shows his costume*], there'd be awful trouble if he saw you gentlemen in modern dress.

Harold. He would think it was some diabolical masquerade.

Di Nolli. As these men seem to be in costume to you, so we appear to be in costume to him, in these modern clothes of ours.

Landolph. It wouldn't matter so much if he wouldn't suppose it to be the work of his mortal enemy.

Belcredi. Pope Gregory VII?

Landolph. Precisely. He calls him "a pagan."

Belcredi. The Pope a pagan? Not bad that!

Landolph. —Yes, sir,—and a man who calls up the dead! He accuses him of all the diabolical arts. He's terribly afraid of him.

Doctor. Persecution mania!

Harold. He'd be simply furious.

Di Nolli [*to* BELCREDI]. But there's no need for you to be there, you know. It's sufficient for the Doctor to see him.

Doctor. —What do you mean? . . . I? Alone?

Di Nolli. —But they are there. [*Indicates the three young men.*]

Doctor. I don't mean that . . . I mean if the Marchioness . . .

Donna Matilda. Of course. I mean to see him too, naturally. I want to see him again.

Frida. Oh, why, mother, why? Do come away with me, I implore you!

Donna Matilda [*imperiously*]. Let me do as I wish!

I came here for this purpose! [*To* LANDOLPH.] I shall be "Adelaide," the mother.

Landolph. Excellent! The mother of the Empress Bertha. Good! It will be enough if her Ladyship wears the ducal crown and puts on a mantle that will hide her other clothes entirely. [*To* HAROLD.] Off you go, Harold!

Harold. Wait a moment! And this gentleman here? . . . [*Alludes to the* DOCTOR.]

Doctor. —Ah yes . . . we decided I was to be . . . the Bishop of Cluny, Hugh of Cluny!

Harold. The gentleman means the Abbot. Very good! Hugh of Cluny.

Landolph. —He's often been here before!

Doctor [*amazed*]. —What? Been here before?

Landolph. —Don't be alarmed! I mean that it's an easily prepared disguise . . .

Harold. We've made use of it on other occasions, you see!

Doctor. But . . .

Landolph. Oh, no, there's no risk of his remembering. He pays more attention to the dress than to the person.

Donna Matilda. That's fortunate for me too then.

Di Nolli. Frida, you and I'll get along. Come on, Tito!

Belcredi. Ah no. If she [*Indicates the* MARCHIONESS.] stops here, so do I!

Donna Matilda. But I don't need you at all.

Belcredi. You may not need me, but I should like to see him again myself. Mayn't I?

Landolph. Well, perhaps it would be better if there were three.

Harold. How is the gentleman to be dressed then?

Belcredi. Oh, try and find some easy costume for me.

Landolph [*to* HAROLD]. Hum! Yes . . . he'd better be from Cluny too.

Belcredi. What do you mean—from Cluny?

Landolph. A Benedictine's habit of the Abbey of Cluny. He can be in attendance on Monsignor. [*To* HAROLD.] Off you go! [*To* BERTHOLD.] And you too get away and keep out of sight all today. No, wait a bit! [*To* BERTHOLD.] You bring here the costumes he will give you. [*To* HAROLD.] You go at once and announce the visit of the "Duchess Adelaide" and "Monsignor Hugh of Cluny." Do you understand? [HAROLD *and* BERTHOLD *go off by the first door on the right.*]

Di Nolli. We'll retire now. [*Goes off with* FRIDA, *left.*]

Doctor. Shall I be a *persona grata* to him, as Hugh of Cluny?

Landolph. Oh, rather! Don't worry about that! Monsignor has always been received here with great respect. You too, my Lady, he will be glad to see. He never forgets that it was owing to the intercession of you two that he was admitted to the Castle of Canossa and the presence of Gregory VII, who didn't want to receive him.

Belcredi. And what do I do?

Landolph. You stand a little apart, respectfully: that's all.

Donna Matilda [*irritated, nervous*]. You would do well to go away, you know.

Belcredi [*slowly, spitefully*]. How upset you seem! . . .

Donna Matilda [*proudly*]. I am as I am. Leave me alone!

[BERTHOLD *comes in with the costumes.*]

Landolph [*seeing him enter*]. Ah, the costumes: here they are. This mantle is for the Marchioness . . .

Donna Matilda. Wait a minute! I'll take off my hat. [*Does so and gives it to* BERTHOLD.]

Landolph. Put it down there! [*Then to the* MARCHIONESS, *while he offers to put the ducal crown on her head.*] Allow me!

Donna Matilda. Dear, dear! Isn't there a mirror here?

Landolph. Yes, there's one there [*Points to the door on the left.*] If the Marchioness would rather put it on herself . . .

Donna Matilda. Yes, yes, that will be better. Give it to me! [*Takes up her hat and goes off with* BERTHOLD, *who carries the cloak and the crown.*]

Belcredi. Well, I must say, I never thought I should be a Benedictine monk! By the way, this business must cost an awful lot of money.

The Doctor. Like any other fantasy, naturally!

Belcredi. Well, there's a fortune to go upon.

Landolph. We have got there a whole wardrobe of costumes of the period, copied to perfection from old models. This is my special job. I get them from the best theatrical costumers. They cost lots of money. [DONNA MATILDA *re-enters, wearing mantle and crown.*]

Belcredi [*at once, in admiration*]. Oh magnificent! Oh, truly regal!

Donna Matilda [*looking at* BELCREDI *and bursting out into laughter*]. Oh no, no! Take it off! You're impossible. You look like an ostrich dressed up as a monk.

Belcredi. Well, how about the Doctor?

The Doctor. I don't think I look so bad, do I?

Donna Matilda. No; the Doctor's all right . . . but you are too funny for words.

The Doctor. Do you have many receptions here then?

Landolph. It depends. He often gives orders that such and such a person appear before him. Then we have to find someone who will take the part. Women too . . .

Donna Matilda [*hurt, but trying to hide the fact*]. Ah, women too?

Landolph. Oh, yes; many at first.

Belcredi [*laughing*]. Oh, that's great! In costume, like the Marchioness?

Landolph. Oh well, you know, women of the kind
that lend themselves to . . .

Belcredi. Ah, I see! [*Perfidiously to the* MARCHIONESS.]
Look out, you know he's becoming dangerous for you.

[*The second door on the right opens, and* HAROLD
*appears making first of all a discreet sign that all
conversation should cease.*]

Harold. His Majesty, the Emperor!

[*The* TWO VALETS *enter first, and go and stand on
either side of the throne. Then* HENRY IV *comes in
between* ORDULPH *and* HAROLD, *who keep a little in
the rear respectfully.*

[HENRY IV *is about 50 and very pale. The hair on the
back of his head is already grey; over the temples
and forehead it appears blond, owing to its having
been tinted in an evident and puerile fashion. On
his cheek bones he has two small, doll-like dabs of
color, that stand out prominently against the rest
of his tragic pallor. He is wearing a penitent's sack
over his regal habit, as at Canossa. His eyes have
a fixed look which is dreadful to see, and this expression is in strained contrast with the sackcloth.*
ORDULPH *carries the Imperial crown;* HAROLD, *the
sceptre with eagle, and the globe with the cross.*]

Henry IV [*bowing first to* DONNA MATILDA *and afterwards to the* DOCTOR]. My lady . . . Monsignor . . .
[*Then he looks at* BELCREDI *and seems about to greet him
too; when, suddenly, he turns to* LANDOLPH, *who has
approached him, and asks him sotto voce and with diffidence.*] Is that Peter Damiani?

Landolph. No, Sire. He is a monk from Cluny who
is accompanying the Abbot.

Henry IV [*looks again at* BELCREDI *with increasing mis-
trust, and then noticing that he appears embarrassed and
keeps glancing at* DONNA MATILDA *and the* DOCTOR, *stands
upright and cries out*]. No, it's Peter Damiani! It's no

use, father, your looking at the Duchess. [*Then turning quickly to* DONNA MATILDA *and the* DOCTOR *as though to ward off a danger.*] I swear it! I swear that my heart is changed towards your daughter. I confess that if he [*Indicates* BELCREDI.] hadn't come to forbid it in the name of Pope Alexander, I'd have repudiated her. Yes, yes, there were people ready to favour the repudiation: the Bishop of Mayence would have done it for a matter of one hundred and twenty farms. [*Looks at* LANDOLPH *a little perplexed and adds.*] But I mustn't speak ill of the bishops at this moment! [*More humbly to* BELCREDI.] I am grateful to you, believe me, I am grateful to you for the hindrance you put in my way!—God knows, my life's been all made of humiliations: my mother, Adalbert, Tribur, Goslar! And now this sackcloth you see me wearing! [*Changes tone suddenly and speaks like one who goes over his part in a parenthesis of astuteness.*] It doesn't matter: clarity of ideas, perspicacity, firmness and patience under adversity that's the thing. [*Then turning to all and speaking solemnly.*] I know how to make amend for the mistakes I have made; and I can humiliate myself even before you, Peter Damiani. [*Bows profoundly to him and remains curved. Then a suspicion is born in him which he is obliged to utter in menacing tones, almost against his will.*] Was it not perhaps you who started that obscene rumor that my holy mother had illicit relations with the Bishop of Augusta?

Belcredi [*since* HENRY IV *has his finger pointed at him*]. No, no, it wasn't I . . .

Henry IV [*straightening up*]. Not true, not true? Infamy! [*Looks at him and then adds.*] I didn't think you capable of it! [*Goes to the* DOCTOR *and plucks his sleeve, while winking at him knowingly.*] Always the same, Monsignor, those bishops, always the same!

Harold [*softly, whispering as if to help out the doctor*]. Yes, yes, the rapacious bishops!

The Doctor [*to* HAROLD, *trying to keep it up*].   Ah, yes, those fellows . . . ah yes . . .

Henry IV.   Nothing satisfies them! I was a little boy, Monsignor . . . One passes the time, playing even, when, without knowing it, one is a king.—I was six years old; and they tore me away from my mother, and made use of me against her without my knowing anything about it . . . always profaning, always stealing, stealing! . . . One greedier than the other . . . Hanno worse than Stephen! Stephen worse than Hanno!

Landolph [*sotto voce, persuasively, to call his attention*].   Majesty!

Henry IV [*turning round quickly*].   Ah yes . . . this isn't the moment to speak ill of the bishops. But this infamy against my mother, Monsignor, is too much. [*Looks at the* MARCHIONESS *and grows tender.*] And I can't even weep for her, Lady . . . I appeal to you who have a mother's heart! She came here to see me from her convent a month ago . . . They had told me she was dead! [*Sustained pause full of feeling. Then smiling sadly.*] I can't weep for her; because if you are here now, and I am like this [*Shows the sackcloth he is wearing.*] it means I am twenty-six years old!

Harold.   And that she is therefore alive, Majesty! . . .

Ordulph.   Still in her convent!

Henry IV [*looking at them*].   Ah yes! And I can postpone my grief to another time. [*Shows the* MARCHIONESS *almost with coquetry the tint he has given to his hair.*] Look! I am still fair . . . [*Then slowly as if in confidence.*] For you . . . there's no need! But little exterior details do help! A matter of time, Monsignor, do you understand me? [*Turns to the* MARCHIONESS *and notices her hair.*] Ah, but I see that you too, Duchess . . . Italian, eh? [*As much as to say "false"; but without any indignation, indeed rather with malicious admiration.*] Heaven forbid that I should show disgust or surprise!

Nobody cares to recognize that obscure and fatal power which sets limits to our will. But I say, if one is born and one dies . . . Did you want to be born, Monsignor? I didn't! And in both cases, independently of our wills, so many things happen we would wish didn't happen, and to which we resign ourselves as best we can! . . .

Doctor [*merely to make a remark, while studying* HENRY IV *carefully*]. Alas! Yes, alas!

Henry IV. It's like this: When we are not resigned, out come our desires. A woman wants to be a man . . . an old man would be young again. Desires, ridiculous fixed ideas of course— But reflect! Monsignor, those other desires are not less ridiculous: I mean, those desires where the will is kept within the limits of the possible. Not one of us can lie or pretend. We're all fixed in good faith in a certain concept of ourselves. However, Monsignor, while you keep yourself in order, holding on with both your hands to your holy habit, there slips down from your sleeves, there peels off from you like . . . like a serpent . . . something you don't notice: life, Monsignor! [*Turns to the* MARCHIONESS.] Has it never happened to you, my Lady, to find a different self in yourself? Have you always been the same? My God! One day . . . how was it, how was it you were able to commit this or that action? [*Fixes her so intently in the eyes as almost to make her blanch.*] Yes, that particular action, that very one: we understand each other! But don't be afraid: I shall reveal it to none. And you, Peter Damiani, how could you be a friend of that man? . . .

Landolph. Majesty!

Henry IV [*at once*]. No, I won't name him! [*Turning to* BELCREDI.] What did you think of him? But we all of us cling tight to our conceptions of ourselves, just as he who is growing old dyes his hair. What does it matter that this dyed hair of mine isn't a reality for you, if it *is*, to some extent, for me?—you, you, my Lady, certainly don't dye your hair to deceive the others, nor even yourself; but only to cheat your own image a little before the looking-glass. I do it for a joke! You do it seriously! But I assure you that you too, Madam, are in masquerade, though it be in all seriousness; and I am not speaking of the venerable crown on your brows or the ducal mantle. I am speaking only of the memory you wish to fix in yourself of your fair complexion one day when it pleased you —or of your dark complexion, if you were dark: the fading image of your youth! For you, Peter Damiani, on the contrary, the memory of what you have been, of what you have done, seems to you a recognition of past realities that remain within you like a dream. I'm in the same case too: with so many inexplicable memories—like dreams! Ah! . . . There's nothing to marvel at in it, Peter Damiani! Tomorrow it will be the same thing with our life of today! [*Suddenly getting excited and taking hold of his sackcloth.*] This sackcloth here . . . [*Beginning to take it off with a gesture of almost ferocious joy while the* THREE VALETS *run over to him, frightened, as if to prevent his doing so.*] Ah, my God! [*Draws back and throws off sackcloth.*] Tomorrow, at Bressanone, twenty-seven German and Lombard bishops will sign with me the act of deposition of Gregory VII! No Pope at all! Just a false monk!

Ordulph [*with the other three*]. Majesty! Majesty! In God's name! . . .

Harold [*inviting him to put on the sackcloth again*]. Listen to what he says, Majesty!

Landolph. Monsignor is here with the Duchess to intercede in your favor. [*Makes secret signs to the* DOCTOR *to say something at once.*]

Doctor [*foolishly*]. Ah yes . . . yes . . . we are here to intercede . . .

Henry IV [*repenting at once, almost terrified, allowing the three to put on the sackcloth again, and pulling it down over him with his own hands*]. Pardon . . . yes . . . yes . . . pardon, Monsignor: forgive me, my Lady . . . I swear to you I feel the whole weight of the anathema. [*Bends himself, takes his face between his hands, as though waiting for something to crush him. Then changing tone, but without moving, says softly to* LANDOLPH, HAROLD *and* ORDULPH.] But I don't know why I cannot be humble before that man there! [*Indicates* BELCREDI.]

Landolph [*sotto voce*]. But why, Majesty, do you insist on believing he is Peter Damiani, when he isn't, at all?

Henry IV [*looking at him timorously*]. He isn't Peter Damiani?

Harold. No, no, he is a poor monk, Majesty.

Henry IV [*sadly with a touch of exasperation*]. Ah! None of us can estimate what we do when we do it from instinct . . . You perhaps, Madam, can understand me better than the others, since you are a woman and a Duchess. This is a solemn and decisive moment. I could, you know, accept the assistance of the Lombard bishops, arrest the Pope, lock him up here in the castle, run to Rome and elect an anti-Pope; offer alliance to Robert Guiscard—and Gregory VII would be lost! I resist the temptation; and, believe me, I am wise in doing so. I feel the atmosphere of our times and the majesty of one who knows how to be what he ought to be! a Pope! Do you feel inclined to laugh at me, seeing me like this? You would be foolish to do so; for you don't understand the political wisdom which makes this penitent's sack advisable. The parts may be changed tomorrow. What would you do then? Would you laugh to see the Pope a prisoner? No! It would come to the same thing: I dressed as a penitent, today; he, as prisoner tomorrow! But woe to him who doesn't know how to wear his mask, be he king or Pope!—Perhaps he is a bit too cruel! No! Yes, yes, maybe!

—You remember, my Lady, how your daughter Bertha, for whom, I repeat, my feelings have changed [*Turns to* BELCREDI *and shouts to his face as if he were being contradicted by him.*]—yes, changed on account of the affection and devotion she showed me in that terrible moment . . . [*Then once again to the* MARCHIONESS.] . . . you remember how she came with me, my Lady, followed me like a beggar and passed two nights out in the open, in the snow? You are her mother! Doesn't this touch your mother's heart? Doesn't this urge you to pity, so that you will beg His Holiness for pardon, beg him to receive us?

Donna Matilda [*trembling, with feeble voice*]. Yes, yes, at once . . .

Doctor. It shall be done!

Henry IV. And one thing more! [*Draws them in to listen to him.*] It isn't enough that he should receive me! You know he can do *everything—everything* I tell you! He can even call up the dead. [*Touches his chest.*] Behold me! Do you see me? There is no magic art unknown to him. Well, Monsignor, my Lady, my torment is really this: that whether here or there [*Pointing to his portrait almost in fear.*] I can't free myself from this magic. I am a penitent now, you see; and I swear to you I shall remain so until he receives me. But you two, when the excommunication is taken off, must ask the Pope to do this thing he can so easily do: to take me away from that; [*Indicating the portrait again.*] and let me live wholly and freely my miserable life. A man can't always be twenty-six, my Lady. I ask this of you for your daughter's sake too; that I may love her as she deserves to be loved, well disposed as I am now, all tender towards her for her pity. There: it's all there! I am in your hands! [*Bows.*] My Lady! Monsignor!

[*He goes off, bowing grandly, through the door by which he entered, leaving everyone stupefied, and the* MARCHIONESS *so profoundly touched, that no sooner has he gone than she breaks out into sobs and sits down almost fainting.*]

ACT II

Another room of the villa, adjoining the throne room. Its furniture is antique and severe. Principal exit at rear in the background. To the left, two windows looking on the garden. To the right, a door opening into the throne room.

Late afternoon of the same day.

DONNA MATILDA, *the* DOCTOR *and* BELCREDI *are on the stage engaged in conversation; but* DONNA MATILDA *stands to one side, evidently annoyed at what the other two are saying; although she cannot help listening, because, in her agitated state, everything interests her in spite of herself. The talk of the other two attracts her attention, because she instinctively feels the need for calm at the moment.*

Belcredi. It may be as you say, Doctor, but that was my impression.

Doctor. I won't contradict you; but, believe me, it is only . . . an impression.

Belcredi. Pardon me, but he even said so, and quite clearly [*Turning to the* MARCHIONESS.] Didn't he, Marchioness?

Donna Matilda [*turning round*]. What did he say? . . . [*Then not agreeing.*] Oh yes . . . but not for the reason you think!

Doctor. He was alluding to the costumes we had slipped on . . . Your cloak [*Indicating the* MARCHIONESS.] our Benedictine habits . . . But all this is childish!

Donna Matilda [*turning quickly, indignant*]. Childish? What do you mean, Doctor?

Doctor. From one point of view, it is—I beg you to let me say so, Marchioness! Yet, on the other hand, it is much more complicated than you can imagine.

Donna Matilda. To me, on the contrary, it is perfectly clear!

Doctor [*with a smile of pity of the competent person towards those who do not understand*]. We must take into account the peculiar psychology of madmen; which, you must know, enables us to be certain that they observe things and can, for instance, easily detect people who are disguised; can in fact recognize the disguise and yet believe in it; just as children do, for whom disguise is both play and reality. That is why I used the word childish. But the thing is extremely complicated, inasmuch as he must be perfectly aware of being an image to himself and for himself—that image there, in fact! [*Alluding to the portrait in the throne room, and pointing to the left.*]

Belcredi. That's what he said!

Doctor. Very well then— An image before which other images, ours, have appeared: understand? Now he, in his acute and perfectly lucid delirium, was able to detect at once a difference between his image and ours: that is, he saw that ours were make-believes. So he suspected us; because all madmen are armed with a special diffidence. But that's all there is to it! Our make-believe, built up all round his, did not seem pitiful to him. While his seemed all the more tragic to us, in that he, as if in defiance—understand?—and induced by his suspicion, wanted to show us up merely as a joke. That was also partly the case with him, in coming before us with painted cheeks and hair, and saying he had done it on purpose for a jest.

Donna Matilda [*impatiently*]. No, it's not that, Doctor. It's not like that! It's not like that!

Doctor. Why isn't it, may I ask?

Donna Matilda [*with decision but trembling*]. I am perfectly certain he recognized me!

Doctor. It's not possible . . . it's not possible!

Belcredi [*at the same time*]. Of course not!

Donna Matilda [*more than ever determined, almost convulsively*]. I tell you, he recognized me! When he came close up to speak to me—looking in my eyes, right into my eyes—he recognized me!

Belcredi. But he was talking of your daughter!

Donna Matilda. That's not true! He was talking of me! Of me!

Belcredi. Yes, perhaps, when he said . . .

Donna Matilda [*letting herself go*]. About my dyed hair! But didn't you notice that he added at once: "or the memory of your dark hair, if you were dark"? He remembered perfectly well that I was dark—then!

Belcredi. Nonsense! nonsense!

Donna Matilda [*not listening to him, turning to the* DOCTOR]. My hair, Doctor, is really dark—like my daughter's! That's why he spoke of her.

Belcredi. But he doesn't even know your daughter! He's never seen her!

Donna Matilda. Exactly! Oh, you never understand anything! By my daughter, stupid, he meant me—as I was then!

Belcredi. Oh, this is catching! This is catching, this madness!

Donna Matilda [*softly, with contempt*]. Fool!

Belcredi. Excuse me, were you ever his wife? Your daughter is his wife—in his delirium: Bertha of Susa.

Donna Matilda. Exactly! Because I, no longer dark —as he remembered me—but *fair*, introduced myself as "Adelaide," the mother. My daughter doesn't exist for him: he's never seen her—you said so yourself! So how can he know whether she's fair or dark?

Belcredi. But he said dark, speaking generally, just as anyone who wants to recall, whether fair or dark, a memory of youth in the color of the hair! And you, as usual, begin to imagine things! Doctor, you said I ought not to have come! It's she who ought not to have come!

Donna Matilda [*upset for a moment by* BELCREDI's *remark, recovers herself. Then with a touch of anger, because doubtful*]. No, no . . . he spoke of me . . . He spoke all the time to me, with me, of me . . .

Belcredi. That's not bad! He didn't leave me a moment's breathing space; and you say he was talking all the time to you? Unless you think he was alluding to you too, when he was talking to Peter Damiani!

Donna Matilda [*defiantly, almost exceeding the limits of courteous discussion*]. Who knows? Can you tell me why, from the outset, he showed a strong dislike for you, for you alone? [*From the tone of the question, the expected answer must almost explicitly be: "because he understands you are my lover."* BELCREDI *feels this so well that he remains silent and can say nothing.*]

Doctor. The reason may also be found in the fact that only the visit of the Duchess Adelaide and the Abbot of Cluny was announced to him. Finding a third person present, who had not been announced, at once his suspicions . . .

Belcredi. Yes, exactly! His suspicion made him see an enemy in me: Peter Damiani! But she's got it into her head, that he recognized her . . .

Donna Matilda. There's no doubt about it! I could see it from his eyes, doctor. You know, there's a way of looking that leaves no doubt whatever . . . Perhaps it was only for an instant, but I am sure!

Doctor. It is not impossible: a lucid moment . . .

Donna Matilda. Yes, perhaps . . . And then his speech seemed to me full of regret for his and my youth—for the horrible thing that happened to him, that has held him in that disguise from which he has never been able to free himself, and from which he longs to be free —he said so himself!

Belcredi. Yes, so as to be able to make love to your daughter, or you, as you believe—having been touched by your pity.

Donna Matilda. Which is very great, I would ask you to believe.

Belcredi. As one can see, Marchioness; so much so that a miracle-worker might expect a miracle from it!

Doctor. Will you let me speak? I don't work miracles, because I am a doctor and not a miracle-worker. I listened very intently to all he said; and I repeat that that certain analogical elasticity, common to all systematized delirium, is evidently with him much . . . what shall I say? —much relaxed! The elements, that is, of his delirium no longer hold together. It seems to me he has lost the equilibrium of his second personality and sudden recollections drag him—and this is very comforting—not from a state of incipient apathy, but rather from a morbid inclination to reflective melancholy, which shows a . . . a very considerable cerebral activity. Very comforting, I repeat! Now if, by this violent trick we've planned . . .

Donna Matilda [*turning to the window, in the tone of a sick person complaining*]. But how is it that the motor has not returned? It's three hours and a half since . . .

Doctor. What do you say?

Donna Matilda. The motor, Doctor! It's more than three hours and a half . . .

Doctor [*taking out his watch and looking at it*]. Yes, more than four hours, by this!

Donna Matilda. It could have reached here an hour ago at least! But, as usual . . .

Belcredi. Perhaps they can't find the dress . . .

Donna Matilda. But I explained exactly where it was!
[*Impatiently.*] And Frida . . . where is Frida?

Belcredi [*looking out of the window*]. Perhaps she is
in the garden with Charles . . .

Doctor. He'll talk her out of her fright.

Belcredi. She's not afraid, Doctor; don't you believe
it: the thing bores her rather . . .

Donna Matilda. Just don't ask anything of her! I
know what she's like.

Doctor. Let's wait patiently. Anyhow, it will soon be
over, and it has to be in the evening . . . It will only be
the matter of a moment! If we can succeed in rousing
him, as I was saying, and in breaking at one go the
threads—already slack—which still bind him to this fiction of his, giving him back what he himself asks for—you
remember, he said: "one cannot always be twenty-six
years old, madam!" if we can give him freedom from this
torment, which even *he* feels is a torment, then if he is
able to recover at one bound the sensation of the distance
of time . . .

Belcredi [*quickly*]. He'll be cured! [*Then emphati-
cally with irony.*] We'll pull him out of it all!

Doctor. Yes, we may hope to set him going again, like
a watch which has stopped at a certain hour . . . just as
if we had our watches in our hands and were waiting for
that other watch to go again.—A shake—so—and let's
hope it'll tell the time again after its long stop. [*At this
point the* MARQUIS CHARLES DI NOLLI *enters from the
principal entrance.*]

Donna Matilda. Oh, Charles! . . . And Frida?
Where is she?

Di Nolli. She'll be here in a moment.

Doctor. Has the motor arrived?

Di Nolli. Yes.

Donna Matilda. Yes? Has the dress come?

Di Nolli. It's been here some time.

Doctor. Good! Good!

Donna Matilda [*trembling*]. Where is she? Where's Frida?

Di Nolli [*shrugging his shoulders and smiling sadly, like one lending himself unwillingly to an untimely joke*]. You'll see, you'll see! . . . [*Pointing towards the hall.*] Here she is! . . . [BERTHOLD *appears at the threshold of the hall, and announces with solemnity.*]

BERTHOLD. Her Highness the Countess Matilda of Canossa! [FRIDA *enters, magnificent and beautiful, arrayed in the robes of her mother as "Countess Matilda of Tuscany," so that she is a living copy of the portrait in the throne room.*]

FRIDA [*passing* BERTHOLD, *who is bowing, says to him with disdain*]. Of Tuscany, of Tuscany! Canossa is just one of my castles!

Belcredi [*in admiration*]. Look! Look! She seems another person . . .

Donna Matilda. One would say it were I! Look!—Why, Frida, look! She's exactly my portrait, alive!

Doctor. Yes, yes . . . Perfect! Perfect! The portrait, to the life.

Belcredi. Yes, there's no question about it. She *is* the portrait! Magnificent!

Frida. Don't make me laugh, or I shall burst! I say, mother, what a tiny waist you had? I had to squeeze so to get into this!

Donna Matilda [*arranging her dress a little*]. Wait! . . . Keep still! . . . These pleats . . . is it really so tight?

Frida. I'm suffocating! I implore you, to be quick! . . .

Doctor. But we must wait till it's evening!

Frida. No, no, I can't hold out till evening!

Donna Matilda. Why did you put it on so soon?

Frida. The moment I saw it, the temptation was irresistible . . .

Donna Matilda. At least you could have called me, or have had someone help you! It's still all crumpled.

Frida. So I saw, mother; but they are old creases; they won't come out.

Doctor. It doesn't matter, Marchioness! The illusion is perfect. [*Then coming nearer and asking her to come in front of her daughter, without hiding her.*] If you please, stay there, there . . . at a certain distance . . . now a little more forward . . .

Belcredi. For the feeling of the distance of time . . .

Donna Matilda [*slightly turning to him*]. Twenty years after! A disaster! A tragedy!

Belcredi. Now don't let's exaggerate!

Doctor [*embarrassed, trying to save the situation*]. No, no! I meant the dress . . . so as to see . . . You know . . .

Belcredi [*laughing*]. Oh, as for the dress, Doctor, it isn't a matter of twenty years! It's eight hundred! An abyss! Do you really want to shove him across it [*Pointing first to* FRIDA *and then to* MARCHIONESS.] from there to here? But you'll have to pick him up in pieces with a basket! Just think now: for us it is a matter of twenty years, a couple of dresses, and a masquerade. But, if, as you say, Doctor, time has stopped for and around him: if he lives there [*Pointing to* FRIDA.] with her, eight hundred years ago . . . I repeat: the giddiness of the jump will be such, that finding himself suddenly among us . . . [*The* DOCTOR *shakes his head in dissent.*] You don't think so?

Doctor. No, because life, my dear baron, can take up its rhythms. This—our life—will at once become real also to him; and will pull him up directly, wresting from him suddenly the illusion, and showing him that the eight hundred years, as you say, are only twenty! It will be like one of those tricks, such as the leap into space, for instance, of the Masonic rite, which appears to be heaven knows how far, and is only a step down the stairs.

Belcredi. Ah! An idea! Yes! Look at Frida and the Marchioness, doctor! Which is more advanced in time? We old people, Doctor! The young ones think they are more ahead; but it isn't true: we are more ahead, because time belongs to us more than to them.

Doctor. If the past didn't alienate us . . .

Belcredi. It doesn't matter at all! How does it alienate us? They [*Pointing to* FRIDA *and* DI NOLLI.] have still to do what we have accomplished, Doctor: to grow old, doing the same foolish things, more or less, as we did . . . This is the illusion: that one comes forward through a door to life. It isn't so! As soon as one is born, one starts dying; therefore, he who started first is the most advanced of all. The youngest of us is father Adam! Look there: [*Pointing to* FRIDA.] eight hundred years younger than all of us—the Countess Matilda of Tuscany. [*He makes her a deep bow.*]

Di Nolli. I say, Tito, don't start joking.

Belcredi. Oh, you think I am joking? . . .

Di Nolli. Of course, of course . . . all the time.

Belcredi. Impossible! I've even dressed up as a Benedictine . . .

Di Nolli. Yes, but for a serious purpose.

Belcredi. Well, exactly. If it has been serious for the others . . . for Frida, now, for instance. [*Then turning to the* DOCTOR.] I swear, Doctor, I don't yet understand what you want to do.

Doctor [*annoyed*]. You'll see! Let me do as I wish . . . At present you see the Marchioness still dressed as . . .

Belcredi. Oh, she also . . . has to masquerade?

Doctor. Of course! of course! In another dress that's

in there ready to be used when it comes into his head he sees the Countess Matilda of Canossa before him.

Frida [*while talking quietly to* Di Nolli *notices the doctor's mistake*]. Of Tuscany, of Tuscany !

Doctor. It's all the same!

Belcredi. Oh, I see! He'll be faced by two of them . . .

Doctor. Two, precisely! And then . . .

Frida [*calling him aside*]. Come here, doctor! Listen!

Doctor. Here I am! [*Goes near the two young people and pretends to give some explanations to them.*]

Belcredi [*softly to* Donna Matilda]. I say, this is getting rather strong, you know!

Donna Matilda [*looking him firmly in the face*]. What?

Belcredi. Does it really interest you as much as all that—to make you willing to take part in . . . ? For a woman this is simply enormous! . . .

Donna Matilda. Yes, for an ordinary woman.

Belcredi. Oh, no, my dear, for all women,—in a question like this! It's an abnegation.

Donna Matilda. I owe it to him.

Belcredi. Don't lie! You know well enough it's not hurting you!

Donna Matilda. Well, then, where does the abnegation come in?

Belcredi. Just enough to prevent you losing caste in other people's eyes—and just enough to offend me! . . .

Donna Matilda. But who is worrying about you now?

Di Nolli [*coming forward*]. It's all right. It's all right. That's what we'll do! [*Turning towards* Berthold.] Here you, go and call one of those fellows!

Berthold. At once! [*Exit.*]

Donna Matilda. But first of all we've got to pretend that we are going away.

Di Nolli. Exactly! I'll see to that . . . [*To* BELCREDI.] you don't mind staying here?

Belcredi [*ironically*]. Oh, no, I don't mind, I don't mind! . . .

Di Nolli. We must look out not to make him suspicious again, you know.

Belcredi. Oh, Lord! *He* doesn't amount to anything!

Doctor. He must believe absolutely that we've gone away. [LANDOLPH *followed by* BERTHOLD *enters from the right.*]

Landolph. May I come in?

Di Nolli. Come in! Come in! I say—your name's Lolo, isn't it?

Landolph. Lolo, or Landolph, just as you like!

Di Nolli. Well, look here: the Doctor and the Marchioness are leaving, at once.

Landolph. Very well. All we've got to say is that they have been able to obtain the permission for the reception from His Holiness. He's in there in his own apartments repenting of all he said—and in an awful state to have the pardon! Would you mind coming a minute? . . . If you would, just for a minute . . . put on the dress again . . .

Doctor. Why, of course, with pleasure . . .

Landolph. Might I be allowed to make a suggestion? Why not add that the Marchioness of Tuscany has interceded with the Pope that he should be received?

Donna Matilda. You see, he has recognized me!

Landolph. Forgive me . . . I don't know my history very well. I am sure you gentlemen know it much better! But I thought it was believed that Henry IV had a secret passion for the Marchioness of Tuscany.

Donna Matilda [*at once*]. Nothing of the kind! Nothing of the kind!

Landolph. That's what I thought! But he says he's

loved her . . . he's always saying it . . . And now he fears that her indignation for this secret love of his will work him harm with the Pope.

Belcredi. We must let him understand that this aversion no longer exists.

Landolph. Exactly! Of course!

Donna Matilda [*to* BELCREDI]. History says—I don't know whether you know it or not—that the Pope gave way to the supplications of the Marchioness Matilda and the Abbot of Cluny. And I may say, my dear Belcredi, that I intended to take advantage of this fact—at the time of the pageant—to show him my feelings were not so hostile to him as he supposed.

Belcredi. You are most faithful to history, Marchioness . . .

Landolph. Well then, the Marchioness could spare herself a double disguise and present herself with Monsignor [*Indicating the* DOCTOR.] as the Marchioness of Tuscany.

Doctor [*quickly, energetically*]. No, no! That won't do at all. It would ruin everything. The impression from the conformation must be a sudden one, give a shock! No, no, Marchioness, you will appear again as the Duchess Adelaide, the mother of the Empress. And then we'll go away. This is most necessary: that he should know we've gone away. Come on! Don't let's waste any more time! There's a lot to prepare.

[*Exeunt the* DOCTOR, DONNA MATILDA, *and* LANDOLPH, *right.*]

Frida. I am beginning to feel afraid again.

Di Nolli. Again, Frida?

Frida. It would have been better if I had seen him before.

Di Nolli. There's nothing to be frightened of, really.

Frida. He isn't furious, is he?

Di Nolli. Of course not! he's quite calm.

Belcredi [*with ironic sentimental affectation*]. Melancholy! Didn't you hear that he loves you?

Frida. Thanks! That's just why I am afraid.

Belcredi. He won't do you any harm.

Di Nolli. It'll only last a minute . . .

Frida. Yes, but there in the dark with him . . .

Di Nolli. Only for a moment; and I will be near you, and all the others behind the door ready to run in. As soon as you see your mother, your part will be finished . . .

Belcredi. I'm afraid of a different thing: that we're wasting our time . . .

Di Nolli. Don't begin again! The remedy seems a sound one to me.

Frida. I think so too! I feel it! I'm all trembling!

Belcredi. But, mad people, my dear friends—though they don't know it, alas—have this felicity which we don't take into account . . .

Di Nolli [*interrupting, annoyed*]. What felicity? Nonsense!

Belcredi [*forcefully*]. They don't reason!

Di Nolli. What's reasoning got to do with it, anyway?

Belcredi. Don't you call it reasoning that he will have to do—according to us—when he sees her [*Indicates* Frida.] and her mother? We've reasoned it all out, surely!

Di Nolli. Nothing of the kind: no reasoning at all! We put before him a double image of his own fantasy, or fiction, as the doctor says.

Belcredi [*suddenly*]. I say, I've never understood why they take degrees in medicine.

Di Nolli [*amazed*]. Who?

Belcredi. The alienists!

Di Nolli. What ought they to take degrees in, then?

Frida. If they are alienists, in what else should they take degrees?

Belcredi. In law, of course! All a matter of talk! The

more they talk, the more highly they are considered. "Analogous elasticity," "the sensation of distance in time!" And the first thing they tell you is that they don't work miracles—when a miracle's just what is wanted! But they know that the more they say they are not miracle-workers, the more folk believe in their seriousness!

Berthold [*who has been looking through the keyhole of the door on right*]. There they are! There they are! They're coming in here.

Di Nolli. Are they?

Berthold. He wants to come with them . . . Yes! . . . He's coming too!

Di Nolli. Let's get away, then! Let's get away, at once! [*To* BERTHOLD.] You stop here!

Berthold. Must I?

[*Without answering him,* DI NOLLI, FRIDA, *and* BEL-CREDI *go out by the main exit, leaving* BERTHOLD *surprised. The door on the right opens, and* LAN-DOLPH *enters first, bowing. Then* DONNA MATILDA *comes in, with mantle and ducal crown as in the first act; also the* DOCTOR *as the* ABBOT OF CLUNY. HENRY IV *is among them in royal dress.* ORDULPH *and* HAROLD *enter last of all.*]

Henry IV [*following up what he has been saying in the other room*]. And now I will ask you a question: how can I be astute, if you think me obstinate?

Doctor. No, no, not obstinate!

Henry IV [*smiling, pleased*]. Then you think me really astute?

Doctor. No, no, neither obstinate, nor astute.

Henry IV [*with benevolent irony*]. Monsignor, if obstinacy is not a vice which can go with astuteness, I hoped that in denying me the former, you would at least allow me a little of the latter. I can assure you I have great need of it. But if you want to keep it all for yourself . . .

Doctor. I? I? Do I seem astute to you?

Henry IV. No. Monsignor! What do you say? Not in the least! Perhaps in this case, I may seem a little obstinate to you [*Cutting short to speak to* DONNA MATILDA.] With your permission: a word in confidence to the Duchess. [*Leads her aside and asks her very earnestly.*] Is your daughter really dear to you?

Donna Matilda [*dismayed*]. Why, yes, certainly . . .

Henry IV. Do you wish me to compensate her with all my love, with all my devotion, for the grave wrongs I have done her—though you must not believe all the stories my enemies tell about my dissoluteness!

Donna Matilda. No, no, I don't believe them. I never have believed such stories.

Henry IV. Well, then are you willing?

Donna Matilda [*confused*]. What?

Henry IV. That I return to love your daughter again? [*Looks at her and adds, in a mysterious tone of warning.*] You mustn't be a friend of the Marchioness of Tuscany!

Donna Matilda. I tell you again that she has begged and tried not less than ourselves to obtain your pardon . . .

Henry IV [*softly, but excitedly*]. Don't tell me that! Don't say that to me! Don't you see the effect it has on me, my Lady?

Donna Matilda [*looks at him; then very softly as if in confidence*]. You love her still?

Henry IV [*puzzled*]. Still? Still, you say? You know, then? But nobody knows! Nobody must know!

Donna Matilda. But perhaps she knows, if she has begged so hard for you!

Henry IV [*looks at her and says*]. And you love your daughter? [*Brief pause. He turns to the* DOCTOR *with laughing accents.*] Ah, Monsignor, it's strange how little I think of my wife! It may be a sin, but I swear to you that I hardly feel her at all in my heart. What is stranger

is that her own mother scarcely feels her in her heart.
Confess, my Lady, that she amounts to very little for you.
[*Turning to* DOCTOR.] She talks to me of that other
woman, insistently, insistently, I don't know why! . . .

Landolph [*humbly*].   Maybe, Majesty, it is to disabuse
you of some ideas you have had about the Marchioness of
Tuscany. [*Then, dismayed at having allowed himself this
observation, adds.*] I mean just now, of course . . .

Henry IV.   You too maintain that she has been
friendly to me?

Landolph.   Yes, at the moment, Majesty.

Donna Matilda.   Exactly! Exactly! . . .

Henry IV.   I understand. That is to say, you don't believe I love her. I see! I see! Nobody's ever believed it,
nobody's ever thought it. Better so, then! But enough,
enough! [*Turns to the* DOCTOR *with changed expression.*]
Monsignor, you see? The reasons the Pope has had for re-
voking the excommunication have got nothing at all to
do with the reasons for which he excommunicated me
originally. Tell Pope Gregory we shall meet again at
Brixen. And you, Madame, should you chance to meet
your daughter in the courtyard of the castle of your
friend the Marchioness, ask her to visit me. We shall see
if I succeed in keeping her close beside me as wife and
Empress. Many women have presented themselves here
already assuring me that they were she. And I thought
to have her—yes, I tried sometimes—there's no shame in
it, with one's wife!—But when they said they were Bertha,
and they were from Susa, all of them—I can't think
why—started laughing! [*Confidentially.*] Understand?—
in bed—I undressed—so did she—yes, by God, undressed
—a man and a woman—it's natural after all! Like that,
we don't bother much about who we are. And one's dress
is like a phantom that hovers always near one. Oh, Monsignor, phantoms in general are nothing more than tri-
fling disorders of the spirit: images we cannot contain

within the bounds of sleep. They reveal themselves even when we are awake, and they frighten us. I . . . ah . . . I am always afraid when, at night time, I see disordered images before me. Sometimes I am even afraid of my own blood pulsing loudly in my arteries in the silence of night, like the sound of a distant step in a lonely corridor! . . . But, forgive me! I have kept you standing too long already. I thank you, my Lady, I thank you, Monsignor. [DONNA MATILDA *and the* DOCTOR *go off bowing. As soon as they have gone,* HENRY IV *suddenly changes his tone.*] Buffoons, buffoons! One can play any tune on them! And that other fellow . . . Pietro Damiani! . . . Caught him out perfectly! He's afraid to appear before me again. [*Moves up and down excitedly while saying this; then sees* BERTHOLD, *and points him out to the other three valets.*] Oh, look at this imbecile watching me with his mouth wide open! [*Shakes him.*] Don't you understand? Don't you see, idiot, how I treat them, how I play the fool with them, make them appear before me just as I wish? Miserable, frightened clowns that they are! And you [*Addressing the* VALETS.] are amazed that I tear off their ridiculous masks now, just as if it wasn't I who had made them mask themselves to satisfy this taste of mine for playing the madman!

Landolph—Harold—Ordulph [*bewildered, looking at one another*]. What? What does he say? What?

Henry IV [*answers them imperiously*]. Enough! enough! Let's stop it. I'm tired of it. [*Then as if the thought left him no peace.*] By God! The impudence! To come here along with her lover! . . . And pretending to do it out of pity! So as not to infuriate a poor devil already out of the world, out of time, out of life! If it hadn't been supposed to be done out of pity, one can well imagine that fellow wouldn't have allowed it. Those people expect others to behave as they wish all the time. And, of course, there's nothing arrogant in that! Oh, no! Oh, no!

It's merely their way of thinking, of feeling, of seeing. Everybody has his own way of thinking; you fellows, too. Yours is that of a flock of sheep—miserable, feeble, uncertain . . . But those others take advantage of this and make you accept their way of thinking; or, at least, they suppose they do; because, after all, what do they succeed in imposing on you? Words, words which anyone can interpret in his own manner! That's the way public opinion is formed! And it's a bad look out for a man who finds himself labelled one day with one of these words which everyone repeats; for example "madman," or "imbecile." Don't you think it is rather hard for a man to keep quiet, when he knows that there is a fellow going about trying to persuade everybody that he is as he sees him, trying to fix him in other people's opinion as a "madman"—according to him? Now I am talking seriously! Before I hurt my head, falling from my horse . . . [*Stops suddenly, noticing the dismay of the four young men.*] What's the matter with you? [*Imitates their amazed looks.*] What? Am I, or am I not, mad? Oh, yes! I'm mad all right! [*He becomes terrible.*] Well, then, by God, down on your knees, down on your knees! [*Makes them go down on their knees one by one.*] I order you to go down on your knees before me! And touch the ground three times with your foreheads! Down, down! That's the way you've got to be before madmen! [*Then annoyed with their facile humiliation.*] Get up, sheep! You obeyed me, didn't you? You might have put the strait jacket on me! . . . Crush a man with the weight of a word—it's nothing —a fly! all our life is crushed by the weight of words: the weight of the dead. Look at me here: can you really suppose that Henry IV is still alive? All the same, I speak, and order you live men about! Do you think it's a joke that the dead continue to live?—Yes, *here* it's a joke! But get out into the live world!—Ah, you say: what a beautiful sunrise—for us! All time is before us!—Dawn! We

will do what we like with this day——. Ah, yes! To Hell
with tradition, the old conventions! Well, go on! You will
do nothing but repeat the old, old words, while you imagine you are living! [*Goes up to* Berthold *who has now
become quite stupid.*] You don't understand a word of
this, do you? What's your name?

Berthold. I? . . . What? . . . Berthold . . .

Henry IV. Poor Berthold! What's your name here?

Berthold. I . . . I . . . my name in Fino.

Henry IV [*feeling the warning and critical glances of
the others, turns to them to reduce them to silence*].
Fino?

Berthold. Fino Pagliuca, sire.

Henry IV [*turning to* Landolph]. I've heard you call
each other by your nick-names often enough! Your name
is Lolo, isn't it?

Landolph. Yes, sire . . . [*Then with a sense of im-
mense joy.*] Oh Lord! Oh Lord! Then he is not mad . . .

Henry IV [*brusquely*]. What?

Landolph [*hesitating*]. No . . . I said . . .

Henry IV. Not mad, any more. No. Don't you see?
We're having a joke on those that think I am mad! [*To*
Harold.] I say, boy, your name's Franco . . . [*To* Or-
dulph] And yours . . .

Ordulph. Momo.

Henry IV. Momo, Momo . . . A nice name that!

Landolph. So he isn't . . .

Henry IV. What are you talking about? Of course
not! Let's have a jolly, good laugh! . . . [*Laughs.*] Ah!
. . . Ah! . . . Ah! . . .

Landolph—Harold—Ordulph [*looking at each other
half happy and half dismayed*]. Then he's cured! . . .
he's all right! . . .

Henry IV. Silence! Silence! . . . [*To* Berthold.]
Why don't you laugh? Are you offended? I didn't mean
it especially for you. It's convenient for everybody to in-

sist that certain people are mad, so they can be shut up.
Do you know why? Because it's impossible to hear them
speak! What shall I say of these people who've just gone
away? That one is a whore, another a libertine, another
a swindler . . . don't you think so? You can't believe
a word he says . . . don't you think so?—By the way,
they all listen to me terrified. And why are they terrified,
if what I say isn't true? Of course, you can't believe what
madmen say—yet, at the same time, they stand there
with their eyes wide open with terror!—Why? Tell me,
tell me, why?—You see I'm quite calm now!

Berthold. But, perhaps, they think that . . .

Henry IV. No, no, my dear fellow! Look me well in
the eyes! . . . I don't say that it's true—nothing is true,
Berthold! But . . . look me in the eyes!

Berthold. Well . . .

Henry IV. You see? You see? . . . You have terror in
your own eyes now because I seem mad to you! There's
the proof of it! [*Laughs.*]

Landolph [*coming forward in the name of the others,
exasperated*]. What proof?

Henry IV. Your being so dismayed because now I
seem again mad to you. You have thought me mad up to
now, haven't you? You feel that this dismay of yours can
become terror too—something to dash away the ground
from under your feet and deprive you of the air you
breathe! Do you know what it means to find yourselves
face to face with a madman—with one who shakes the
foundations of all you have built up in yourselves, your
logic, the logic of all your constructions? Madmen, lucky
folk! construct without logic, or rather with a logic that
flies like a feather. Voluble! Voluble! Today like this and
tomorrow—who knows? You say: "This cannot be"; but
for them everything can be. You say: "This isn't true!"
And why? Because it doesn't seem true to you, or you, or
you . . . [*Indicates the three of them in succession.*] . . .

and to a hundred thousand others! One must see what
seems true to these hundred thousand others who are not
supposed to be mad! What a magnificent spectacle they
afford, when they reason! What flowers of logic they scatter! I know that when I was a child, I thought the moon
in the pond was real. How many things I thought real!
I believed everything I was told—and I was happy! Because it's a terrible thing if you don't hold on to that
which seems true to you today—to that which will seem
true to you tomorrow, even if it is the opposite of that
which seemed true to you yesterday. I would never wish
you to think, as I have done, on this horrible thing which
really drives one mad: that if you were beside another
and looking into his eyes—as I one day looked into somebody's eyes—you might as well be a beggar before a door
never to be opened to you; for he who does enter there
will never be you, but someone unknown to you with his
own different and impenetrable world . . . [*Long pause.
Darkness gathers in the room, increasing the sense of
strangeness and consternation in which the four young
men are involved.* HENRY IV *remains aloof, pondering on
the misery which is not only his, but everybody's. Then
he pulls himself up, and says in an ordinary tone.*] It's
getting dark here . . .

Ordulph.   Shall I go for a lamp?

Henry IV [*ironically*].   The lamp, yes the lamp! . . .
Do you suppose I don't know that as soon as I turn my
back with my oil lamp to go to bed, you turn on the elec-
tric light for yourselves, here, and even there, in the
throne room? I pretend not to see it!

Ordulph.   Well, then, shall I turn it on now?

Henry IV.   No, it would blind me! I want my lamp!

Ordulph.   It's ready here behind the door. [*Goes to
the main exit, opens the door, goes out for a moment,
and returns with an ancient lamp which is held by a ring
at the top.*]

Henry IV. Ah, a little light! Sit there around the table, no, not like that; in an elegant, easy, manner! . . . [*To* HAROLD.] Yes, you, like that! [*Poses him.*] [*Then to* BERTHOLD.] You, so! . . . and I, here! [*Sits opposite them.*] We could do with a little decorative moonlight. It's very useful for us, the moonlight. I feel a real necessity for it, and pass a lot of time looking up at the moon from my window. Who would think, to look at her that she knows that eight hundred years have passed, and that I, seated at the window, cannot really be Henry IV gazing at the moon like any poor devil? But, look, look! See what a magnificent night scene we have here: the emperor surrounded by his faithful counsellors! . . . How do you like it?

Landolph [*softly to* HAROLD, *so as not to break the enchantment*]. And to think it wasn't true! . . .

Henry IV. True? What wasn't true?

Landolph [*timidly as if to excuse himself*]. No . . . I mean . . . I was saying this morning to him [*Indicates* BERTHOLD.]—he has just entered on service here—I was saying: what a pity that dressed like this and with so many beautiful costumes in the wardrobe . . . and with a room like that . . . [*Indicates the throne room.*]

Henry IV. Well? what's the pity?

Landolph. Well . . . that we didn't know . . .

Henry IV. That it was all done in jest, this comedy?

Landolph. Because we thought that . . .

Harold [*coming to his assistance*]. Yes . . . that it was done seriously!

Henry IV. What do you say? Doesn't it seem serious to you?

Landolph. But if you say that . . .

Henry IV. I say that—you are fools! You ought to have known how to create a fantasy for yourselves, not to act it for me, or anyone coming to see me; but naturally, simply, day by day, before nobody, feeling yourselves alive

in the history of the eleventh century, here at the court
of your emperor, Henry IV! You, Ordulph [*Taking him
by the arm.*], alive in the castle of Goslar, waking up in
the morning, getting out of bed, and entering straightway
into the dream, clothing yourself in the dream that would
be no more a dream, because you would have lived it,
felt it all alive in you. You would have drunk it in with
the air you breathed; yet knowing all the time that it was
a dream, so you could better enjoy the privilege afforded
you of having to do nothing else but live this dream, this
far off and yet actual dream! And to think that at a distance of eight centuries from this remote age of ours, so
colored and so sepulchral, the men of the twentieth
century are torturing themselves in ceaseless anxiety to
know how their fates and fortunes will work out!
Whereas you are already in history with me . . .

Landolph. Yes, yes, very good!

Henry IV. . . . Everything determined, everything
settled!

Ordulph. Yes, yes!

Henry IV. And sad as is my lot, hideous as some of the
events are, bitter the struggles and troublous the time—
still all history! All history that cannot change, understand? All fixed for ever! And you could have admired at
your ease how every effect followed obediently its cause
with perfect logic, how every event took place precisely
and coherently in each minute particular! The pleasure,
the pleasure of history, in fact, which is so great, was
yours.

Landolph. Beautiful, beautiful!

Henry IV. Beautiful, but it's finished! Now that you
know, I could not do it any more! [*Takes his lamp to go
to bed.*] Neither could you, if up to now you haven't
understood the reason of it! I am sick of it now. [*Almost
to himself with violent contained rage.*] By God, I'll make
her sorry she came here! Dressed herself up as a mother-

in-law for me . . . ! And he as an abbot . . . ! And they bring a doctor with them to study me . . . ! Who knows if they don't hope to cure me? . . . Clowns . . . ! I'd like to smack one of them at least in the face: yes, that one—a famous swordsman, they say! . . . He'll kill me . . . Well, we'll see, we'll see! . . . [*A knock at the door.*] Who is it?

The Voice of John.   Deo Gratias!

Harold [*very pleased at the chance for another joke*]. Oh, it's John, it's old John, who comes every night to play the monk.

Ordulph [*rubbing his hands*].   Yes, yes! Let's make him do it!

Henry IV [*at once, severely*].   Fool, why? Just to play a joke on a poor old man who does it for love of me?

Landolph [*to* ORDULPH].   It has to be as if it were true.

Henry IV.   Exactly, as if true! Because, only so, truth is not a jest [*Opens the door and admits* JOHN *dressed as a humble friar with a roll of parchment under his arm.*] Come in, come in, father! [*Then assuming a tone of tragic gravity and deep resentment.*] All the documents of my life and reign favorable to me were destroyed deliberately by my enemies. One only has escaped destruction, this, my life, written by a humble monk who is devoted to me. And you would laugh at him! [*Turns affectionately to* JOHN, *and invites him to sit down at the table.*] Sit down, father, sit down! Have the lamp near you! [*Puts the lamp near him.*] Write! Write!

John [*opens the parchment and prepares to write from dictation*].   I am ready, your Majesty!

Henry IV [*dictating*].   "The decree of peace proclaimed at Mayence helped the poor and the good, while it damaged the powerful and the bad. [*Curtain begins to fall.*] It brought wealth to the former, hunger and misery to the latter . . ."

Curtain.

ACT III

The throne room so dark that the wall at the bottom is hardly seen. The canvases of the two portraits have been taken away; and, within their frames, FRIDA, dressed as the "Marchioness of Tuscany" and CHARLES DI NOLLI, as "Henry IV," have taken the exact positions of the portraits.

For a moment, after the raising of curtain, the stage is empty. Then the door on the left opens; and HENRY IV, holding the lamp by the ring on top of it, enters. He looks back to speak to the four young men, who, with JOHN, are presumedly in the adjoining hall, as at the end of the second act.

Henry IV. No, stay where you are, stay where you are. I shall manage all right by myself. Good night! [*Closes the door and walks, very sad and tired, across the hall towards the second door on the right, which leads into his apartments.*]

Frida [*as soon as she sees that he has just passed the throne, whispers from the niche like one who is on the point of fainting away with fright*]. Henry . . .

Henry IV [*stopping at the voice, as if someone had stabbed him traitorously in the back, turns a terror-stricken face towards the wall at the bottom of the room; raising an arm instinctively, as if to defend himself and ward off a blow*]. Who is calling me? [*It is not a question, but an exclamation vibrating with terror, which does not expect a reply from the darkness and the terrible silence of the hall, which suddenly fills him with the suspicion that he is really mad.*]

Frida [*at his shudder of terror, is herself not less frightened at the part she is playing, and repeats a little more loudly*]. Henry! . . . [*But, although she wishes to act the part as they have given it to her, she stretches her head a little out of the frame towards the other frame.*]

Henry IV [*gives a dreadful cry; lets the lamp fall from his hands to cover his head with his arms, and makes a movement as if to run away*].

Frida [*jumping from the frame on to the stand and shouting like a mad woman*]. Henry! . . . Henry! . . . I'm afraid! . . . I'm terrified! . . .

[*And while* DI NOLLI *jumps in turn on to the stand and thence to the floor and runs to* FRIDA *who, on the verge of fainting, continues to cry out, the* DOCTOR, DONNA MATILDA, *also dressed as "Matilda of Tuscany,"* TITO BELCREDI, LANDOLPH, BERTHOLD *and* JOHN *enter the hall from the doors on the right and on the left. One of them turns on the light: a strange light coming from lamps hidden in the ceiling so that only the upper part of the stage is well lighted. The others without taking notice of* HENRY IV, *who looks on astonished by the unexpected inrush, after the moment of terror which still causes him to tremble, run anxiously to support and comfort the still shaking* FRIDA, *who is moaning in the arms of her fiancé. All are speaking at the same time.*]

Di Nolli. No, no, Frida . . . Here I am . . . I am beside you!

Doctor [*coming with the others*]. Enough! Enough! There's nothing more to be done! . . .

Donna Matilda. He is cured, Frida. Look! He is cured! Don't you see?

Di Nolli [*astonished*]. Cured?

Belcredi. It was only for fun! Be calm!

Frida. No! I am afraid! I am afraid!

Donna Matilda. Afraid of what? Look at him! He was never mad at all! . . .

Di Nolli. That isn't true! What are you saying? Cured?

Doctor.   It appears so. I should say so . . .

Belcredi.   Yes, yes! They have told us so. [*Pointing to the four young men.*]

Donna Matilda.   Yes, for a long time! He has confided in them, told them the truth!

Di Nolli [*now more indignant than astonished*].   But what does it mean? If, up to a short time ago . . . ?

Belcredi.   Hum! He was acting, to take you in and also us, who in good faith . . .

Di Nolli.   Is it possible? To deceive his sister, also, right up to the time of her death?

Henry IV [*remains apart, peering at one and now at the other under the accusation and the mockery of what all believe to be a cruel joke of his, which is now revealed. He has shown by the flashing of his eyes that he is meditating a revenge, which his violent contempt prevents him from defining clearly, as yet. Stung to the quick and with a clear idea of accepting the fiction they have insidiously worked up as true, he bursts forth at this point*].   Go on, I say! Go on!

Di Nolli [*astonished at the cry*].   Go on! What do you mean?

Henry IV.   It isn't *your* sister only that is dead!

Di Nolli.   My sister? Yours, I say, whom you compelled up to the last moment, to present herself here as your mother Agnes!

Henry IV.   And was she not *your* mother?

Di Nolli.   My mother? Certainly my mother!

Henry IV.   But your mother is dead for me, *old and far away!* You have just got down now from there. [*Pointing to the frame from which he jumped down.*] And how do you know whether I have not wept her long in secret, dressed even as I am?

Donna Matilda [*dismayed, looking at the others*]. What does he say? [*Much impressed, observing him.*] Quietly! quietly, for Heaven's sake!

Henry IV. What do I say? I ask all of you if Agnes was not the mother of Henry IV? [*Turns to* FRIDA *as if she were really the "Marchioness of Tuscany."*] You, Marchioness, it seems to me, ought to know.

Frida [*still frightened, draws closer to* DI NOLLI]. No, no, I don't know. Not I!

Doctor. It's the madness returning. . . . Quiet now, everybody!

Belcredi [*indignant*]. Madness indeed, Doctor! He's acting again! . . .

Henry IV [*suddenly*]. I? You have emptied those two frames over there, and he stands before my eyes as Henry IV . . .

Belcredi. We've had enough of this joke now.

Henry IV. Who said joke?

Doctor [*loudly to* BELCREDI]. Don't excite him, for the love of God!

Belcredi [*without lending an ear to him, but speaking louder*]. But they have said so [*Pointing again to the four young men.*], they, they!

Henry IV [*turning round and looking at them*]. You? Did you say it was all a joke?

Landolph [*timid and embarrassed*]. No . . . really we said that you were cured.

Belcredi. Look here! Enough of this! [*To* DONNA MATILDA.] Doesn't it seem to you that the sight of him, [*Pointing to* DI NOLLI.] Marchioness, and that of your daughter dressed so, is becoming an intolerable puerility?

Donna Matilda. Oh, be quiet! What does the dress matter, if he is cured?

Henry IV. Cured, yes! I am cured! [*To* BELCREDI.] ah, but not to let it end this way all at once, as you suppose! [*Attacks him.*] Do you know that for twenty years nobody has ever dared to appear before me here like you and that gentleman? [*Pointing to the* DOCTOR.]

Belcredi. Of course I know it. As a matter of fact, I too appeared before you this morning dressed . . .

Henry IV. As a monk, yes!

Belcredi. And you took me for Peter Damiani! And I didn't even laugh, believing, in fact, that . . .

Henry IV. That I was mad! Does it make you laugh seeing her like that, now that I am cured? And yet you might have remembered that in my eyes her appearance now . . . [*Interrupts himself with a gesture of contempt.*] Ah! [*Suddenly turns to the* DOCTOR.] You are a doctor, aren't you?

Doctor. Yes.

Henry IV. And you also took part in dressing her up as the Marchioness of Tuscany? To prepare a counter-joke for me here, eh?

Donna Matilda [*impetuously*]. No, no! What do you say? It was done for you! I did it for your sake.

Doctor [*quickly*]. To attempt, to try, not knowing . . .

Henry IV [*cutting him short*]. I understand. I say counter-joke, in his case [*Indicates* BELCREDI.] because he believes that I have been carrying on a jest . . .

Belcredi. But excuse me, what do you mean? You say yourself you are cured.

Henry IV. Let me speak! [*To the* DOCTOR.] Do you know, Doctor, that for a moment you ran the risk of making me mad again? By God, to make the portraits speak; to make them jump alive out of their frames . . .

Doctor. But you saw that all of us ran in at once, as soon as they told us . . .

Henry IV. Certainly! [*Contemplates* FRIDA *and* DI NOLLI, *and then looks at the* MARCHIONESS, *and finally at his own costume.*] The combination is very beautiful . . . Two couples . . . Very good, very good, Doctor! For a madman, not bad! . . . [*With a slight wave of his hand to* BELCREDI.] It seems to him now to be a carnival out of season, eh? [*Turns to look at him.*] We'll get rid now of this masquerade costume of mine, so that I may come away with you. What do you say?

Belcredi. With me? With us?

Henry IV. Where shall we go? To the Club? In dress coats and with white ties? Or shall both of us go to the Marchioness' house?

Belcredi. Wherever you like! Do you want to remain here still, to continue—alone—what was nothing but the unfortunate joke of a day of carnival? It is really incredible, incredible how you have been able to do all this, freed from the disaster that befell you!

Henry IV. Yes, you see how it was! The fact is that falling from my horse and striking my head as I did, I was really mad for I know not how long . . .

Doctor. Ah! Did it last long?

Henry IV [*very quickly to the* DOCTOR]. Yes, Doctor, a long time! I think it must have been about twelve years. [*Then suddenly turning to speak to* BELCREDI.] Thus I saw nothing, my dear fellow, of all that, after that day of carnival, happened for you but not for me: how things changed, how my friends deceived me, how my place was taken by another, and all the rest of it! And suppose my place had been taken in the heart of the woman I loved? . . . And how should I know who was dead or who had disappeared? . . . All this, you know, wasn't exactly a jest for me, as it seems to you . . .

Belcredi. No, no! I don't mean that if you please. I mean after . . .

Henry IV. Ah, yes? After? One day [*Stops and addresses the* DOCTOR.]—A most interesting case, Doctor! Study me well! Study me carefully! [*Trembles while speaking.*] All by itself, who knows how, one day the trouble here [*Touches his forehead.*] mended. Little by little, I open my eyes, and at first I don't know whether I am

asleep or awake. Then I know I am awake. I touch this
thing and that; I see clearly again . . . Ah!—then, as *he*
says [*Alludes to* BELCREDI.] away, away with this masquerade, this incubus! Let's open the windows, breathe life
once again! Away! Away! Let's run out! [*Suddenly pulling himself up.*] But where? And to do what? To show
myself to all, secretly, as Henry IV, not like this, but arm
in arm with you, among my dear friends?

Belcredi. What are you saying?

Donna Matilda. Who could think it? It's not to be
imagined. It was an accident.

Henry IV. They all said I was mad before. [*To* BEL-
CREDI.] And you know it! You were more ferocious than
any one against those who tried to defend me.

Belcredi. Oh, that was only a joke!

Henry IV. Look at my hair! [*Shows him the hair on
the nape of his neck.*]

Belcredi. But mine is grey too!

Henry IV. Yes, with this difference: that mine went
grey here, as Henry IV, do you understand? And I never
knew it! I perceived it all of a sudden, one day, when I
opened my eyes; and I was terrified because I understood
at once that not only had my hair gone grey, but that I
was all grey, inside; that everything had fallen to pieces,
that everything was finished; an I was going to arrive,
hungry as a wolf, at a banquet which had already been
cleared away . . .

Belcredi. Yes, but, what about the others? . . .

Henry IV [*quickly*]. Ah, yes, I know! They couldn't
wait until I was cured, not even those, who, behind my
back, pricked my saddled horse till it bled. . . .

Di Nolli [*agitated*]. What, what?

Henry IV. Yes, treacherously, to make it rear and
cause me to fall.

Donna Matilda [*quickly, in horror*]. This is the first
time I knew that.

Henry IV. That was also a joke, probably!

Donna Matilda. But who did it? Who was behind us, then?

Henry IV. It doesn't matter who it was. All those that went on feasting and were ready to leave me their scrapings, Marchioness, of miserable pity, or some dirty remnant of remorse in the filthy plate! Thanks! [*Turning quickly to the* DOCTOR.] Now, Doctor, the case must be absolutely new in the history of madness; I preferred to remain mad—since I found everything ready and at my disposal for this new exquisite fantasy. I would live it— this madness of mine—with the most lucid consciousness; and thus revenge myself on the brutality of a stone which had dinted by head. The solitude—this solitude—squalid and empty as it appeared to me when I opened my eyes again— I determined to deck it out with all the colors and splendors of that far off day of carnival, when you [*Looks at* DONNA MATILDA *and points* FRIDA *out to her.*] —when you, Marchioness, triumphed. So I would oblige all those who were around me to follow, by God, at my orders that famous pageant which had been—for you and not for me—the jest of a day. I would make it become— for ever—no more a joke but a reality, the reality of a real madness: here, all in masquerade, with throne room, and these my four secret counsellors: secret and, of course, traitors. [*He turns quickly towards them.*] I should like to know what you have gained by revealing the fact that I was cured! If I am cured, there's no longer any need of you, and you will be discharged! To give anyone one's confidence . . . that is really the act of a madman. But now I accuse you in my turn. [*Turning to the others.*] Do you know? They thought [*Alludes to the* VALETS.] they could make fun of me too with you. [*Bursts out laughing. The others laugh, but shamefacedly, except* DONNA MATILDA.]

Belcredi [*to* DI NOLLI]. Well, imagine that . . . That's not bad . . .

Di Nolli [*to the* FOUR YOUNG MEN]. You?

Henry IV. We must pardon them. This dress [*Plucking his dress.*] which is for me the evident, involuntary caricature of that other continuous, everlasting masquerade, of which we are the involuntary puppets [*Indicates* BELCREDI.], when, without knowing it, we mask ourselves with that which we appear to be . . . ah, that dress of theirs, this masquerade of theirs, of course, we must forgive it them, since they do not yet see it is identical with themselves . . . [*Turning again to* BELCREDI.] You know, it is quite easy to get accustomed to it. One walks about as a tragic character, just as if it were nothing . . . [*Imitates the tragic manner.*] in a room like this . . . Look here, doctor! I remember a priest, certainly Irish, a nice-looking priest, who was sleeping in the sun one November day, with his arm on the corner of the bench of a public garden. He was lost in the golden delight of the mild sunny air which must have seemed for him almost summery. One may be sure that in that moment he did not know any more that he was a priest, or even where he was. He was dreaming . . . A little boy passed with a flower in his hand. He touched the priest with it here on the neck. I saw him open his laughing eyes, while all his mouth smiled with the beauty of his dream. He was forgetful of everything . . . But all at once, he pulled himself together, and stretched out his priest's cassock; and there came back to his eyes the same seriousness which you have seen in mine; because the Irish priests defend the seriousness of their Catholic faith with the same zeal with which I defend the sacred rights of hereditary monarchy! I am cured, gentlemen: because I can act the madman to perfection, here; and I do it very quietly, I'm only sorry for you that have to live your madness so agitatedly, without knowing it or seeing it.

Belcredi. It comes to this, then, that it is we who are mad. That's what it is!

Henry IV [*containing his irritation*]. But if you weren't mad, both you and she [*Indicating the* MARCHIONESS.] would you have come here to see me?

Belcredi. To tell the truth, I came here believing that you were the madman.

Henry IV [*suddenly indicating the* MARCHIONESS]. And she?

Belcredi. Ah, as for her . . . I can't say. I see she is all fascinated by your words, by this *conscious* madness of yours. [*Turns to her.*] Dressed as you are [*Speaking to her.*], you could even remain here to live it out, Marchioness.

Donna Matilda. You are insolent!

Henry IV [*conciliatingly*]. No, Marchioness, what he means to say is that the miracle would be complete, according to him, with you here, who—as the Marchioness of Tuscany, you well know,—could not be my friend, save, as at Canossa, to give me a little pity . . .

Belcredi. Or even more than a little! She said so herself!

Henry IV [*to the* MARCHIONESS, *continuing*]. And even, shall we say, a little remorse! . . .

Belcredi. Yes, that too she has admitted.

Donna Matilda [*angry*]. Now look here . . .

Henry IV [*quickly, to placate her*]. Don't bother about him! Don't mind him! Let him go on infuriating me—though the Doctor's told him not to. [*Turns to* BELCREDI.] But do you suppose I am going to trouble myself any more about what happened between us—the share you had in my misfortune with her [*Indicates the* MARCHIONESS *to him and pointing* BELCREDI *out to her.*] the part he has now in your life? This is my life! Quite a different thing from your life! Your life, the life in which

you have grown old—I have not lived that life. [*To*
DONNA MATILDA.] Was this what you wanted to show me
with this sacrifice of yours, dressing yourself up like this,
according to the Doctor's idea? Excellently done, Doctor!
Oh, an excellent idea:—"As we were then, eh? and as we
are now?" But I am not a madman according to your way
of thinking, Doctor. I know very well that that man
there [*Indicates* DI NOLLI.] cannot be me; because I
am Henry IV, and have been, these twenty years, cast in
this eternal masquerade. She has lived these years! [*Indicates the* MARCHIONESS.] She has enjoyed them and has
become—look at her!—a woman I can no longer recognize. It is so that I knew her! [*Points to* FRIDA *and draws
near her.*] This is the Marchioness I know, always this
one! . . . You seem a lot of children to be so easily
frightened by me . . . [*To* FRIDA.] And you're frightened
too, little girl, aren't you, by the jest that they made you
take part in—though they didn't understand it wouldn't
be the jest they meant it to be, for me? Oh miracle of
miracles! Prodigy of prodigies! The dream alive in you!
More than alive in you! It was an image that wavered
there and they've made you come to life! Oh, mine!
You're mine, mine, mine, in my own right! [HE *holds her
in his arms, laughing like a madman, while all stand still
terrified. Then as they advance to tear* FRIDA *from his
arms, he becomes furious, terrible and cries imperiously
to his* VALETS.] Hold them! Hold them! I order you to
hold them!

   [*The* FOUR YOUNG MEN *amazed, yet fascinated, move to
     execute his orders, automatically, and seize* DI NOLLI,
     the DOCTOR, *and* BELCREDI.]

   Belcredi [*freeing himself*]. Leave her alone! Leave her
alone! You're no madman!

   Henry IV [*in a flash draws the sword from the side of*
LANDOLPH, *who is close to him*]. I'm not mad, eh! Take
that, you! . . . [*Drives sword into him. A cry of horror*

goes up. All rush over to assist BELCREDI, *crying out together.*]

Di Nolli.   Has he wounded you?

Berthold.   Yes, yes, seriously!

Doctor.   I told you so!

Frida.   Oh God, oh God!

Di Nolli.   Frida, come here!

Donna Matilda.   He's mad, mad!

Di Nolli.   Hold him!

Belcredi [*while* THEY *take him away by the left exit,* HE *protests as he is borne out*].   No, no, you're not mad! You're not mad. He's not mad!

[THEY *go out by the left amid cries and excitement. After a moment, one hears a still sharper, more piercing cry from* DONNA MATILDA, *and then, silence.*]

Henry IV [*who has remained on the stage between* LANDOLPH, HAROLD *and* ORDULPH, *with his eyes almost starting out of his head, terrified by the life of his own masquerade which has driven him to crime.*]   Now, yes . . . . we'll have to [*Calls his* VALETS *around him as if to protect him.*] here we are . . . together . . . for ever!

Curtain.

PREMISE

(To *Six Characters in Search of an Author, Each in His Own Way,* and *Tonight We Improvise*)

EACH of the three works collected in this first volume of my plays presents characters, events, and passions peculiar to it and having nothing to do with those of the other two; but the three together, however different, form something of a trilogy of the theatre in the theatre, not only because there is action both on the stage and in the auditorium, in a box and in the corridors and in the foyer of a theatre, but also because the whole complex of theatrical elements, characters and actors, author and actor-manager or director, dramatic critics and spectators (external or involved) present every possible conflict.

The difference between the three works, beyond being a difference of plot, stems from the mode and quality of these conflicts between the theatrical elements. In the first the conflict is between the Characters and the Actors and the Actor-Manager; in the second, between the Spectators and the Author and the Actors; in the third, between the Actors become Characters and their Director. Where the comedy is "in the making" as in the first, to be improvised as in the third, the conflict (not the same nor even similar, but rather exactly opposite) prevents the play from being created and the improvisation from being regulated and controlled, from proceeding logically to a conclusion; where the comedy is already created, as in the second, the conflict sends the presentation—the performance—up in smoke. But what was to be presented was precisely this different conflict in each of the three works, and just for that reason, if they remain incomplete or interrupted in their pretexts or plots, they are in themselves complete and finished and can go together to form, as has just been said, a trilogy of the theatre in the theatre.

It goes without saying that one is speaking here of the artistic structure of the three works and of the reason why they are collected in a group. As to whatever else each may contain within itself, this is not the place or the occasion to speak of it—nor is it for me to do so.

L.P., 1933
(translated E.B., 1950)

NOTE: Technical limitations of space prevent the inclusion of *Tonight We Improvise*, the third play of this trilogy; it is, however, available in a separate volume.

SIX CHARACTERS IN SEARCH OF AN AUTHOR

(Sei personaggi in cerca d'autore)

A COMEDY IN THE MAKING

English version by
EDWARD STORER

CHARACTERS OF THE COMEDY IN THE MAKING

THE FATHER
THE MOTHER
THE STEP-DAUGHTER
THE SON

THE BOY
THE CHILD
(*The last two do not speak*)
MADAME PACE

ACTORS OF THE COMPANY

THE MANAGER
LEADING LADY
LEADING MAN
SECOND LADY
LEAD
L'INGÉNUE
JUVENILE LEAD

OTHER ACTORS AND ACTRESSES
PROPERTY MAN
PROMPTER
MACHINIST
MANAGER'S SECRETARY
DOOR-KEEPER
SCENE-SHIFTERS

Daytime. The Stage of a Theatre

N. B. *The Comedy is without acts or scenes. The performance is interrupted once, without the curtain being lowered, when the manager and the chief characters withdraw to arrange the scenario. A second interruption of the action takes place when, by mistake, the stage hands let the curtain down.*

ACT I

The spectators will find the curtain raised and the stage as it usually is during the day time. It will be half dark, and empty, so that from the beginning the public

211

may have the impression of an impromptu performance.

Prompter's box and a small table and chair for the manager.

Two other small tables and several chairs scattered about as during rehearsals.

The ACTORS *and* ACTRESSES *of the company enter from the back of the stage:*
first one, then another, then two together; nine or ten in all. They are about to rehearse a Pirandello play: Mixing It Up. *Some of the company move off towards their dressing rooms. The* PROMPTER *who has the "book" under his arm, is waiting for the manager in order to begin the rehearsal.*

The ACTORS *and* ACTRESSES, *some standing, some sitting, chat and smoke. One perhaps reads a paper; another cons his part.*

Finally, the MANAGER *enters and goes to the table prepared for him. His* SECRETARY *brings him his mail, through which he glances. The* PROMPTER *takes his seat, turns on a light, and opens the "book."*

The Manager [*throwing a letter down on the table*]. I can't see [*To* PROPERTY MAN.] Let's have a little light, please!

Property Man. Yes sir, yes, at once. [*A light comes down on to the stage.*]

The Manager [*clapping his hands*]. Come along! Come along! Second act of "Mixing It Up." [*Sits down.*]

[*The* ACTORS *and* ACTRESSES *go from the front of the stage to the wings, all except the three who are to begin the rehearsal.*]

The Prompter [*reading the "book"*]. "Leo Gala's house. A curious room serving as dining-room and study."

The Manager [*to* PROPERTY MAN]. Fix up the old red room.

* i.e. *Il giuoco delle parti.*

Property Man [*noting it down*]. Red set. All right!

The Prompter [*continuing to read from the "book"*]. "Table already laid and writing desk with books and papers. Book-shelves. Exit rear to Leo's bedroom. Exit left to kitchen. Principal exit to right."

The Manager [*energetically*]. Well, you understand: The principal exit over there; here, the kitchen. [*Turning to actor who is to play the part of* SOCRATES.] You make your entrances and exits here. [*To* PROPERTY MAN.] The baize doors at the rear, and curtains.

Property Man [*noting it down*]. Right!

Prompter [*reading as before*]. "When the curtain rises, Leo Gala, dressed in cook's cap and apron is busy beating an egg in a cup. Philip, also dresesd as a cook, is beating another egg. Guido Venanzi is seated and listening."

Leading Man [*To* MANAGER]. Excuse me, but must I absolutely wear a cook's cap?

The Manager [*annoyed*]. I imagine so. It says so there anyway. [*Pointing to the "book."*]

Leading Man. But it's ridiculous!

The Manager [*jumping up in a rage*]. Ridiculous? Ridiculous? Is it my fault if France won't send us any more good comedies, and we are reduced to putting on Pirandello's works, where nobody understands anything, and where the author plays the fool with us all? [*The* ACTORS *grin. The* MANAGER *goes to* LEADING MAN *and shouts.*] Yes sir, you put on the cook's cap and beat eggs. Do you suppose that with all this egg-beating business you are on an ordinary stage? Get that out of your head. You represent the shell of the eggs you are beating! [*Laughter and comments among the* ACTORS.] Silence! and listen to my explanations, please! [*To* LEADING MAN.] "The empty form of reason without the fullness of instinct, which is blind."—You stand for reason, your wife is instinct. It's a mixing up of the parts, according to which

you who act your own part become the puppet of yourself. Do you understand?

Leading Man. I'm hanged if I do.

The Manager. Neither do I. But let's get on with it.
It's sure to be a glorious failure anyway. [*Confidentially.*]
But I say, please face three-quarters. Otherwise, what with
the abstruseness of the dialogue, and the public that won't
be able to hear you, the whole thing will go to hell. Come
on! come on!

Prompter. Pardon sir, may I get into my box? There's
a bit of a draught.

The Manager. Yes, yes, of course!

At this point, the DOOR-KEEPER *has entered from the
stage door and advances towards the manager's table, taking off his braided cap. During this manoeuvre, the* SIX
CHARACTERS *enter, and stop by the door at back of stage,
so that when the* DOOR-KEEPER *is about to announce their
coming to the* MANAGER, *they are already on the stage. A
tenuous light surrounds them, almost as if irradiated by
them—the faint breath of their fantastic reality.*

*This light will disappear when they come forward to-
wards the actors. They preserve, however, something of
the dream lightness in which they seem almost suspended;
but this does not detract from the essential reality of their
forms and expressions.*

He who is known as THE FATHER *is a man of about 50:
hair, reddish in colour, thin at the temples; he is not bald,
however; thick moustaches, falling over his still fresh
mouth, which often opens in an empty and uncertain
smile. He is fattish, pale; with an especially wide forehead. He has blue, oval-shaped eyes, very clear and
piercing. Wears light trousers and a dark jacket. He is
alternatively mellifluous and violent in his manner.*

THE MOTHER *seems crushed and terrified as if by an intolerable weight of shame and abasement. She is dressed*

in modest black and wears a thick widow's veil of crêpe. When she lifts this, she reveals a wax-like face. She always keeps her eyes downcast.

THE STEP-DAUGHTER, *is dashing, almost impudent, beautiful. She wears mourning too, but with great elegance. She shows contempt for the timid half-frightened manner of the wretched* BOY *(14 years old, and also dressed in black); on the other hand, she displays a lively tenderness for her little sister,* THE CHILD *(about four), who is dressed in white, with a black silk sash at the waist.*

THE SON *(22) tall, severe in his attitude of contempt for* THE FATHER, *supercilious and indifferent to* THE MOTHER. *He looks as if he had come on the stage against his will.*

Door-keeper [*cap in hand*].   Excuse me, sir . . .

The Manager [*rudely*].   Eh? What is it?

Door-keeper [*timidly*].   These people are asking for you, sir.

The Manager [*furious*].   I am rehearsing, and you know perfectly well no one's allowed to come in during rehearsals! [*Turning to the* CHARACTERS.] Who are you, please? What do you want?

The Father [*coming forward a little, followed by the others who seem embarrassed*].   As a matter of fact . . . we have come here in search of an author . . .

The Manager [*half angry, half amazed*].   An author? What author?

The Father.   Any author, sir.

The Manager.   But there's no author here. We are not rehearsing a new piece.

The Step-Daughter [*vivaciously*].   So much the better, so much the better! We can be your new piece.

An Actor [*coming forward from the others*].   Oh, do you hear that?

The Father [to STEP-DAUGHTER]. Yes, but if the author isn't here . . . [*To* MANAGER.] unless you would be willing . . .

The Manager. You are trying to be funny.

The Father. No, for Heaven's sake, what are you saying? We bring you a drama, sir.

The Step-Daughter. We may be your fortune.

The Manager. Will you oblige me by going away? We haven't time to waste with mad people.

The Father [*mellifluously*]. Oh sir, you know well that life is full of infinite absurdities, which, strangely enough, do not even need to appear plausible, since they are true.

The Manager. What the devil is he talking about?

The Father. I say that to reverse the ordinary process may well be considered a madness: that is, to create credible situations, in order that they may appear true. But permit me to observe that if this be madness, it is the sole *raison d'être* of your profession, gentlemen. [*The* ACTORS *look hurt and perplexed.*]

The Manager [*getting up and looking at him*]. So our profession seems to you one worthy of madmen then?

The Father. Well, to make seem true that which isn't true . . . without any need . . . for a joke as it were . . . Isn't that your mission, gentlemen: to give life to fantastic characters on the stage?

The Manager [*interpreting the rising anger of the* COMPANY]. But I would beg you to believe, my dear sir, that the profession of the comedian is a noble one. If today, as things go, the playwrights give us stupid comedies to play and puppets to represent instead of men, remember we are proud to have given life to immortal works here on these very boards! [*The* ACTORS, *satisfied, applaud their* MANAGER.]

The Father [*interrupting furiously*]. Exactly, perfectly, to living beings more alive than those who breathe and wear clothes: beings less real perhaps, but truer! I agree with you entirely. [*The* ACTORS *look at one another in amazement.*]

The Manager. But what do you mean? Before, you said . . .

The Father. No, excuse me, I meant it for you, sir, who were crying out that you had no time to lose with madmen, while no one better than yourself knows that nature uses the instrument of human fantasy in order to pursue her high creative purpose.

The Manager. Very well,—but where does all this take us?

The Father. Nowhere! It is merely to show you that one is born to life in many forms, in many shapes, as tree, or as stone, as water, as butterfly, or as woman. So one may also be born a character in a play.

The Manager [*with feigned comic dismay*]. So you and these other friends of yours have been born characters?

The Father. Exactly, and alive as you see! [MANAGER *and* ACTORS *burst out laughing.*]

The Father [*hurt*]. I am sorry you laugh, because we carry in us a drama, as you can guess from this woman here veiled in black.

The Manager [*losing patience at last and almost indignant*]. Oh, chuck it! Get away please! Clear out of here! [*To* PROPERTY MAN.] For Heaven's sake, turn them out!

The Father [*resisting*]. No, no, look here, we . . .

The Manager [*roaring*]. We come here to work, you know.

Leading Actor. One cannot let oneself be made such a fool of.

The Father [*determined, coming forward*]. I marvel at your incredulity, gentlemen. Are you not accustomed to see the characters created by an author spring to life in yourselves and face each other? Just because there is no "book" [*Pointing to the* PROMPTER'S *box.*] which contains us, you refuse to believe . . .

The Step-Daughter [*advances towards* MANAGER, *smiling and coquettish*]. Believe me, we are really six most interesting characters, sir; side-tracked however.

The Father. Yes, that is the word! [*To* MANAGER *all at once.*] In the sense, that is, that the author who created us alive no longer wished, or was no longer able, materially to put us into a work of art. And this was a real crime, sir; because he who has had the luck to be born a character can laugh even at death. He cannot die. The man, the writer, the instrument of the creation will die, but his creation does not die. And to live for ever, it does not need to have extraordinary gifts or to be able to work wonders. Who was Sancho Panza? Who was Don Abbondio? Yet they live eternally because—live germs as they were—they had the fortune to find a fecundating matrix, a fantasy which could raise and nourish them: make them live for ever!

The Manager. That is quite all right. But what do you want here, all of you?

The Father. We want to live.

The Manager [*ironically*]. For Eternity?

The Father. No, sir, only for a moment . . . in you.

An Actor. Just listen to him!

Leading Lady. They want to live, in us . . . !

Juvenile Lead [*pointing to the* STEP-DAUGHTER]. I've no objection, as far as that one is concerned!

The Father. Look here! look here! The comedy has to be made. [*To the* MANAGER.] But if you and your actors are willing, we can soon concert it among ourselves.

The Manager [*annoyed*]. But what do you want to concert? We don't go in for concerts here. Here we play dramas and comedies!

The Father. Exactly! That is just why we have come to you.

The Manager. And where is the "book"?

The Father. It is in us! [*The* ACTORS *laugh.*] The drama is in us, and we are the drama. We are impatient to play it. Our inner passion drives us on to this.

The Step-Daughter [*disdainful, alluring, treacherous, full of impudence*]. My passion, sir! Ah, if you only knew! My passion for him! [*Points to the* FATHER *and makes a pretence of embracing him. Then she breaks out into a loud laugh.*]

The Father [*angrily*]. Behave yourself! And please don't laugh in that fashion.

The Step-Daughter. With your permission, gentlemen, I, who am a two months' orphan, will show you how I can dance and sing. [*Sings and then dances* Prenez garde à Tchou-Tchin-Tchou.]

> Les chinois sont un peuple malin,
> De Shangaî à Pekin,
> Ils ont mis des écriteaux partout:
> Prenez garde à Tchou-Tchin-Tchou.

Actors and Actresses. Bravo! Well done! Tip-top!

The Manager. Silence! This isn't a café concert, you know! [*Turning to the* FATHER *in consternation.*] Is she mad?

The Father. Mad? No, she's worse than mad.

The Step-Daughter [*to* MANAGER]. Worse? Worse? Listen! Stage this drama for us at once! Then you will see that at a certain moment I . . . when this little darling here . . . [*Takes the* CHILD *by the hand and leads her to the* MANAGER.] Isn't she a dear? [*Takes her up and kisses her.*] Darling! Darling! [*Puts her down again and adds feelingly.*] Well, when God suddenly takes this dear little child away from that poor mother there; and this imbecile here [*Seizing hold of the* Boy *roughly and pushing him forward.*] does the stupidest things, like the fool he is, you will see me run away. Yes, gentlemen, I shall be off. But the moment hasn't arrived yet. After what has taken place between him and me [*indicates the* FATHER *with a horrible wink.*] I can't remain any longer in this society, to have to witness the anguish of this mother here for that fool . . . [*Indicates the* SON.] Look at him! Look at him! See how indifferent, how frigid he is, because he is the legitimate son. He despises me, despises him [*Pointing to the* Boy.], despises this baby here; because . . . we are bastards. [*Goes to the* MOTHER *and embraces her.*] And he doesn't want to recognize her as his mother —she who is the common mother of us all. He looks down upon her as if she were only the mother of us three bastards. Wretch! [*She says all this very rapidly, excitedly. At the word "bastards" she raises her voice, and almost spits out the final "Wretch!"*]

The Mother [*to the* MANAGER, *in anguish*]. In the name of these two little children, I beg you . . . [*She grows faint and is about to fall.*] Oh God!

The Father [*coming forward to support her as do some of the* ACTORS]. Quick, a chair, a chair for this poor widow!

The Actors. Is it true? Has she really fainted?

The Manager. Quick, a chair! Here!

[*One of the* ACTORS *brings a chair, the* OTHERS *proffer assistance. The* MOTHER *tries to prevent the* FATHER *from lifting the veil which covers her face.*]

The Father. Look at her! Look at her!

The Mother. No, no; stop it please!

The Father [*raising her veil*]. Let them see you!

The Mother [*rising and covering her face with her hands, in desperation*]. I beg you, sir, to prevent this man from carrying out his plan which is loathsome to me.

The Manager [*dumbfounded*]. I don't understand at all. What is the situation? Is this lady your wife? [*To the* FATHER.]

The Father. Yes, gentlemen: my wife!

The Manager. But how can she be a widow if you are alive? [*The* ACTORS *find relief for their astonishment in a loud laugh.*]

The Father. Don't laugh! Don't laugh like that, for Heaven's sake. Her drama lies just here in this: she has had a lover, a man who ought to be here.

The Mother [*with a cry*]. No! No!

The Step-Daughter. Fortunately for her, he is dead. Two months ago as I said. We are in mourning, as you see.

The Father. He isn't here you see, not because he is dead. He isn't here—look at her a moment and you will understand—because her drama isn't a drama of the love of two men for whom she was incapable of feeling anything except possibly a little gratitude—gratitude not for me but for the other. She isn't a woman, she is a mother, and her drama—powerful sir, I assure you—lies, as a matter of fact, all in these four children she has had by two men.

The Mother. I had them? Have you got the courage to say that I wanted them? [*To the* COMPANY.] It was his doing. It was he who gave me that other man, who forced me to go away with him.

The Step-Daughter. It isn't true.

The Mother [*startled*]. Not true, isn't it?

The Step-Daughter. No, it isn't true, it just isn't true.

The Mother. And what can you know about it?

The Step-Daughter. It isn't true. Don't believe it. [*To* MANAGER.] Do you know why she says so? For that fellow there. [*Indicates the* SON.] She tortures herself, destroys herself on account of the neglect of that son there; and she wants him to believe that if she abandoned him when he was only two years old, it was because he [*Indicates the* FATHER.] made her do so.

The Mother [*vigorously*].   He forced me to it, and I call God to witness it. [*To the* MANAGER.] Ask him [*Indicates* HUSBAND.] if it isn't true. Let him speak. You [*To* DAUGHTER.] are not in a position to know anything about it.

The Step-Daughter.   I know you lived in peace and happiness with my father while he lived. Can you deny it?

The Mother.   No, I don't deny it . . .

The Step-Daughter.   He was always full of affection and kindness for you. [*To the* BOY, *angrily*.] It's true, isn't it? Tell them! Why don't you speak, you little fool?

The Mother.   Leave the poor boy alone. Why do you want to make me appear ungrateful, daughter? I don't want to offend your father. I have answered him that I didn't abandon my house and my son through any fault of mine, nor from any wilful passion.

The Father.   It is true. It was my doing.

Leading Man [*to the* COMPANY].   What a spectacle!

Leading Lady.   We are the audience this time.

Juvenile Lead.   For once, in a way.

The Manager [*beginning to get really interested*]. Let's hear them out. Listen!

The Son.   Oh yes, you're going to hear a fine bit now. He will talk to you of the Demon of Experiment.

The Father.   You are a cynical imbecile. I've told you so already a hundred times. [*To the* MANAGER.] He tries to make fun of me on account of this expression which I have found to excuse myself with.

The Son [*with disgust*].   Yes, phrases! phrases!

The Father.   Phrases! Isn't everyone consoled when faced with a trouble or fact he doesn't understand, by a word, some simple word, which tells us nothing and yet calms us?

The Step-Daughter. Even in the case of remorse. In fact, especially then.

The Father. Remorse? No, that isn't true. I've done more than use words to quieten the remorse in me.

The Step-Daughter. Yes, there was a bit of money too. Yes, yes, a bit of money. There were the hundred lire he was about to offer me in payment, gentlemen . . . [*Sensation of horror among the* ACTORS.]

The Son [*to the* STEP-DAUGHTER]. This is vile.

The Step-Daughter. Vile? There they were in a pale blue envelope on a little mahogany table in the back of Madame Pace's shop. You know Madame Pace—one of those ladies who attract poor girls of good family into their ateliers, under the pretext of their selling *robes et manteaux.*

The Son. And he thinks he has bought the right to tyrannize over us all with those hundred lire he was going to pay; but which, fortunately—note this, gentlemen— he had no chance of paying.

The Step-Daughter. It was a near thing, though, you know! [*Laughs ironically.*]

The Mother [*protesting*]. Shame, my daughter, shame!

The Step-Daughter. Shame indeed! This is my revenge! I am dying to live that scene . . . The room . . . I see it . . . Here is the window with the mantles exposed, there the divan, the looking-glass, a screen, there in front of the window the little mahogany table with the blue envelope containing one hundred lire. I see it. I see it. I could take hold of it . . . But you, gentlemen, you ought to turn your backs now: I am almost nude, you know. But I don't blush: I leave that to him. [*Indicating* FATHER.]

The Manager. I don't understand this at all.

The Father. Naturally enough. I would ask you, sir, to exercise your authority a little here, and let me speak

before you believe all she is trying to blame me with.
Let me explain.

The Step-Daughter. Ah yes, explain it in your own
way.

The Father. But don't you see that the whole trouble
lies here. In words, words. Each one of us has within him
a whole world of things, each man of us his own special
world. And how can we ever come to an understanding if
I put in the words I utter the sense and value of things as
I see them; while you who listen to me must inevitably
translate them according to the conception of things each
one of you has within himself. We think we understand
each other, but we never really do. Look here! This
woman [*Indicating the* MOTHER.] takes all my pity for her
as a specially ferocious form of cruelty.

The Mother. But you drove me away.

The Father. Do you hear her? I drove her away! She
believes I really sent her away.

The Mother. You know how to talk, and I don't;
but, believe me, sir [*To* MANAGER.], after he had married
me . . . who knows why? . . . I was a poor insignificant
woman . . .

The Father. But, good Heavens! it was just for your
humility that I married you. I loved this simplicity in you.
[*He stops when he sees she makes signs to contradict him,
opens his arms wide in sign of desperation, seeing how
hopeless it is to make himself understood.*] You see she
denies it. Her mental deafness, believe me, is phenome-
nal, the limit: [*Touches his forehead.*] deaf, deaf, men-
tally deaf! She has plenty of feeling. Oh yes, a good heart
for the children; but the brain—deaf, to the point of
desperation——!

The Step-Daughter. Yes, but ask him how his intelligence has helped us.

The Father. If we could see all the evil that may
spring from good, what should we do? [*At this point the*

LEADING LADY *who is biting her lips with rage at seeing the* LEADING MAN *flirting with the* STEP-DAUGHTER, *comes forward and says to the* MANAGER.]

Leading Lady. Excuse me, but are we going to rehearse today?

Manager. Of course, of course; but let's hear them out.

Juvenile Lead. This is something quite new.

L'Ingénue. Most interesting!

Leading Lady. Yes, for the people who like that kind of thing. [*Casts a glance at* LEADING MAN.]

The Manager [*to* FATHER]. You must please explain yourself quite clearly. [*Sits down.*]

The Father. Very well then: listen! I had in my service a poor man, a clerk, a secretary of mine, full of devotion, who became friends with her. [*Indicating the* MOTHER.] They understood one another, were kindred souls in fact, without, however, the least suspicion of any evil existing. They were incapable even of thinking of it.

The Step-Daughter. So he thought of it—for them!

The Father. That's not true. I meant to do good to them—and to myself, I confess, at the same time. Things had come to the point that I could not say a word to either of them without their making a mute appeal, one to the other, with their eyes. I could see them silently asking each other how I was to be kept in countenance, how I was to be kept quiet. And this, believe me, was just about enough of itself to keep me in a constant rage, to exasperate me beyond measure.

The Manager. And why didn't you send him away then—this secretary of yours?

The Father. Precisely what I did, sir. And then I had to watch this poor woman drifting forlornly about the house like an animal without a master, like an animal one has taken in out of pity.

The Mother.   Ah yes . . . !

The Father [*suddenly turning to the* MOTHER]. It's true about the son anyway, isn't it?

The Mother.   He took my son away from me first of all.

The Father.   But not from cruelty. I did it so that he should grow up healthy and strong by living in the country.

The Step-Daughter [*pointing to him ironically*]. As one can see.

The Father [*quickly*]. Is it my fault if he has grown up like this? I sent him to a wet nurse in the country, a peasant, as *she* did not seem to me strong enough, though she is of humble origin. That was, anyway, the reason I married her. Unpleasant all this may be, but how can it be helped? My mistake possibly, but there we are! All my life I have had these confounded aspirations towards a certain moral sanity. [*At this point the* STEP-DAUGHTER *bursts into a noisy laugh.*] Oh, stop it! Stop it! I can't stand it.

The Manager.   Yes, please stop it, for Heaven's sake.

The Step-Daughter.   But imagine moral sanity from him, if you please—the client of certain ateliers like that of Madame Pace!

The Father.   Fool! That is the proof that I am a man! This seeming contradiction, gentlemen, is the strongest proof that I stand here a live man before you. Why, it is just for this very incongruity in my nature that I have had to suffer what I have. I could not live by the side of that woman [*Indicating the* MOTHER.] any longer; but not so much for the boredom she inspired me with as for the pity I felt for her.

The Mother.   And so he turned me out—.

The Father.   —well provided for! Yes, I sent her to that man, gentlemen . . . to let her go free of me.

The Mother. And to free himself.

The Father. Yes, I admit it. It was also a liberation for me. But great evil has come of it. I meant well when I did it; and I did it more for her sake than mine. I swear it. [*Crosses his arms on his chest; then turns suddenly to the* MOTHER.] Did I ever lose sight of you until that other man carried you off to another town, like the angry fool he was? And on account of my pure interest in you . . . my pure interest, I repeat, that had no base motive in it . . . I watched with the tenderest concern the new family that grew up around her. She can bear witness to this. [*Points to the* STEP-DAUGHTER.]

The Step-Daughter. Oh yes, that's true enough. When I was a kiddie, so so high, you know, with plaits over my shoulders and knickers longer than my skirts, I used to see him waiting outside the school for me to come out. He came to see how I was growing up.

The Father. This is infamous, shameful!

The Step-Daughter. No. Why?

The Father. Infamous! infamous! [*Then excitedly to* MANAGER *explaining.*] After she [*Indicating* MOTHER.] went away, my house seemed suddenly empty. She was my incubus, but she filled my house. I was like a dazed fly alone in the empty rooms. This boy here [*Indicating the* SON.] was educated away from home, and when he came back, he seemed to me to be no more mine. With no mother to stand between him and me, he grew up entirely for himself, on his own, apart, with no tie of intellect or affection binding him to me. And then—strange but true —I was driven, by curiosity at first and then by some tender sentiment, towards her family, which had come into being through my will. The thought of her began gradually to fill up the emptiness I felt all around me. I wanted to know if she were happy in living out the simple daily duties of life. I wanted to think of her as fortunate and happy because far away from the complicated torments of my spirit. And so, to have proof of this, I used to watch that child coming out of school.

The Step-Daughter. Yes, yes. True. He used to follow me in the street and smiled at me, waved his hand, like this. I would look at him with interest, wondering who he might be. I told my mother, who guessed at once. [*The* MOTHER *agrees with a nod.*] Then she didn't want to send me to school for some days; and when I finally went back, there he was again—looking so ridiculous—with a paper parcel in his hands. He came close to me, caressed me, and drew out a fine straw hat from the parcel, with a bouquet of flowers—all for me!

The Manager. A bit discursive this, you know!

The Son [*contemptuously*]. Literature! Literature!

The Father. Literature indeed! This is life, this is passion!

The Manager. It may be, but it won't act.

The Father. I agree. This is only the part leading up. I don't suggest this should be staged. She [*Pointing to the* STEP-DAUGHTER.], as you see, is no longer the flapper with plaits down her back—.

The Step-Daughter. —and the knickers showing below the skirt!

The Father. The drama is coming now, sir; something new, complex, most interesting.

The Step-Daughter. As soon as my father died . . .

The Father. —there was absolute misery for them. They came back here, unknown to me. Through her stupidity! [*Pointing to the* MOTHER.] It is true she can barely write her own name; but she could anyhow have got her daughter to write to me that they were in need . . .

The Mother. And how was I to divine all this sentiment in him?

The Father. That is exactly your mistake, never to have guessed any of my sentiments.

The Mother. After so many years apart, and all that had happened . . .

The Father. Was it my fault if that fellow carried you away? It happened quite suddenly; for after he had obtained some job or other, I could find no trace of them; and so, not unnaturally, my interest in them dwindled. But the drama culminated unforeseen and violent on their return, when I was impelled by my miserable flesh that still lives . . . Ah! what misery, what wretchedness is that of the man who is alone and disdains debasing *liaisons!* Not old enough to do without women, and not young enough to go and look for one without shame. Misery? It's worse than misery; it's a horror; for no woman can any longer give him love; and when a man feels this . . . One ought to do without, you say? Yes, yes, I know. Each of us when he appears before his fellows is clothed in a certain dignity. But every man knows what unconfessable things pass within the secrecy of his own heart. One gives way to the temptation, only to rise from it again, afterwards, with a great eagerness to re-establish one's dignity, as if it were a tombstone to place on the grave of one's shame, and a monument to hide and sign the memory of our weaknesses. Everybody's in the same case. Some folks haven't the courage to say certain things, that's all!

The Step-Daughter. All appear to have the courage to do them though.

The Father. Yes, but in secret. Therefore, you want more courage to say these things. Let a man but speak these things out, and folks at once label him a cynic. But it isn't true. He is like all the others, better indeed, because he isn't afraid to reveal with the light of the intelligence the red shame of human bestiality on which most men close their eyes so as not to see it.

Woman—for example, look at her case! She turns tantalizing inviting glances on you. You seize her. No sooner does she feel herself in your grasp than she closes her eyes. It is the sign of her mission, the sign by which she says to man: "Blind yourself, for I am blind."

The Step-Daughter. Sometimes she can close them no more: when she no longer feels the need of hiding her shame to herself, but dry-eyed and dispassionately, sees only that of the man who has blinded himself without love. Oh, all these intellectual complications make me sick, disgust me—all this philosophy that uncovers the beast in man, and then seeks to save him, excuse him . . . I can't stand it, sir. When a man seeks to "simplify" life bestially, throwing aside every relic of humanity, every chaste aspiration, every pure feeling, all sense of ideality, duty, modesty, shame . . . then nothing is more revolting and nauseous than a certain kind of remorse—crocodiles' tears, that's what it is.

The Manager. Let's come to the point. This is only discussion.

The Father. Very good, sir! But a fact is like a sack which won't stand up when it is empty. In order that it may stand up, one has to put into it the reason and sentiment which have caused it to exist. I couldn't possibly know that after the death of that man, they had decided to return here, that they were in misery, and that she [*Pointing to the* MOTHER.] had gone to work as a modiste, and at a shop of the type of that of Madame Pace.

The Step-Daughter. A real high-class modiste, you must know, gentlemen. In appearance, she works for the leaders of the best society; but she arranges matters so that these elegant ladies serve her purpose . . . without prejudice to other ladies who are . . . well . . . only so so.

The Mother. You will believe me, gentlemen, that it

never entered my mind that the old hag offered me work because she had her eye on my daughter.

The Step-Daughter. Poor mamma! Do you know, sir, what that woman did when I brought her back the work my mother had finished? She would point out to me that I had torn one of my frocks, and she would give it back to my mother to mend. It was I who paid for it, always I; while this poor creature here believed she was sacrificing herself for me and these two children here, sitting up at night sewing Madame Pace's robes.

The Manager. And one day you met there . . .

The Step-Daughter. Him, him. Yes sir, an old client. There's a scene for you to play! Superb!

The Father. She, the Mother arrived just then . . .

The Step-Daughter [*treacherously*]. Almost in time!

The Father [*crying out*]. No, in time! in time! Fortunately I recognized her . . . in time. And I took them back home with me to my house. You can imagine now her position and mine; she, as you see her; and I who cannot look her in the face.

The Step-Daughter. Absurd! How can I possibly be expected—after that—to be a modest young miss, a fit person to go with his confounded aspirations for "a solid moral sanity"?

The Father. For the drama lies all in this—in the conscience that I have, that each one of us has. We believe this conscience to be a single thing, but it is many-sided. There is one for this person, and another for that. Diverse consciences. So we have this illusion of being one person for all, of having a personality that is unique in all our acts. But it isn't true. We perceive this when, tragically perhaps, in something we do, we are as it were, suspended, caught up in the air on a kind of hook. Then we perceive that all of us was not in that act, and that it would be an atrocious injustice to judge us by that

action alone, as if all our existence were summed up in
that one deed. Now do you understand the perfidy of
this girl? She surprised me in a place, where she ought
not to have known me, just as I could not exist for her;
and she now seeks to attach to me a reality such as I
could never suppose I should have to assume for her in
a shameful and fleeting moment of my life. I feel this
above all else. And the drama, you will see, acquires a
tremendous value from this point. Then there is the
position of the others . . . his . . . [*Indicating the* SON.]

The Son [*shrugging his shoulders scornfully*]. Leave
me alone! I don't come into this.

The Father. What? You don't come into this?

The Son. I've got nothing to do with it, and don't
want to have; because you know well enough I wasn't
made to be mixed up in all this with the rest of you.

The Step-Daughter. We are only vulgar folk! He is
the fine gentleman. You may have noticed, Mr. Manager,
that I fix him now and again with a look of scorn while
he lowers his eyes—for he knows the evil he has done me.

The Son [*scarcely looking at her*]. I?

The Step-Daughter. You! you! I owe my life on the
streets to you. Did you or did you not deny us, with
your behaviour, I won't say the intimacy of home, but
even that mere hospitality which makes guests feel at
their ease? We were intruders who had come to disturb
the kingdom of your legitimacy. I should like to have
you witness, Mr. Manager, certain scenes between him
and me. He says I have tyrannized over everyone. But it
was just his behaviour which made me insist on the
reason for which I had come into the house,—this reason
he calls "vile"—into his house, with my mother who is
his mother too. And I came as mistress of the house.

The Son. It's easy for them to put me always in the
wrong. But imagine, gentlemen, the position of a son,
whose fate it is to see arrive one day at his home a young

woman of impudent bearing, a young woman who in-
quires for his father, with whom who knows what business she has. This young man has then to witness her
return bolder than ever, accompanied by that child
there. He is obliged to watch her treat his father in an
equivocal and confidential manner. She asks money of
him in a way that lets one suppose he must give it her,
must, do you understand, because he has every obligation
to do so.

The Father. But I have, as a matter of fact, this obligation. I owe it to your mother.

The Son. How should I know? When had I ever seen
or heard of her? One day there arrive with her [*Indicating* STEP-DAUGHTER.] that lad and this baby here. I am
told: "This is *your* mother too, you know." I divine from
her manner [*Indicating* STEP-DAUGHTER *again.*] why it is
they have come home. I had rather not say what I feel
and think about it. I shouldn't even care to confess to
myself. No action can therefore be hoped for from me in
this affair. Believe me, Mr. Manager, I am an "unreal-
ized" character, dramatically speaking; and I find myself
not at all at ease in their company. Leave me out of it,
I beg you.

The Father. What? It is just because you are so
that . . .

The Son. How do you know what I am like? When
did you ever bother your head about me?

The Father. I admit it. I admit it. But isn't that a
situation in itself? This aloofness of yours which is so
cruel to me and to your mother, who returns home and
sees you almost for the first time grown up, who doesn't
recognize you but knows you are her son . . . [*Pointing
out the* MOTHER *to the* MANAGER.] See, she's crying!

The Step-Daughter [*angrily, stamping her foot*].   Like
a fool!

The Father [*indicating* STEP-DAUGHTER].   She can't

stand him you know. [*Then referring again to the* SON.] He says he doesn't come into the affair, whereas he is really the hinge of the whole action. Look at that lad who is always clinging to his mother, frightened and humiliated. It is on account of this fellow here. Possibly his situation is the most painful of all. He feels himself a stranger more than the others. The poor little chap feels mortified, humiliated at being brought into a home out of charity as it were. [*In confidence.*] He is the image of his father. Hardly talks at all. Humble and quiet.

The Manager. Oh, we'll cut him out. You've no notion what a nuisance boys are on the stage . . .

The Father. He disappears soon, you know. And the baby too. She is the first to vanish from the scene. The drama consists finally in this: when that mother re-enters my house, her family born outside of it, and shall we say superimposed on the original, ends with the death of the little girl, the tragedy of the boy and the flight of the elder daughter. It cannot go on, because it is foreign to its surroundings. So after much torment, we three remain: I, the mother, that son. Then, owing to the disappearance of that extraneous family, we too find ourselves strange to one another. We find we are living in an atmosphere of mortal desolation which is the revenge, as he [*Indicating* SON.] scornfully said of the Demon of Experiment, that unfortunately hides in me. Thus, sir, you see when faith is lacking, it becomes impossible to create certain states of happiness, for we lack the necessary humility. Vaingloriously, we try to substitute ourselves for this faith, creating thus for the rest of the world a reality which we believe after their fashion, while, actually, it doesn't exist. For each one of us has his own reality to be respected before God, even when it is harmful to one's very self.

The Manager. There is something in what you say. I assure you all this interests me very much. I begin to think there's the stuff for a drama in all this, and not a bad drama either.

The Step-Daughter [*coming forward*]. When you've got a character like me.

The Father [*shutting her up, all excited to learn the decision of the* MANAGER]. You be quiet!

The Manager [*reflecting, heedless of interruption*]. It's new . . . hem . . . yes . . .

The Father. Absolutely new!

The Manager. You've got a nerve though, I must say, to come here and fling it at me like this . . .

The Father. You will understand, sir, born as we are for the stage . . .

The Manager. Are you amateur actors then?

The Father. No. I say born for the stage, be-cause . . .

The Manager. Oh, nonsense. You're an old hand, you know.

The Father. No sir, no. We act that rôle for which we have been cast, that rôle which we are given in life. And in my own case, passion itself, as usually happens, becomes a trifle theatrical when it is exalted.

The Manager. Well, well, that will do. But you see, without an author . . . I could give you the address of an author if you like . . .

The Father. No, no. Look here! You must be the author.

The Manager. I? What are you talking about?

The Father. Yes, you, you! Why not?

The Manager. Because I have never been an author: that's why.

The Father. Then why not turn author now? Every-body does it. You don't want any special qualities. Your task is made much easier by the fact that we are all here alive before you . . .

The Manager. It won't do.

The Father. What? When you see us live our drama . . .

The Manager. Yes, that's all right. But you want someone to write it.

The Father. No, no. Someone to take it down, possibly, while we play it, scene by scene! It will be enough to sketch it out at first, and then try it over.

The Manager. Well . . . I am almost tempted. It's a bit of an idea. One might have a shot at it.

The Father. Of course. You'll see what scenes will come out of it. I can give you one, at once . . .

The Manager. By Jove, it tempts me. I'd like to have a go at it. Let's try it out. Come with me to my office. [*Turning to the* Actors.] You are at liberty for a bit, but don't step out of the theatre for long. In a quarter of an hour, twenty minutes, all back here again! [*To the* Father.] We'll see what can be done. Who knows if we don't get something really extraordinary out of it?

The Father. There's no doubt about it. They [*Indicating the* Characters.] had better come with us too, hadn't they?

The Manager. Yes, yes. Come on! come on! [*Moves away and then turning to the* Actors.] *Be punctual, please!* [Manager *and the* Six Characters *cross the stage and go off. The other* Actors *remain, looking at one another in astonishment.*]

Leading Man. Is he serious? What the devil does he want to do?

Juvenile Lead. This is rank madness.

Third Actor. Does he expect to knock up a drama in five minutes?

Juvenile Lead. Like the improvisers!

Leading Lady. If he thinks I'm going to take part in a joke like this . . .

Juvenile Lead. I'm out of it anyway.

Fourth Actor. I should like to know who they are. [*Alludes to* CHARACTERS].

Third Actor. What do you suppose? Madmen or rascals!

Juvenile Lead. And he takes them seriously!

L'Ingénue. Vanity! He fancies himself as an author now.

Leading Man. It's absolutely unheard of. If the stage has come to this . . . well I'm . . .

Fifth Actor. It's rather a joke.

Third Actor. Well, we'll see what's going to happen next.

[*Thus talking, the* ACTORS *leave the stage; some going out by the little door at the back; others retiring to their dressing-rooms.*

The curtain remains up.

The action of the play is suspended for twenty minutes].

ACT II

The stage call-bells ring to warn the company that the play it about to begin again.

The STEP-DAUGHTER *comes out of the* MANAGER'S *office along with the* CHILD *and the* BOY. *As she comes out of the office, she cries:—*

Nonsense! nonsense! Do it yourselves! I'm not going to mix myself up in this mess. [*Turning to the* CHILD *and coming quickly with her on to the stage.*] Come on, Rosetta, let's run!

[*The* BOY *follows them slowly, remaining a little behind and seeming perplexed.*]

The Step-Daughter [*stops, bends over the* CHILD *and takes the latter's face between her hands*]. My little darling! You're frightened, aren't you? You don't know where we are, do you? [*Pretending to reply to a question of the* CHILD.] What is the stage? It's a place, baby, you know, where people play at being serious, a place where they act comedies. We've got to act a comedy now, dead serious, you know; and you're in it also, little one. [*Embraces her, pressing the little head to her breast,. and rocking the* CHILD *for a moment*.] Oh darling, darling, what a horrid comedy you've got to play! What a wretched part they've found for you! A garden . . . a fountain . . . look . . . just suppose, kiddie, it's here. Where, you say? Why, right here in the middle. It's all pretence you know. That's the trouble, my pet: it's all make-belive here. It's better to imagine it though, because if they fix it up for you, it'll only be painted cardboard, painted cardboard for the rockery, the water, the plants . . . Ah, but I think a baby like this one would sooner have a make-believe fountain than a real one, so she could play with it. What a joke it'll be for the others! But for you, alas! not quite such a joke: you who are real, baby dear, and really play by a real fountain that is big and green and beautiful, with ever so many bamboos around it that are reflected in the water, and a whole lot of little ducks swimming about . . . No, Rosetta, no, your mother doesn't bother about you on account of that wretch of a son there. I'm in the devil of a temper, and as for that lad . . . [*Seizes* BOY *by the arm to force him to take one of his hands out of his pockets.*] What have you got there? What are you hiding? [*Pulls his hand out of his pocket, looks into it and catches the glint of a revolver.*] Ah! where did you get this? [*The* BOY, *very pale in the face, looks at her, but does not answer*]. Idiot! If I'd been in your place, instead of killing myself, I'd have shot one of those two, or both of them: father and son.

[*The* FATHER *enters from the office, all excited from his work. The* MANAGER *follows him.*]

The Father. Come on, come on dear! Come here for a minute! We've arranged everything. It's all fixed up.

· *The Manager* [*also excited*]. If you please, young lady, there are one or two points to settle still. Will you come along?

The Step-Daughter [*following him towards the office*]. Ouff! what's the good, if you've arranged everything.

[*The* FATHER, MANAGER *and* STEP-DAUGHTER *go back into the office again (off) for a moment. At the same time, The* SON *followed by The* MOTHER, *comes out.*]

The Son [*looking at the three entering office*]. Oh this is fine, fine! And to think I can't even get away!

[*The* MOTHER *attempts to look at him, but lowers her eyes immediately when* HE *turns away from her.* SHE *then sits down. The* BOY *and The* CHILD *approach her.* SHE *casts a glance again at the* SON, *and speaks with humble tones, trying to draw him into conversation.*]

The Mother. And isn't my punishment the worst of all? [*Then seeing from the* SON's *manner that he will not bother himself about her.*] My God! Why are you so cruel? Isn't it enough for one person to support all this torment? Must you then insist on others seeing it also?

The Son [*half to himself, meaning the* MOTHER *to hear, however*]. And they want to put it on the stage! If there was at least a reason for it! He thinks he has got at the meaning of it all. Just as if each one of us in every circumstance of life couldn't find his own explanation of it! [*Pauses.*] He complains he was discovered in a place where he ought not to have been seen, in a moment of his life which ought to have remained hidden and kept out of the reach of that convention which he has to maintain for other people. And what about my case?

Haven't I had to reveal what no son ought ever to reveal: how father and mother live and are man and wife for themselves quite apart from that idea of father and mother which we give them? When this idea is revealed, our life is then linked at one point only to that man and that woman; and as such it should shame them, shouldn't it?

[*The* Mother *hides her face in her hands. From the dressing-rooms and the little door at the back of the stage the* Actors *and* Stage Manager *return, followed by the* Property Man, *and the* Prompter. *At the same moment, The* Manager *comes out of his office, accompanied by the* Father *and the* Step-Daughter.]

The Manager.   Come on, come on, ladies and gentlemen! Heh! you there, machinist!

Machinist.   Yes sir?

The Manager.   Fix up the white parlor with the floral decorations. Two wings and a drop with a door will do. Hurry up!

[*The* Machinist *runs off at once to prepare the scene, and arranges it while The* Manager *talks with the* Stage Manager, *the* Property Man, *and the* Prompter *on matters of detail.*]

The Manager [*to* Property Man].   Just have a look, and see if there isn't a sofa or divan in the wardrobe . . .

Property Man.   There's the green one.

The Step-Daughter.   No no! Green won't do. It was yellow, ornamented with flowers—very large! and most comfortable!

Property Man.   There isn't one like that.

The Manager.   It doesn't matter. Use the one we've got.

The Step-Daughter.   Doesn't matter? It's most important!

The Manager.   We're only trying it now. Please don't

interfere. [*To* PROPERTY MAN.] See if we've got a shop window—long and narrowish.

The Step-Daughter. And the little table! The little mahogany table for the pale blue envelope!

Property Man [*to* MANAGER]. There's that little gilt one.

The Manager. That'll do fine.

The Father. A mirror.

The Step-Daughter. And the screen! We must have a screen. Otherwise how can I manage?

Property Man. That's all right, Miss. We've got any amount of them.

The Manager [*to the* STEP-DAUGHTER]. We want some clothes pegs too, don't we?

The Step-Daughter. Yes, several, several!

The Manager. See how many we've got and bring them all.

Property Man. All right!

[*The* PROPERTY MAN *hurries off to obey his orders. While he is putting the things in their places, the* MANAGER *talks to the* PROMPTER *and then with the* CHARACTERS *and the* ACTORS.]

The Manager [*to* PROMPTER]. Take your seat. Look here: this is the outline of the scenes, act by act. [*Hands him some sheets of paper.*] And now I'm going to ask you to do something out of the ordinary.

Prompter. Take it down in shorthand?

The Manager [*pleasantly surprised*]. Exactly! Can you do shorthand?

Prompter. Yes, a little.

The Manager. Good! [*Turning to a* STAGE HAND.] Go and get some paper from my office, plenty, as much as you can find.

[*The* STAGE HAND *goes off, and soon returns with a handful of paper which he gives to the* PROMPTER.]

The Manager [*to* PROMPTER]. You follow the scenes

as we play them, and try and get the points down, at any
rate the most important ones. [*Then addressing the* Actors.] Clear the stage, ladies and gentlemen! Come over
here [*Pointing to the left.*] and listen attentively.

Leading Lady. But, excuse me, we . . .

The Manager [*guessing her thought*]. Don't worry!
You won't have to improvise.

Leading Man. What have we to do then?

The Manager. Nothing. For the moment you just
watch and listen. Everybody will get his part written out
afterwards. At present we're going to try the thing as best
we can. They're going to act now.

The Father [*as if fallen from the clouds into the confusion of the stage*]. We? What do you mean, if you
please, by a rehearsal?

The Manager. A rehearsal for them. [*Points to the*
Actors.]

The Father. But since we are the characters . . .

The Manager. All right: "characters" then, if you
insist on calling yourselves such. But here, my dear sir,
the characters don't act. Here the actors do the acting.
The characters are there, in the "book" [*Pointing towards* Prompter's *box.*]—when there is a "book"!

The Father. I won't contradict you; but excuse me,
the actors aren't the characters. They want to be, they
pretend to be, don't they? Now if these gentlemen here
are fortunate enough to have us alive before them . . .

The Manager. Oh this is grand! You want to come
before the public yourselves then?

The Father. As we are . . .

The Manager. I can assure you it would be a magnificent spectacle!

Leading Man. What's the use of us here anyway
then?

The Manager. You're not going to pretend that you

can act? It makes me laugh! [*The* ACTORS *laugh.*] There, you see, they are laughing at the notion. But, by the way, I must cast the parts. That won't be difficult. They cast themselves. [*To the* SECOND LADY LEAD.] You play the Mother. [*To the* FATHER.] We must find her a name.

The Father. Amalia, sir.

The Manager. But that is the real name of your wife. We don't want to call her by her real name.

The Father. Why ever not, if it is her name? . . . Still, perhaps, if that lady must . . . [*Makes a slight motion of the hand to indicate the* SECOND LADY LEAD.] I see this woman here [*Means the* MOTHER.] as Amalia. But do as you like. [*Gets more and more confused.*] I don't know what to say to you. Already, I begin to hear my own words ring false, as if they had another sound . . .

The Manager. Don't you worry about it. It'll be our job to find the right tones. And as for her name, if you want her Amalia, Amalia it shall be; and if you don't like it, we'll find another! For the moment though, we'll call the characters in this way: [*To* JUVENILE LEAD.] You are the Son. [*To the* LEADING LADY.] You naturally are the Step-Daughter . . .

The Step-Daughter [*excitedly*]. What? what? I, that woman there? [*Bursts out laughing.*]

The Manager [*angry*]. What is there to laugh at?

Leading Lady [*indignant*]. Nobody has ever dared to laugh at me. I insist on being treated with respect; otherwise I go away.

The Step-Daughter. No, no, excuse me . . . I am not laughing at you . . .

The Manager [*to* STEP-DAUGHTER]. You ought to feel honored to be played by . . .

Leading Lady [*at once, contemptuously*]. "That woman there" . . .

The Step-Daughter. But I wasn't speaking of you,

you know. I was speaking of myself—whom I can't see at all in you! That is all. I don't know . . . but . . . you . . . aren't in the least like me . . .

The Father. True. Here's the point. Look here, sir, our temperaments, our souls . . .

The Manager. Temperament, soul, be hanged! Do you suppose the spirit of the piece is in you? Nothing of the kind!

The Father. What, haven't we our own temperaments, our own souls?

The Manager. Not at all. Your soul or whatever you like to call it takes shape here. The actors give body and form to it, voice and gesture. And my actors—I may tell you—have given expression to much more lofty material than this little drama of yours, which may or may not hold up on the stage. But if it does, the merit of it, believe me, will be due to my actors.

The Father. I don't dare contradict you, sir; but, believe me, it is a terrible suffering for us who are as we are, with these bodies of ours, these features to see . . .

The Manager [*cutting him short and out of patience*]. Good heavens! The make-up will remedy all that, man, the make-up . . .

The Father. Maybe. But the voice, the gestures . . .

The Manager. Now, look here! On the stage, you as yourself, cannot exist. The actor here acts you, and that's an end to it!

The Father. I understand. And now I think I see why our author who conceived us as we are, all alive, didn't want to put us on the stage after all. I haven't the least desire to offend your actors. Far from it! But when I think that I am to be acted by . . . I don't know by whom . . .

Leading Man [*on his dignity*]. By me, if you've no objection!

The Father [*humbly, mellifously*]. Honored, I assure you, sir. [*Bows.*] Still, I must say that try as this gentleman may, with all his good will and wonderful art, to absorb me into himself . . .

Leading Man. Oh chuck it! "Wonderful art!" Withdraw that, please!

The Father. The performance he will give, even doing his best with make-up to look like me . . .

Leading Man. It will certainly be a bit difficult! [*The* ACTORS *laugh.*]

The Father. Exactly! It will be difficult to act me as I really am. The effect will be rather—apart from the make-up—according as to how he supposes I am, as he senses me—if he does sense me—and not as I inside of myself feel myself to be. It seems to me then that account should be taken of this by everyone whose duty it may become to criticize us . . .

The Manager. Heavens! The man's starting to think about the critics now! Let them say what they like. It's up to us to put on the play if we can. [*Looking around.*] Come on! come on! Is the stage set? [*To the* ACTORS *and* CHARACTERS.] Stand back—stand back! Let me see, and don't let's lose any more time! [*To the* STEP-DAUGHTER.] Is it all right as it is now?

The Step-Daughter. Well, to tell the truth, I don't recognize the scene.

The Manager. My dear lady, you can't possibly suppose that we can construct that shop of Madame Pace piece by piece here? [*To the* FATHER.] You said a white room with flowered wall paper, didn't you?

The Father. Yes.

The Manager. Well then. We've got the furniture right more or less. Bring that little table a bit further forward. [*The* STAGE HANDS *obey the order. To* PROPERTY MAN.] You go and find an envelope, if possible, a pale blue one; and give it to that gentleman. [*Indicates* FATHER.]

Property Man. An ordinary envelope?

Manager and Father. Yes, yes, an ordinary envelope.

Property Man. At once, sir. [*Exit.*]

The Manager. Ready, everyone! First scene—the Young Lady. [*The* LEADING LADY *comes forward.*] No, no, you must wait. I meant her [*Indicating the* STEP-DAUGHTER.] You just watch—

The Step-Daughter [*adding at once*]. How I shall play it, how I shall live it! . . .

Leading Lady [*offended*]. I shall live it also, you may be sure, as soon as I begin!

The Manager [*with his hands to his head*]. Ladies and gentlemen, if you please! No more useless discussions! Scene I: the young lady with Madame Pace: Oh! [*Looks around as if lost.*] And this Madame Pace, where is she?

The Father. She isn't with us, sir.

The Manager. Then what the devil's to be done?

The Father. But she is alive too.

The Manager. Yes, but where is she?

The Father. One minute. Let me speak! [*Turning to the* ACTRESSES.] If these ladies would be so good as to give me their hats for a moment . . .

The Actresses [*half surprised, half laughing, in chorus*]. What?

Why?

Our hats?

What does he say?

The Manager. What are you going to do with the ladies' hats? [*The* ACTORS *laugh.*]

The Father. Oh nothing. I just want to put them on these pegs for a moment. And one of the ladies will be so kind as to take off her mantle . . .

The Actors. Oh, what d'you think of that?

Only the mantle?

He must be mad.

Some Actresses. But why?

Mantles as well?

The Father. To hang them up here for a moment. Please be so kind, will you?

The Actresses [*taking off their hats, one or two also their cloaks, and going to hang them on the racks*]. After all, why not?

There you are!

This is really funny.

We've got to put them on show.

The Father. Exactly; just like that, on show.

The Manager. May we know why?

The Father. I'll tell you. Who knows if, by arranging the stage for her, she does not come here herself, attracted by the very articles of her trade? [*Inviting the* Actors *to look towards the exit at back of stage.*] Look! Look!

[*The door at the back of stage opens and* Madame Pace *enters and takes a few steps forward. She is a fat, oldish woman with puffy oxygenated hair. She is rouged and powdered, dressed with a comical elegance in black silk. Round her waist is a long silver chain from which hangs a pair of scissors. The* Step-Daughter *runs over to her at once amid the stupor of the actors.*]

The Step-Daughter [*turning towards her*]. There she is! There she is!

The Father [*radiant*]. It's she! I said so, didn't I? There she is!

The Manager [*conquering his surprise, and then becoming indignant*]. What sort of a trick is this?

Leading Man [*almost at the same time*]. What's going to happen next?

Juvenile Lead. Where does *she* come from?

L'Ingénue. They've been holding her in reserve, I guess.

Leading Lady. A vulgar trick!

The Father [*dominating the protests*]. Excuse me, all of you! Why are you so anxious to destroy in the name of a vulgar, commonplace sense of truth, this reality which comes to birth attracted and formed by the magic of the stage itself, which has indeed more right to live here than you, since it is much truer than you—if you don't mind my saying so? Which is the actress among you who is to play Madame Pace? Well, here is Madame Pace herself. And you will allow, I fancy, that the actress who acts her will be less true than this woman here, who is herself in person. You see my daughter recognized her and went over to her at once. Now you're going to witness the scene!

[*But the scene between the* STEP-DAUGHTER *and* MA-DAME PACE *has already begun despite the protest of the actors and the reply of The* FATHER. *It has begun quietly, naturally, in a manner impossible for the stage. So when the actors, called to attention by The* FATHER, *turn round and see* MADAME PACE, *who has placed one hand under the* STEP-DAUGHTER'S *chin to raise her head, they observe her at first with great attention, but hearing her speak in an unintelligible manner their interest begins to wane.*]

The Manager. Well? well?

Leading Man. What does she say?

Leading Lady. One can't hear a word.

Juvenile Lead. Louder! Louder please!

The Step-Daughter [*leaving* MADAME PACE, *who smiles a Sphinx-like smile, and advancing towards the actors*]. Louder? Louder? What are you talking about? These aren't matters which can be shouted at the top of one's voice. If I have spoken them out loud, it was to shame him and have my revenge. [*Indicates* FATHER.] But for Madame it's quite a different matter.

The Manager. Indeed? indeed? But here, you know, people have got to make themselves heard, my dear. Even we who are on the stage can't hear you. What will it be when the public's in the theatre? And anyway, you can very well speak up now among yourselves, since we shan't be present to listen to you as we are now. You've got to pretend to be alone in a room at the back of a shop where no one can hear you.

[*The* STEP-DAUGHTER *coquettishly and with a touch of malice makes a sign of disagreement two or three times with her finger.*]

The Manager. What do you mean by no?

The Step-Daughter [*sotto voce, mysteriously*]. There's someone who will hear us if she [*Indicating* MADAME PACE.] speaks out loud.

The Manager [*in consternation*]. What? Have you got someone else to spring on us now? [*The* ACTORS *burst out laughing.*]

The Father. No, no sir. She is alluding to me. I've got to be here—there behind that door, in waiting; and Madame Pace knows it. In fact, if you will allow me, I'll go there at once, so I can be quite ready. [*Moves away.*]

The Manager [*stopping him*]. No! Wait! wait! We must observe the conventions of the theatre. Before you are ready . . .

The Step-Daughter [*interrupting him*]. No, get on with it at once! I'm just dying, I tell you, to act this scene. If he's ready, I'm more than ready.

The Manager [*shouting*]. But, my dear young lady, first of all, we must have the scene between you and this lady . . . [*Indicates* MADAME PACE.] Do you under-stand? . . .

The Step-Daughter. Good Heavens! She's been tell-ing me what you know already: that mamma's work is badly done again, that the material's ruined; and that if I want her to continue to help us in our misery I must be patient . . .

Madame Pace [*coming forward with an air of great*

importance]. Yes indeed, sir, I no wanta take advantage of her, I no wanta be hard . . .

[*Note.* MADAME PACE *is supposed to talk in a jargon half Italian, half English.*]

The Manager [*alarmed*]. What? What? She talks like that? [*The* ACTORS *burst out laughing again.*]

The Step-Daughter [*also laughing*]. Yes yes, that's the way she talks, half English, half Italian! Most comical it is!

Madame Pace. Itta seem not verra polite gentlemen laugha atta me eef I trya best speaka English.

The Manager. Diamine! Of course! Of course! Let her talk like that! Just what we want. Talk just like that, Madame, if you please! The effect will be certain. Exactly what was wanted to put a little comic relief into the crudity of the situation. Of course she talks like that! Magnificent!

The Step-Daughter. Magnificent? Certainly! When certain suggestions are made to one in language of that kind, the effect is certain, since it seems almost a joke. One feels inclined to laugh when one hears her talk about an "old signore" "who wanta talka nicely with you." Nice old signore, eh, Madame?

Madame Pace. Not so old my dear, not so old! And even if you no lika him, he won't make any scandal!

The Mother [*jumping up amid the amazement and consternation of the actors who had not been noticing her.* THEY *move to restrain her*]. You old devil! You murderess!

The Step-Daughter [*running over to calm her* MOTHER]. Calm yourself, Mother, calm yourself! Please don't . . .

The Father [*going to her also at the same time*]. Calm yourself! Don't get excited! Sit down now!

The Mother. Well then, take that woman away out of my sight!

The Step-Daughter [*to* MANAGER]. It is impossible for my mother to remain here.

The Father [*to* MANAGER]. They can't be here together. And for this reason, you see: that woman there was not with us when we came . . . If they are on together, the whole thing is given away inevitably, as you see.

The Manager. It doesn't matter. This is only a first rough sketch—just to get an idea of the various points of the scene, even confusedly . . . [*Turning to the* MOTHER *and leading her to her chair.*] Come along, my dear lady, sit down now, and let's get on with the scene . . .

[*Meanwhile, the* STEP-DAUGHTER, *coming forward again, turns to* MADAME PACE.]

The Step-Daughter. Come on, Madame, come on!

Madame Pace [*offended*]. No, no, *grazie*. I not do anything witha your mother present.

The Step-Daughter. Nonsense! Introduce this "old signore" who wants to talk nicely to me. [*Addressing the* COMPANY *imperiously.*] We've got to do this scene one way or another, haven't we? Come on! [*To* MADAME PACE.] You can go!

Madame Pace. Ah yes! I go'way! I go'way! Certainly! [*Exits furious.*]

The Step-Daughter [*to the* FATHER]. Now you make your entry. No, you needn't go over here. Come here. Let's suppose you've already come in. Like that, yes! I'm here with bowed head, modest like. Come on! Out with your voice! Say "Good morning, Miss" in that peculiar tone, that special tone . . .

The Manager. Excuse me, but are you the Manager, or am I? [*To the* FATHER, *who looks undecided and perplexed.*] Get on with it, man! Go down there to the back of the stage. You needn't go off. Then come right forward here.

[*The* FATHER *does as he is told, looking troubled and perplexed at first. But as soon as he begins to move, the reality of the action affects him, and he begins to smile and to be more natural. The* ACTORS *watch intently.*]

The Manager [*sotto voce, quickly to the* PROMPTER *in his box*]. Ready! ready? Get ready to write now.

The Father [*coming forward and speaking in a different tone*]. Good afternoon, Miss!

The Step-Daughter [*head bowed down slightly, with restrained disgust*]. Good afternoon!

The Father [*looks under her hat which partly covers her face. Perceiving she is very young, he makes an exclamation, partly of surprise, partly of fear lest he compromise himself in a risky adventure*]. Ah . . . but . . . ah . . . I say . . . this is not the first time that you have come here, is it?

The Step-Daughter [*modestly*]. No sir.

The Father. You've been here before, eh? [*Then seeing her nod agreement.*] More than once? [*Waits for her to answer, looks under her hat, smiles, and then says.*] Well then, there's no need to be so shy, is there? May I take off your hat?

The Step-Daughter [*anticipating him and with veiled disgust*]. No sir . . . I'll do it myself. [*Takes it off quickly.*]

[*The* MOTHER, *who watches the progress of the scene with The* SON *and the other two children who cling to her, is on thorns; and follows with varying expressions of sorrow, indignation, anxiety, and horror the words and actions of the other two. From time to time* SHE *hides her face in her hands and sobs.*]

The Mother. Oh, my God, my God!

The Father [*playing his part with a touch of gallantry*]. Give it to me! I'll put it down. [*Takes hat from her hands.*] But a dear little head like yours ought to have a smarter hat. Come and help me choose one from the stock, won't you?

L'Ingénue [*interrupting*]. I say . . . those are our hats you know.

The Manager [*furious*]. Silence! silence! Don't try and be funny, if you please . . . We're playing the scene now I'd have you notice. [*To the* STEP-DAUGHTER.] Begin again, please!

The Step-Daughter [*continuing*]. No thank you, sir.

The Father. Oh, come now. Don't talk like that. You must take it. I shall be upset if you don't. There are some lovely little hats here; and then—Madame will be pleased. She expects it, anyway, you know.

The Step-Daughter. No, no! I couldn't wear it!

The Father. Oh, you're thinking about what they'd say at home if they saw you come in with a new hat? My dear girl, there's always a way round these little matters, you know.

The Step-Daughter [*all keyed up*]. No, it's not that. I couldn't wear it because I am . . . as you see . . . you might have noticed . . . [*Showing her black dress.*]

The Father. . . . in mourning! Of course: I beg your pardon: I'm frightfully sorry . . .

The Step-Daughter [*forcing herself to conquer her indignation and nausea*]. Stop! Stop! It's I who must thank you. There's no need for you to feel mortified or specially sorry. Don't think any more of what I've said. [*Tries to smile.*] I must forget that I am dressed so . . .

The Manager [*interrupting and turning to the* PROMPTER]. Stop a minute! Stop! Don't write that down. Cut out that last bit. [*Then to the* FATHER *and* STEP-DAUGHTER.] Fine! it's going fine! [*To the* FATHER *only*.] And now you can go on as we arranged. [*To the* ACTORS.] Pretty good that scene, where he offers her the hat, eh?

The Step-Daughter. The best's coming now. Why can't we go on?

The Manager. Have a little patience! [*To the Ac-*
TORS.] Of course, it must be treated rather lightly.

Leading Man. Still, with a bit of go in it!

Leading Lady. Of course! It's easy enough! [*To*
LEADING MAN.] Shall you and I try it now?

Leading Man. Why, yes! I'll prepare my entrance.
[*Exit in order to make his entrance.*]

The Manager [*to* LEADING LADY]. See here! The scene
between you and Madame Pace is finished. I'll have it
written out properly after. You remain here . . . oh,
where are you going?

Leading Lady. One minute. I want to put my hat on
again. [*Goes over to hat-rack and puts her hat on her
head.*]

The Manager. Good! You stay here with your head
bowed down a bit.

The Step-Daughter. But she isn't dressed in black.

Leading Lady. But I shall be, and much more effectively than you.

The Manager [*to* STEP-DAUGHTER]. Be quiet please,
and watch! You'll be able to learn something. [*Clapping
his hands.*] Come on! come on! Entrance, please!

[*The door at rear of stage opens, and the* LEADING MAN
*enters with the lively manner of an old gallant. The
rendering of the scene by the* ACTORS *from the very
first words is seen to be quite a different thing,
though it has not in any way the air of a parody.
Naturally, the* STEP-DAUGHTER *and the* FATHER, *not
being able to recognize themselves in the* LEADING
LADY *and the* LEADING MAN, *who deliver their words
in different tones and with a different psychology,
express, sometimes with smiles, sometimes with gestures, the impression they receive.*]

Leading Man. Good afternoon, Miss . . .

The Father [*at once unable to contain himself*]. No!
no!

[*The* STEP-DAUGHTER *noticing the way the* LEADING MAN *enters, bursts out laughing.*]

The Manager [*furious*]. Silence! And you please just stop that laughing. If we go on like this, we shall never finish.

The Step-Daughter. Forgive me, sir, but it's natural enough. This lady [*Indicating* LEADING LADY.] stands there still; but if she is supposed to be me, I can assure you that if I heard anyone say "Good afternoon" in that manner and in that tone, I should burst out laughing as I did.

The Father. Yes, yes, the manner, the tone . . .

The Manager. Nonsense! Rubbish! Stand aside and let me see the action.

Leading Man. If I've got to represent an old fellow who's coming into a house of an equivocal character . . .

The Manager. Don't listen to them, for Heaven's sake! Do it again! It goes fine. [*Waiting for the* ACTORS *to begin again.*] Well?

Leading Man. Good afternoon, Miss.

Leading Lady. Good afternoon.

Leading Man [*imitating the gesture of the* FATHER *when he looked under the hat, and then expressing quite clearly first satisfactin and then fear*]. Ah, but . . . I say . . . this is not the first time that you have come here, is it?

The Manager. Good, but not quite so heavily. Like this. [*Acts himself.*] "This isn't the first time that you have come here" . . . [*To* LEADING LADY.] And you say: "No, sir."

Leading Lady. No, sir.

Leading Man. You've been here before, more than once.

The Manager. No, no, stop! Let her nod "yes" first. "You've been here before, eh?" [*The* LEADING LADY *lifts up her head slightly and closes her eyes as though in dis-gust. Then* SHE *inclines her head twice.*]

The Step-Daughter [*unable to contain herself*]. Oh my God! [*Puts a hand to her mouth to prevent herself from laughing.*]

The Manager [*turning round*]. What's the matter?

The Step-Daughter. Nothing, nothing!

The Manager [*to* LEADING MAN]. Go on!

Leading Man. You've been here before, eh? Well then, there's no need to be so shy, is there? May I take off your hat?

[*The* LEADING MAN *says this last speech in such a tone and with such gestures that the* STEP-DAUGHTER, *though she has her hand to her mouth, cannot keep from laughing.*]

Leading Lady [*indignant*]. I'm not going to stop here to be made a fool of by that woman there.

Leading Man. Neither am I! I'm through with it!

The Manager [*shouting to* STEP-DAUGHTER]. Silence! for once and all, I tell you!

The Step-Daughter. Forgive me! forgive me!

The Manager. You haven't any manners: that's what it is! You go too far.

The Father [*endeavouring to intervene*]. Yes, it's true, but excuse her . . .

The Manager. Excuse what? It's absolutely disgusting.

The Father. Yes, sir, but believe me, it has such a strange effect when . . .

The Manager. Strange? Why strange? Where is it strange?

The Father. No, sir; I admire your actors—this gen-tleman here, this lady; but they are certainly not us!

The Manager. I should hope not. Evidently they can-not be you, if they are actors.

The Father. Just so: actors! Both of them act our parts exceedingly well. But, believe me, it produces quite

a different effect on us. They want to be us, but they
aren't, all the same.

The Manager. What is it then anyway?

The Father. Something that is . . . that is theirs—
and no longer ours . . .

The Manager. But naturally, inevitably. I've told you
so already.

The Father. Yes, I understand . . . I understand . . .

The Manager. Well then, let's have no more of it!
[*Turning to the* ACTORS.] We'll have the rehearsals by
ourselves, afterwards, in the ordinary way. I never could
stand rehearsing with the author present. He's never
satisfied! [*Turning to* FATHER *and* STEP-DAUGHTER.] Come
on! Let's get on with it again; and try and see if you
can't keep from laughing.

The Step-Daughter. Oh, I shan't laugh any more.
There's a nice little bit coming for me now: you'll see.

The Manager. Well then: when she says "Don't think
any more of what I've said. I must forget, etc.," you [*Addressing the* FATHER.] come in sharp with "I understand,
I understand"; and then you ask her . . .

The Step-Daughter [*interrupting*]. What?

The Manager. Why she is in mourning.

The Step-Daughter. Not at all! See here: when I told
him that it was useless for me to be thinking about my
wearing mourning, do you know how he answered me?
"Ah well," he said, "then let's take off this little frock."

The Manager. Great! Just what we want, to make a
riot in the theatre!

The Step-Daughter. But it's the truth!

The Manager. What does that matter? Acting is our
business here. Truth up to a certain point, but no further.

The Step-Daughter. What do you want to do then?

The Manager. You'll see, you'll see! Leave it to me.

The Step-Daughter. No sir! What you want to do is
to piece together a little romantic sentimental scene out

of my disgust, out of all the reasons, each more cruel and viler than the other, why I am what I am. He is to ask me why I'm in mourning; and I'm to answer with tears in my eyes, that it is just two months since papa died. No sir, no! He's got to say to me; as he did say: "Well, let's take off this little dress at once." And I; with my two months' mourning in my heart, went there behind that screen, and with these fingers tingling with shame . . .

The Manager [*running his hands through his hair*]. For Heaven's sake! What are you saying?

The Step-Daughter [*crying out excitedly*]. The truth! The truth!

The Manager. It may be. I don't deny it, and I can understand all your horror; but you must surely see that you can't have this kind of thing on the stage. It won't go.

The Step-Daughter. Not possible, eh? Very well! I'm much obliged to you—but I'm off!

The Manager. Now be reasonable! Don't lose your temper!

The Step-Daughter. I won't stop here! I won't! I can see you've fixed it all up with him in your office. All this talk about what is possible for the stage . . . I understand! He wants to get at his complicated "cerebral drama," to have his famous remorses and torments acted; but I want to act my part, *my part!*

The Manager [*annoyed, shaking his shoulders*]. Ah! Just *your* part! But, if you will pardon me, there are other parts than yours: His [*Indicating the* FATHER.] and hers! [*Indicating the* MOTHER.] On the stage you can't have a character becoming too prominent and overshadowing all the others. The thing is to pack them all into a neat little framework and then act what is actable. I am aware of the fact that everyone has his own interior life which he wants very much to put forward. But the difficulty lies in this fact: to set out just so much as is necessary for the stage, taking the other characters into consideration, and at the same time hint at the unrevealed interior life of each. I am willing to admit, my dear young lady, that from your point of view it would be a fine idea if each character could tell the public all his troubles in a nice monologue or a regular one hour lecture. [*Good humoredly.*] You must restrain yourself, my dear, and in your own interest, too; because this fury of yours, this exaggerated disgust you show, may make a bad impression, you know. After you have confessed to me that there were others before him at Madame Pace's and more than once . . .

The Step-Daughter [*bowing her head, impressed*]. It's true. But remember those others mean him for me all the same.

The Manager [*not understanding*].   What? The others? What do you mean?

The Step-Daughter.   For one who has gone wrong, sir, he who was responsible for the first fault is responsible for all that follow. He is responsible for my faults, was, even before I was born. Look at him, and see if it isn't true!

The Manager.   Well, well! And does the weight of so much responsibility seem nothing to you? Give him a chance to act it, to get it over!

The Step-Daughter.   How? How can he act all his "noble remorses," all his "moral torments," if you want to spare him the horror of being discovered one day—after he had asked her what he did ask her—in the arms of her, that already fallen woman, that child, sir, that child he used to watch come out of school? [SHE *is moved.*]

[*The* MOTHER *at this point is overcome with emotion, and breaks out into a fit of crying. ALL are touched. A long pause.*]

The Step-Daughter [*as soon as the* MOTHER *becomes a little quieter, adds resolutely and gravely*].   At present, we are unknown to the public. Tomorrow, you will act us as you wish, treating us in your own manner. But do you really want to see drama, do you want to see it flash out as it really did?

The Manager. Of course! That's just what I do want, so I can use as much of it as is possible.

The Step-Daughter. Well then, ask that Mother there to leave us.

The Mother [*changing her low plaint into a sharp cry*]. No! No! Don't permit it, sir, don't permit it!

The Manager. But it's only to try it.

The Mother. I can't bear it. I can't.

The Manager. But since it has happened already . . . I don't understand!

The Mother. It's taking place now. It happens all the time. My torment isn't a pretended one. I live and feel every minute of my torture. Those two children there—have you heard them speak? They can't speak any more. They cling to me to keep up my torment actual and vivid for me. But for themselves, they do not exist, they aren't any more. And she [*Indicating the* STEP-DAUGHTER.] has run away, she has left me, and is lost. If I now see her here before me, it is only to renew for me the tortures I have suffered for her too.

The Father. The eternal moment! She [*Indicating the* STEP-DAUGHTER.] is here to catch me, fix me, and hold me eternally in the stocks for that one fleeting and shameful moment of my life. She can't give it up! And you sir, cannot either fairly spare me it.

The Manager. I never said I didn't want to act it. It will form, as a matter of fact, the nucleus of the whole first act right up to her surprise. [*Indicates the* MOTHER.]

The Father. Just so! This is my punishment: the passion in all of us that must culminate in her final cry.

The Step-Daughter. I can hear it still in my ears. It's driven me mad, that cry!—You can put me on as you like; it doesn't matter. Fully dressed, if you like—provided I have at least the arm bare; because, standing like this [*She goes close to the* FATHER *and leans her head on his breast.*] with my head so, and my arms round his neck, I saw a vein pulsing in my arm here; and then, as if that live vein had awakened disgust in me, I closed my eyes like this, and let my head sink on his breast. [*Turning to the* MOTHER.] Cry out mother! Cry out! [*Buries head in* FATHER'S *breast, and with her shoulders raised as if to prevent her hearing the cry, adds in tones of intense emotion.*] Cry out as you did then!

The Mother [*coming forward to separate them*]. No! My daughter, my daughter! [*And after having pulled her away from him.*] You brute! you brute! She is my daughter! Don't you see she's my daughter?

The Manager [*walking backwards towards footlights*]. Fine! fine! Damned good! And then, of course—curtain!

The Father [*going towards him excitedly*]. Yes, of course, because that's the way it really happened.

The Manager [*convinced and pleased*]. Oh, yes, no doubt about it. Curtain here, curtain!

[*At the reiterated cry of* The MANAGER, *The* MACHINIST *lets the curtain down, leaving The* MANAGER *and The* FATHER *in front of it before the footlights.*]

The Manager. The darned idiot! I said "curtain" to show the act should end there, and he goes and lets it down in earnest. [*To the* FATHER, *while he pulls the curtain back to go on to the stage again.*] Yes, yes, it's all right. Effect certain! That's the right ending. I'll guarantee the first act at any rate.

ACT III

When the curtain goes up again, it is seen that the stage hands have shifted the bit of scenery used in the last part, and have rigged up instead at the back of the stage a drop,

with some trees, and one or two wings. A portion of a
fountain basin is visible. The MOTHER *is sitting on the*
right with the two children by her side. The SON *is on*
the same side, but away from the others. He seems bored,
angry, and full of shame. The FATHER *and the* STEP-
DAUGHTER *are also seated towards the right front. On*
the other side (left) are the ACTORS, *much in the positions*
they occupied before the curtain was lowered. Only the
MANAGER *is standing up in the middle of the stage, with*
his hand closed over his mouth in the act of meditating.

The Manager [*shaking his shoulders after a brief
pause*]. Ah yes: the second act! Leave it to me, leave it
all to me as we arranged, and you'll see! It'll go fine!

The Step-Daughter. Our entry into his house [*Indicates* FATHER.] in spite of him . . . [*Indicates the* SON.]

The Manager [*out of patience*]. Leave it to me, I tell
you!

The Step-Daughter. Do let it be clear, at any rate,
that it is in spite of my wishes.

The Mother [*from her corner, shaking her head*]. For
all the good that's come of it . . .

The Step-Daughter [*turning towards her quickly*].
It doesn't matter. The more harm done us, the more remorse for him.

The Manager [*impatiently*]. I understand! Good
Heavens! I understand! I'm taking it into account.

The Mother [*supplicatingly*]. I beg you, sir, to let it
appear quite plain that for conscience' sake I did try in
every way . . .

The Step-Daughter [*interrupting indignantly and continuing for the* MOTHER]. . . . to pacify me, to dissuade
me from spiting him. [*To* MANAGER.] Do as she wants:
satisfy her, because it is true! I enjoy it immensely. Anyhow, as you can see, the meeker she is, the more she tries

to get at his heart, the more distant and aloof does he become.

The Manager. Are we going to begin this second act or not?

The Step-Daughter. I'm not going to talk any more now. But I must tell you this: you can't have the whole action take place in the garden, as you suggest. It isn't possible!

The Manager. Why not?

The Step-Daughter. Because he [*Indicates the* Son *again.*] is always shut up alone in his room. And then there's all the part of that poor dazed-looking boy there which takes place indoors.

The Manager. Maybe! On the other hand, you will understand—we can't change scenes three or four times in one act.

The Leading Man. They used to once.

The Manager. Yes, when the public was up to the level of that child there.

The Leading Lady. It makes the illusion easier.

The Father [*irritated*]. The illusion! For Heaven's sake, don't say illusion. Please don't use that word, which is particularly painful for us.

The Manager [*astounded*]. And why, if you please?

The Father. It's painful, cruel, really cruel; and you ought to understand that.

The Manager. But why? What ought we to say then? The illusion, I tell you, sir, which we've got to create for the audience . . .

The Leading Man. With our acting.

The Manager. The illusion of a reality.

The Father. I understand; but you, perhaps, do not understand us. Forgive me! You see . . . here for you and your actors, the thing is only—and rightly so . . . a kind of game . . .

The Leading Lady [*interrupting indignantly*]. A game! We're not children here, if you please! We are serious actors.

The Father. I don't deny it. What I mean is the game, or play, of your art, which has to give, as the gentleman says, a perfect illusion of reality.

The Manager. Precisely—!

The Father. Now, if you consider the fact that we [*Indicates himself and the other five* CHARACTERS.], as we are, have no other reality outside of this illusion . . .

The Manager [*astonished, looking at his* ACTORS, *who are also amazed*]. And what does that mean?

The Father [*after watching them for a moment with a wan smile*]. As I say, sir, that which is a game of art for you is our sole reality. [*Brief pause. He goes a step or two nearer the* MANAGER *and adds.*] But not only for us, you know, by the way. Just you think it over well. [*Looks him in the eyes.*] Can you tell me who you are?

The Manager [*perplexed, half smiling*]. What? Who am I? I am myself.

The Father. And if I were to tell you that that isn't true, because you and I . . . ?

The Manager. I should say you were mad—! [*The* ACTORS *laugh.*]

The Father. You're quite right to laugh: because we are all making believe here. [*To* MANAGER.] And you can therefore object that it's only for a joke that that gentleman there [*Indicates the* LEADING MAN.], who naturally is himself, has to be me, who am on the contrary myself— this thing you see here. You see I've caught you in a trap! [*The* ACTORS *laugh.*]

The Manager [*annoyed*]. But we've had all this over once before. Do you want to begin again?

The Father. No, no! That wasn't my meaning! In fact, I should like to request you to abandon this game of art [*Looking at the* LEADING LADY *as if anticipating her.*]

which you are accustomed to play here with your actors, and to ask you seriously once again: who are you?

The Manager [*astonished and irritated, turning to his* ACTORS]. If this fellow here hasn't got a nerve! A man who calls himself a character comes and asks me who I am!

The Father [*with dignity, but not offended*]. A character, sir, may always ask a man who he is. Because a character has really a life of his own, marked with his especial characteristics; for which reason he is always "somebody." But a man—I'm not speaking of you now— may very well be "nobody."

The Manager. Yes, but you are asking these questions of me, the boss, the manager! Do you understand?

The Father. But only in order to know if you, as you really are now, see yourself as you once were with all the illusions that were yours then, with all the things both inside and outside of you as they seemed to you—as they were then indeed for you. Well, sir, if you think of all those illusions that mean nothing to you now, of all those things which don't even *seem* to you to exist any more, while once they *were* for you, don't you feel that—I won't say these boards—but the very earth under your feet is sinking away from you when you reflect that in the same way this *you* as you feel it today—all this present reality of yours—is fated to seem a mere illusion to you tomorrow?

The Manager [*without having understood much, but astonished by the specious argument*]. Well, well! And where does all this take us anyway?

The Father. Oh, nowhere! It's only to show you that if we [*Indicating the* CHARACTERS.] have no other reality beyond the illusion, you too must not count overmuch on your reality as you feel it today, since, like that of yesterday, it may prove an illusion for you tomorrow.

The Manager [*determining to make fun of him*]. Ah,

excellent! Then you'll be saying next that you, with this comedy of yours that you brought here to act, are truer and more real than I am.

The Father [*with the greatest seriousness*]. But of course; without doubt!

The Manager. Ah, really?

The Father. Why, I thought you'd understand that from the beginning.

The Manager. More real than I?

The Father. If your reality can change from one day to another . . .

The Manager. But everyone knows it can change. It is always changing, the same as anyone else's.

The Father [*with a cry*]. No, sir, not ours! Look here! That is the very difference! Our reality doesn't change: it can't change! It can't be other than what it is, because it is already fixed for ever. It's terrible. Ours is an immutable reality which should make you shudder when you approach us if you are really conscious of the fact that your reality is a mere transitory and fleeting illusion, taking this form today and that tomorrow, according to the conditions, according to your will, your sentiments, which in turn are controlled by an intellect that shows them to you today in one manner and tomorrow . . . who knows how? . . . Illusions of reality represented in this fatuous comedy of life that never ends, nor can ever end! Because if tomorrow it were to end . . . then why, all would be finished.

The Manager. Oh for God's sake, will you *at least* finish with this philosophizing and let us try and shape this comedy which you yourself have brought me here? You argue and philosophize a bit too much, my dear sir. You know you seem to me almost, almost . . . [*Stops and looks him over from head to foot.*] Ah, by the way, I think you introduced yourself to me as a—what shall . . . we say—a "character," created by an author who did not afterward care to make a drama of his own creations.

The Father. It is the simple truth, sir.

The Manager. Nonsense! Cut that out, please! None of us believes it, because it isn't a thing, as you must recognize yourself, which one can believe seriously. If you want to know, it seems to me you are trying to imitate the manner of a certain author whom I heartily detest—I warn you—although I have unfortunately bound myself to put on one of his works. As a matter of fact, I was just starting to rehearse it, when you arrived. [*Turning to the* ACTORS.] And this is what we've gained—out of the frying-pan into the fire!

The Father. I don't know to what author you may be alluding, but believe me I feel what I think; and I seem to be philosophizing only for those who do not think what they feel, because they blind themselves with their own sentiment. I know that for many people this self-blinding seems much more "human"; but the contrary is really true. For man never reasons so much and becomes so introspective as when he suffers; since he is anxious to get at the cause of his sufferings, to learn who has produced them, and whether it is just or unjust that he should have to bear them. On the other hand, when he is happy, he takes his happiness as it comes and doesn't analyze it, just as if happiness were his right. The animals suffer without reasoning about their sufferings. But take the case of a man who suffers and begins to reason about it. Oh no! it can't be allowed! Let him suffer like an animal, and then—ah yet, he is "human"!

The Manager. Look here! Look here! You're off again, philosophizing worse than ever.

The Father. Because I suffer, sir! I'm not philosophizing: I'm crying aloud the reason of my sufferings.

The Manager [*makes brusque movement as he is taken with a new idea*]. I should like to know if anyone has

ever heard of a character who gets right out of his part
and perorates and speechifies as you do. Have you ever
heard of a case? I haven't.

The Father. You have never met such a case, sir,
because authors, as a rule, hide the labour of their creations. When the characters are really alive before their
author, the latter does nothing but follow them in their
action, in their words, in the situations which they suggest to him; and he has to will them the way they will
themselves—for there's trouble if he doesn't. When a
character is born, he acquires at once such an independ-
ence, even of his own author, that he can be imagined
by everybody even in many other situations where the
author never dreamed of placing him; and so he acquires
for himself a meaning which the author never thought of
giving him.

The Manager. Yes, yes, I know this.

The Father. What is there then to marvel at in us?
Imagine such a misfortune for characters as I have described to you: to be born of an author's fantasy, and be
denied life by him; and then answer me if these characters left alive, and yet without life, weren't right in doing
what they did do and are doing now, after they have
attempted everything in their power to persuade him to
give them their stage life. We've all tried him in turn, I,
she [*Indicating the* STEP-DAUGHTER.] and she. [*Indicating
the* MOTHER.]

The Step-Daughter. It's true. I too have sought to
tempt him, many, many times, when he has been sitting
at his writing table, feeling a bit melancholy, at the twilight hour. He would sit in his armchair too lazy to
switch on the light, and all the shadows that crept into
his room were full of our presence coming to tempt him.
[*As if she saw herself still there by the writing table, and
was annoyed by the presence of the* ACTORS.] Oh, if you
would only go away, go away and leave us alone—mother

here with that son of hers—I with that Child—that Boy there always alone—and then I with him [*Just hints at the* FATHER.]—and then I alone, alone . . . in those shadows! [*Makes a sudden movement as if in the vision she has of herself illuminating those shadows she wanted to seize hold of herself.*] Ah! my life! my life! Oh, what scenes we proposed to him—and I tempted him more than any of the others!

The Father. Maybe. But perhaps it was your fault that he refused to give us life: because you were too insistent, too troublesome.

The Step-Daughter... Nonsense! Didn't he make me so himself? [*Goes close to the* MANAGER *to tell him as if in confidence.*] In my opinion he abandoned us in a fit of depression, of disgust for the ordinary theatre as the public knows it and likes it.

The Son. Exactly what it was, sir; exactly that!

The Father. Not at all! Don't believe it for a minute. Listen to me! You'll be doing quite right to modify, as you suggest, the excesses both of this girl here, who wants to do too much, and of this young man, who won't do anything at all.

The Son. No, nothing!

The Manager. You too get over the mark occasionally, my dear sir, if I may say so.

The Father. I? When? Where?

The Manager. Always! Continuously! Then there's this insistence of yours in trying to make us believe you are a character. And then too, you must really argue and philosophize less, you know, much less.

The Father. Well, if you want to take away from me the possibility of representing the torment of my spirit which never gives me peace, you will be suppressing me: that's all. Every true man, sir, who is a little above the level of the beasts and plants does not live for the sake of living, without knowing how to live; but he lives so as to give a meaning and a value of his own to life. For me this is *everything*. I cannot give up this, just to represent a mere fact as she [*Indicating the* STEP-DAUGHTER.] wants. It's all very well for her, since her "vendetta" lies in the "fact." I'm not going to do it. It destroys my *raison d'être*.

The Manager. Your *raison d'être*! Oh, we're going ahead fine! First she starts off, and then you jump in. At this rate, we'll never finish.

The Father. Now, don't be offended! Have it your own way—provided, however, that within the limits of the parts you assign us each one's sacrifice isn't too great.

The Manager. You've got to understand that you can't go on arguing at your own pleasure. Drama is action, sir, action and not confounded philosophy.

The Father. All right. I'll do just as much arguing and philosophizing as everybody does when he is considering his own torments.

The Manager. If the drama permits! But for Heaven's sake, man, let's get along and come to the scene.

The Step-Daughter. It seems to me we've got too much action with our coming into his house. [*Indicating* FATHER.] You said, before, you couldn't change the scene every five minutes.

The Manager. Of course not. What we've got to do is to combine and group up all the facts in one simultaneous, close-knit, action. We can't have it as you want, with your little brother wandering like a ghost from room to room, hiding behind doors and meditating a project which—what did you say it did to him?

The Step-Daughter. Consumes him, sir, wastes him away!

The Manager. Well, it may be. And then at the same time, you want the little girl there to be playing in the garden . . . one in the house, and the other in the garden: isn't that it?

The Step-Daughter. Yes, in the sun, in the sun! That is my only pleasure: to see her happy and careless in the garden after the misery and squalor of the horrible room where we all four slept together. And I had to sleep with her—I, do you understand?—with my vile contaminated body next to hers; with her folding me fast in her loving little arms. In the garden, whenever she spied me, she would run to take me by the hand. She didn't care for the big flowers, only the little ones; and she loved to show me them and pet me.

The Manager. Well then, we'll have it in the garden. Everything shall happen in the garden; and we'll group the other scenes there. [*Calls a* STAGE HAND.] Here, a back-cloth with trees and something to do as a fountain basin. [*Turning round to look at the back of the stage.*] Ah, you've fixed it up. Good! [*To* STEP-DAUGHTER.] This is just to give an idea, of course. The Boy, instead of hiding behind the doors, will wander about here in the garden, hiding behind the trees. But it's going to be rather difficult to find a child to do that scene with you where she shows you the flowers. [*Turning to the* BOY.] Come forward a little, will you please? Let's try it now! Come along! come along! [*Then seeing him come shyly forward, full of fear and looking lost.*] It's a nice business, this lad here. What's the matter with him? We'll have to give him a word or two to say. [*Goes close to him, puts a hand on his shoulders, and leads him behind one of the trees.*] Come on! come on! Let me see you a little! Hide here . . . yes, like that. Try and show your head just a little as if you were looking for someone . . . [*Goes back to observe the effect, when the* BOY *at once goes through the action.*] Excellent! fine! [*Turning to* STEP-DAUGHTER.] Suppose the little girl there were to surprise him as he looks round, and run over to him, so we could give him a word or two to say?

The Step-Daughter. It's useless to hope he will speak, as long as that fellow there is here . . . [*Indicates the* SON.] You must send him away first.

The Son [*jumping up*]. Delighted! Delighted! I don't ask for anything better. [*Begins to move away.*]

The Manager [*at once stopping him*]. No! No! Where are you going? Wait a bit!

[*The* MOTHER *gets up alarmed and terrified at the thought that he is really about to go away. Instinctively she lifts her arms to prevent him, without, however, leaving her seat.*]

The Son [*to* MANAGER *who stops him*]. I've got nothing to do with this affair. Let me go please! Let me go!

The Manager. What do you mean by saying you've got nothing to do with this?

The Step-Daughter [*calmly, with irony*]. Don't bother to stop him: he won't go away.

The Father. He has to act the terrible scene in the garden with his mother.

The Son [*suddenly resolute and with dignity*]. I shall act nothing at all. I've said so from the very beginning. [*To the* MANAGER.] Let me go!

The Step-Daughter [*going over to the* MANAGER]. Allow me? [*Puts down the* MANAGER'S *arm which is restraining the* SON.] Well, go away then, if you want to! [*The* SON *looks at her with contempt and hatred. She laughs and says.*] You see, he can't, he can't go away! He is obliged to stay here, indissolubly bound to the chain. If I, who fly off when that happens which has to happen, because I can't bear him—if I am still here and support that face and expression of his, you can well imagine that he is unable to move. He has to remain here, has to stop with that nice father of his, and that mother whose only son he is. [*Turning to the* MOTHER.] Come on, mother, come along! [*Turning to* MANAGER *to indicate her.*] You see, she was getting up to keep him back. [*To the* MOTHER, *beckoning her with her hand.*] Come on! come on! [*Then to* MANAGER.] You can imagine how little she wants to show these actors of yours what she really feels; but so eager is she to get near him that . . . There, you see? She is willing to act her part. [*And in fact, the* MOTHER *approaches him; and as soon as the* STEP-DAUGHTER *has finished speaking, opens her arms to signify that she consents.*]

The Son [*suddenly*]. No! no! If I can't go away, then I'll stop here; but I repeat: I act nothing!

The Father [*to* MANAGER *excitedly*]. You can force him, sir.

The Son. Nobody can force me.

The Father. I can.

The Step-Daughter. Wait a minute, wait . . . First of all, the baby has to go to the fountain . . . [*Runs to take the* CHILD *and leads her to the fountain.*]

The Manager. Yes, yes of course; that's it. Both at the same time.

[*The second* LADY LEAD *and the* JUVENILE LEAD *at this point separate themselves from the group of* ACTORS. *One watches the* MOTHER *attentively; the other moves about studying the movements and manner of the* SON *whom he will have to act.*]

The Son [*to* MANAGER]. What do you mean by both at the same time? It isn't right. There was no scene between me and her. [*Indicates the* MOTHER.] Ask her how it was!

The Mother. Yes, it's true. I had come into his room . . .

The Son. Into my room, do you understand? Nothing to do with the garden.

The Manager. It doesn't matter. Haven't I told you we've got to group the action?

The Son [*observing the* JUVENILE LEAD *studying him*]. What do you want?

The Juvenile Lead. Nothing! I was just looking at you.

The Son [*turning towards the second* LADY LEAD]. Ah! she's at it too: to re-act her part! [*Indicating the* MOTHER.]

The Manager. Exactly! And it seems to me that you ought to be grateful to them for their interest.

The Son. Yes, but haven't you yet perceived that it isn't possible to live in front of a mirror which not only freezes us with the image of ourselves, but throws our likeness back at us with a horrible grimace?

The Father. That is true, absolutely true. You must see that.

The Manager [*to second* LADY LEAD *and* JUVENILE LEAD]. He's right! Move away from them!

The Son. Do as you like. I'm out of this!

The Manager. Be quiet, you, will you? And let me hear your mother! [*To* MOTHER.] You were saying you had entered . . .

The Mother. Yes, into his room, because I couldn't stand it any longer. I went to empty my heart to him of all the anguish that tortures me . . . But as soon as he saw me come in . . .

The Son. Nothing happened! There was no scene. I went away, that's all! I don't care for scenes!

The Mother. It's true, true. That's how it was.

The Manager. Well now, we've got to do this bit between you and him. It's indispensable.

The Mother. I'm ready . . . when you are ready. If you could only find a chance for me to tell him what I feel here in my heart.

The Father [*going to* SON *in a great rage*]. You'll do this for your mother, for your mother, do you understand?

The Son [*quite determined*]. I do nothing!

The Father [*taking hold of him and shaking him*].

For God's sake, do as I tell you! Don't you hear your mother asking you for a favor? Haven't you even got the guts to be a son?

The Son [*taking hold of the* FATHER]. No! No! And for God's sake stop it, or else . . . [*General agitation. The* MOTHER, *frightened, tries to separate them.*]

The Mother [*pleading*]. Please! please!

The Father [*not leaving hold of the* SON]. You've got to obey, do you hear?

The Son [*almost crying from rage*]. What does it mean, this madness you've got? [*They separate.*] Have you no decency, that you insist on showing everyone our shame? I won't do it! I won't! And I stand for the will of our author in this. He didn't want to put us on the stage, after all!

The Manager. Man alive! You came here . . .

The Son [*indicating* FATHER]. *He* did! I didn't!

The Manager. Arent't you here now?

The Son. It was his wish, and he dragged us along with him. He's told you not only the things that did happen, but also things that have never happened at all.

The Manager. Well, tell me then what did happen. You went out of your room without saying a word?

The Son. Without a word, so as to avoid a scene!

The Manager. And then what did you do?

The Son. Nothing . . . walking in the garden . . . [*Hesitates for a moment with expression of gloom.*]

The Manager [*coming closer to him, interested by his extraordinary reserve*]. Well, well . . . walking in the garden . . .

The Son [*exasperated*]. Why on earth do you insist? It's horrible! [*The* MOTHER *trembles, sobs, and looks towards the fountain.*]

The Manager [*slowly observing the glance and turning towards the* SON *with increasing apprehension*]. The baby?

The Son. There in the fountain . . .

The Father [*pointing with tender pity to the* MOTHER].
She was following him at the moment . . .

The Manager [*to the* SON *anxiously*]. And then
you . . .

The Son. I ran over to her; I was jumping in to drag
her out when I saw something that froze my blood . . .
the boy standing stock still, with eyes like a madman's,
watching his little drowned sister, in the fountain! [*The*
STEP-DAUGHTER *bends over the fountain to hide the*
CHILD. *She sobs.*] Then . . . [*A revolver shot rings out
behind the trees where the* BOY *is hidden.*]

The Mother [*with a cry of terror runs over in that direction together with several of the* ACTORS *amid general
confusion*]. My son! My son! [*Then amid the cries and
exclamations one hears her voice.*] Help! Help!

The Manager [*pushing the* ACTORS *aside while* THEY
lift up the BOY *and carry him off.*] Is he really wounded?

Some Actors. He's dead! dead!

Other Actors. No, no, it's only make believe, it's only
pretence!

The Father [*with a terrible cry*]. Pretence? Reality,
sir, reality!

The Manager. Pretence? Reality? To hell with it all!
Never in my life has such a thing happened to me. I've
lost a whole day over these people, a whole day!

Curtain.

EACH IN HIS OWN WAY

(Ciascuno a suo modo)

A COMEDY IN TWO OR THREE ACTS WITH CHORAL INTERLUDES

English version by

ARTHUR LIVINGSTON

CHARACTERS OF THE COMEDY ON THE STAGE

DELIA MORELLO (*referred to in the interludes as "the leading lady"*)
MICHELE ROCCA
DONNA LIVIA PALEGARI (*an old lady*)
HER GUESTS (*men and women of her own age who feel quite at home in her house*)
DORO PALEGARI (*her son*)

DIEGO CINCI (*a young friend of Palegari*)
FILIPPO (*a butler of long service in the Palegari household*)
FRANCESCO SAVIO (*who starts the quarrel*)
PRESTINO (*one of several other friends of Savio*)
FENCING MASTER
BUTLER (*in Francesco Savio's house*)

"REAL" PEOPLE, APPEARING IN THE
THEATRE LOBBY

DELIA MORENO (*whose connection with the play everybody understands*)
BARON NUTI
STAGE MANAGER
LEADING LADY (*who is the same as Delia Morello in the play*)
OWNER OF THE THEATRE
BUSINESS MANAGER
USHERS
POLICEMEN
FIVE DRAMATIC CRITICS
OLD AUTHOR (*who never had a play accepted*)

YOUNG AUTHOR
LITERARY MAN (*who would write if the public were not beneath his contempt*)
GOOD-NATURED SPECTATOR
BAD-HUMORED SPECTATOR
A MAN WHO UNDERSTANDS
A MAN WHO NEVER UNDERSTANDS
ONE OR TWO SUPPORTERS OF PIRANDELLO
AN ARMY OF ANTAGONISTS
SPECTATOR FROM THE SOCIAL SET
LADIES AND GENTLEMEN (*from the audience*)

The public is requested to remain seated at the end of the first
and second acts, for the curtain will at once rise again for the choral
interludes. The number of acts in the comedy cannot be made more
specific in view of unpleasant incidents that will arise during the
course of the performance.

ACT I

The ancient palace of DONNA LIVIA PALEGARI. *It is tea
time, and the guests are about to leave. Through the back
drop, which presents three arches and two columns, a
sumptuous drawing-room brightly lighted and with an
animated company—ladies and gentlemen—can be seen.
The front of the stage, less brightly lighted, is a smaller
parlor ornately decorated in damask, and with ancient
paintings (of religious subjects for the most part) on the
walls. As we look at the stage we should get the impression of being in a shrine in a church, of which the drawing-room beyond the columns might be the nave—the
sacred chapel of a very worldly church! The parlor in the
foreground is unfurnished save for one or two benches or
wooden stools for the convenience of people desirous of
studying the paintings on the walls. There are no doors.
The guests will come into this retreat two or three at a
time to exchange confidences in private; and in fact as
the curtain rises, we meet there: an* OLD FRIEND *of* DONNA
LIVIA *and a* YOUNG MAN *(one of the guests), engaged in
conversation.*

   Young Man.   Well, what's your idea of it?
   Old Man [*with a sigh*].   My idea of it? [*Pause.*] I
really couldn't explain. [*Pause.*] What are other people
saying?
   Young Man.   Oh, some one thing, some another.
   Old Man.   Of course, each his own private opinion!
   Young Man.   But none of them, when you come down
to it, seem to be sure of themselves. They are all like you.

Before they'll tell you what they think, they want to know what others are saying.

Old Man. Oh, as for me, I am absolutely sure. But . . . it's common sense, isn't it? I'm not anxious to make a fool of myself. Before I say anything definite I ought to know whether other people may not have some information which I have not yet had and which might in part modify my judgment.

Young Man. But what do you think, so far as you know?

Old Man. Oh, my dear boy, we never know everything!

Young Man. Well, in that case, what are opinions worth?

Old Man. Dear me, opinions? My opinion is a view that I hold until—well—until I find out something that changes it.

Young Man. Not at all, if I may press the point. The moment you say that we never know everything, you take it for granted that facts exist which would change your mind.

Old Man [*looking at him thoughtfully and smiling*]. Are you trying to corner me? You're trying to make me say that I have no opinion?

Young Man. How can you? From your point of view I shouldn't think anyone could have an opinion.

Old Man. Well, refusing to have an opinion is a way of having one, isn't it?

Young Man. Yes, but in a purely negative way.

Old Man. A negative way is better than no way at all though, my boy. [*He takes the young man by the arm and starts back with him toward the drawing-room, where some girls can be seen serving tea and cookies to the guests. A pause. Two* YOUNG LADIES *steal cautiously into the parlor.*]

First Young Lady [*eagerly*]. So you know all about it then? Oh, you darling! Tell me! Tell me!

Second Young Lady. But remember, it's only an impression I have.

First Young Lady. When *you* have an impression it's sure to be worth hearing. Was he pale? And you said he was sad!

Second Young Lady. He seemed that way to me.

First Young Lady. I should never have let him go away! Oh, and I felt that way at the time—here, in my heart. I went as far as the door with him, his hand in mine. He was a step outside, and still I held his hand. We had kissed each other good-bye. We had separated—but our hands—no, no—they just refused to let go! But tell me, won't you? He made no reference—?

Second Young Lady. Reference to what?

First Young Lady. No—I mean—well—I mean whether—well, you know—speaking in a general way as one often does—

Second Young Lady. No, he said nothing in particular. He was listening to what the others were saying.

First Young Lady. Ah yes. Because he—*he* knows. He knows what harm we do through this silly habit of talking we all have. Whereas, so long as we have the slightest doubt, we ought to keep our lips shut, tight. But we talk—we talk—and we don't know what we are talking about, ourselves! But you said he was pale—and sad! You don't remember what the others were saying, do you?

Second Young Lady. No, I really don't. However, I shouldn't like to have you disappointed, my dear. You know how it is—we are so easily mistaken. It may have been indifference, but it seemed to me that he was pale; and when he smiled it was such a sad smile. Wait. I do remember! When somebody said—

First Young Lady. What did somebody say?

Second Young Lady. What was it now? Wait—somebody said: "Women are like dreams—they are never the way you would like to have them."

First Young Lady. He didn't say that, did he? You are sure?

Second Young Lady. No, it wasn't he.

First Young Lady. Oh my, my, my! Anyhow, I don't know whether I am making a mistake or not. I've always been proud of acting in my own way under all circumstances. I'm a very good-natured person; but I can be spiteful on occasion. And if I ever am—well—it'll go hard with him!

Second Young Lady. I hope you will never be any different from what you are, dear.

First Young Lady. But what am I, really? I'm sure I don't know. I assure you I don't know—even myself! All this way and that, fickle, changing, my feet off the ground! First I'm here and then I'm there. I laugh. I go off into a corner to have a good cry all by myself. Oh, how terrible it is! Sometimes I just have to hide my face to keep from seeing myself. I am so ashamed at realizing how different, how incoherent, how unreliable I am from time to time.

[*At this moment other guests come into the room; two* YOUNG MEN (*dressed in the height of fashion*) *much bored with the party; and, with them,* DIEGO CINCI.]

First Young Man. Hope we're not intruding?

Second Young Lady. Not in the least. Please, do come in!

Second Young Man. So here's the chapel! The confessional, you might almost call it, eh?

Diego. Yes. There's only one thing lacking. Donna Livia ought to have a father confessor here for the convenience of her guests!

First Young Man. And why a priest, pray? We have our own consciences.

Diego. Yes, but what do you do with your conscience?

First Young Man. My conscience?

Second Young Man [*solemnly*]. "Mea mihi conscientia pluris est quam hominum sermo."

Second Young Lady. Why, that was Latin, wasn't it?

Second Young Man. Exactly, Signorina. A quotation from Cicero. I remember it from my school days.

First Young Lady. And what does it mean?

Second Young Man [*solemnly*]. "I care more for what my conscience says than for what the world says!"

First Young Man. We have a popular saying something like that. "With conscience clear, never fear!"

Diego. If we were the only ones—

Second Young Man [*not understanding*]. What do you mean? If we were the only ones—?

Diego. I mean that then the approval of our own consciences would be sufficient. But in that case it would hardly be a question of conscience any longer. Unfortunately, my friends, I'm here, and you're here! Unfortunately!

First Young Lady. Unfortunately, he says!

Second Young Lady. And not very nice of him either!

Diego. Why, I mean—we've always got to consider other people, my dear young lady.

Second Young Man. Not at all, not at all. When my own conscience approves—

Diego. But don't you see that that blessed conscience of yours is nothing but other people inside you?

First Young Man. Your usual philosophical clap-trap!

Diego. But it's not so hard to understand. [*To the* SECOND YOUNG MAN.] When you say that you are satisfied with the approval of your own conscience, what do you mean? You mean that other people may think of you and judge you as they choose—even unjustly, let us say; but that you, meantime, will hold your own head high in the assurance that you have done no wrong. Isn't that what you mean?

Second Young Man. Yes, I guess so.

Diego. Well, then, how do you acquire that assurance except from other people? Who can assure you you have done no wrong?

Second Young Man. I do myself. It's my conscience. What else?

Diego. All you're saying is that other people in your place, meeting, in other words, circumstances similar to yours, would have done as you have done. That's all you are saying, isn't it? Or indeed, you mean that above and beyond definite concrete situations in life, certain abstractions, certain general principles, exist on which we can all agree—and why not?—since agreement, in the case of principles merely, costs so little! But notice now: if you shut yourself up disdainfully in your ivory tower and insist that you have your own conscience and are satisfied with its approval, it is because you know that everybody is criticizing you, condemning you, or laughing at you—otherwise you would never think of saying such a thing. The fact is that the general principles in question ever remain abstractions. No one is able to recognize them as you do in the situation in which you find yourself, nor are people able to see themselves acting just as you acted in doing what you did. So then you say that the approval of your own conscience is sufficient—but sufficient for what, if you please? Does it enable you to enjoy standing all by yourself against the world? Not at all, not at all! As a matter of fact, you are afraid of being at outs with everybody. So what do you do? You imagine that there are any number of heads all made like your own, heads in fact that are duplicates, replicas, of your head. And you think you can shake those heads to say 'yes' or 'no,' 'no' or 'yes,' just as you please; and that comforts you and makes you sure of yourself. Oh, interesting game, I grant you! But what else does that conscience of yours amount to?

Second Young Man. But what do *you* do, may I ask?

Diego. Oh, I play the game the same as you. I have my conscience too, I should say so!

First Young Lady. Oh, how interesting! But, I'm sure it's getting late! I think I must be going!

Second Young Lady. Yes, yes, everybody seems to be going. [*Turning to* DIEGO *and pretending that she is much offended.*] How entertaining you have been!

First Young Man. Hadn't we better be going too? [THEY *step back into the drawing-room to pay their respects to the hostess and to take their leave. The company in the parlor, meantime, has thinned out perceptibly. The last guests are bowing to* DONNA LIVIA, *who finally steps forward into the parlor, great anxiety written on her face. She is leading* DIEGO CINCI *by the hand. The* OLD MAN *whom we saw at the rising of the curtain and a* SECOND OLD MAN *follow after her.*]

Donna Livia [*to* DIEGO]. Oh no, Diego, please don't go! Please don't go! You are the best friend my son has in the world, and I am quite beside myself. Tell me, is it true? Is it true—what these dear old friends of mine have been saying?

First Old Man. I was careful to point out, Donna Livia, that we had no real information to go on.

Diego. You are talking about Doro? What's happened to him?

Donna Livia [*in surprise*]. What? Haven't you heard?

Diego. I haven't heard anything. Nothing serious, I trust. If it had been, I am sure I should have heard.

Second Old Man [*half closing his eyes to soften the shock of what he is about to reveal*]. We were referring to the trouble last night! A bit of a scandal, you know . . .

Donna Livia. . . . at the Avanzi's! Doro stood up for that—that—what's her name?—that woman!

Diego. Scandal! What woman?

First Old Man [*as above*]. Why, that Morello person. Who else?

Diego. Oh, you are talking about Delia Morello!

Donna Livia. So you know her then?

Diego. Know her? Who doesn't know her, Signora?

Donna Livia. So Doro knows her too? It is true then! He knows her!

Diego. Why, I suppose so. Why shouldn't he? And what was the trouble about?

Donna Livia [*turning to the* First Old Man]. And you said he didn't!

Diego. He knows her the way everybody knows her, Signora. But what happened?

First Old Man. But remember, remember! I was careful to say just what I said: that he stood up for the woman, *perhaps without ever having spoken to her in his life!*

Second Old Man. Yes, that's the way he knew her. Just her general reputation!

Donna Livia. And yet he stood up for her, even to the point of coming to blows?

Diego. Blows? With whom?

Second Old Man. With Francesco Savio.

Donna Livia. Why, it's incredible! The idea of starting a fight—a fight—in a respectable house, of respectable people! And for a woman of that breed!

Diego. Why, perhaps in the course of an argument . . .

First Old Man. . . . Just so . . . in the heat of an argument . . .

Second Old Man. . . . as so often happens . . .

Donna Livia. Please, gentlemen, don't try to spare my feelings. [*To* DIEGO.] *You* tell me, Diego, *you* tell me! *You* know all about Doro.

Diego. But why so wrought up, my dear Signora?

Donna Livia [*putting her foot down*]. No! You pretend to be a real friend of my son. In that case it is your duty to tell me frankly all you know about the matter.

Diego. But I know nothing whatever about the matter. Surely it can't be of much importance. Why so excited over a mere word or two?

First Old Man. Ah, as for that—now you're going a step too far! I don't follow you! . . .

Second Old Man. You can't deny that the affair made a very great impression on everybody present.

Diego. But what affair, for heaven's sake?

Donna Livia. Why, he stood up for the woman! Why, he actually came to her defense! Does that seem to you a matter of no consequence?

Diego. But, my dear Signora, the whole town has been talking about Delia Morello for three weeks past. She is the topic of conversation in the cafés, in the clubs, on the sidewalks, wherever you go. She is in the headlines of the papers. You must have read about her yourself.

Donna Livia. Yes, a man committed suicide on her account.

First Old Man. A young painter he was, named Salvi.

Diego. Giorgio Salvi, yes!

Second Old Man. A youth of great promise, it seems.

Diego. And it seems that there was someone before him.

Donna Livia. What! Another man?

First Old Man. Yes, it was mentioned in one of the papers . . .

Second Old Man. . . . . that *he* committed suicide too.

Diego. Yes, he was a Russian. That, however, happened some years ago at Capri.

Donna Livia [*shuddering and hiding her face in her hands*]. Oh dear! Oh dear! Oh dear!

Diego. But for heaven's sake, you're not afraid that Doro is going to be the third, are you? I must say, Signora, that we all have a right to deplore the tragedy that has robbed us of an artist like Giorgio Salvi; but after all, when we know the situation as it actually was, it is quite possible—possible, notice—to say something in defense of the woman.

Donna Livia. So you defend her too?

Diego. Yes, I too, to that extent! Why not?

Second Old Man. Challenging the indignation of all decent people in town, I suppose!

Diego. Perhaps! I was simply observing that something may be said for the woman.

Donna Livia. But my own son, my Doro! I always thought he kept the best of company.

First Old Man. He was a good boy . . .

Second Old Man. . . . always knew how to behave himself.

Diego. But it was an argument, wasn't it? Well, in an argument he may have said more than he really meant. He may have exaggerated.

Donna Livia. No! No! Don't you try to spare my feelings! Don't you conceal anything from me! Delia Morello—she's an actress, isn't she?

Diego. I should call her a lunatic, Signora.

First Old Man. She has been on the stage.

Diego. But she couldn't hold her job anywhere. No manager dares take the risk of hiring her any more. Delia Morello can't be her real name. That must be just the way she is known on the stage. No one knows who she really is, nor where she comes from.

Donna Livia.   Is she a good-looking woman?

Diego.   They call her beautiful.

Donna Livia.   Oh, they're all beautiful—those actresses! I suppose Doro met her in some theatre.

Diego.   I believe he did. But at the most it couldn't have been more than an introduction, a visit to her dressing-room, back-stage, perhaps. And that is not such a terrible thing as many good people imagine, Signora. Please don't worry!

Donna Livia.   But here two men have gone and killed themselves on her account!

Diego.   I would not have killed myself for her!

Donna Livia.   But she made those two fellows lose their heads.

Diego.   I wouldn't have lost mine!

Donna Livia.   But I'm not worried on your account—I am thinking of Doro!

Diego.   Never fear, Signora! And one more thing: if that unhappy woman has done wrong to other people, she has always done the greatest wrong to herself. She's one of those women who are made haphazard, so to speak, who seem unable to get hold of themselves—wanderers astray on the face of the earth, never knowing where they're going nor where they will end. And yet sometimes, you know, she seems to be just a poor little child afraid of the world and appealing to you for help.

Donna Livia [*much impressed, and seizing him by both elbows*].   Diego, look me in the eye: you got that from Doro!

Diego.   No, Signora!

Donna Livia [*insisting*].   Tell me the truth, Diego. Doro is in love with that woman!

Diego.   I am sure he isn't.

Donna Livia [*still insisting*].   He is! He is! He is in love with her. What you have just said only a man in love with her could say!

Diego. But they're my words, not Doro's!

Donna Livia. That isn't so. Doro talked that way about her to you. And no one can convince me that he didn't!

Diego [*shrinking before her persistence*]. Oh! Oh! [*Then with a sudden eloquence, his voice becoming clear and light, caressing, inviting.*] Signora, can't you imagine —imagine—a carriage—driving along a country road— through the open fields—on a bright afternoon in summer time?

Dona Livia [*dumbfounded*]. A carriage—on a country road! What's that got to do with it?

Diego [*angrily and deeply moved*]. Signora, can you imagine the condition I was in when I sat up all night watching at the bedside of my mother, dying? I sat there —and do you know what I was doing? I was staring at a fly, a fly that had fallen into a glass of water on the lamp-stand and was swimming about, his wings flat on the surface of the water—And I sat there watching him. I didn't even notice when my poor mother died! I was all taken up in admiring the confidence that poor fly seemed to have in the strength of his two hind legs. They were longer than the others. They were made for him to get his start with. He kept swimming about desperately, always confident that those two hind legs would finally lift him above the liquid surface were he was caught. But whenever he tried to jump, he would find that something was sticking to the ends of them. So every time he failed, he would rub them together furiously, to clean them—and then he would try again! I sat there watching him for more than half an hour; and then I saw him die —and I did not see my poor mother die! Now then, do you understand? Let me alone!

Donna Livia [*dumbfounded, bewildered, stands there looking first at one and then at the other of the two* OLD

MEN *who are as much at sea as she is*]. I beg your pardon—I don't see the connection!

Diego. Does it seem to you so absurd? Well, tomorrow now, I assure you, you will laugh . . . you will laugh at all these fancied terrors you are feeling for your son when you think of that carriage on the country road which I have just trundled along before your mind's eye the better to confuse you. But please realize that I can never laugh as I think of that poor fly that came before my eyes while I was sitting there watching at my mother's bedside. [*A pause.* DONNA LIVIA *and the two* OLD MEN *stand looking at each other after this abrupt diversion, more than ever confused, unable in spite of all their efforts to make this carriage on the country road and this fly in the glass of water fit into the subject which they had just been discussing.* DIEGO CINCI *is all absorbed in memories of his mother's death; so that when* DORO PALEGARI *enters, at just this moment,* DORO *will find* CINCI *in a very unusual frame of mind.*]

Doro [*looking first at one and then at the other of the company in surprise*]. Why, what's the matter?

Donna Livia [*coming to herself*]. Oh, it's you! Doro, my boy, what have you been doing? What have you been doing? These gentlemen have been telling me—

Doro [*snapping angrily*]. About the "scandal," I suppose? Saying that I am in love, head over heels in love, with Delia Morello, eh? I suppose so! All my friends wink at me as I pass them on the street. "Eh, how's Delia, old boy?" Heavens above! What's got into you? Have you all lost your minds?

Donna Livia. But if you—

Doro. If I, what? I can't understand it, upon my word! And a scandal made of it, within twenty-four hours!

Donna Livia. But you came to the defense of that—

Doro. I came to nobody's defense.

Donna Livia. At the Avanzi's last evening!

Doro. At the Avanzi's last evening I heard Francesco Savio express, in regard to the tragic suicide of Giorgio Salvi—about whom, by the way, everybody is having his say—an opinion which did not seem to me a fair one. So I contested it! That's all there is to it!

Donna Livia. But you said certain things. . . .

Doro. Oh, I may have talked a lot of nonsense. All I said I really can't remember. In an argument one word follows on another. I may have exaggerated! But hasn't a fellow a right to his opinion on topics of the day? It seems to me we can interpret certain episodes in one fashion or another as we see fit. Today it is this way, tomorrow it's another. For example, if I happen to see Francesco Savio tomorrow, I shall be quite ready to admit that he was right and that I was wrong.

First Old Man. Oh, in that case, very well.

Donna Livia. Do so, please, Doro! Please do so! By all means!

Second Old Man. . . . to put an end to all this gossip, you understand.

Doro. Oh, not for that reason. I don't care a hang about the gossip! I would be doing it only to get rid of the mortification I feel myself!

First Old Man. Quite so. Yes, quite so . . .

Second Old Man. . . . at seeing yourself so misunderstood!

Doro. Not at all, not at all! The mortification I feel at having let myself go so far—an anger justified perhaps by the spectacle of Francesco Savio sitting there, stupidly arguing, with his facts all wrong; though he after all— well yes—he was right, substantially! So now, when I've cooled off a bit, I'm ready—yes, I'm quite ready—to apologize. And I will do so. I will apologize in the presence of everybody, to put an end to this absurd dispute. My, what a row over nothing! I'm disgusted.

Donna Livia. Well, I'm much relieved, Doro, much relieved! And I'm glad to hear you admit right here in the presence of a friend of yours that nothing can be said in defense of such a woman.

Doro. Why, was he trying to defend her too?

First Old Man. Yes, he was—that is to say, after a fashion . . .

Second Old Man. Not in earnest, you understand! Just to soothe your mother's feelings.

Donna Livia. Yes, and I must say he wasn't succeeding very well. But now what you have said is a great relief to me. And thank you, thank you ever so much, my boy.

Doro [*angry, irritated at the implication of his mother's gratitude*]. But—you're really serious? You—why, mother, you make me angrier than ever! I'm getting mad, clear through!

Donna Livia. Angry—because I am thanking you?

Doro. Well, I must say? Why do you thank me, in fact? Why are you so much relieved now! I see, you thought that . . . I swear, mother, I'll be flying off the handle!

Donna Livia. No, no, don't be angry! Let's say no more about it!

Doro [*turning to* Diego]. So you think something can be said for Delia Morello?

Diego. Oh, let's drop the subject—now that your mother is quite herself again.

Doro. No, I insist on knowing. I insist on knowing.

Diego. So you want to start the argument over again with me?

Donna Livia. Please don't, Doro.

Doro [*to his mother*]. No, it was just a matter of curiosity. [*To* Diego.] I wanted to see whether you were making the same points that I brought up last evening in my quarrel with Francesco Savio.

Diego. And suppose I were. You don't mean to say you would be on the other side now?

Doro. Do you think I'm a whirligig? Last evening I took this position: I said: "You can't claim that Delia Morello intended to encompass the ruin of Giorgio Salvi because of the simple fact that the night before she was to be married to him she went off on a lark with another man; since the real ruin of Salvi would have been for him to marry her!"

Diego. Exactly! Just my view of it. And the Morello woman knew this too; and, precisely because she knew it, she was determined to prevent it.

Doro. Nothing of the kind! Savio was right in holding that she went off with that other fellow, Michele Rocca, to push her vengeance on Giorgio Salvi to the limit—because there is no escaping the fact that in all this affair she acted at all times and under all circumstances with the most refined treachery toward him. There!

Diego. So that's your view of it? Well, keep to that opinion. And much good may it do you! At any rate, let's drop the subject now!

First Old Man. Wisely said! And now we must be going, Donna Livia. [*He kisses her hand.*]

Second Old Man. . . . delighted that everything has been cleared up now! [*He also kisses her hand. Then turning to the others.*] Good afternoon, Doro, and you too, Cinci.

Diego. Good afternoon! Good afternoon!

Donna Livia [*turning to the first of the two friends and starting back with them to the drawing-room, from which* THEY *will depart through an exit to the right*]. So then, when you get to Christina's—just tell her that I'll be calling, and ask her to be ready. [DONNA LIVIA *withdraws. For a moment* DORO *and* DIEGO *stand there without speaking. The empty drawing-room brightly lighted in the background behind them should give an interesting effect.*]

Diego [*spreading the fingers of his two hands fan-shaped, then crossing one hand over the other so as to form a network of his fingers, finally stepping up to* DORO *to attract the latter's attention*]. This is the way it is—look!—this way—exactly!

Doro. What?

Diego. That conscience we were talking about in here just before you came. A net, an elastic net! You slacken it up a little like this and good-bye!—the madness we each have in us runs amuck!

Doro [*after a brief silence, worried, suspicious*]. You mean that for me?

Diego [*almost talking to himself*]. Before your mind the images, the memories, piled up during the years, begin to crowd—fragments of the life which you have lived perhaps, but which never gains the forefront of your consciousness because you have never been willing or able to view it in the clear light of reason . . . questionable things you may have done; lies of which you would be ashamed; thoughts that are mean, petty, unworthy of you; crimes you have thought out and planned in their minutest particulars; desires unconfessed and unconfessable—and it all, all, all comes up in your mind and throws you off your balance, till you don't know where you're at, leaving you disconcerted, bewildered, terrified!

Doro [*as above*]. What are you talking about, man?

Diego [*gazing fixedly into space*]. And I hadn't slept for nine nights in succession. . . . [*He turns vehemently upon* DORO.] Try it for yourself! Nine successive nights without a wink of sleep! The white mug on the table beside your bed has a single blue line around it—and that infernal bell! Ding! Ding! Ding! Ding! Eight . . . nine! I used to count them! Ten . . . eleven! The clock striking, you see! Twelve! Not to mention the quarters and the halves . . . ! There's no human affection strong enough to hold its own when you've neglected those primal needs of the body which must—must, I tell you! —be satisfied! There I was, outraged at the cruel fate which had fallen upon the ghastly, unconscious, unrecognizable body of my poor mother—nothing but body left of her, poor thing—well, do you know what I thought? I kept thinking: "God! I wish she'd stop that gasping!"

Doro. But my dear Diego! Your mother . . . why . . . she's been dead at least two years, hasn't she?

Diego. Yes! And you have no idea how surprised I was when the gasping did stop for a moment. The room fell into a terrible silence, and I turned—I don't know why—and I looked into the mirror on the dressing-table. I was bending over the bed to see whether perchance she might have died. But the mirror was so placed that I couldn't help seeing—seeing what the expression on my face was like, the expression, that is, which I was wearing as I bent over to look at her . . . a sort of joyous terror, a sort of terrible joy, the joy that would welcome my liberation. . . . But she gave another gasp, and that gasp gave me such a shudder of loathing for the thought I had been thinking that I buried my face in my two hands as though I had committed a crime. And I began to weep—to weep like the child I once had been—for my poor mamma, whose pity . . . yes! yes! it was her pity I wanted, pity for the fatigue I felt, the fatigue I felt for having been there nine sleepless nights in succession! You see . . . yes . . . at that instant I had ceased to hope that she would die. Poor, poor mamma! How many nights' sleep had she lost when I was a little child—and sick?

Doro. Would you mind explaining why you talk about your mother this way, all of a sudden?

Diego. I don't know, I'm sure. Won't you tell me why you got angry when your mother thanked you for having put her mind at ease?

Doro. Why, it was because she actually suspected for a moment, herself—

Diego. Oh, get out! You can't make me swallow that.

Doro [*shrugging his shoulders*]. I don't know what you're driving at.

Diego. If such a suspicion on her part had not been well founded, you would have laughed instead of getting angry.

Doro. What do you mean? You don't seriously think . . . ?

Diego. I? You are the one who is thinking it?

Doro. But now I'm taking Savio's view of the matter.

Diego. So you see. . . . First here and then there! You are even angry at yourself—for your exaggerations, as you called them!

Doro. That is because I now see . . .

Diego. No! No! Be frank with yourself! Read your own thoughts, accurately!

Doro. But what thoughts shall I read, man alive?

Diego. You're now agreeing with Francesco Savio! But do you know why? It's to hide a feeling which you've had inside you without your knowing that it was there.

Doro. Nothing of the kind! You make me laugh!

Diego. It's true! It's true!

Doro. You make me laugh, I say!

Diego. In the excitement of the argument last evening that feeling suddenly came to the top in your mind. It caught you off your guard . . and you said things you didn't realize you were saying. . . . Of course you didn't! Of course you didn't! And you imagine you never even thought those things! And yet you did think them . . . you did think them! . . .

Doro.   What do you mean? When?

Diego.   Secretly . . . unknown even to yourself! Oh, my dear Doro, just as we sometimes have illegitimate children, so we sometimes have illegitimate thoughts!

Doro.   Speak for yourself, eh!

Diego.   Yes, I'll speak also for myself! . . . We all yearn to marry, and for our whole life long, some one particular soul . . . the soul which seems most convenient, most useful, to us . . . the soul which brings us in dowry the faculties and qualities most likely to help us attain the goals to which we aspire. But later on, outside the honest, conjugal household of our consciousness, we have . . . well . . . one affair after another, numberless little sins with all those other souls which we have rejected and buried in the depths of our being, and from which actions and thoughts are born—actions and thoughts which we refuse to recognize, but which, when we are forced to it, we adopt or legitimize . . . with appropriate adaptations, reserves, and cautions. Now, in this case, one of your own poor, fatherless thoughts has come home to you. You deny paternity . . . but look it over carefully! It's yours! It's yours! You were really in love with Delia Morello . . . head-over-heels in love, as you said!

Doro.   Hah! Hah! Hah! Hah! Hah! Hah! Hah! You make me laugh! You make me laugh!

[*At this point the butler,* FILIPPO, *enters the room.*]

Filippo.   Signor Francesco Savio, sir.

Doro.   Oh, here he is now! [*To* FILIPPO.] Show him in!

Diego.   And I will leave you alone with him!

Doro.   No! Wait! I want you to see how much in love I am with Delia Morello! [FRANCESCO SAVIO *appears in the drawing-room.*]

Doro.   Come in here, Francesco, won't you?

Francesco.   Why, my dear Doro! And how are you, Cinci?

Diego.   Glad to see you, Savio!

Francesco [*addressing* DORO].   I came to tell you how sorry I was about our little squabble last evening.

Doro.   I was just on the point of going to look you up to tell you how sorry I was.

Francesco [*taking his hand warmly*].   That's good news, Doro, my boy! You have taken a great weight off my mind!

Diego.   I should like to have a picture of you two fellows, upon my word!

Francesco [*to* DIEGO].   You know, Diego, we two have been friends all our lives . . . and we were on the point of breaking over nothing!

Doro.   Oh, it wasn't quite so bad as that, was it!

Francesco.   Why, it was on my mind all last evening! I can't understand how I could have helped recognizing the generosity which prompted you . . .

Diego [*breaking in*].   Exactly! The *generosity* which prompted him to defend Delia Morello!

Francesco.   Yes! And so that everybody could hear too! And it took some courage . . . with all those people yelping against her!

Doro [*puzzled*].   But . . . do you mean to say . . . ?

Diego [*to* FRANCESCO].   And you more rabid than any of the rest!

Francesco [*warmly*].   Yes. Because I had not given enough weight to certain considerations, one more sound and convincing than the other, which Doro, here, brought forward!

Doro [*with rising anger*].   Ah! So *that's* it! So you now . . . so you now! . . .

Diego [*breaking in*].   Exactly! So you now are standing up for the woman, are you not?

Francesco.   But Doro stood out against the whole crowd! He held his ground in the face of all those fools, and they couldn't find a thing to answer him with!

Doro [*to* FRANCESCO, *at the height of his irritation*]. Listen! You know what you are? . . . You're an ordinary circus clown!

Francesco. What do you mean? I came here to see you to admit that you were right! . . .

Doro. Yes! And that is why I say: you are just an ordinary circus clown!

Diego. You see, just as you now have come to the point of agreeing with him, he had already come to the point of agreeing with you!

Francesco. Agreeing with me?

Diego. Yes, with you . . . with you because of the things you said *against* Delia Morello! . . .

Doro. . . . and now you have the impudence to come and tell me that I was right!

Francesco. But—simply because I have thought over all you said!

Diego. Exactly! Don't you see? Just as *he* has thought over what *you* said! . . .

Francesco. And now he says *I* was right . . .

Diego. Just as you say *he* was right!

Doro. Yes! You say that now . . . after you made a fool of me last night . . . in the presence of everybody! Set them all talking about me . . . and nearly drove my poor mother out of her mind! . . .

Francesco. I? . . .

Doro. Yes! You! You! You just drew me on . . . getting me into an argument . . . trying to compromise me . . . making me say things that I would otherwise never have dreamed of saying! [*He steps up to* FRANCESCO *and faces him angrily.*] Just take a suggestion from me! You be very careful not to go around saying to anybody that I was right! . . .

Diego [*pressing his point*]. Because you see, you recognize the generosity which prompted him! . . .

Francesco. But I do . . . I do! . . .

Doro. You're just an ordinary circus clown!

Diego. You see . . . if you go around saying that he was right that will show that you, too, know the truth now . . . the truth, that is, that *he is in love* with Delia Morello . . . and that he came to her defense *on that account!*

Francesco. That is the third time you've called me a clown, notice!

Doro. But it won't be the last! I'll say you're a clown one hundred times . . . today . . . tomorrow . . . always!

Francesco. Please remember that I am in your house!

Doro. In my house I say that you're a clown . . . but even when I'm not in my own house I'll say you're a clown! You're a clown! A clown! A clown!

Francesco. Very well! Very well! In that case . . . good afternoon! And we'll see each other later, eh? . . . [*He starts to leave the room.*]

Diego [*in an effort to detain him*]. One moment . . . one moment! Let's not go too fast!

Doro [*restraining him*]. No, let him go!

Diego. Are you crazy, man? This will compromise you for good!

Doro. I don't care a damn!

Diego [*breaking away from him*]. But you're crazy, I say! Let me go! [*He dashes out of the room in an effort to overtake* FRANCESCO SAVIO.]

Doro [*calling after him*]. Mind your own business, Diego! [DIEGO, *however, does not stop.*]

Doro [*begins walking up and down the room, muttering furiously to himself*]. Huh! That's a good one! And he has the impudence to come and tell me that I was right! . . . The clown! After making it look to everybody as though . . . [*At this point the* BUTLER *hurries in in some alarm with a visiting card in his hand.*]

Filippo. May I come in, sir?

Doro. . . Well, what's the matter?

Filippo. A lady calling, sir.

Doro. A lady?

Filippo. Here's her card. [*He holds out a visiting card.*]

Doro [*in great agitation after reading the name on the card*]. Where . . . where is she?

Filippo. She is in the hall, sir, waiting.

Doro [*he looks around him in perplexity. Finally, and with a great effort to conceal his anxiety and confusion*]. Has mamma gone out?

Filippo. Yes, sir, she left a moment ago!

Doro. Show the lady in! Show her in here! [FILIPPO *withdraws.* DORO *advances toward the drawing-room to receive the visitor. He is standing under the central arch between the two columns when* FILIPPO *reappears, introducing* DELIA MORELLO. SHE *is soberly but elegantly costumed, and wears a thick veil.* FILIPPO *withdraws, bowing.*]

Doro. You? Delia? Here?

Delia. I came to thank you. Oh, can I ever tell you how grateful I am, my good, kind, friend!

Doro. Please, please, don't say that!

Delia. Yes! I must say just that! [DORO *has extended his hand.* DELIA *bends over as though to kiss it.*] I must thank you! Thank you, indeed!

Doro. But no . . . no . . . please! . . . I, rather, should warn you that . . .

Delia. Thank you for the kindness . . . the great kindness you did me!

Doro. But what kindness? I simply said . . .

Delia. No! Oh, I see! . . . You thought I was thanking you for having stood up for me? Not at all! What do I care whether people accuse me or defend me? I am my own judge, and my own tormentor! My gratitude, rather, is for what you thought and felt inside yourself

. . . and not because you took the trouble to express it in the presence of other people.

Doro [*in great bewilderment*]. I thought . . . yes . . . what . . . knowing the facts as I did . . . it seemed to me . . . what it seemed to me was just to think.

Deliá. Just or unjust . . . what do I care? The fact is that what you said of me suddenly made me see myself . . . you understand . . . see myself—the moment I heard it!

Doro [*in growing bewilderment, but striving to appear indifferent*]. Ah, so then . . . so then . . . I guessed right?

Delia. As right as though you had lived my life to the bottom . . . but understanding me in a way I never understood myself! Never! Never! And a great shudder went over me! . . . I cried . . . Yes! Yes! . . . "That's just the way I am! That's just the way I am!" . . . And you can't imagine with what joy and with what anguish I recognized myself, saw myself . . . in all the things you found to say of me!

Doro. I am happy . . . happy . . . most happy . . . happy because it all seemed to me so clear at the time, when in fact I did discover those things—without reflection . . . you understand . . . as though by an inspiration coming to me directly from you. Later on, I confess, I did not feel the same way.

Delia. Ah! Later on—you changed?

Doro. Yes. But if now you tell me that you recognize yourself in what I said of you . . . if you tell me that I was right . . .

Delia. I have been living all day on that inspiration of yours—inspiration you may well call it. What I don't understand is how you could see through me so easily, and so clearly—you who scarcely know me, after all. Whereas I . . . well . . . it's terrible . . . I struggle and struggle, suffering all the while—I don't know—as though—as though I were not quite myself, as though I were constantly groping around to find myself . . . to understand the woman that I really am, to ask her what she really wants, why she is suffering so, and what I ought to do to tame her, pacify her, give her a little peace . . .

Doro. That's it . . . a little peace, a little quiet! That's what you need!

Delia. I have him constantly before my eyes . . . just as I saw him there at my feet . . . pale . . . lifeless . . . a dead thing! It all came over me in a flash! I felt myself—I don't know—dying—and I bent over to look at him . . . trying to grasp from the abyss of that instant the eternity of the sudden death I could see before my eyes, there, in his face, a face which in a second had lost consciousness of everything . . . Ah, I knew . . . I alone knew . . . the life there had been in that poor body which had destroyed itself for me, for me who am nothing . . . nothing. Ah! I was quite mad! Imagine the state I must be in at present!

Doro. But quiet, now! Please, be calm!

Delia. Oh, I am calm enough . . . But see . . . when I try to be calm . . . well . . . it's this way . . . I'm stunned, stunned, that's it! All feeling seems to leave me! Just that . . . just that! I pinch myself, but I don't feel it! My hands . . . I look at them, and they don't seem to be mine! And then all the things I have to do—I don't know why I have to do them—I open my handbag and take out my mirror and I am horror-stricken at the pallor and at the coldness that has come over me! Well . . . you can't imagine the impression I get, there, in the circle of that mirror, of my painted lips and my painted eyes! . . .

Doro. That's because you don't see yourself as others see you.

Delia. So you say that, too? Must I actually hate—

hate as my enemies—all the people I have anything to do with—that they may help me to understand myself?

Doro. Why no . . . why should you?

Delia. Why, I see them walk in front of me and they seem—well—to be dazzled by my eyes, by my lips, by my beauty, in short; but no one cares for me . . . no one cares for what most concerns me.

Doro. Your real self, that is! . . .

Delia. So then I punish them in the things they really desire. Those desires disgust me, but first I do my best to fan them, make them worse in order to get my revenge . . . and that revenge I get by giving myself away, suddenly, capriciously, to the person whom they would have least expected to win me! [Doro *nods with a suggestion of reproach.*] I do that, I suppose, to show them my contempt for the things they most highly prize in me. [*Again* Doro *nods.*] Have I harmed myself? Always . . . always! But better worthless men like that . . . worthless men who have no pretensions, and who know how little they amount to . . . people who bore you, perhaps, but who do not disappoint you . . . and who may even have their good points, too—certain fresh and honest qualities which are the more delightful because you least expect to find them, just there.

Doro [*surprised*]. Well, that was almost exactly what I said! Almost exactly!

Delia [*with great emotion*]. Yes! Yes!

Doro. That was the way I explained certain incomprehensible acts of yours! . . .

Delia. Incomprehensible? Yes . . . caprices . . . impulses of the moment . . . leaps into space with my eyes closed! . . . [*She stands there for a moment, gazing vacantly into void, as though fascinated by some distant vision.*] Just imagine . . . [*And then she continues as though speaking to herself.*] somersaults you might call them . . . yes . . . somersaults . . . [*falling into her abstraction again*]. There was a little girl, and the gypsies taught her to turn somersaults . . . handsprings . . . wheeling hand over hand on a green lawn near my house in the country when I was a child! . . . [*Still in her abstraction.*] Was I ever a child? [*A memory of the way her mother used to call her comes into her mind and she shouts:*] "Lilly dear! Lilly dear! Lilli! Lilli!" Hahah! Hahah! She was afraid of those gypsies, poor, dear mamma! She was afraid they would suddenly break camp and carry me off. [*Comes to herself again.*] The gypsies never carried me off. I learned to turn handsprings and somersaults all by myself after I had come away from the country here to town . . . here, where everything is false, fictitious . . . falser and more fictitious every day. And we can't shake it off; because when we try to get back to simplicity again . . . make ourselves true and honest again, our very honesty and our very simplicity seem false and counterfeit! It all seems that way because it is . . . because it is false and counterfeit! Haha! Truth? What is truth? . . . Nothing is true! I should like to see with my eyes, or hear with my ears, or feel with my fingers, one thing . . . just one thing . . . that is true . . . really true . . . in me!

Doro. There is one thing in you that I imagine is true . . . the goodness and kindness that you have at bottom—a goodness and a kindness hidden from other people, and perhaps even from yourself—a goodness, at any rate, that I tried, in the quarrel yesterday, to make other people see.

Delia. Yes! Yes! And I'm very grateful! Yes! Goodness . . . you call me "good"—but a goodness so complicated, so complex that when you tried to make people understand it, when you tried to make it look simple and clear, they grew angry at you and laughed at you. . . . But you have explained it, even to me. . . . Yes, people dislike me, just as you say. I was kept at a distance

by everybody—there, at Capri. I'm sure that some of
them thought I was a spy! But what a discovery I made
there, Doro. . . . Love for humanity! Do you know
what it means to love humanity? It means just this: when
you say you are in love with humanity, you are satisfied
with yourself! When a person is satisfied with himself
. . . happy with himself . . . he loves humanity! Full
of just such love, and happy . . . oh, so happy *he* must
have been when *he* came to Capri, after the last exhibi-
tion of his paintings at Naples!

Doro.   Giorgio Salvi, you mean?

Delia.   He had been working on some Neapolitan
studies, as he called them, and he found me when he was
in just that state of mind.

Doro.   There you are! Just as I said! All taken up
with his own art . . . and as for feelings! . . . no feelings for anything except for his art!

Delia.   Color . . . ah, color . . . everything was
color with him! Feeling with him was nothing but color!

Doro.   So he asked you to sit for a portrait? . . .

Delia.   In the beginning . . . yes! But later on . . .
he had a way of his own in asking for anything he wanted
—so funny—petulant, almost impudent—he was like a
spoiled child! So I became his model! . . . It was very,
very true what you said: nothing is more irritating than
to be held aloof, excluded from a joy which . . .

Doro.   . . . which is living, present, before us, around
us, and the reason for which we can neither discover nor
define! . . .

Delia.   Exactly! It was a joy . . . well, a pure joy,
but only for his *eyes* . . . and it proved to me that, after
all, at bottom he saw in me . . . he prized in me . . .
only my body! My body was the only thing he wanted
from me! Oh, don't misunderstand me! Not as other
men wanted me—out of a low desire—oh no!

Doro. But that, in the long run, could only have irritated you the more.

Delia. Precisely! Because if I was disgusted, nauseated, when other men failed to help me in my own spiritual uncertainties and troubles, my disgust at a man who also wanted my body and nothing else—but only to get from me a purely . . . a purely . . .

Doro. . . . ideal joy . . .

Delia. . . . and a joy exclusively his own . . .

Doro. . . . must have been all the stronger precisely because every tangible motive for anger was lacking . . .

Delia. . . . and it was impossible for me to have the satisfaction of that vengeance which at least I was able to inflict upon other men by suddenly giving myself to someone else! Oh, for a woman I assure you, an angel is always more irritating than a beast!

Doro [*triumphantly*]. Well! Well! Well! I used those very words! Absolutely! Those very words!

Delia. Yes, but you forget—I am only repeating them, after you, just as they were reported to me. You see, they suddenly made so many things clear to me!

Doro. Why, yes . . . revealing a real reason . . .

Delia. . . . for what I did! Yes . . . yes . . . it's true: to get my revenge on him, I tried to bring my body gradually to life before him so that it should no longer exist merely for the delight of his eyes . . .

Doro. . . . and later, when you saw that he had become your slave as so many others had been, then, to taste your vengeance to the full, you forbade him any other joy than the one with which, up to that time, he had been content . . .

Delia. Since that was all he had ever asked for . . . since that was the only one truly worthy of him! . . .

Doro. That's enough! I understand! I understand! In that way your vengeance was complete! You never wanted him to marry you, did you? In fact, you were determined that he shouldn't?

DELIA. Yes! Yes! For a long time I struggled . . . I did my best to dissuade him . . . But in the end, driven to a fury, beside himself . . . exasperated beyond endurance by my obstinate refusals, he threatened to do something rash . . . It was then that I decided to go away . . . disappear forever!

Doro. And then it was that you imposed upon him conditions which you knew would be terribly hard for him! . . . You imposed them deliberately upon him! . . .

Delia. Deliberately . . . yes . . . on purpose!

Doro. The condition that he would introduce you formally, as his fiancée, to his mother and to his sister! . . .

Delia. Yes . . . yes . . . because they were proud and haughty women, of the most inaccessible aristocracy —not my kind at all—and he was proud of their pride and jealous of their high position. Yes, I did it deliberately, so that he would say no! Oh, how he used to talk of his little sister! . . .

Doro. Exactly! Just as I contended, then! Tell me the truth now . . . when Rocca, his sister's fiancé . . .

Delia [*horror-stricken*]. Oh, no, no! Don't speak of him . . . don't speak of him, please!

Doro. But here we would have the real proof of the position I maintained! You must tell me! You must tell me that what I said is true!

Delia. Yes, I did go away with him! I did spend a night with him . . . because I was desperate . . . desperate . . . unable to see any other means of escape!

Doro. Exactly! Exactly!

Delia. And under such circumstances that Giorgio would be sure to find us together—yes—find me with Rocca and thus refuse to go on with our marriage . . . which would have been the ruin of him—utter·unhappiness—and the ruin of me also. I would have been wretched, too.

Doro [*triumphantly*]. Exactly! Absolutely what I said! So I defended you—and that fool there saying I was wrong—saying that your refusals of Giorgio . . . all your struggles, all your threats . . . your attempt to run away . . . were just part of a cheap game you were playing to lead him on.

Delia [*alarmed*]. He said that? . . .

Doro. Yes! Treachery premeditated . . . carefully thought out . . . aiming to reduce Salvi to utter despair, after you had made him fall in love with you, after you had led him on!

Delia [*alarmed*]. I . . . led him on . . . I?

Doro. Exactly! And the more desperate he got, the more you held out in order to gain many many things which he would never have granted you otherwise.

Delia [*more and more alarmed and gradually losing her confidence again*]. What things?

Doro. Well, first of all, an introduction to his mother and to his sister, and to the latter's fiancé, social recognition from the three of them!

Delia. Ah! And he didn't see that I hoped to find in Giorgio's refusal to give me those introductions a pretext for breaking off my engagement to him?

Doro. No . . . no! He claimed you had another scheme in that!

Delia [*in utter desperation*]. What scheme?

Doro. He said you wanted to parade your victory in public, before all society, by being seen in the presence of that little sister of his . . . you a model of the studios . . . you an actress . . . you, an adventuress! . . .

Delia [*stabbed to the heart*]. Oh, that is what he said? [*She stands there looking blankly into space, overwhelmed.*]

Doro. That is exactly what he said! And furthermore,

he said that when the introduction you had insisted upon was postponed from day to day, you discovered that the postponement was due to the flat refusal of Rocca, the sister's fiancé, to meet you!

Delia. And so to show my power over Rocca . . . to humiliate him . . . to get even with him! . . . That's the idea, isn't it?

Doro. Yes . . . you sank your claws into Rocca, twisting him around your finger like a blade of grass, quite forgetting Salvi, meantime—just for the pleasure of showing that sister of his and her mother, what the pride and respectability of the pillars of public morals amounted to! [*For a time* DELIA *stands in silence her eyes fixed apparently upon something in distant space. Finally* SHE *covers her face with both her hands and remains in that attitude for some seconds.* DORO *considers her, in perplexity and surprise. Then he asks:*] What's the matter? [DELIA *still keeps her hands to her face, but finally* SHE *lowers them and is again seen staring with the same blank expression into space. Then, opening her two arms in a gesture of discouragement.*]

Delia. And who knows! Who knows! Who knows that those weren't the reasons?

Doro [*startled*]. Weren't the reasons? . . . What do you mean? If they were . . . [*At this moment* DONNA LIVIA *appears in the brightly lighted drawing-room and comes forward on the stage in great agitation, calling, before* SHE *reaches the parlor:*]

Donna Livia. Doro! Doro!

Doro [*leaping to his feet in alarm at the sound of his mother's voice*]. My mother is coming!

Donna Livia [*rushing into the room*]. Doro! Is this true? I've been told that the trouble last evening is to result in a duel!

Doro. Duel? Who ever said such a thing?

Donna Livia [*noticing* DELIA *and turning disdainfully*

upon her].   Ah! Indeed! So I find this woman in my own house!

Doro [*firmly, and stressing the important words*].   Yes, in your house! In *your* house, mamma! You call it *your* house!

Delia.   Oh, but I'm going away . . . I'm going away! But don't be alarmed, Signora! There will be no duel . . . there will be no duel! I assure you, Signora! Don't worry on that account! I will prevent it . . . I will find a way to prevent it! . . . [*With a sob, she starts rapidly for the other room.*]

Doro [*following after her and calling*].   Signora, don't you dare! Please, Signora, don't try to interfere! [DELIA *goes out.*]

Donna Livia [*trying to stop* DORO *and almost in a scream*].   So it's true then?

Doro [*turning and answering vehemently*].   True? What is true? That I'm going to fight a duel? Perhaps! And why? For something that no one understands . . . neither he, nor I, nor the woman herself . . . ah . . . nor the woman herself! . . .

Curtain.

The curtain falls, but almost immediately rises again, uncovering a section of the theatre lobby opening on the orchestra. SPECTATORS, *one by one, are seen coming out of the main hall of the theatre, at the end of the first act. It may be taken for granted that other spectators are similarly entering the corridors that lie invisible to right and left. In fact, newcomers keep appearing from other parts of the lobby from time to time.*

This scene in the lobby—SPECTATORS *coming out of a theatre—will show what was first presented on the stage as life itself to be a fiction of art; and the substance of the comedy will accordingly be pushed back, as it were, into a secondary plane of actuality or reality. But later on, toward the end of this interlude, the scene in the lobby will, in its turn, be expelled from the foreground, when it transpires that the comedy which has been witnessed on the stage is a "comedy with a key"—a comedy, that is, based upon an episode in real life, an episode, moreover, with which the newspapers have been recently dealing as a feature: the famous triangular situation between a certain* MORENO WOMAN *(whom everybody recognizes in the* DELIA MORELLO *of the comedy): a certain* BARON NUTI, *and the sculptor,* GIACOMO LA VELA *(who has committed suicide). The* MORENO WOMAN *and* BARON NUTI *are present in the theatre among the spectators. Their appearance, therefore, suddenly and violently establishes a plane of reality still closer to real life, leaving the spectators who are discussing the fictitious reality of the staged play on a plane midway between. In the interlude at the end of the second act these three planes of reality will come into conflict with one another, as the participants in the drama of real life attack the participants in the comedy, the* SPECTATORS, *meantime, trying to interfere. Under such circumstances it need not be observed, a comedy cannot go on.*

In the production of this first interlude the greatest naturalness, volubility, and vivacity are necessary. The presupposition is that at the end of every act of these unintelligible, implausible, paradoxical—and what not —comedies of PIRANDELLO, *arguments and conflicts are bound to occur. The* DEFENDERS OF PIRANDELLO *should show toward his uncompromising antagonists a smiling humility of countenance which has the effect of exasperating hostilities rather than the contrary.*

Various groups of people form in the lobby. Individuals may be seen going from one group to the other in quest of light. Comic effects should be derived from their changes of opinion according to the group they hit upon.

*A few placid individuals are smoking unconcernedly,
and the way they smoke will show their boredom, if they
are bored, or their doubts, if they are in doubt; because
smoking, like all vices that become habitual, has this sad
shortcoming: that it eventually fails to satisfy, by itself,
but takes its flavor from the moment in which it is indulged and from the state of mind in which it is indulged.
It follows that even people who dislike* PIRANDELLO'S
*plays may console themselves with a good cigar, if they
choose, on occasion.*

*Conspicuous in the crowd in the lobby, the uniforms
of two* POLICEMEN *(carabinieri) may be seen. An* USHER
or two and a TICKET TAKER; *two or three* MAIDS *dressed
in black with white aprons. A* NEWSBOY *intrudes from the
street, calling his headlines. In the groups, arguing and
gesticulating here and there, a few women may be observed. Some of them also are smoking (but not with the
author's approval); others may be seen going in and out
of the doors to the boxes, where they are visiting friends.*

The FIVE DRAMATIC CRITICS *are naturally much in evidence.* THEY *keep away from each other at first, and if
anyone questions them they maintain a stolid silence
(they have to, you see, to live up to a reputation for
"reserve" and "balance"). Gradually, however, they drift
together to get a line on each other's "dope." Individuals
who recognize them edge up as close as possible (without
impoliteness) to hear what these celebrities are saying.
The interest these people manifest gradually attracts a
crowd, whereupon the* CRITICS *either crawl into their
shells or walk away. It is quite possible that here in the
lobby some of the* CRITICS *will say very sharp things about
the comedy and its author; though they will have only
praise for both in the articles they write for their papers
the next day. A profession is one thing, while the man
who professes it is quite another: a critic may have plenty
of reasons for sacrificing as a writer his sincerity as a man*

*—granted, of course, that such sacrifice be possible,
granted, I mean to say, that he have some sincerity to
sacrifice. So with the spectators. Many of those who here
appear as bitter critics of the play clapped it uproariously
in the theatre at the end of the first act.*

*It is hardly worth while writing out the dialogue of
this choral interlude. People say much the same things
and express much the same judgments about all plays
and all authors—which, and who, are "good," "bad,"
"well constructed," "badly constructed," "obscure," "absurd," "improbable," "paradoxical," "cerebral—all from
the brain," and so on. Nevertheless, we must here note
down such exchanges as are indispensable between the
actors who are actors for the moment in this interlude;
though the stage manager is intentionally left a free hand
to introduce anything he can devise to keep the lobby in
a state of lively and confused animation.*

*At first: monosyllables, exclamations, grunts, brief
questions and answers, from phlegmatic* SPECTATORS *who
make for the lobby at the earliest possible moment (those
really interested in the play are still inside witnessing or
fomenting the uproar following on the first act).*

Two People [*coming out in a hurry*].   I'll just go upstairs and look for him.

Number eight, second row, balcony. But be sure you
find him, eh?

Don't worry, I'll get him all right. [*The* SECOND *starts
away to the left.*]

A Man [*meeting him*].   Hello! So you managed to get
in?

The Second of the First Two.   As you see. However,
I'll be back in a moment. I'm just going upstairs. [*Other*
SPECTATORS *come on from the left where a great deal of
talking can be heard.* OTHERS *are appearing through the
main and side entrances.*]

Somebody [*anybody*]. Good house tonight!
Another. Full up!
A Third. See them anywhere?
A Fourth. I don't think they got past the box-office;
but they were beauts!

[*In the general confusion exchanges of greetings:*
"Good evening!" "Good evening!"—*Smatterings of light
talk; one word comments on the play:* "Some show!"
"Bunk!" *etc., etc. A few introductions. A* NEWSBOY *enters
from the street calling his papers. A* MAN *buys one. An
eruption from the theatre—a number of* SPECTATORS *favorable to the author. Enthusiastic, eager, eyes gleaming,*
THEY *crowd together in a group and begin exchanging
first impressions. Later* THEY *scatter in various directions,
approaching this or that hostile circle, defending their
author and his comedy now good-humoredly, now bad-
humoredly, now with irony. Their* ADVERSARIES *have also
been organizing, meantime.*]

Friends of Pirandello.
   Here we are! Here! This way!
   I'll be right there!
   All together now, if there's trouble!
   A great success, it seems to me!
   Splendid! Splendid!
   Seems to have gotten away with it!
   That last scene with the woman . . . !
   Real acting, I say!
   Those fellows both changed their minds!
   The whole act's a ripper!
Opponents.
   His usual line of nonsense!
   What does he think we are, fools?
   Pirandello's in the same old rut!
   You can't make head or tail to the thing!

What's it all mean?

That bird's getting away with murder!

Two dollars, to listen to that stuff!

[*One of the* ADVERSARIES, *calling to the group of* PIRANDELLO'S FRIENDS.] But you fellows, you understand it all, eh?

Another of the Adversaries. Of course they do. They're a bunch of wise ones, all right!

One of Pirandello's Friends [*approaching*]. You said that for my benefit?

The First of the Two Adversaries. No, I didn't mean you—I meant him. [*And he points to another man.*]

The Latter [*advancing*]. You meant that for me?

Adversary. Yes, I meant it for you! I meant it for you! You wouldn't understand "Punch and Judy" if you had it explained to you!

The Man in Question. Yes, but *you* understand, don't you! At least, you understand enough to say it's bunk, don't you?

Voices from Neighboring Groups.

But what is there to understand, anyhow?

Didn't you hear . . . ?

Nobody knows what it's all about!

First it's this, and then it's something else!

First they said one thing, but now they say the opposite!

It's a joke on the audience!

What are those people staring at?

That poor mother dying, eh? . . .

. . . And that carriage on the country road! . . .

And it never gets anywhere! Some flivver!

A Man [*going from one group to another*]. So it's a joke on the audience! A joke on the audience! What's it all mean? No one knows what it means! No one can make head or tail to it!

Another Group [*coming into the foreground*].

But it certainly makes you think, eh?

But why is he always harping on this illusion and reality string?

That's not my view of it!

It's just a way of saying things!

Hasn't he expressed it?

Well, expression is art, and art is expression!

But damned if I can see what he's expressed!

But I saw you clapping . . . yes, you did . . . yes, you did . . . I saw you . . . I saw you! . . .

But a single conception may present different phases, according as you look at it, providing it be a whole conception of life.

Conception be damned! Can you tell me what the conception in this first act is?

Yes, but supposing it didn't pretend to have any meaning! . . .

The Same Man [*going to another group*]. Yes! Exactly! I see! It isn't supposed to have any meaning! Clever, eh? Clever!

A Third Group [*gathering around the critics*]. Nonsense! Just plain damn nonsense! But you critics—you understand the dra-ama! Pray enlighten us. What's it all mean?

First Critic. The construction . . . not bad . . . not bad. Of course one or two places could be left out . . .

One of the Spectators. What was the point in all that high-brow stuff about conscience?

A Second Critic. But gentlemen, gentlemen, you have seen only the first act! . . .

Third Critic. But, honest now . . . is it permissible, I ask you, to play with character that way? There ought to be a law against it . . . and an act without either head or tail? Here we have a drama based, almost casually, you might say, on a discussion that is not even held on the stage! . . .

Fourth Critic. But the discussion is about the play itself. It is the play itself!

Second Critic. And the play gets going at last when the woman comes on!

Third Critic. But why not give us the play then, and have done with it?

A Friend of Pirandello. But that woman is well conceived!

One of the Adversaries. It isn't so much the character, though. It's the girl who takes the part. [*He will name the actress doing* DELIA MORELLO.]

The Man [*leaving this group and going back to the first one*]. The drama gets going finally, when the woman comes on! She is well conceived, there's no denying that! Everybody is saying so!

A Man in the First Group [*answering angrily*]. Oh, give us a rest! This play is just one jumble of words!

Another Man [*vehemently*]. He took the plot out of the newspapers! Sheer impudence!

Third [*just as vehemently*]. One trick after another! Just word play! All on the surface!

The Man [*going from the first to the second group*]. Yes, he got the plot from the newspapers! There's no denying it! Everybody says so!

Fourth Critic [*speaking to the third*]. But what characters, in the name of heaven! Where do you find people like that in life?

Third Critic. That's a great idea! People can talk, can't they, and the moment they talk . . . !

Fourth Critic. Talk? Exactly! Talk! And you can do what you want when you're playing with words!

Fifth Critic. But I ask you now, if the theatre is art! . . .

One of the Adversaries. Art . . . exactly . . . poetry . . . poetry!

Fifth Critic. But why not controversy? Admirable,

that, I grant you. Conflict . . . the shock of opposite opinions . . . just that!

One of the Friends of Pirandello. But you people are making the controversy, it seems to me. I didn't notice so much of it on the stage!

One of the Adversaries. Yes . . . here we have a great author, haven't we? At least you say so!

The Old Author [*who never had a play produced*]. So far as I am concerned, if you like this play, you're welcome! What I think—you know already!

Voices. No! Tell us! Tell us! What do you think? Let's have it!

Old Author. Oh, little tricks of the mind . . . intellectual altogether, gentlemen . . . little problems . . . what shall I say—little problems of philosophy, as philosophy is studied by men who are not philosophers! . . .

Fourth Critic. I don't agree! I don't agree!

Old Author [*raising his voice*]. But no great travail of the spirit, as we say! Nothing really straightforward and convincing.

Fourth Critic. Yes, we all know what you call straightforward and convincing! . . .

A Literary Man [*who never writes*]. If you ask me, the most objectionable thing about the play is . . . well . . . it's the disagreeableness of the situation itself!

Second Critic. Why, no! This time it seems to me we have an atmosphere much more wholesome than usual.

Literary Man. But no real artistic urge! Why anybody could write like that!

Fourth Critic. For my part, not having seen the whole play as yet, I shouldn't risk a final judgment; but I think there is going to be something to it. It's as though you were looking into a looking-glass that had gone crazy somehow and . . .

[*On the left at this moment a violent clamor is heard.*

Screams. Shouts.] "Lunatic! Fraud! Fraud! Lunatic! Call the ambulance!" [PEOPLE *all look in that direction.*] What's going on in there?

The Bad-Humored Spectator. Can't a fellow ever come to see a play of this fellow Pirandello without getting mixed up in a scrap?

Good-Humored Spectator. Let's hope there'll be no heads broken.

One of the Friends of Pirandello. If you want to sleep, why don't you stick to the other plays? With them you can just lean back in your seat and take what is sent you across the footlights. But with a comedy of Pirandello's you have to be on your pins. You sit up straight and dig your finger nails into the arms of your chair as though you were going to be knocked down by what the author has to say! You hear a word . . . any word at all . . . "chair" for instance! Now with most people that would mean "chair," but with Pirandello you say "A chair? . . . No sir! He isn't going to get away with that! I'm going to find out what's under the chair!"

One of the Adversaries. Yes, yes! That's right! Pirandello gives you everything except a little sentiment! But not a bit of sentiment!

Other Adversaries. That's it! That's it! Not a bit of sentiment . . . and you've got to have sentiment!

One of Pirandello's Friends. If you want sentiment go and find it under the chair that fellow is talking about.

The Adversaries. But let us have done with these spasms, this nihilism . . . this delight he takes in denying everything! We're tired of tearing down. Let us begin to build up!

First of Pirandello's Friends [*vehemently*]. Who is tearing anything down? You people are the Bolshevists!

One of the Adversaries [*storming back at him*]. We, tearing down? We never denied that reality exists!

First of Pirandello's Friends. But who denies your reality, if you never succeeded in creating one?

A Second Friend. You deny the truth as other people see it, you claim that there is only one way of looking at things.

First Friend. The way you look at them yourself, today!

Second Friend. Forgetting how you looked at them yesterday!

First Friend. Because you . . . you people get your reality from others—it's a convention . . . a mere convention . . . an empty word . . . any word at all: mountain, tree, stream. You think that reality is something fixed, something definite, and you feel as though you were being cheated if someone comes along and shows you that it was all an illusion on your part. Idiots! This comedy tells you that everyone must build a foundation for himself under his own feet, bit by bit, step by step, if he is to advance. You must kick aside a reality that does not belong to you, for the simple reason that you have not made it for yourselves, but are using it as parasites—yes, gentlemen, as parasites—mourning that old-fashioned sentimentality of yours that we've driven from the stage at last, thank God!

Baron Nuti [*pale, disheveled, in a rage, comes in from the left accompanied by two other* SPECTATORS *who are trying to restrain him*]. And something else, it seems to me, this comedy teaches, my dear sir! It teaches you to malign the dead and to slander the living!

One of the Men with Him [*seizing him by an arm and trying to drag him away*]. But please . . . no . . . please . . . come away . . . come away!

The Other Man with Him [*talking at the same time*]. Yes . . . hush . . . hush! Come . . . come . . . please come! Come!

Baron Nuti [*as he is being dragged off to the left, turns*

and shouts back].   To malign the dead and to slander
the living!

Voices [*amid general surprise*].

What's the matter? Who's that man?

Who's that man?

What a face!

Has he gone crazy?

What's the matter?

Who is he?

Spectator from the Social Set.   It's Baron Nuti.
Voices.

Baron Nuti? Who is Baron Nuti?

Why did he say what he said?

Spectator from the Social Set.   But don't you people
understand that there is a key to this comedy?

One of the Critics.   A key? What do you mean . . .
a key?

Spectator from the Social Set.   Why yes! This comedy
is based on the Moreno affair! Almost word for word!
The author has taken it from real life!

Voices.

The Moreno case?

The Moreno woman?

Who is she?

Who is she?

Why, she's that actress that was in Germany for so
long!

She's well known in Turin!

Ah, yes, she was mixed up in the suicide of that
sculptor named La Vela some months ago!

What do you think of that?

And Pirandello . . . is Pirandello getting so low
that he makes comedies on society gossip?

Looks that way . . . looks that way!

And it's not the first time, you know!

But there's nothing wrong in making comedy out of the day's gossip, is there?

No, unless, as that man just said, you use your comedy to malign the dead and slander the living.

But Nuti . . . who is Nuti?

Spectator from the Social Set. He is the other fellow in the triangle! La Vela killed himself on Nuti's account! Nuti was to marry La Vela's sister!

One of the Critics. And he spent the night with the Moreno woman—the night before her marriage to La Vela?

Voices from the Hostile Group. The same situation to a T! It's a crime . . . a downright crime!

Other Voices from the Same Group. And the actors in the real drama have been here in the theatre?

A Third [*calling attention to* NUTI *off the stage, to the left*]. There he is . . . there he is!

Spectator from the Social Set. The Moreno woman has a seat in a box upstairs. She recognized herself immediately in the comedy. They'd better watch out for her! She's a terror when she gets started! She bit her handkerchief to shreds during the first act! She'll be making a noise, you'll see! She'll turn the place upside down!

Voices.

Serve them right if she did!

The idea of putting a woman in a pillory like that!

Her own case right before her eyes on the stage, and that Nuti fellow, too!

He had murder in his eye!

There's going to be trouble here . . . there's going to be trouble!

[*A bell rings, announcing the beginning of the second act.*]

There's the bell . . . there's the bell!

The curtain's going up!

Let's hurry! We mustn't miss anything!

[*There is a general movement toward the entrances to the theatre proper. Exclamations, comments, murmurings continue as the news spreads. Three individuals from the group favorable to* PIRANDELLO *bring up the rear, so that they are present on the stage—that is to say, in the theatre lobby, now virtually cleared of people— when the* MORENO WOMAN *appears from the left. She has come tearing down from her box upstairs despite the efforts of* THREE MALE FRIENDS *who are trying to get her out of the theatre to prevent trouble. The* TICKET TAKERS *at the theatre doors are at first caught by surprise; but then they do their best to quiet the disturbance so that the play inside will not be interrupted. The three partisans of* PIRANDELLO *stand aside listening in amazement and consternation.*]

Signora Moreno. No . . . no! I will! I will! Let me alone . . . let me alone!

One of Her Friends. But it's madness . . . it's sheer madness! What can you do about it?

Signora Moreno. I am going behind the scenes!

A Second of Her Friends. What can you do in there? Have you lost your mind?

Signora Moreno. Let me alone! Let me alone!

The Third of Her Friends. Now I'll just take you to my car.

Other Two [*in chorus*]. Yes, yes, let's all go home! Please, now, come along with us!

Signora Moreno. I won't! I won't! Let go of me! Let go of me! It's a disgrace! It's an insult! And they won't get away with it scot free!

The First Friend. But what's the idea? What's the idea? . . . On the stage . . . in front of everybody there?

Signora Moreno. Let go of me, I tell you! Let go of me! Yes, there on the stage, in front of everybody!

Second Friend. Ah, no, not a bit of it! Not a bit of it! We won't let you make a show of yourself like that!

Signora Moreno. Let go of me, won't you? I'm going in there behind the scenes. . . .

Third Friend. But the actors are out on the stage again!

First Friend. The second act has begun!

Signora Moreno [*suddenly growing calmer*]. Ah, they have begun again? I must hear what they have to say! I'm going back! [*She starts off toward the left again.*]

Her Friends [*all together*]. No! No! Please, let's go away! Do as we say! Please! Please! Let's go home!

Signora Moreno [*virtually dragging them after her*]. No! I'm going back in again! I want to see the rest of it! I will! I will!

One of the Friends [*as they withdraw to the left*]. But why torment yourself any further?

One of the Ticket Takers [*addressing the three partisans of* PIRANDELLO]. What's the matter with those people? Gone nutty? . . .

The First of the Partisans [*to the other two*]. Did you understand? Did you understand?

The Second. It's the Moreno woman!

The Third. But say, is Pirandello in the theatre?

The First. He may be. I think I'll just step inside and advise him to run, while the running is good. This evening there's going to be a rumpus, and no mistake.

Curtain.

ACT II

The house of FRANCESCO SAVIO *the morning after.*

A sort of lounge opening on a wide veranda, where SAVIO *habitually practices fencing. On the veranda, ac-*

*cordingly, as we view it through the large windows which
occupy almost all the rear wall of the room, there are one
or two stools, a long bench for spectators, fencing masks
and gloves, chest protectors, sabres, rapiers. A green cloth
curtain hangs on the inside of the window and may be
run back and forth on rings so as to cut off the view of
the veranda and give a little privacy to the room. A similar curtain, stretched between the posts on the veranda,
is already drawn, cutting off the veranda from the garden
which is supposed to lie beyond, and of which a glimpse
will be had at certain moments as some of the characters
draw the curtain aside to go down the steps into the garden.*

*The room is furnished with green wicker furniture—
two chairs, a table, a stand, two divans. There must be a
door to the right, in addition to one opening upon the
veranda, and a small window to the left.*

As the curtain rises, FRANCESCO SAVIO *and the* FENCING
MASTER, *with masks, protectors, and gloves on, are fencing on the veranda.* PRESTINO *and two other* FRIENDS
stand looking on.

   The Fencing Master.   Eh-eh-eh! Look out! Look out!
[*He lunges and* FRANCESCO *parries.*] Good! No . . . let's
try that again! Eh-eh-eh-eh! [*They cross their rapiers, the
fencing master lunges, and* FRANCESCO *parries as before.*]
Well done! Well done! Now look out . . . look out! In
position! Now attack . . . now attack! That feint is no
good! That feint is no good! It leaves you open over here!
This way . . . see? There you are! All right! Alt! [THEY
lower their rapiers. The practice bout is over.] Keep at it
that way and you'll come through all right! [THEY *take
off their masks.*]
   Francesco.   Yes! I'm sure I will! But I think I have
had enough! Thanks, maestro! [*He shakes hands with the
fencing master.*]

Prestino.   Yes, better not keep it up too long!

Fencing Master [*taking off his glove and then the protector*].   But I'll tell you one thing . . . you're not going to find Palegari easy! He's a tough customer when he attacks!

One of the Two Friends.   And he parries splendidly! Don't give him a chance at you!

The Second.   He's as quick as a flash!

Francesco.   Yes, I knew that. [*Taking off his glove and protector.*]

The First of His Friends.   You keep your eye peeled to the right!

Fencing Master.   The main point is to keep your iron on his.

Francesco.   I understand . . . I understand!

The Second Friend.   The straight lunge works best against Doro.

First Friend.   Not a bit of it! You just meet his rush . . . just meet his rush! You take it from me . . . let him alone and he'll beat himself! Keep a stiff arm and he'll spit himself on your weapon!

Fencing Master.   Meantime, I must congratulate you . . . you have an air-tight defense!

Prestino.   Follow my advice and don't do any attacking! Keep him coming on and you'll get a chance at him sooner or later! Meantime I propose a round of drinks to your good luck! [*He comes forward into the room with the others.*]

Francesco.   Yes, yes, right you are! [*He pushes a button in the wall; then turning to the* FENCING MASTER]: And you, maestro, what'll you have?

The Fencing Master.   Nothing for me—I never drink in the forenoon.

Francesco.   I have some first rate beer.

Prestino.   That's the talk! A mug of beer!

First of the Two Friends. Same here! [*The* BUTLER *appears from the door to the right.*]

Francesco. Bring in four or five bottles of beer right away. [*The* BUTLER *goes out, returning almost immediately, however, with bottles and glasses on a tray. He pours the beer, passes it around and withdraws again.*]

First Friend. This will be the craziest duel on record. Your name will go down in history, Francesco.

Second Friend. It certainly will. I doubt whether two men ever cut themselves up before, each for the privilege of saying that the other one was right.

Prestino. But it's all very natural, however.

First Friend. Natural? What is there natural about it?

Prestino. Why, here the two of them were on opposite sides of the same question. They both changed their minds at the same time, each coming around to the view of the other. Naturally, they collided in the process.

Fencing Master. Of course, if while the one who was first attacking has now passed to the defense and fights just as fiercely as before, each of them, meantime, using the arguments of the other . . .

First Friend. Are you sure of that?

Francesco. I assure you I went to his house with the most sincere and cordial intentions.

First Friend. And not because you felt—

Francesco. No, there is no question of pride at all!

First Friend. That isn't what I was going to say. It's not because you felt you had gone a bit too far in publicly assailing the Morello woman so bitterly?

Francesco. Not at all . . . not at all! Why . . . I . . .

First Friend. Wait! Let me finish. I was going to say: without taking account of a fact that was perfectly obvious to everybody that evening?

Second Friend. That he was defending the woman because he was in love with her?

Francesco. Not at all . . . not at all! It was because I had not been thinking of any of those things that all the trouble has arisen. We must look like two blamed fools! This is what I get for letting myself go, for being quite spontaneous and frank for once in my life! What a nuisance! I had planned on a quiet little visit to my sister and her husband in the country day after tomorrow.

Prestino. Nevertheless, you had had a rather heated argument the evening before.

Francesco. But—as I tell you again—without thinking of anything but the merits of the case, and without dreaming that he had any secret passion for the woman!

Second Friend. But are you sure he has?

First Friend. Certainly he has!

Prestino. He must have . . . certainly!

Francesco. If I had even remotely suspected such a thing I would not have gone to his house to admit that he was right, certain as I could be that that would make him furious!

The Second Friend [*violently*]. I wanted to say this . . . [*He breaks off short and* THEY *all turn to look at him in surprise.*]

First Friend [*after waiting a second*]. You wanted to say what?

Second Friend. I wanted to say . . . oh, I have forgotten what. [*At this moment* DIEGO CINCI *appears in the doorway to the right.*]

Diego. Am I intruding?

Francesco [*in surprise*]. Oh, Diego, you here?

Prestino. Has someone sent you?

Diego [*shrugging his shoulders*]. Why should anyone have sent me? Good day, maestro!

Fencing Master. Good day, Cinci! But I must be going. [*Shakes hands with* Savio *warmly.*] See you tomorrow, Savio . . . and don't stay awake, worrying!

Francesco. Never was cooler in my life, don't fear! Thank you, maestro!

Fencing Master [*bowing to the others*]. Gentlemen, I am sorry I can't stay in your good company, but I have an important engagement. [*The* Others *bow to him.*]

Francesco. Look, maestro, if you prefer, you can go out this way. [*He points toward the veranda.*] Just draw the curtain aside and you'll see the stairs. The garden opens on the street.

Fencing Master. Ah, that's a good idea. I'll do that. Once more . . . good morning! [*He withdraws.*]

First Friend [*to* Diego]. We were expecting you to be one of Doro Palegari's seconds.

Diego [*shaking his finger in silent negation*]. No, I couldn't, you see, I was caught between two fires last evening. Good friends of them both! . . . I had to keep out of it.

The Second Friend. But why have you come here now, then?

Diego. To say that I am delighted that there is going to be a duel! Delighted! Delighted! [*The* Others *laugh.*] And I hope that both get hurt! Not mortally, of course . . . not mortally! A little blood-letting would do them both good! A cut, besides, is something you can see and be sure about! A cut two . . . three . . . five inches long! [*He takes* Francesco *by the forearm and looks under the sleeve of his coat.*] Let me look at your wrist! All sound! Well, tomorrow morning you're going to have a cut from here to here. It will be something you can look at!

Francesco. A fine consolation! [*The* Others *laugh again.*]

Diego [*speaking up quickly*]. But Doro will get his too, let us hope! Doro, too! Let's be quite impartial! I have a surprise for you! You know who came to Palegari's shortly after you went away and I followed you?

Prestino. Delia Morello!

The Second Friend. I suppose she went to thank him for standing up for her!

Diego. Yes, except that when she found out just why you accused her . . . well . . . you know what she did?

Francesco. What did she do?

Diego. She admitted that you were right!

Francesco, Prestino, and the First Friend [*all together*]. She did? Really? That's a great idea! And Doro . . . how about him?

Diego. You can imagine how he took it!

Second Friend. He can't have the least idea now why he is going to fight.

Francesco. No, he knows the reason for that! He's going to fight because he insulted me in your presence while I, as I was saying here to my two friends and as you know yourself, had simply gone to him to admit that he was right!

Diego. Now . . .

Francesco. Now what?

Diego. Now that you know that Delia Morello says that you were right . . .

Francesco. Oh, well, if she herself—

Diego. No, my dear boy, no; Hold your ground . . . hold your ground . . . because now Delia Morello is in greater need of a defender than ever, and the job falls to you! You were the first to accuse her!

Prestino. Let's get this straight! Francesco must defend her against herself, now that she's accused herself before the man who at first tried to defend her!

Diego. Exactly! Exactly! And my admiration for her has increased one hundredfold since I found that out! [*Turns suddenly on* FRANCESCO.] You—who are you? [*Then turning to* PRESTINO.] Who are you? Who am I?

Who are we all? Your name is Francesco Savio; mine is Diego Cinci; yours is Prestino. We have of each other reciprocally, and each has of himself, knowledge of some small, insignificant certainty of today, which is not the certainty it was yesterday and will not be the certainty of tomorrow. Francesco, you are living on your income and you are bored!

Francesco. No . . . who told you that?

Diego. You are not bored? Lucky man! I have worn my soul out digging, digging tunnels—to China! [*To* PRESTINO.] What do you do?

Prestino. Nothing!

Diego. A fine profession! But even people who work, my dear friends—decent, respectable people like me—we are all, all alike! This life that is in us and around us—well examine it as closely as you wish. It is such a continuous, changing thing that if our deepest affections cannot endure against it, imagine what the case with the ideas, the opinions, the judgments which we succeed in forming for ourselves, must be! All our ideas, in short, change in the restless turmoil we call life. We think we catch a glimpse of a situation! But let us just discover something contrary to what we thought! So-and-so was a white man, eh? Well at once he's a black man! Our impressions of things change from hour to hour! A word is often sufficient or even just the manner in which it is said—to change our minds completely! And then besides, quite without our knowledge, images of hundreds and hundreds of things are flitting through our minds, suddenly causing our tempers to vary in the strangest way! Here along a road darkening with the approach of evening we are walking, sad, gloomy, despondent. We raise our eyes and we see a cottage still blazing under the setting sun. . . . Or we see a red geranium burning in a stray burst of sunlight. . . . And we change . . . we change . . . we brighten! A wave of tenderness sweeps over us!

Prestino.   And where does all that get us?

Diego.   Nowhere! Where are we trying to get, for that matter? I was telling you how things are . . . everything vague, indefinite, changing, insubstantial! Finally, to get hold of something solid, to feel the firm ground under your feet, you drop back into the weariness and affliction of your little certainty of today! . . . of that little which you succeed in knowing about yourself . . . your name, let us say . . . how much money you have in your pocket . . . the number of the house on the street where you live . . . your habits . . . your feelings . . . all these things which are customary, established, fixed, in your existence . . . that poor body of yours, for example, which still moves and can follow the flux of life, until its movements, which grow less and less vigorous every-day and less and less supple the older you get, finally cease altogether and—good night!

Francesco.   But you were talking of Delia Morello!

Diego.   Ah, yes! I was trying to make you understand my great admiration for her; or rather I was trying to make you feel what a joy it is, what a wonderful—though terrible—joy it is, when, caught by the tide of life in one of its moments of tempest, we are able actually to witness the collapse of all those fictitious forms around which our stupid daily life has solidified; and under the dikes, beyond the seawalls, which we had thrown up to isolate, to create, a definite consciousness for ourselves at all hazards, to build a personality of some kind, we are able to see that bit of tide—which was not wholly unknown to us and which seemed something tangible to us because we had carefully harnessed it to serve our feelings, draining it off into the duties which we had assumed, into the habits which we had created—suddenly break forth in a magnificent, overwhelming flood and turns everything topsy-turvy! Ah, at last!—A whirlwind! A volcanic eruption! An earthquake! A cataclysm!

Everybody [*in chorus*].   You like that, eh? No, thank you! None of those things for me! The Lord deliver us!

Diego.   But, my dear friends, after we have witnessed the farce of our own absurd changes of opinion, we have before us the tragedy of a bewildered spirit, gone astray and unable to find its way again. And it's not only Delia Morello! Wait, Francesco, you'll see! Soon you'll have them both on your hands! Both here and the other fellow!

Francesco.   The other fellow? What other fellow? Michele Rocca?

Diego.   Yes, Michele Rocca, himself!

First Friend.   He came in last evening from Naples.

Second Friend.   Ah, I have it! That was what I was trying to tell you fellows some time ago. I learned that he was looking for Palegari . . . to slap his face!

Prestino.   Yes, but we knew all that! [*To* FRANCESCO.] I told you so, didn't I?

Francesco [*to* DIEGO].   But why should he come here to see me just now?

Diego.   Because he insists on fighting a duel with Doro Palegari before you do! But now it would seem that he ought to have the duel with you!

Francesco.   What do you mean . . . with me?

The Others [*all together*].   Why with Francesco? Why with Savio?

Diego.   With you, of course! You have changed your mind, haven't you, honestly, sincerely? And thereby you assume responsibility for everything said by Palegari against him . . . at the Avanzi's the other night! What could be clearer? You have inverted your respective positions! It is obvious then! Rocca ought to make his fight with you!

Francesco. Not so fast, not so fast! What in the deuce are you talking about?

Diego. Excuse me . . . you are fighting this duel with Doro simply because he insulted you, are you not? Well, why did Doro insult you?

Francesco [*in some irritation*]. Why, of course, of course . . . because I . . .

Diego [*speaking up quickly and carrying on the thought*]. . . . because you, *loyally, sincerely* . . .

The Two Friends [*without letting him finish*]. Yes, yes, he's right! Diego is right!

Diego. So the rôles have been inverted! You are left to defend Delia Morello, putting all the blame on Michele Rocca!

Prestino [*shocked*]. Oh, let's quit joking!

Diego. Joking? [*To* FRANCESCO.] Oh, if you ask me . . . you can boast this time of being right!

Francesco. So you want me to have a duel with Michele Rocca, too?

Diego. Ah, I couldn't say that! A duel with a man in his frame of mind would be a very serious matter! The poor fellow is desperate!

The First Friend. I should say so! With Salvi's corpse lying between him and the girl he was going to marry.

Second Friend. The marriage broken off! . . .

Diego. And Delia Morello making a fool of him!

Francesco [*with a rising irritation*]. What do you mean . . . a fool of him? You are saying she made a fool of him, now!

Diego. That she did use him for her own purposes, no one can deny!

Francesco. Treacherously, therefore, as I claimed at first!

Diego [*trying to stop him with a reproof*]. Ah-ah-ah-ah, ah-ah-ah! There you go! Listen! The annoyance you

now feel for having gotten into this mess ought not make
you change your mind for still a third time!

Francesco. Not at all! Not at all! Excuse me . . . you
said yourself that she went and confessed to Doro Palegari
that I was right in accusing her of treachery!

Diego. You see? You see?

Francesco. But what do I see, damn it all? If I discover that she is now accusing herself and saying that I
was right, why—of course—I change my mind and go
back to my first position! [*Turning to the others.*] Don't
you think I have a right to, you people?

Diego [*vehemently*]. But I tell you that she used him
treacherously . . . yes . . . if you insist on that word
. . . but only in order to free Giorgio Salvi from the
danger he was running in marrying her! Understand?
You have absolutely no right to claim that that was
treachery toward Salvi. On the contrary, I am ready to
defend her myself, even if she herself be her own accuser
. . . I'll defend her even against herself. . . .

Francesco [*giving ground with some irritation*]. . . .
In view of the reasons . . . yes . . . of the reasons advanced by Doro Palegari . . .

Diego. . . . on account of which you . . .

Francesco. . . . yes, . . . changed my mind . . .
changed my mind . . . exactly. . . . But the fact remains that as regards Rocca she was really treacherous
all the time.

Diego. Treacherous? She was just a woman! Why not
stop at that? He approached her with the idea of having
his fun with her, giving her that impression also, so that
she in her turn made a fool of him. That really is what's
the matter with Michele Rocca! He is stung in his pride
as a man and as a male! He is not yet ready to admit that
he was just a helpless, stupid thing in the hands of a
woman, a doll which Delia Morello tossed aside and
broke to pieces after amusing herself in making it open

and close its arms in prayer—just by pressing the spring
of passion which that doll had in its insides somewhere!
Huh! The doll has been picked up again and set in place,
the wax nose of its wax face broken, the wax fingers on
its wax hands gone—cracks in its wax head and in its wax
body, and the spring—the spring of passion that it had in
its gizzard—has broken through the cloth covering and
is sticking out! But yet . . . no . . . the doll will not
have it that way! The doll keeps crying at the top of its
voice that it's not true; that that woman didn't make it
say its prayers; that that woman did not use it as a play-
thing, breaking it to pieces when the game was done! No
. . . no . . . it cries! Well, I ask you, did you ever see a
more absurd spectacle than that?

Prestino [*losing control of himself and almost shaking
his fist in* DIEGO's *face*].   Why are you trying to make us
laugh at such a serious matter, you clown?

Diego [*looking at* PRESTINO *in amazement, as the*
OTHERS *do also*].   I?

Prestino.   You! Yes, you! Ever since you've been in
here, you've been playing the clown, trying to make a
fool of him, of me, of us, of everybody!

Diego.   But also of myself, don't you think?

Prestino.   Keep your compliments for yourself! It's
easy to laugh the way you do, making us all out so many
cocks on a weather vane which turns this way or that,
according as the wind blows! I'm tired of this nonsense!
How shall I describe it? When you talk that way you
seem to put poison in my soul!

Diego.   Not at all, my dear boy! I laugh because I
have reasoned my heart dry!

Prestino.   You said as much yourself . . . there is
nothing in your heart! It is empty, cold, dead . . . that
is why you laugh!

Diego.   That is why you *think* I laugh!

Prestino.   I think so because it's so! Even if it were

true that people are as you say we are, I should think
you would feel more like pitying us than laughing at us.

Diego [*offended in his turn, advancing toward* PRE-
STINO *aggressively, placing his two hands on the latter's
two shoulders, and bringing his face up close, looking the
man fixedly in the eye*]. Pity? Yes . . . if you let yourself be examined this way . . .

Prestino [*puzzled*]. What way?

Diego. This way . . . in the eye . . . just like this!
No . . . look at me! This way . . . naked as you are
. . . with all the filth and muck and smallness there is
in you! In you as in me . . . in me as in you—all the
fears—all the self-reproaches—all the hesitations and con-
tradictions! Shake yourself free from the manikin you
create out of a false interpretation of what you do and
what you feel, and you'll at once see that the manikin
you make yourself is nothing at all like what you really
are or what you can really be! Nothing at all like what
is in you without your knowing that it is there—a terrible
avenger if you resist it; though it at once becomes chari-
table toward all your shortcomings if you just give in
and do not try to justify and delude yourself! Oh, I
know . . . to cast aside that manikin, that fiction, seems
in a certain way to be a denial of one's self, something
unworthy of a man; and it will always be that way so long
as we believe that humanness consists in what we call
conscience, in that courage, if you wish, which we have
shown on one single occasion rather than in the coward-
ice which on many occasions has counselled prudence.
You have agreed to act as Savio's second in this stupid
duel of Palegari's. [*Talking to* SAVIO.] And you thought
that Palegari kept calling you a clown yesterday? Huh!
He was calling names at that manikin which he could not
see in himself, but which he could see in you because you
showed it to him as in a mirror! I laugh . . . yes . . . I

laugh in my own way, and my ridicule falls upon myself sooner than on anyone else!

[*A pause.* THEY *all fall silent, each absorbed in his own thoughts. The following lines will be pronounced at intervals between pauses, as though each were talking to himself.*]

Francesco.   Of course, I have no real animosity against Doro Palegari. He kept leading me on from one thing to another. [*A pause.*]

Prestino [*after some seconds*].   So many times we have to pretend we are sure; and if such pretense only hurts us the more deeply, we are not more worthy of blame, but more worthy of pity.

First Friend [*after another pause, as though he were reading* FRANCESCO SAVIO'S *thoughts*].   Who knows? It must be splendid out in the country today!

Francesco [*answering quickly and without surprise, as though to justify himself*].   Why I had actually bought some playthings to carry out to my sister's little girl.

Second Friend.   A cute little tot she was that time I saw her.

Francesco.   Oh, a dear little thing! Prettiest child I ever set my eyes on! So wise, as she looks up at you out of her big eyes! An angel! A cherub!

Diego [*to* FRANCESCO].   Listen! If I were you, Francesco . . . [*The* BUTLER *appears in the doorway to the right.*]

Butler.   May I interrupt, sir?

Francesco.   What is it, Giovanni?

Butler.   A message for you, sir.

Francesco [*approaching the* BUTLER *and listening to what he has to say. Then with evident annoyance*]. Now? How can I? Impossible! [*He turns and stands looking at his friends, hesitant, in great perplexity.*]

Diego [*understanding*]. She is here?

Prestino. You cannot receive her! You must not!

First Friend. Of course not! You cannot while this point of honor is still pending!

Diego. Not at all! She has nothing to do with that!

Prestino. What do you mean? Why, she is the cause of the whole trouble? However, I won't argue the point. I am your second in this affair and I say no! I say you mustn't let her come in!

Second Friend. But you can't send a lady away like that, without even finding out what she's come for!

Diego. I really have no right to say anything.

First Friend [*to* FRANCESCO]. You might find out what she wants!

Second Friend. Yes, and if perchance . . .

Francesco. . . . she tries to put in a word about the duel . . .

Prestino. . . . end the interview at once! On that basis I consent!

Francesco. Very well! Very well! I'll tell her to go on about her business! That's what I'll do! Just leave it to me! [FRANCESCO *withdraws, followed by the* BUTLER.]

Diego. My only suggestion would be that he should advise her to . . . [*At this moment the veranda curtain is torn furiously aside and* MICHELE ROCCA *breaks in from the garden in the throes of a dangerous excitement which he has difficulty in restraining.* HE *is a person about thirty years old—black hair, dark complexion, traces of bitterness, of remorse, of passion, in the lines of his face. His whole expression, the nervous movements of his body, the twitching of his features, show that he is ready to go to any extreme.*]

Rocca. If I may! [*Then surprised at seeing so many people he had not expected to find.*] Is this the place? I have come to the right house?

Prestino [*voicing his own amazement and that of the others*]. Who are you?

Rocca. Michele Rocca.

Diego. Ah, so here he is!

Rocca [*to* Diego]. You are Signor Francesco Savio?

Diego. No, I am not. Savio is in the other room. [*He points to the door on the right.*]

Prestino. But if I may ask . . . how did you get in here in this way?

Rocca. I was shown to this entrance.

Diego. The porter thought he was one of Savio's friends!

Rocca. Am I mistaken? Did not a lady enter this house a few seconds before me?

Prestino. You mean that you were following her?

Rocca. Yes, I was following her. I knew that she was to come here.

Diego. So did I . . . and I knew that you would come here too.

Rocca. The most outrageous things are being said about me all over town! I know that Signor Savio, without ever having met me, has come to my defense. Now, he must not listen to that woman! He must not . . . without first hearing from me exactly how matters stand!

Prestino. But it's too late now, my dear sir!

Rocca. Too late? What do you mean?

Prestino. I said it was too late! Arbitration is now out of the question!

First Friend. A challenge has been made and accepted!

Second Friend. And the conditions signed!

Diego. And they both have changed their minds!

Prestino [*angrily to* Diego]. You will be so good as to refrain from any further interference! To put it plainly, please mind your own damn business!

First Friend. Why do you keep trying to mix things up?

Diego. I'm not mixing anything up. I'm making it clearer! This gentleman came here under the impression that Savio has been defending him. I am simply pointing out that Savio has changed his mind, and is defending him no longer!

Rocca. Ah, I see! So now *he* is blaming me, too!

Diego. He is not the only one, notice!

Rocca. You too, for instance?

Diego. Yes, yes! I—and everybody else here, as you may see!

Rocca. I can well believe it! So far, you've been talking only with her!

Diego. No! No! Not at all! None of us has seen her nor has Savio, until just now! He has this minute stepped into the other room to find out what she wants!

Rocca. Why do you blame me then? And why does Savio? At first he took my side! If he has changed his mind, why is he having his duel with Signor Palegari?

Diego. My dear sir, in your case—as I understand very well—in your case, madness assumes its most spectacular forms; but believe me, as I was saying just now, all of us are crazy in one way or another! This duel, as you must know, is being fought precisely because both the litigants have changed their minds!

First Friend [*along with the others, in some heat*]. Don't listen to this fellow! He is quite mistaken!

Second Friend. They're going on with the duel because, after the trouble night before last, Palegari got angry . . .

First Friend [*raising his voice*] . . . and called Signor Savio a clown!

Prestino [*raising his voice still higher*]. Signor Savio took offense at the insult and issued a challenge . . .

Diego [*raising his voice till it overrides the others*].

. . . though by that time they were both in perfect agreement!

Rocco [*vehemently*]. In agreement in condemning me without having heard my case? I should like to know— how is this worthless woman able to get everybody on her side like that?

Diego. Everybody except herself . . . except herself!

Rocca. Except herself?

Diego. Not quite that! Don't imagine that she is on one side or on the other! She doesn't know exactly where she stands! Examine your own state of mind, a little more carefully, Signor Rocca, and you will see that even you are not quite sure where you stand!

Rocca. I'm glad you enjoy your own jokes! However, will you kindly announce me, one of you gentlemen? Say that Signor Michele Rocca would like to be received by Signor Francesco Savio.

Prestino. But what do you want to see him about? I repeat, it's too late!

Rocca. What do you know about it? If he's against me now, all the better!

Prestino. But he's in the other room there with the lady!

Rocca. Better still! I followed her to this house on purpose! Perhaps it is just as well for her that I am meeting her with other people, in the presence, in fact, of a stranger whom chance has seen fit to involve in our troubles. So then, I have made up my mind—for anything! I was blind . . . blind . . . but now the simple fact that I find myself here unexpectedly with all you gentlemen . . . the simple fact that I must speak . . . answer your questions . . . well . . . I feel as though . . . I could—all of a sudden—breathe more easily . . . as though the atmosphere had been cleared! I had been keeping to myself for days and days! You gentlemen can't understand the agony I have been through! I tried to save the man whose sister I was to marry, a man I had come to love as my own brother . . . !

Prestino. You tried to save him? That's a good one!

First Friend. By running off with the girl he was in love with!

Second Friend. The night before he was to marry her!

Rocca. No! No! Listen . . . listen, please! Not at all! I wasn't trying to steal his girl . . . and you say he was going to marry her! It wasn't much of a job to save him! It was sufficient to demonstrate to him, to make him see beyond any question of doubt that the woman he was going to marry because he wanted her could be his—as she could be anybody's—without any question of marriage!

Prestino. Anyhow, you spent the night with her . . . !

Rocca. But on a bet . . . on a bet!

First Friend. On what bet?

Second Friend. Bet with whom?

Rocca. Let me finish! Let me finish! A bet with him! You see, it was by arrangement with his sister and his mother! He had introduced her to the family, doing violence thereby to all his feelings of propriety; and I, by an arrangement I made with his sister and his mother, followed the two of them to Naples with the excuse of helping them get settled in their new house! He was to marry the girl a few months later. However, there was a quarrel . . . one of those quarrels that often arise between people about to get married. She lost her temper and left him for some days! [*He covers his eyes with a hand as though to hide a vision that tempts and horrifies at the same time.*] Oh, she went away . . . and I can see her . . . I can see her! . . . [*He lowers his hand, his face showing greater and greater emotion.*] For I was present at the quarrel! . . . [*Mastering his feelings.*] I seized that occasion as a favorable opportunity for demonstrating to Giorgio the absurdity of what he was about to do. It's in-

credible, isn't it? Incredible! And yet those women are
often that way, it seems! Do you know, she never gave
him the slightest concession?

First Friend [*intent, as all the others are, on the narrative*]. Of course!

Rocca. Not only that. At Capri there, she had shown
herself disdainful and contemptuous toward all the men,
keeping to herself . . . proud and reserved! "Well, I'll
bet you," said he to me, "I'll bet you!" And he challenged
me to do what I bet him that I could do, promising that
if I won the bet, he'd break with the girl and have nothing more to do with her! Well, instead, he shot himself!

First Friend. But I don't understand! You lent yourself to such a scheme!

Rocca. It was a bet! To save him!

Second Friend. But the treachery of it all!

Rocca. Yes, horrible . . . horrible!

Second Friend. But his treachery toward you, I mean!

Rocca. Yes, he did not play fair with me!

Second Friend. He shot himself!

Prestino. It's incredible . . . incredible!

Rocca. . . . that I lent myself to such a thing? . . .

Prestino. . . . No, that he allowed you to strike such
a bargain with him!

Rocca. But don't you see? He did it on purpose! Because he had noticed . . . noticed right away, you understand . . . that she had tried—from the very moment
when she saw me with his sister—she had tried spitefully,
with the most evil intent, to attract me . . . attract me
to herself, wheedling me with all her artfulness! Why, it
was Giorgio himself who called my attention to it! So it
was easy, you understand—it was easy to make the proposal I made at that moment, saying to him: "Why, you
know she would give herself even to me!"

Prestino. And in that case . . . well, I give up. He
dared you—but he was really daring himself!

Rocca. But he ought to have told me! He ought to have shouted it into my ears if necessary! He should have made me understand that he was lost, poisoned forever! That it was useless for me to try to cure him of a venom from that viper's fangs which had sunk so deep into his soul!

Diego. Viper? Viper? No, excuse me! I would hardly say viper!

Rocca. Viper! Viper! Viper!

Diego. I wonder . . . I wonder! A bit too ingenuous it seems to me, a bit too ingenuous, for a viper. If there was so much poison in her fangs, why should she have bitten you so soon, so immediately, I might even say?

Prestino. But she may have been bent on ruining Giorgio Salvi, breaking his heart, encompassing his death!

Rocca. She may.

Diego. And how is that possible? She had succeeded in forcing him to marry her, hadn't she? Why spoil everything before getting what she wanted?

Rocca. But she never suspected . . .

Diego. Why do you call her a viper then? A viper is always deliberate. A snake such as you say she is would have bitten afterwards, but not before! If now she did bite nevertheless, it means either that she is not so bad as you say she is, or else that she was not trying to harm Giorgio Salvi!

Rocca. So you think then . . .

Diego. It is you who make me think so, understand! You are trying to tell me that she is a treacherous woman. I am keeping to what you say yourself . . . and the case for perfidy doesn't hang together! You say she was trying to trick him into marrying her, but then just before the wedding she gives herself to you!

Rocca [*jumping to his feet*]. Gives herself to me? Who ever said she gave herself to me? I had nothing to do with the woman . . . nothing at all! And you imagine I ever could have thought of such a thing?

Diego [*in astonishment, like the rest*]. Ah, really?

The Others. What! Is it possible?

Rocca. You see, all I wanted was proof . . . proof that she . . . something in short to convince *him!* [*At this moment the door on the right opens and* FRANCESCO SAVIO *appears in great excitement and commotion. He has been in the other room with* DELIA MORELLO. *Fulfilling her promise to prevent the duel between him and* DORO PALEGARI, *she has used all her arts upon him, intoxicating him with herself. He at once assails* MICHELE ROCCA *vehemently.*]

Francesco. And what is this? What are you doing here? What do you want in my house? What mess are you trying to stir up here?

Rocca. I came to tell you . . .

Francesco. There is nothing you need to tell me!

Rocca. You are mistaken! I have something to say, and not only to you!

Francesco. I should advise you not to be quite so positive in your threats!

Rocca. I am making no threats. I was anxious to talk with you.

Francesco. You have been following a lady to my house!

Rocca. Ah, I have just been explaining to your friends here . . .

Francesco. What do I care about your explanations to my friends? You have been following a woman who was coming to see me! Do you deny it?

Rocca. Yes, because if you intend to fight a duel with Signor Palegari . . .

Francesco. What duel? Nonsense! I am not going to fight a duel with anybody!

Prestino [*in amazement*]. What is that you say? No duel?

Francesco. I am calling it off!

First Friend, Diego, Second Friend [*speaking at once*]. Are you crazy? Do you mean it? That's ridiculous!

Rocca [*also speaking at the same time, but in a louder voice, with a guffaw*]. Of course, you're calling it off! It's *her* work!

Francesco [*about to attack him physically*]. Shut your mouth or I . . .

Prestino [*running in front of him and holding him back*]. No! First you must answer me! You're calling this duel with Palegari off?

Francesco. Yes, I am calling it off! It's all nonsense, and I have no right to add to a woman's despair.

Prestino. But it will be worse, if you don't fight! The conditions of the duel have been drawn up and the papers signed!

Francesco. But it's sheer nonsense to have a duel with Palegari now! It's ridiculous!

Prestino. Why so ridiculous?

Francesco. Ridiculous! It's ridiculous because we are in entire agreement . . . Oh, you understand, Prestino, when you have a chance to figure in some affair like this, you are ready for a week's holiday!

Prestino. But Palegari insulted you, and you challenged him!

Francesco. But nonsense, nonsense, just as Doro said, nonsense! I am calling it off!

Prestino. This is incredible . . . incredible!

Rocca. He promised her he wouldn't fight with her champion?

Francesco. Yes, why shouldn't I, since I have you here?

Rocca. I see! That is why you promised not to?

Francesco. No, since you are here insulting me in my own house! What do you want of that lady, anyhow?

Prestino. You can't do that!

Francesco. He's been following her around for a day or more!

Prestino. But you can't fight with *him* now!

Francesco. No one can say I am challenging a less dangerous opponent!

Prestino. Not at all! Not at all! That won't make any difference! Because if I should go now and offer to fight Palegari in your place . . .

First Friend [almost shouting at FRANCESCO]. You will be disqualified!

Rocca. But I can ignore the disqualification!

First Friend. No, because we would prevent you!

Prestino [to FRANCESCO]. And you won't find a soul to act as your second! However, you have all day to think it over. I can't stay here any longer, so I'm going away!

Diego. He'll think it over, all right!

Prestino [to the two friends]. This is no place for us! Let's be going! [*The* THREE OF THEM *withdraw by way of the garden, rear.*]

Diego [walking out on the veranda after them and calling]. Not too fast, gentlemen, not too fast! [*Then turning to* FRANCESCO.] And you had better watch your step!

Francesco. You go to the devil! [*Again assailing* ROCCA.] And you!—you will find the door this way! Please make use of it! I am at your service when, where, and as, you wish! [*At this point* DELIA MORELLO *appears at the doorway to the right. The moment* SHE *sees* MICHELE ROCCA, *so changed from what he had been, another person in fact, she suddenly finds the mask lifted from her eyes—the mask, the fiction, which both she and he have hitherto been using to defend themselves against the secret passion by which from the very beginning they*

*have been madly attracted toward one another, a passion
which they have been translating before their own minds
into terms of pity and interest for* GIORGIO SALVI, *each
pretending to be trying to save him from one or the
other. With this fiction gone, destroyed by the sudden
shock they feel at being brought thus face to face,* THEY
stand looking at each other, pale and trembling.]

Rocca [*with a sob*]. Delia! Delia! [*He advances to
embrace her.*]

Delia [*sinking into his arms and accepting his kiss*].
No! No! My poor boy! My poor boy! [*To the horror and
disgust of* FRANCESCO *and* DIEGO, THEY *embrace fran-
tically.*]

Rocca. Delia! My Delia!

Diego. That is the way they hate each other! Ah, how
they hate each other! You see? You see?

Francesco. But it's absurd! It's monstrous! With the
corpse of a man between them!

Rocca [*gathering* DELIA *into his arms, like an animal
turning ravenously upon its prey*]. Monstrous? Yes! But
she must belong to me! She must suffer with me . . .
with me!

Delia [*suddenly horrified, and tearing herself loose
ferociously*]. No! No! Go away! Go away! Don't touch
me!

Rocca [*struggling to hold her*]. No! No! Mine! Mine!
Here, with me, in my despair! Here!

Delia [*still struggling*]. Let me go, I tell you! Let me
go! Murderer!

Francesco. Yes! Let her go! I say let her go!

Rocca. You keep your distance!

Delia [*freeing herself at last*]. Let me go! [FRANCESCO
and DIEGO *restrain* ROCCA *from throwing himself upon
her.*] I am not afraid of you! No! No! No harm can come
to me from you! Not even if you kill me!

Rocca [*speaking at the same time, struggling with the*

two men and shouting].   Delia! Delia! You must belong
to me! You are mine! You must belong to me! I cannot
live without you!

Delia.   I am free! I am free! I feel nothing, nothing
whatever! It was an illusion! I thought it was compassion
. . . fear . . . but no, it was nothing . . . nothing!

Rocca [*still struggling*].   Let me alone! Let me alone!

Francesco and Diego [*talking together*].   You are two
wild beasts! Monstrous! Two monsters!

Delia.   Let him go! I am not afraid of him! I let
him kiss me! But it was coldly, without passion! It was
not fear! It was not pity!

Rocca.   Yes, you wretch! I know! I know your kisses
are worthless, but I want you! I am going to have you!

Delia.   Any harm you might do me, even if you killed
me, would not be so bad as that! Another crime! Poison!
Death itself! I want to remain as I am! I want to suffer
as I am!

Rocca [*still struggling to free himself from the two
men*].   Her love is worth nothing, but all that I have
suffered on her account gives it value to me! It is not love
I feel for you! It's hatred! It's hatred!

Delia.   Hatred! Yes, it's hatred with me, too! Hatred!

Rocca.   The very blood that has been shed on her
account! [*With a sudden burst of violence he succeeds in
freeing his arms.*] Have pity on me . . . pity on me! [*He
pursues her about the room.*]

Delia [*trying to keep away*].   No! No! Don't you touch
me! It will be the worse for you!

Diego and Francesco [*getting hold of him again*].   But
keep away, won't you? You must answer for this with me!

Delia.   It will be the worse for him if he tries to
arouse my pity either for myself or for him! I have none!
But if you have any regard for him, send him away from
here! Send him away!

Rocca. How can I go away? You know that my life was drowned forever in Giorgio's blood!

Delia. The brother of the girl you were to marry! And you did not try to save him from dishonor!

Rocca. You lie! That is not true! You know that we have both been lying!

Delia. Yes, we have both been lying! Two falsehoods!

Rocca. You have wanted me as I have wanted you, from the moment when we first saw each other!

Delia. Yes! Yes! But it was to punish you!

Rocca. Yes, so with me! It was to punish you! But your life, too, has been drowned, drowned forever in Giorgio's blood!

Delia. Yes, you are right! You are right! [*She runs to him like a flame, pushing aside the two men who are restraining him.*] Yes, it is true! It is true!

Rocca [*embracing her again desperately*]. So we must both drown in that blood, but drown together . . . this way . . . in each other's arms . . . not I alone . . . not you alone . . . but both together! This way! This way!

Diego. If they don't change their minds!

Rocca [*carrying* DELIA *in his arms toward the door into the garden, leaving the two men standing there in utter astonishment and stupefaction*]. Yes . . . with me . . . with me! Come! Come! With me . . . away, with me . . . away, with me!

Francesco. Two lunatics!

Diego. You don't see yourself!

SECOND CHORAL INTERLUDE

Again the curtain rises as soon as possible after it has fallen on the second act; and again the theatre lobby appears with the entrances leading to the hall of the theatre. But this time no one comes out for some moments. The TICKET TAKER, *one or two* USHERS, MAIDS *from the*

*women's room are standing about in some apprehension;
because, along toward the end of the second act, they
have seen the* MORENO WOMAN, *despite the interference
of her* THREE MALE FRIENDS, *run through the corridor toward the stage entrance. Now the sound of shouting, clapping, hissing, comes out from the theatre, growing louder
and louder all the time, either because the actors have not
yet appeared before the curtain to make their bows to
the audience or because something strange and unusual
is going on inside.*

One of the Ticket Takers. What the devil is the matter in there?

Another Ticket Taker. Isn't it Pirandello tonight?
What else can you expect?

An Usher. No, the audience is applauding, but the
actors refuse to come out.

A Maid. But there's shouting and screaming on the
stage, don't you hear?

Another Usher. And the house is in an uproar!

Second Maid. Has that woman anything to do with
it?

Ticket Taker. I imagine she has. The men with her
were having a devil of a time keeping her quiet!

First Maid. She got in behind the scenes!

First Ticket Taker. She was trying to get in at the end
of the first act!

Another Maid. But hell is let loose in there! Don't
you hear? [*Two or three of the doors into the theatre are
thrown open and some* SPECTATORS *dash out into the
lobby, the uproar in the auditorium becoming louder for
the moment.*]

The Spectators. But she got in there on the stage!
What's the matter? Are they fighting? [*Shouting. Scream-
ing.*] And the actors are not answering their curtain call!
[*More* SPECTATORS *appear, coming through the doors into*

the lobby and looking toward the stage entrance to the right. THEY *are followed by a great number of* SPECTA-TORS *who come on through the left. They are all shout-ing:*] What's the matter? What's going on? What's the trouble?

Confused Voices. There's a fight on behind the scenes! There . . . do you hear? On the stage! Why? Why? Who knows?

Gangway, please! What's happened? What's going on? Trouble tonight, all right! Let me get by! Is the play over? Isn't there a third act? There must be a third act! Make way there, please! Yes, at four o'clock sharp, so long! . . . Don't forget! But did you hear that? They're fighting! I am going in there myself! Do you hear that? It's scandalous! They've no right to! What's it all about? Why it seems that . . . God only knows! What the deuce! Why . . . why . . . there . . . there! The door is opening!

[*The stage entrance is thrown open, and for the mo-ment the uproar on the stage—shrieks from the* ACTRESSES, *oaths from* ACTORS *and from the* STAGE MANAGER, *the voices of the* MORENO WOMAN *and her* THREE FRIENDS— *become louder. These noises will be drowned eventually by the confusion among the* SPECTATORS *crowding around the stage entrance, varied by the angry protests of a few people, some of whom are trying to get to the stage and others are trying to get away and out of the theatre.*]

Voices from the Stage [ACTORS *speaking*]. Get out of here! Get out of there! Back where you belong! Get that woman away! Have her arrested! She'll pay me for that! Back where you belong! Get out of here!

Voice of the Moreno Woman. It's a disgrace! It's a crime! I won't! I won't!

Voice of the Stage Manager. You just be moving along!

Voice of the Moreno Woman. You're insulting me publicly!

Voice of One of Her Friends. Remember she's a woman!

Voice of Another of Her Friends. Don't you dare strike a woman!

Voice of One of the Actors. Woman? Nonsense! She's making all the trouble! Get her out of here! Get her out of here!

Voices of Some Actresses. What a cat! For shame! For shame!

Voices of Some Actors. Lucky for her she's a woman! She deserves every bit of it! Get her out of here!

Stage Manager. Clear that doorway, there! Clear that doorway!

Voices from the Crowd of Spectators [*all talking at once, with occasional hoots, jeers, and applause*]. Signora Moreno! The Moreno woman! Who is she! She slapped the leading lady's face! Who? Who slapped her? Signora Moreno! The Moreno woman! Who is she? The leading lady! No! No! It was the author's face she slapped? Pirandello? She slapped his face! Who? Who slapped his face? Signora Moreno! No! The leading lady! The author slapped her face? No! No! The other way about! The leading lady slapped the author's face! Not at all! Not at all! Signora Moreno assaulted the leading lady and pulled her hair!

Voices from the Stage. Enough of this! Out of here! Put her out! Put her out! Cowards! Wretches! Call the police! What a woman! Put her out! Put her out!

Voices from the Spectators. Go on with the play! Put them out! Less noise! Shut up! Signora Moreno! Put her out! The third act! We want the third act! Pirandello!

Put him out! A speech! A speech from Pirandello! Put
him out! A speech! He's to blame! Sh-sh-sh-sh! Make way
there! The third act! Clear the way! Clear the way!

[*Some* ACTORS *and* ACTRESSES *from the play on the stage,
more especially those appearing in the third act, elbow
their way through the crowd gathered before the stage
entrance. With them appear the* STAGE MANAGER *and the*
TREASURER *of the theatre, the latter trying to persuade
them to go on with the play. The lobby is thrown into
the greatest agitation. At first the* SPECTATORS *are silent,
eagerly listening to the dialogue of the stage people;
though later on they will break occasionally into noisy
comment of approval or disapproval.*]

Treasurer of the Theatre. But for heaven's sake, use
your brains. The crowd will want its money back! You
want to stop the play?

Actors and Actresses [*talking all at the same time*].
Not on your life! I am going home! We won't put up
with this! We are all going home! This is too much! It's a
disgrace! We refuse to put up with it! We are going to
strike in protest!

Stage Manager. Protest? Who are you protesting
against?

One of the Actresses. Against the author, and rightly
so!

One of the Actors. And against the producer! Who
ever thought of producing such a comedy as this!

Treasurer. But you can't protest this way! If you
go away and don't finish the play, we are ruined! This
is pure Bolshevism!

Voices from Among the Spectators. Fine! Fine!
That's the way to talk! Not at all! The actors are right!
They're right!

The Actors [*all speaking together*].   Yes! Yes! We protest! We protest!

An Actor.   You can't compel us to play a comedy with a key!

Voices from Some Ingenuous Spectators.   A key? Where's the key? What's a comedy with a key?

Actors.   We refuse! We refuse!

Voices of Other Spectators.   Of course! Everybody knows it! It's disgraceful! It's scandalous! You can't help seeing! The Moreno case! She's here! In the theatre! She got in behind the scenes! She slapped the leading lady's face!

Voices of Spectators and Friends of Pirandello [*all talking together and in great confusion*].   But nobody noticed! It's a good play! We want the third act! Give us our money back! We bought our tickets! The third act! The third act!

One of the Actors.   But we refuse to have our faces slapped!

An Actor.   Let's all go home! I, for my part, am going home!

An Actress.   The leading lady has already gone home!

Voices of Spectators.   Gone home? How did she go out? Through the stage entrance! Why?

Actress.   Because a woman came in on the stage and slapped her face!

Voices of Spectators in Argument.   Slapped her face? Yes! Yes! Signora Moreno! And she was right! Who was right? The Moreno woman? Why did she slap her face? The leading lady!

One of the Actors.   Because she saw an allusion to herself in the play!

Another Actor.   And she thought we had conspired with the author to make fun of her?

First Actress.   We refuse to be treated that way!

Baron Nuti [*accompanied by* Two Friends *as in the first interlude, more than ever excited and confused, pushes his way forward*].   It's true! It's unheard of! It's a disgrace! You're right in stopping the show!

One of His Friends.   Hush! Don't make matters worse! Let's go home!

Baron Nuti.   It's a disgrace, ladies and gentlemen! Two people pilloried in public! The private affairs of two people exposed to public ridicule!

Treasurer [*in despair*].   The play seems to have moved from the stage to the lobby!

Voices of Spectators Hostile to the Author.   He's right! He's right! It's a disgrace! They ought to put a stop to it! They're right! They're right!

Voices of Spectators Favorable to Pirandello.   Not at all! Not at all! It was a good show! The third act! Where is the third act. Give us the third act! Disgrace? Nonsense! It could be anybody! Where's the slander?

Treasurer [*to the actors*].   Shall we go on with the show or shall we not?

Baron Nuti [*seizing one of the* Spectators *by the front of his coat and addressing him so violently that everyone falls silent at the spectacle of his fury*].   You say it's all right? You approve? They have a right to take me and expose me there on the stage in public? Show me off, and all my sorrows, in the presence of a crowd? Make me say things that I never thought of saying and do things that I never thought of doing? [*In the silence that greets* Baron Nuti's *harangue, the* Stage Manager *will appear from the stage entrance, walking a few steps ahead of the* Moreno Woman *who, weeping, disheveled, half fainting, is being rather dragged than led out of the theatre by her* Three Male Companions. *The exchange of sentences between the* Stage Manager *and* Signora Moreno *will fall upon the silence as a reply to* Baron Nuti's *words. Everyone meantime will turn toward the stage entrance, mak-*

ing way for SIGNORA MORENO *and her* COMPANIONS. NUTI *will release his grasp on the* SPECTATOR *he has been assailing, and turns to ask:*] What's the matter?

Stage Manager. But you know very well that neither the author nor the leading lady have ever met you! They don't know you at all!

Signora Moreno. She mimicked my voice! She used my manner—all my gestures! She was imitating me! I recognized myself!

Stage Manager. But why should you believe it was you?

Signora Moreno. No! No! That isn't so! It was so terrible to see myself there on the stage acting that way! The idea! Why! I . . . I . . . kissing that man! [*She suddenly becomes aware of* BARON NUTI'S *presence and utters a shriek, covering her face with her hands.*] Oh! Oh! There he is! There he is! There!

Baron Nuti. Amelia! Amelia!

[*General commotion among the* SPECTATORS, *who can scarcely believe their eyes, as they see the very characters and the very scene they have witnessed at the end of the second act, present now before them. Their astonishment should be manifested, however, only by facial expression, by brief comments delivered in low tones, and a few hushed exclamations.*]

Voices of Spectators. Oh! Look! Look! There they are! Oh! In real life! Both of them! The same scene over again! Look! Look!

Signora Moreno [*desperately, to the* THREE MEN *with her*]. Take him away! Take him away!

Her Companions. Yes! Let's go away! Let's go away!

Baron Nuti [*dashing upon her*]. No! No! You must come with me! You must come with me!

Signora Moreno [*tearing herself from his grasp*]. No!

Let me alone! Let me alone! Don't touch me! Murderer!
Murderer!

Baron Nuti. You heard that on the stage!

Signora Moreno. Let me alone! I am not afraid of
you!

Baron Nuti. But it was true! It's our punishment!
It's our punishment! And we must suffer it together!
Your place is with me! Come! Come!

Signora Moreno. Let me alone, I say! I hate you! I
hate you!

Baron Nuti. We are drowning . . . drowning in his
blood! It was true! Come with me! Come! [*He drags her
off to the left.*]

[*Most of the* SPECTATORS *follow with noisy comments
and exclamations.*]

Spectators. Oh! Really! It can't be! Incredible! How
horrible! There they are! Look! Delia Morello and
Michele Rocca! [*Other* SPECTATORS *continue standing in
the lobby, but looking after them and making more or
less the same remarks.*]

A Spectator [*who has not grasped the situation*]. And
they complain because the same thing was done on the
stage!

Stage Manager. Yes, and the leading lady had the
courage to come and slap my face . . . there, on the
stage!

Many Voices. Incredible! Incredible! Absurd!

A Spectator Who Understands. But no! It's all natural enough! They rebelled because they saw themselves
there, as in a mirror, forced into a situation that has the
eternity of art!

Stage Manager. They did it over again to the very
gesture!

A Spectator Who Understands. And that's natural,
too! They have done, here before our eyes and quite

involuntarily, something that the author had foreseen!
[*Some of the* SPECTATORS *approve.* OTHERS *laugh.*]

Treasurer of the Theatre to the Stage Manager.   But
I should like to know whether you intend holding a
debate right here?

Stage Manager.   You want to close the theatre? What
have I got to do with that? Tell them to get out!

Treasurer.   Well, I can't have the third act! The
actors have gone home!

Stage Manager.   Post a placard calling the show off!

Treasurer.   But some of the audience are still in their
seats!

Stage Manager.   Very well! I'll make the announce-
ment from behind the footlights!

Treasurer.   Yes, that's the way out of it! Go and do
that! [*The* STAGE MANAGER *starts for the stage entrance,
while the* TREASURER *begins shooing people out of the
lobby.*] We are closing up, gentlemen! We are closing up!
If you please, gentlemen, the play is over for tonight! The
play is over for tonight!

[*The curtain falls, but immediately the* STAGE MAN-
AGER *will make his way through the central opening of
the curtain and come forward to the footlights.*]

Stage Manager.   The management is grieved to announce that in view of unfortunate incidents which took
place at the end of the second act, we shall be unable to
continue the performance this evening.

APPENDIX I

PREFACE

to

Six Characters in Search of an Author

by

Luigi Pirandello

(1925)

It seems like yesterday but is actually many years ago that a nimble little maidservant entered the service of my art. However, she always comes fresh to the job.

She is called Fantasy.

A little puckish and malicious, if she likes to dress in black no one will wish to deny that she is often positively bizarre and no one will wish to believe that she always does everything in the same way and in earnest. She sticks her hand in her pocket, pulls out a cap and bells, sets it on her head, red as a cock's comb, and dashes away. Here today, there tomorrow. And she amuses herself by bringing to my house—since I derive stories and novels and plays from them—the most disgruntled tribe in the world, men, women, children, involved in strange adventures which they can find no way out of; thwarted in their plans; cheated in their hopes; with whom, in short, it is often torture to deal.

Well, this little maidservant of mine, Fantasy, several years ago, had the bad inspiration or ill-omened caprice to bring a family into my house. I wouldn't know where she fished them up or how, but, according to her, I could find in them the subject for a magnificent novel.

I found before me a man about fifty years old, in a dark

jacket and light trousers, with a frowning air and ill-natured, mortified eyes; a poor woman in widow's weeds leading by one hand a little girl of four and by the other a boy of rather more than ten; a cheeky and "sexy" girl, also clad in black but with an equivocal and brazen pomp, all atremble with a lively, biting contempt for the mortified old man and for a young fellow of twenty who stood on one side closed in on himself as if he despised them all. In short, the six characters who are seen coming on stage at the beginning of the play. Now one of them and now another—often beating down one another—embarked on the sad story of their adventures, each shouting his own reasons, and projecting in my face his disordered passions, more or less as they do in the play to the unhappy Manager.

What author will be able to say how and why a character was born in his fantasy? The mystery of artistic creation is the same as that of birth. A woman who loves may desire to become a mother; but the desire by itself, however intense, cannot suffice. One fine day she will find herself a mother without having any precise intimation when it began. In the same way an artist imbibes very many germs of life and can never say how and why, at a certain moment, one of these vital germs inserts itself into his fantasy, there to become a living creature on a plane of life superior to the changeable existence of every day.

I can only say that, without having made any effort to seek them out, I found before me, alive—you could touch them and even hear them breathe—the six characters now seen on the stage. And they stayed there in my presence, each with his secret torment and all bound together by the one common origin and mutual entanglement of their affairs, while I had them enter the world of art, constructing from their persons, their passions, and their adventures a novel, a drama, or at least a story.

Born alive, they wished to live.

To me it was never enough to present a man or a woman and what is special and characteristic about them simply for the pleasure of presenting them; to narrate a particular affair, lively or sad, simply for the pleasure of narrating it; to describe a landscape simply for the pleasure of describing it.

There are some writers (and not a few) who do feel this pleasure and, satisfied, ask no more. They are, to speak more precisely, historical writers.

But there are others who, beyond such pleasure, feel a more profound spiritual need on whose account they admit only figures, affairs, landscapes which have been soaked, so to speak, in a particular sense of life and acquire from it a universal value. These are, more precisely, philosophical writers.

I have the misfortune to belong to these last.

I hate symbolic art in which the presentation loses all spontaneous movement in order to become a machine, an allegory —a vain and misconceived effort because the very fact of giving an allegorical sense to a presentation clearly shows that we have to do with a fable which by itself has no truth either fantastic or direct; it was made for the demonstration of some moral truth. The spiritual need I speak of cannot be satisfied—or seldom, and that to the end of a superior irony, as for example in Ariosto—by such allegorical symbolism. This latter starts from a concept, and from a concept which creates or tries to create for itself an image. The former on the other hand seeks in the image—which must remain alive and free throughout— a meaning to give it value.

Now, however much I sought, I did not succeed in uncovering this meaning in the six characters. And I concluded therefore that it was no use making them live.

I thought to myself: "I have already afflicted my readers with hundreds and hundreds of stories. Why should I afflict them now by narrating the sad entanglements of these six unfortunates?"

And, thinking thus, I put them away from me. Or rather I did all I could to put them away.

But one doesn't give life to a character for nothing.

Creatures of my spirit, these six were already living a life which was their own and not mine any more, a life which it was not in my power any more to deny them.

Thus it is that while I persisted in desiring to drive them out of my spirit, they, as if completely detached from every narrative support, characters from a novel miraculously emerging from the pages of the book that contained them, went on living on their own, choosing certain moments of the day to reappear before me in the solitude of my study and coming— now one, now the other, now two together—to tempt me, to propose that I present or describe this scene or that, to explain the effects that could be secured with them, the new interest which a certain unusual situation could provide, and so forth.

For a moment I let myself be won over. And this condescension of mine, thus letting myself go for a while, was enough, because they drew from it a new increment of life, a greater degree of clarity and addition, consequently a greater degree of persuasive power over me. And thus as it became gradually harder and harder for me to go back and free myself from them, it became easier and easier for them to come back and tempt me. At a certain point I actually became obsessed with them. Until, all of a sudden, a way out of the difficulty flashed upon me.

"Why not," I said to myself, "present this highly strange fact of an author who refuses to let some of his characters live though they have been born in his fantasy, and the fact that these characters, having by now life in their veins, do not resign themselves to remaining excluded from the world of art? They are detached from me; live on their own; have acquired voice and movement; have by themselves—in this struggle for existence that they have had to wage with me—become dramatic characters, characters that can move and talk on their own initiative; already see themselves as such; have learned to defend themselves against me; will even know how to defend themselves against others. And so let them go where dramatic characters do go to have life: on a stage. And let us see what will happen."

That's what I did. And, naturally, the result was what it had to be: a mixture of tragic and comic, fantastic and realistic, in a humorous situation that was quite new and infinitely complex, a drama which is conveyed by means of the characters, who carry it within them and suffer it, a drama, breathing, speaking, self-propelled, which seeks at all costs to find the means of its own presentation; and the comedy of the vain attempt at an improvised realization of the drama on stage. First, the surprise of the poor actors in a theatrical company rehearsing a play by day on a bare stage (no scenery, no flats). Surprise and incredulity at the sight of the six characters announcing themselves as such in search of an author. Then, immediately afterwards, through that sudden fainting fit of the Mother veiled in black, their instinctive interest in the drama of which they catch a glimpse in her and in the other members of the strange family, an obscure, ambiguous drama, coming about so unexpectedly on a stage that is empty and unprepared to receive it. And gradually the growth of this interest to the bursting forth of the contrasting passions of Father, of Step-Daughter, of Son, of that poor Mother, passions seeking, as I said, to overwhelm each other with a tragic, lacerating fury.

And here is the universal meaning at first vainly sought in the six characters, now that, going on stage of their own accord, they succeed in finding it within themselves in the excitement of the desperate struggle which each wages against the other and all wage against the Manager and the actors, who do not understand them.

Without wanting to, without knowing it, in the strife of their bedevilled souls, each of them, defending himself against the accusations of the others, expresses as his own living passion and torment the passion and torment which for so many years have been the pangs of my spirit: the deceit of mutual understanding irremediably founded on the empty abstraction of the words, the multiple personality of everyone corresponding to the possibilities of being to be found in each of us, and finally the inherent tragic conflict between life (which is always moving and changing) and form (which fixes it, immutable).

Two above all among the six characters, the Father and the Step-Daughter, speak of that outrageous unalterable fixity of their form in which he and she see their essential nature expressed permanently and immutably, a nature that for one means punishment and for the other revenge; and they defend it against the factitious affectations and unaware volatility of the actors, and they try to impose it on the vulgar Manager who would like to change it and adapt it to the so-called exigencies of the theatre.

If the six characters don't all seem to exist on the same plane, it is not because some are figures of first rank and others of the second, that is, some are main characters and others minor ones—the elementary perspective necessary to all scenic or narrative art—nor is it that any are not completely created—for their purpose. They are all six at the same point of artistic realization and on the same level of reality, which is the fantastic level of the whole play. Except that the Father, the Step-Daughter, and also the Son are realized as mind; the Mother as nature; the Boy as a presence watching and performing a gesture and the Baby unaware of it all. This fact creates among them a perspective of a new sort. Unconsciously I had had the impression that some of them needed to be fully realized (artistically speaking), others less so, and others merely sketched in as elements in a narrative or presentational sequence: the most alive, the most completely created, are the Father and the Step-Daughter who naturally stand out more and lead the way, dragging themselves along beside the almost dead weight of the others—first, the Son, holding back; second, the Mother, like a victim resigned to her fate, between the two children who have hardly any substance beyond their appearance and who need to be led by the hand.

And actually! actually they had each to appear in that stage of creation which they had attained in the author's fantasy at the moment when he wished to drive them away.

If I now think about these things, about having intuited that necessity, having unconsciously found the way to resolve it by means of a new perspective, and about the way in which I actually obtained it, they seem like miracles. The fact is that the play was really conceived in one of those spontaneous illuminations of the fantasy when by a miracle all the elements of the mind answer to each other's call and work in divine accord. No human brain, working "in the cold," however stirred up it might be, could ever have succeeded in penetrating far enough, could ever have been in a position to satisfy all the exigencies of the play's form. Therefore the reasons which I will give to clarify the values of the play must not be thought of as intentions that I conceived beforehand when I prepared myself for the job and which I now undertake to defend, but only as discoveries which I have been able to make afterwards in tranquillity.

I wanted to present six characters seeking an author. Their play does not manage to get presented—precisely because the author whom they seek is missing. Instead is presented the comedy of their vain attempt with all that it contains of tragedy by virtue of the fact that the six characters have been rejected.

But can one present a character while rejecting him? Obviously, to present him one needs, on the contrary, to receive him into one's fantasy before one can express him. And I have actually accepted and realized the six characters: I have, however, accepted and realized them as rejected: in search of *another* author.

What have I rejected of them? Not themselves, obviously, but their drama, which doubtless is what interests them above all but which did not interest me—for the reasons already indicated.

And what is it, for a character—his drama?

Every creature of fantasy and art, in order to exist, must have his drama, that is, a drama in which he may be a character and for which he *is* a character. This drama is the character's *raison d'être*, his vital function, necessary for his existence.

In these six, then, I have accepted the "being" without the reason for being. I have taken the organism and entrusted to it, not its own proper function, but another more complex function into which its own function entered, if at all, only as a datum. A terrible and desperate situation especially for the two—Father and Step-Daughter—who more than the others

crave life and more than the others feel themselves to be characters, that is, absolutely need a drama and therefore their own
drama—the only one which they can envisage for themselves
yet which meantime they see rejected: an "impossible" situation
from which they feel they must escape at whatever cost; it is a
matter of life and death. True, I have given them another
raison d'être, another function: precisely that "impossible"
situation, the drama of being in search of an author and rejected. But that this should be a *raison d'être,* that it should
have become their real function, that it should be necessary,
that it should suffice, they can hardly suppose; for they have a
life of their own. If someone were to tell them, they wouldn't
believe him. It is not possible to believe that the sole reason
for our living should lie in a torment that seems to us unjust
and inexplicable.

I cannot imagine, therefore, why the charge was brought
against me that the character of the Father was not what it
should have been because it stepped out of its quality and position as a character and invaded at times the author's province
and took it over. I who understand those who don't quite understand me see that the charge derives from the fact that the
character expresses and makes his own a torment of spirit which
is recognized as mine. Which is entirely natural and of absolutely no significance. Aside from the fact that this torment of
spirit in the character of the Father derives from causes, and is
suffered and lived for reasons, that have nothing to do with the
drama of my personal experience, a fact which alone removes
all substance from the criticism, I want to make it clear that the
inherent torment of my spirit is one thing, a torment which I
can legitimately—provided that it be organic—reflect in a character, and that the activity of my spirit as revealed in the realized work, the activity that succeeds in forming a drama out of
the six characters in search of an author is another thing. If the
Father participated in this latter activity, if he competed in
forming the drama of the six characters without an author, then
and only then would it by all means be justified to say that he
was at times the author himself and therefore not the man he
should be. But the Father suffers and does not create his existence as a character in search of an author. He suffers it as an
inexplicable fatality and as a situation which he tries with all
his powers to rebel against, which he tries to remedy: hence it
is that he is a character in search of an author and nothing
more, even if he expresses as his own the torment of my spirit.
If he, so to speak, assumed some of the author's responsibilities,

the fatality would be completely explained. He would, that is to say, see himself accepted, if only as a rejected character, accepted in the poet's heart of hearts, and he would no longer have any reason to suffer the despair of not finding someone to construct and affirm his life as a character. I mean that he would quite willingly accept the *raison d'être* which the author gives him and without regrets would forego his own, throwing over the Manager and the actors to whom in fact he runs as his only recourse.

There is one character, that of the Mother, who on the other hand does not care about being alive (considering being alive as an end in itself). She hasn't the least suspicion that she is *not* alive. It has never occurred to her to ask how and why and in what manner she lives. In short, she is not aware of being a character, inasmuch as she is never, even for a moment, detached from her role. She doesn't know she has a role.

This makes her perfectly organic. Indeed, her role of Mother does not of itself, in its natural essence, embrace mental activity. And she does not exist as a mind. She lives in an endless continuum of feeling, and therefore she cannot acquire awareness of her life—that is, of her existence as a character. But with all this, even she, in her own way and for her own ends, seeks an author, and at a certain stage seems happy to have been brought before the Manager. Because she hopes to take life from him, perhaps? No: because she hopes the Manager will have her present a scene with the Son in which she would put so much of her own life. But it is a scene which does not exist, which never has and never could take place. So unaware is she of being a character, that is, of the life that is possible to her, all fixed and determined, moment by moment, in every action, every phrase.

She appears on stage with the other characters but without understanding what the others make her do. Obviously, she imagines that the itch for life with which the husband and the daughter are afflicted and for which she herself is to be found on stage is no more than one of the usual incomprehensible extravagances of this man who is both tortured and torturer and—horrible, most horrible—a new equivocal rebellion on the part of that poor erring girl. The Mother is completely passive. The events of her own life and the values they assume in her eyes, her very character, are all things which are "said" by the others and which she only once contradicts, and that because the maternal instinct rises up and rebels within her to make it clear that she didn't at all wish to abandon either the son or the husband: the Son was taken from her and the husband forced her to abandon him. She is only correcting data; she explains and knows nothing.

In short, she is nature. Nature fixed in the figure of a mother.

This character gave me a satisfaction of a new sort, not to be ignored. Nearly all my critics, instead of defining her, after their habit, as "unhuman"—which seems to be the peculiar and incorrigible characteristic of all my creatures without exception —had the goodness to note "with real pleasure" that at last a *very human* figure had emerged from my fantasy. I explain this praise to myself in the following way: since my poor Mother is entirely limited to the natural attitude of a Mother with no possibility of free mental activity, being, that is, little more than a lump of flesh completely alive in all its functions—procreation, lactation, caring for and loving its young—without any need therefore of exercising her brain, she realizes in her person the true and complete "human type." That must be how it is, since in a human organism nothing seems more superfluous than the mind.

But the critics have tried to get rid of the Mother with this praise without bothering to penetrate the nucleus of poetic values which the character in the play represents. A very human figure, certainly, because mindless, that is, unaware of being what she is or not caring to explain it to herself. But not knowing that she is a character doesn't prevent her from being one. That is her drama in my play. And the most living expression of it comes spurting out in her cry to the Manager who wants her to think all these things have happened already and therefore cannot now be a reason for renewed lamentations: "No, it's happening now, it's happening always! My torture is not a pretence, signore! I am alive and present, always, in every moment of my torture: it is renewed, alive and present, always!" This she *feels,* without being conscious of it, and feels it therefore as something inexplicable: but she feels it so terribly that she doesn't think it *can* be something to explain either to herself or to others. She feels it and that is that. She feels it as pain, and this pain is immediate; she cries it out. Thus she reflects the growing fixity of life in a form—the same thing, which in another way, tortures the Father and the Step-Daughter. In them, mind. In her, nature. The mind rebels and, as best it may, seeks an advantage; nature, if not aroused by sensory stimuli, weeps.

Conflict between life-in-movement and form is the inexorable condition not only of the mental but also of the physical order.

The life which in order to exist has become fixed in our corporeal form little by little kills that form. The tears of a nature thus fixed lament the irreparable, continuous aging of our bodies. Hence the tears of the Mother are passive and perpetual. Revealed in three faces, made significant in three distinct and simultaneous dramas, this inherent conflict finds in the play its most complete expression. More: the Mother declares also the particular value of artistic form—a form which does not delimit or destroy its own life and which life does not consume —in her cry to the Manager. If the Father and Step-Daughter began their scene a hundred thousand times in succession, always, at the appointed moment, at the instant when the life of the work of art must be expressed with that cry, it would always be heard, unaltered and unalterable in its form, not as a mechanical repetition, not as a return determined by external necessities, but on the contrary, alive every time and as new, suddenly born *thus forever!* embalmed alive in its incorruptible form. Hence, always, as we open the book, we shall find Francesca alive and confessing to Dante her sweet sin, and if we turn to the passage a hundred thousand times in succession, a hundred thousand times in succession Francesca will speak her words, never repeating them mechanically, but saying them as though each time were the first time with such living and sudden passion that Dante every time will turn faint. All that lives, by the fact of living, has a form, and by the same token must die—except the work of art which lives forever in so far as it *is* form.

The birth of a creature of human fantasy, a birth which is a step across the threshold between nothing and eternity, can also happen suddenly, occasioned by some necessity. An imagined drama needs a character who does or says a certain necessary thing; accordingly this character is born and is precisely what he had to be. In this way Madame Pace is born among the six characters and seems a miracle, even a trick, realistically portrayed on the stage. It is no trick. The birth is real. The new character is alive not because she was alive already but because she is now happily born as is required by the fact of her being a character—she is obliged to be as she is. There is a break here, a sudden change in the level of reality of the scene, because a character can be born in this way only in the poet's fancy and not on the boards of a stage. Without anyone's noticing it, I have all of a sudden changed the scene: I have gathered it up again into my own fantasy without removing it from the spectator's eyes. That is, I have shown them,

instead of the stage, my own fantasy in the act of creating—
my own fantasy in the form of this same stage. The sudden and
uncontrollable changing of a visual phenomenon from one
level of reality to another is a miracle comparable to those of
the saint who sets his own statue in motion: it is neither wood
nor stone at such a moment. But the miracle is not arbitrary.
The stage—a stage which accepts the fantastic reality of the six
characters—is no fixed, immutable datum. Nothing in this play
exists as given and preconceived. Everything is in the making,
is in motion, is a sudden experiment: even the place in which
this unformed life, reaching after its own form, changes and
changes again contrives to shift position organically. The level
of reality changes. When I had the idea of bringing Madame
Pace to birth right there on the stage, I felt I could do it and
I did it. Had I noticed that this birth was unhinging and
silently, unnoticed, in a second, giving another shape, another
reality to my scene, I certainly wouldn't have brought it about.
I would have been afraid of the apparent lack of logic. And I
would have committed an ill-omened assault on the beauty of
my work. The fervor of my mind saved me from doing so. For,
despite appearances, with their specious logic, this fantastic
birth is sustained by a real necessity in mysterious, organic relation with the whole life of the work.

That someone now tells me it hasn't all the value it could
have because its expression is not constructed but chaotic, because it smacks of romanticism, makes me smile.

I understand why this observation was made to me: because
in this work of mine the presentation of the drama in which
the six characters are involved appears tumultuous and never
proceeds in an orderly manner. There is no logical development, no concatenation of the events. Very true. Had I hunted
it with a lamp I couldn't have found a more disordered, crazy,
arbitrary, complicated, in short, romantic way of presenting
"the drama in which the six characters are involved." Very
true. But I have not presented that drama. I have presented
another—and I won't undertake to say again what!—in which,
among the many fine things that everyone, according to his
tastes, can find, there is a discreet satire on romantic procedures: in the six characters thus excited to the point where they
stifle themselves in the roles which each of them plays in a
certain drama while I present them as characters in another
play which they don't know and don't suspect the existence of,
so that this inflammation of their passions—which belongs to
the realm of romantic procedures—is humorously "placed,"

located in the void. And the drama of the six characters presented not as it would have been organized by my fantasy had it been accepted but in this way, as a rejected drama, could not exist in the work except as a "situation," with some little development, and could not come out except in indications, stormily, disorderedly, in violent foreshortenings, in a chaotic manner: continually interrupted, sidetracked, contradicted (by one of its characters), denied, and (by two others) not even seen.

There is a character indeed—he who denies the drama which makes him a character, the Son—who draws all his importance and value from being a character not of the comedy in the making—which as such hardly appears—but from the presentation that I made of it. In short, he is the only one who lives solely as "a character in search of an author"—inasmuch as the author he seeks is not a dramatic author. Even this could not be otherwise. The character's attitude is an organic product of my conception, and it is logical that in the situation it should produce greater confusion and disorder and another element of romantic contrast.

But I had precisely to *present* this organic and natural chaos. And to present a chaos is not at all to present chaotically, that is, romantically. That my presentation is the reverse of confused, that it is quite simple, clear, and orderly, is proved by the clarity which the intrigue, the characters, the fantastic and realistic, dramatic and comic levels of the work have had for every public in the world and by the way in which, for those with more searching vision, the unusual values enclosed within it come out.

Great is the confusion of tongues among men if criticisms thus made find words for their expression. No less great than this confusion is the intimate law of order which, obeyed in all points, makes this work of mine classical and typical and at its catastrophic close forbids the use of words. Though the audience eventually understands that one does not create life by artifice and that the drama of the six characters cannot be presented without an author to give them value with his spirit, the Manager remains vulgarly anxious to know how the thing turned out, and the "ending" is remembered by the Son in its sequence of actual moments, but without any sense and therefore not needing a human voice for its expression. It happens stupidly, uselessly, with the going-off of a mechanical weapon on stage. It breaks up and disperses the sterile experiment of the characters and the actors, which has apparently been made without the assistance of the poet.

The poet, unknown to them, as if looking on at a distance during the whole period of the experiment, was at the same time busy creating—with it and of it—his own play.

(Translated E.B.   1950)

APPENDIX II

BIOGRAPHICAL AND HISTORICAL

In the Garibaldian era the Pirandello family were ardent partisans of that great rebel, but when Luigi Pirandello was born
in 1867 the rebellion was over and Italians were eating the
tasteless fruits of victory. Luigi's father was by now a fairly
prosperous sulphur dealer in Agrigento, Sicily. Luigi was des-
tined for a business career too. A studious bent, however, soon
made itself felt, and he received a literary schooling at Palermo,
Rome, and Bonn. His doctoral thesis at Bonn Universtiy (1891)
was a study of his native Sicilian dialect. The young scholar
also translated Goethe's Roman elegies.

Pirandello's first creative efforts were in the realm of verse.
But when he settled down to taste the literary life of Rome, the
influence he fell under was that of the Sicilian novelist, Capuana, who became his friend and adviser. Capuana turned his
interest from what we would call "late-Victorian versifying" to
naturalistic fiction. In 1893 *The Outcast* was written: the tal-
ent that is not so evident in the poems looks through all the
cracks of this first novel.

Pirandello married, became the father of three and, because
he thought it would be good to have a job for a time, accepted
a post as teacher at a girls' school in Rome. When both his own
family and his wife's lost their money in a mining disaster, the
job became a necessity and a bugbear. The drudgery of it became one of the two great burdens he had to carry.

The other was his wife, who went insane. Nor, for many
years, was she taken off Pirandello's hands and placed in a
home. She persecuted him with an unprovoked and crazy jealousy.

As Dr. Johnson paid for his mother's funeral with his admirable story *Rasselas*, so Luigi Pirandello met the family's
financial misfortune with his first widely recognized work: *The*

Late Mattia Pascal (1904). Before the First World War broke out ten years later, Pirandello had published two more novels and a good many short stories.

Although he had been induced to write a play or two at an earlier date, it was not till 1916 that further persuasion from actors precipitated a flood of dramatic works, beginning with *Pensaci, Giacomino!* (*Better Think Twice About It!*), and *Liolà*, and *Così è* (*se vi pare*) (*It Is So!, If You Think So*): they took, respectively, three days, a week, and six days to write. The first Pirandello play to enjoy a notable public success was *Come prima, meglio di prima* (*As Before, Better than Before*) in 1920. In a five-week writing bout Pirandello then created *Six Characters in Search of an Author* (three weeks) and *Henry IV* (two weeks). The first had a *succès de scandale* in Rome and a success without scandal in Milan. In the following year (1922) came the openings of *Henry IV* and *Vestire gli ignudi* (*Naked*), both successes. Komisarjevsky directed *Six Characters* in London. Brock Pemberton saw the production and proceeded to direct the play himself on Broadway. Reinhardt secured the German rights.

Between 1922 and 1924 Pirandello became a public figure, both at home and abroad. He and Mussolini announced their admiration for each other in the press. In Paris, Charles Dullin did *Il piacere dell'onestà* (*The Pleasure of Honesty*), and Georges Pitoëff did *Six Characters*. Pirandello himself went not only to Paris (where he received the Legion of Honor), but also to New York (where Pemberton planned to stage a whole cycle of his plays at the Forty-Fourth Street Theatre).

With the help of Mussolini, who graced the first performance with his presence, Pirandello opened his own Art Theatre in Rome in 1925. His company subsequently took his plays to London, Paris, Vienna, Prague, Budapest, the leading cities of Germany, and ultimately to the Argentine and Brazil. In 1931 Judith Anderson appeared in *Come tu mi vuoi* (As You Desire Me) on Broadway, and the Shuberts began buying even the maestro's untranslated plays. Miss Anderson was replaced in the film of *As You Desire Me* by a yet bigger name: Greta Garbo. In 1934 Pirandello was awarded the Nobel Prize. At his death in 1936 he was under contract to appear as the author in a Hollywood film of *Six Characters*.

Pirandello's whole life after 1918 was a success story. His wife was put in a home, and royalties enabled him to give up teaching. Pirandello's enthusiastic espousal of fascism, which appears to many non-Italians as a surprising blot upon his career, was an integral part of it. Opposition to the fascist regime would have made serious difficulties for him; acceptance of it meant subsidies and publicity. One should not imagine he had anti-fascist scruples to overcome; he accepted money from the fascist government in entire good faith. Nor can one believe reports that he later regretted the zeal of the early fascist years. On his last appearance at the port of New York he handed out a statement in favor of Italy's annexation of Abyssinia. He gave his Nobel medal to be melted down for the Abyssinian campaign.

Under fascism, Pirandello's playwriting entered a third and more problematic phase. The first phase had been that of the Sicilian folk-comedies like *Better Think Twice About It!*, *Liolà*, and *Il berretto a sonagli* (*Cap and Bells*). The second was that of the philosophical comedies in which Pirandello is less Sicilian than European: the phase of *Six Characters* and *Henry IV*. In his third phase, Pirandello withdraws into a strange, subjective world of his own—or, as he would probably prefer to say, tries to create myths. Thus we have the social myth of *La nuova colonia* (*The New Colony*), the religious myth of *Lazzaro* (*Lazarus*), and the myth of art that is *I giganti della montagna* (*Giants of the Mountain*). It would be either a stupid or an over-ingenious critic who would stamp any of these works as fascist. They illustrate at most the plight of a playwright in a fascist state. They show that, in some degree, Pirandello lived in an "inner emigration" like many German writers under Hitler. *The Giants of the Mountain* can be interpreted as showing Pirandello's growing realization that the fascist-giants were hostile to culture. A definitely fascist mentality is present only in the anti-liberal animus of *The New Colony* and the miracle-mongering of *Lazarus*.

The point is that Pirandello's success story of a career was just as sad as most American ones. The strain and stress are apparent in the whole last phase, and one play—*Quando si è qualcuno* (*When You Are Somebody*)—presents the Pirandellian portrait of the literary bigshot: he is nameless and turns to stone before our eyes. Pirandello was no happier as an international bigwig that he had been as a college professor. And, if his marriage was a failure, it doesn't seem that the *grande passion* which dominated his later life proved a satisfying alternative.

At Pirandello's death the fascists came to dress Pirandello in a black shirt and give him a state funeral. But the maestro had left instructions. "When I am dead, do not clothe me. Wrap me naked in a sheet. No flowers on the bed and no lighted candle. A pauper's cart. Naked. And let no one accompany me, neither relatives nor friends. The cart, the horse, the coachman, *e basta*. Burn me . . ." This last "burn me" ended another flirtation of Pirandello's: one with the church, an almost necessary flirtation for a career man in Italy. The church does not believe in cremation and the party did not want a world-famous fascist to slip off naked—i.e., without his black shirt. These words of Pirandello's will sound a little melodramatic to non-Italian ears, yet if we ponder them we can begin to understand in what an agony of apartness this successful man lived. Apartness from church and state, the very sources and symbols of success. Small wonder that, in his creative life, he was not the celebrant of success, but the poet of apartness.

His influence has been considerable. The two principal Italian playwrights of today—Eduardo de Filippo and Ugo Betti—might almost be described as suffering under it. Outside Italy, Pirandello's influence has been most strongly felt in France. The French are most hospitable to a foreign writer whom they regard as a fascinating child of nature, whose barbarism will become significant when assimilated to their own civilization. So it is with Faulkner or Henry Miller today, and so it was with the Sicilian country boy, Luigi Pirandello. Crommelynk, who translated one of his plays *Come prima, meglio di prima*, is distinctly Pirandellian in his own work; and from Crommelynk to Anouilh is but a step. While Lenormand, in such a play as *Le Crépuscule du théâtre*,[1] takes over easily separable technical features of *Six Characters*, Crommelynk and Anouilh are Pirandellian in a deeper sense: they share his metaphysical anguish and, like him, they express it in a version of erotic relations *in extremis*.

In the American theatre I notice nothing so unequivocally Pirandellian.[2] At the first night of *Death of a Salesman* in Rome, everyone talked of *pirandellismo*, yet what has Miller

[1] English version: *In Theatre Street* by Ashley Dukes. Gollancz, London, 1937.

[2] In a note on Pirandello's influence (*Meridiano di Roma*, December 20, 1936), Silvio D'Amico mentions Eugene O'Neill, and specifically *The Great God Brown;* but how many American readers would feel convinced of Pirandellian influence here? The other writers mentioned by D'Amico are Marcel Achard, Denys Amiel (*L'Image*), Henri Bernstein (*Galerie des Spectres*), Jean Giraudoux (*Siegfried*), Kurt Goetz, László Krakatos, Henri Marx, Alfred Savoir, all of them European, all, except Goetz and Krakatos, French.

done to earn the description except write of illusion and reality and find the former more powerful? And surely Miller criticizing Willie Loman's popular Pirandellism—his belief that what your customer thinks you are is more real that what you actually are? An American playwright much more likely to have been directly affected by Pirandello is that avid reader and linguist, Thornton Wilder. Use of commentators and plays within plays no longer indicates knowledge of Pirandello or any other author previous to 1936, but Thornton Wilder's interest in the perspectives that such devices provide in a world in which reality itself resembles concentric circles of meaning, suggests that he may have known his Pirandello before writing *Our Town* and *The Skin of Our Teeth*.

And there is much more in Pirandello for younger men to find.

APPENDIX III

THEATRICAL AND BIBLIOGRAPHICAL

A. The following is a list of Pirandello's plays with the date of the first Italian performance. When a play has been published in English, the English title is also given.

La morsa, 1910. (*The Vise*)
Lumie di Sicilia, 1910. (*Sicilian Limes*)
Il dovere del medico, 1913. (*The Doctor's Duty*)
Se non così. 1915.
Pensaci, Giacomino!, 1916.
Liolà, 1916. (First published in the present volume, title unchanged)
Così è (se vi pare), 1917. (*It Is So!, If You Think So*)
Il berretto a sonagli, 1917.
La giara, 1917.
Il piacere dell'onestà, 1917. (*The Pleasure of Honesty*)
Ma non è una cosa seria, 1918.
Il giuoco delle parti, 1918.
L'innesto, 1919.
La patente, 1919.
L'uomo, la bestia, e la virtù, 1919.
Tutto per bene, 1920.
Come prima, meglio di prima, 1920.
Cecè, 1920. (*Chee-Chee*)
La Signora Morli, una e due, 1920.
Sei personaggi in cerca d'autore, 1921. (*Six Characters in Search of an Author*)
Enrico IV, 1922. (*Henry IV*)
All'uscita, 1922. (*At the Gate*)
L'imbecille, 1922. (*The Imbecile*)
Vestire gli ignudi, 1922. (*Naked*)
L'uomo dal fiore in bocca, 1923. (*The Man with the Flower in His Mouth*)

La vita che ti diedi, 1923.
L'altro figlio, 1923. *(The House with the Column)*
Ciascuno a suo modo, 1924. *(Each in His Own Way)*
Sagra del Signore della nave, 1925. *(Our Lord of the Ship)*
Diana e la Tuda, 1927.
L'amica delle mogli, 1927.
Bellavita, 1927. *(Bellavita)*
Scamandro, 1928.
La nuova colonia, 1928.
O di uno o di nessuno, 1929.
Lazzaro, 1929.
Come tu mi vuoi, 1930. *(As You Desire Me)*
Questa sera si recita a soggetto, 1930. *(Tonight We Improvise)*
Trovarsi, 1932.
Quando si è qualcuno, 1933.
La Favola del figlio cambiato, 1934.
Non si sa come, 1935.
Sogno (ma forse no), 1936. *(Dream, But Perhaps Not)*
I giganti della montagna, 1937.

B. The plays of Pirandello are today available collected in four volumes under the title *Maschere Nude* (Mondadori, Milan, 1948-9). In English they are represented by five volumes, excluding the present one, as follows:

Three Plays. (Six Characters, Henry IV, It Is So!). E. P. Dutton & Co., Inc., New York, 1922; J. M. Dent & Sons, Ltd., London, 1922.
Each in His Own Way and Two Other Plays. (The Pleasure of Honesty, Naked). E. P. Dutton & Co., Inc., New York, 1923; J. M. Dent & Sons, Ltd., London, 1924.
The One-Act Plays. (The Imbecile, By Judgment of Court, Our Lord of the Ship, The Doctor's Duty, Chee-Chee, The Man with the Flower in His Mouth, At the Gate, The Vise, The House with the Column, Sicilian Limes, The Jar). E. P. Dutton & Co., Inc., New York, 1928.
As You Desire Me. E. P. Dutton & Co., Inc., New York, 1931.
Tonight We Improvise. E. P. Dutton & Co., Inc., New York, 1932.

One other play is known to have been published in English: *Dream, But Perhaps Not* in *This Quarter*, Volume II, No. 4, June 1930.

Some of the above plays have been performed in other than
the published translations.

Some Pirandello plays have been performed in English but not
published. Among these are known to be: *Come prima,
meglio di prima* (*Floriani's Wife*), *La vita che ti diedi* (*The
Life I Gave You*), *L'uomo, la bestia, e la virtù* (*Say It with
Flowers*), and *Lazzaro* (*Lazarus*).

Some plays have been translated but neither published nor
performed.

There are further details on these points (not always accurate,
however) in the official Pirandello Bibliography (as listed
below).

C. There are two books on Pirandello in English, and one in
which he occupies a central place:

> *Luigi Pirandello: 1867-1936.* By Walter Starkie. Second Edi-
> tion, John Murray, London, 1937; E. P. Dutton & Co., Inc.,
> New York, 1937.
> *The Drama of Luigi Pirandello.* By Domenico Vittorini.
> University of Pennsylvania Press, Philadelphia, 1935.
> *The Age of Pirandello.* By Lander McClintock. Indiana
> University Press, Bloomington, 1951.

In Italian there is a large number of books and booklets on
Pirandello, among which the following are the most interesting
either for information, critical insight, or the typicality of the
point of view:

> Alvaro, Corrado: *Prefazione.* (Unpublished.)
> Bàccolo, Luigi: *Luigi Pirandello.* Second Edition, Bocca,
> Milan, 1949.
> Di Pietro, Antonio: *Pirandello.* Second Edition, Vita e Pen-
> siero, Milan, 1950.
> Janner, Arminio: *Luigi Pirandello.* "La Nuova Italia," Flor-
> ence, 1948.
> Lo Vecchio Musti, Manlio: *L'opera di Luigi Pirandello.*
> Paravia, Turin, 1939.
> Mignosi, Pietro: *Il segreto di Pirandello.* Second Edition,
> "La Tradizione," Milan, 1937.
> Nardelli, F. V.: *L'uomo segreto, vita e croci di Luigi Piran-
> dello.* Mondadori, Milan, 1932 and 1944.
> Pasini, Ferdinando: *Luigi Pirandello* (*come mi pare*). "La
> Vedetta Italiana," Trieste, 1927.

Petronio, Giuseppe: *Pirandello novelliere e la crisi del realismo.* "Lucentia," Lucca, 1950.

Puliatti, Pietro and Bottino, Egle: *Lineamenti sull'arte di Luigi Pirandello.* Intelisano, Catania, 1941.

Most of the really critical comment on Pirandello, as one would expect, is hidden away in periodicals and books on other subjects. The only systematic guide to this literature is the bibliography of Di Pietro (above), and even this is confessedly incomplete. The present editor has found the following especially suggestive:

Bontempelli, Massimo: "Luigi Pirandello," first published in *La Nuova Antologia,* February 1, 1937; reprinted in *Pirandello Leopardi D'Annunzio,* Bompiani, Milan, 1939; also in Lo Vecchio Musti's bibliography as listed below.

Brancati, Vitaliano: "Pirandello Diabolico?" in *Il Tempo,* March 8, 1948.

Debenedetti, Giacomo: " 'Una Giornata' di Pirandello," *Saggi Critici, Nuova Serie,* Edizioni del Secolo, Rome, 1945.

Gobetti, Piero: *Opera Critica.* Especially the Second Part, Section One, Chapters 7 and 14.

Gramsci, Antonio: "Il teatro di Pirandello," *Letteratura e Vita Nazionale,* Einaudi, Turin, 1950. (See also Second Part.)

Moravia, Alberto: "La lezione di Pirandello," in *Sipario,* November-December, 1946. (Reprinted in *La Fiera Letteraria,* December 12, 1946.)

Pandolfi, Vito: "Gramsci individua Luigi Pirandello," in *Il Dramma,* November 15, 1950.

Russo, Luigi: "Il noviziato letterario di Luigi Pirandello," in *Paesaggio,* April-May, June-July, August-November, 1946.

Tilgher, Adriano: "Il teatro di Luigi Pirandello," *Studi sul teatro contemporaneo.* Third edition. Libreria di Scienze e Lettere, Rome, 1928.

For further data, the reader must go to the official *Bibliografia di Pirandello,* of which a new and up-to-date edition is announced. The edition available to the present editor is in two volumes, dated 1937 and 1940 respectively, published by Mondadori, Milan, and edited by Manlio Lo Vecchio Musti. The first volume lists all Italian editions of the major works

of Pirandello up to 1937. It lists and gives particulars of first
Italian performances of his plays. It provides facts as to translation in and out of dialect; movie scenarios; opera librettos.
It includes thirty-three photographs of the maestro and essays
by Bontempelli and Stefano Pirandello, not to mention a
preface by His Excellency Dino Alfieri.[1] Volume Two is chiefly
devoted to translations of Pirandello (thirty languages); scattered facts on foreign productions are also provided; and the
listing of Pirandello's works in the original is completed with
his contributions to newspapers and periodicals.

[1] See the official bibliographer's *L'opera di Luigi Pirandello* (1939),
page 23: "The Italian government ordered the compilation of his
bibliography for the first anniversary of his death."